We Shall Be No More

We Shall Be No More

Suicide and Self-Government in the Newly United States

RICHARD BELL

Harvard University Press
Cambridge, Massachusetts, and London, England
2012

Library of Congress Cataloging-in-Publication Data

Bell, Richard, 1978–
We shall be no more : suicide and self-government in the newly United States / Richard Bell.
p. cm.
Includes bibliographical references and index.
ISBN 978-0-674-06372-3 (alk. paper)
1. Suicide—United States—History. 2. Suicide—Political aspects—United States. 3. Suicide—Moral and ethical aspects—United States. 4. Suicide in mass media. 5. Suicide—Social aspects—United States. I. Title.
HV6548.U5B45 2012
362.280973—dc23 2011019574

For Sunshine

Contents

We Shall Be No More

There was never a democracy that did not commit suicide.

John Adams, 1814

Introduction: Alarming Progress

On a bright New York day in May 1807, Samuel Miller received an unsigned letter. "Rev. Sir," it began, "I have no doubt it will give you pleasure to be informed, that you have been the means, through the blessing of God, of saving a miserable creature from perpetrating the horrid crime of suicide." Purportedly mailed from a debtors' prison, the letter explained how its author, a man "reduced from a respectable standing in society to the most embarrassed circumstances," had made up his mind to relieve his sufferings by taking his own life. He had penned parting notes to the parents, wife, and child he would leave behind and had smuggled into the prison a dagger sharp enough for his purpose. It was simply by chance, he told the thirty-seven-year-old Presbyterian pastor, that "I took up a paper, published this day, containing an extract from your excellent discourse [against] Suicide." Once he began reading, he could not put it down; it was as if Miller was speaking to him personally through the pages of the newspaper. "Had you known every circumstance of my life, had you known my present situation, you could not have made an address more applicable. . . .

Every sentence struck me to the heart." By the time this troubled soul had finished reading, his resolve to die had melted away to nothing: "I paused—I reflected—I threw the murdering instrument aside, and determined to live."[1]

To Samuel Miller, this letter was a vindication, a much-prayed-for first fruit of his two-year-old crusade to stem the tide of self-destructive behavior he saw engulfing young America. The "excellent discourse" the letter referred to was *The Guilt, Folly, and Sources of Suicide* (1805), a bumper-sized pamphlet that Miller had stuffed full of pro-life messages. It was aimed squarely at the nation's youth, the group Miller believed "most apt to fall into the crime of suicide." According to the Manhattan papers, teenage suicide—and self-destruction more generally—had become rampant there of late. Miller had read of at least nine suicides in New York in the last three months alone: "this number, in a city, the population of which does not exceed 70,000, must be considered as enormous." The crime, he fretted, "has become alarmingly frequent in our land, and in our city."[2]

Miller was not the only person convinced that the land was in the grip of an escalating epidemic. Prior to the Revolution, colonists had often remarked on the low number of suicides in America as compared to England. Yet by the late eighteenth century, claims that "numerous instances of Suicide . . . have occurred within a year past" began to turn up in the early national press with distressing regularity. "Repeated instances of suicide . . . of late have tingled in our ears," Boston's *Independent Chronicle* reported on its front page on January 30, 1783. "Suicide is making a most alarming progress in these states," the *Pennsylvania Evening Herald* announced in June 1785, before detailing the deaths of "three persons . . . who have dared to rush into the presence of their Creator." "Suicide is often committed in these our days," the *Massachusetts Gazette* agreed in August 1788. An essayist in a Vermont paper voiced similar concern soon afterward, directing readers' attention to "the many self murders which have been mentioned of late in the public papers."[3]

A decade later, as Samuel Miller set about making a name for himself in New York City, the same dreadful refrains still showed no signs of quieting. If anything, the clamor was growing louder. In September 1801 a Baltimore paper remarked how suicides now appeared "almost daily" in its pages. According to a contributor to a sister sheet in Connecticut,

"Scarce a Gazette is issued to the publick, but it contains some record" of a person taking his or her own life. "The many instances of Suicide which have lately occured, present a most horrible and alarming proof of the increasing depravity and irreligion of the times," Boston's *People's Friend* lamented a few years later. If the newspapers were to be believed, the new nation was awash with self-destruction. By the time Samuel Miller's 1805 pamphlet appeared under the arms of book peddlers across the Northeast, any diligent urban reader could have collected hundreds of press clippings like these.[4]

For a long time, nobody questioned the fact that so many of these bleak diagnoses referenced newspaper coverage of suicide as the source of their information. Prior to the 1840s, most municipal governments did not collate and distribute mortality statistics, and those that did so typically limited themselves to counting interments in churchyards and other sacred burial grounds, thereby overlooking the potters' fields to which the bodies of unambiguous suicides were unceremoniously consigned. Instead, everyone relied upon trends in press coverage to gauge the frequency of suicide beyond their immediate communities. And those trends were startling. In Annapolis the *Maryland Gazette* published three times as many reports of completed suicide during the 1790s as it had in the decade prior. In New York City the *Weekly Museum* reported four times as many self-destructive acts during the 1800s as it had ten years earlier. Even allowing for the fact that many commercially oriented papers paid scant attention to social news, a broad survey of newspapers published in the mid-Atlantic states reveals that readers at the turn of the nineteenth century confronted vastly more (166 percent) suicide reports than their parents had a generation earlier.[5]

If the newspapers were to be credited, suicide was now so common that it had become a defining feature of life in the early United States. Before the Revolution, colonists had often referred to self-destruction as "the English malady," not least because their local papers typically reported twice as many British suicides as they did American. Yet as these proportions reversed after the break with Britain—the result not only of changing political imperatives but also of structural changes in the way news was gathered and distributed—it was as if the English malady had infected America. Accounts of deaths in European capitals now had to jostle for column inches with more and more news of tragedies in distant and not-so-distant corners of the Union. In Pennsylvania more than half of all reports of completed suicide published in the *Carlisle Gazette* between 1785 and 1815 now focused on domestic subjects, while all but 5 of the 119 named suicides to appear in the pages of New York City's *Weekly Museum* between 1790 and 1817 occurred within the borders of the newly United States. Everywhere readers looked, coverage of suicide was becoming more keenly focused on men and women who took their lives on American soil. In April 1772 the *Pennsylvania Journal* had reported that one London gentleman "went out of the world in the English way." Over the decades that followed, readers of northeastern newspapers found cause to wonder whether perhaps their fellow Americans had since developed their own defining proclivity for suicide.[6]

It seemed that no one was safe. As this tide of newspaper reporting made terrifyingly clear, suicide was not the sole prerogative of one social group or another but was commonly committed by Americans from all walks. Stories informed subscribers such as Samuel Miller of acts committed by "respectable wealthy citizen[s]," those "in affluent circumstances," in "good circumstances," and the "tolerabl[y] well-dressed," like the Connecticut lawyer who took his own life with a horse pistol in 1796. The gentleman, the *Philadelphia Minerva* reported, was "held in high respect and esteemed by his acquaintance, [and] was possessed of a handsome fortune." In addition to lawyers, the papers brought word of the suicides of well-to-do judges, doctors, divines, and even a state governor, Meriwether Lewis, who shot himself in 1809. Suicides from the middling ranks paraded through the same pages. The deaths of postmasters, landlords, teachers, sheriffs, actors, musicians, barbers, weavers, distillers, butchers, and carpenters all shared space in the public prints. The lower orders, too, were distressingly well represented. The last moments of poor women and laboring men were featured alongside the suicides of impoverished ex-soldiers, debtors, servants, slaves, and women of the "frail sisterhood."[7]

Nor were newspapers the only source of this emerging moral panic. Depictions of men and women laying hands on themselves bombarded early national readers no matter where they turned. Newly popular novels and short stories fetishized self-destruction, turning romantic suicide into a central motif of sentimental writing. *The Sorrows of Young Werther*

(1774), a German import wildly popular with teenage readers during the 1780s, fostered a taste for scenes of sentimental suicide that aspiring local authors worked hard to satisfy. Indeed, the very first American novel, William Hill Brown's *The Power of Sympathy* (1789), featured not one but three characters convinced that the best way to exhibit their exquisite sensibility was by taking their own lives. To the dismay of parents of adolescent fiction lovers, almost half of all American novels published between 1789 and 1800—including four works by Charles Brockden Brown and two by Susanna Rowson—built their plots around the suicides of disappointed young romantics.[8]

Anxiety about the spread of suicide even inflected political writing. In an attempt to harness emerging literary tastes for the purpose of reform, early national antislavery activists filled popular magazines with poetic, sometimes sentimental, testimony to the "thousands" of enslaved people whose self-inflicted deaths on board slave ships or on plantations bore witness to America's original sin. In similar fashion it became common for patriot leaders such as George Washington and Alexander Hamilton (not to mention many others) to describe political decisions they perceived as imperiling the fledgling nation in terms that gestured toward the alarming incidence of self-destruction among its constituents. Thus divisions between the leadership of the Continental Army and the Continental Congress threatened "political Suicide," while the attempt to scale back the armed forces after the end of the war was "a species of national suicide." Likewise, during the Constitutional Convention of 1787 and the ensuing debates over ratification, delegates impugned various schemes put forward to settle constitutional problems—representation in the Senate, the role of the militia in peacetime, the interstate commerce clause, the scheduling of congressional elections, and the balance between federal power and states' rights—as "act[s] of suicide." Over the following years, politicians and pundits used the same metaphor to criticize all manner of policy decisions, not least the passage of the Alien and Sedition Acts (1798), Jefferson's embargo restricting American ships from engaging in foreign trade (1807–1809), and Federalist opposition to war with England (1812–1815).[9]

Beyond the corridors of Congress, panic about the rising incidence of self-destruction ensured that moral reformers and social activists turned to antisuicide rhetoric with equally unprecedented enthusiasm. Whether mobilized against the demon drink, unregulated lotteries and backroom gambling dens, the fashionable tight-lacing of ladies' corsets, or the cult of dueling, no metaphorical device was used more frequently, consistently, and zealously in early national moral reform campaigns than the likening of the particular vice to suicide. Temperance was a case in point. Benjamin Rush, the Philadelphia physician and founding father of this movement, built his crusade against distilled spirits around the central idea that inebriates were "guilty of a species of suicide." Were those who drank themselves to death, Rush often asked, any different from those who might willfully jump "from the mast of a ship full sail into the sea?" After his death in 1813, his many disciples copied this rhetoric into their own persuasive pamphlets, ensuring that claims insisting habitual drinking was gradual suicide remained at the forefront of temperance literature for the next twenty years.[10]

Activists frustrated by the failure of legal sanctions to curb the fashion for dueling in postrevolutionary America employed identical tactics, mounting an audacious campaign to invert the moral associations between dueling and honor. To make their case to an ambivalent public, reformers recast dueling not as an honor ritual but as a unique form of homicide, a fatal compact of suicide and murder. "In fine, Duellists are always self-murderers, if not willful murderers of their adversaries," the Newburyport Congregationalist Samuel Spring wrote in the aftermath of Alexander Hamilton's death at the hands of Aaron Burr in 1804. "Who with honor can plead their cause?" Between 1801 and 1850 half of all antidueling pamphlets described pistols at ten paces as a species of self-destruction. Dueling is "suicide of the highest grade, and in the first degree," pronounced Virginia minister Samuel Low in 1811.[11]

Wherever one looked, there was evidence that alarm about the spread of self-destructive behavior now gripped the American imagination. To determine whether or not the escalating epidemic described in the press was confined to the white inhabitants of the United States, social scientists such as Benjamin Rush set about questioning native leaders like Alexander McGillivray and frontiersmen like Meriwether Lewis as to whether "suicide [is] ever known among the Indians. And from what causes, if it be?" By the turn of the century, students at colleges such as Harvard, Yale, and the College of New Jersey (later Princeton) had taken to debating whether the strength of legal injunctions against self-murder was still sufficient. In literary and intellectual circles, clubs such as the Society for the Attainment of Useful Knowledge in Philadelphia held special meetings to ask: "Is Suicide Justifiable?" To capitalize on mounting public unease, opportunistic self-promoters such as a Mr. Ogilvie in Salem, Massachusetts, scheduled speaking engagements devoted to the subject. Elsewhere, friends gathered around dining tables and in parlors to confide their concerns and discuss what to do. At one such get-together in New York City in 1795, a group of young provocateurs decided to play devil's advocate. They reported to the editor of the city's *Weekly Chronicle* that their supper-time discussion had concluded that "there sometimes did, and very often might, happen cases wherein suicide would be perfectly justifiable" and facetiously requested that "some of your ingenious correspondents . . . give us their thoughts therein in your next number."[12]

No one was amused. Judging by surviving diaries and correspondence, few serious-minded newspaper readers welcomed this sort of mischief-making. On the contrary, many prominent citizens were so unnerved by news items suggesting that every corner of the country was now blighted by an unprecedented amount of self-destructive behavior that they began to worry about the number of recent suicides in their own families and neighborhoods. In fact, one of the defining features of postrevolutionary diaries is the care many authors took to document the extent of self-destruction in their communities. Take Philadelphia: in February 1802 Benjamin Rush noted in his commonplace book that "Three instances of suicide have occurred within the last month in this city." On April 19, 1806, a merchant across town confided to his journal that three suicides had been committed that day alone. The very same week, Elizabeth Drinker, a seventy-one-year-old Quaker, compared her own tally with what she had read in a local paper: "The Newspaper tells us of 3 Cases of suecide [*sic*], that has very lately occur'd—we have heard of 4. The man that cut his throat, one that shot himself in prison and another who took a large dose of La[u]danum, also a woman who had been married a few months, that hanged herself."[13]

In Manhattan, Rev. Samuel Miller was hardly the only resident keeping count. In August 1800, Judge Samuel Bayard wrote to Rush with the disturbing news that "there had been 24 instances of suicide in New York . . . since last spring, 3 of whom were servant girls." Between 1804 and 1806, Samuel Latham Mitchill, a doctor and an amateur statistician, counted fifty-one more. While calculations like these typically derived wholly or in great part from newspaper reports, only one state's civic leaders took the time to try to corroborate such worrisome numbers. To do so, members of the Connecticut Academy of Arts and Sciences sent out a questionnaire to the state's 107 townships that asked local officials to count up "instances of suicide, within twenty years" and specify—in language that betrayed their assumption that self-destruction was linked to rising mobility and in-migration—"whether committed by natives" or those born out-of-state. The relative rarity of such incidents in the replies they received—sixty-five deaths across an entire state over two decades—proved puzzling to say the least.[14]

Elsewhere in New England, there was no such confusion. Diarists across the region filled page after page of their private journals with notes that together attest to the extent of the suicide panic. In Salem, Rev. William Bentley seemed to be constantly on guard: his multivolume opus bulged with details of forty-five men and women who retreated to the grave between 1788 and 1813. Martha Ballard reported twelve more in and around the tiny town of Hallowell, Maine, in her diary over the same period, while to the south, in Boston, Josiah Williston carefully recorded the suicides of thirteen people between 1809 and 1813, listing them all by name. In nearby Brookline, Rev. John Pierce kept scrupulous confidential notes on all the members of his congregation who destroyed themselves, usually offering his own speculations as to their motives and even copying out a suicide note that came into his possession.[15]

Everywhere one turned, nervous people were obsessing about suicide—its causes, its consequences and, most of all, its frequency. Diarists up and down the coast, especially parents and ministers living in urban centers, had become hypersensitized to the subject, thanks in no small part to the continuing uproar in the press that suicide was making "alarming progress" throughout the Northeast and the mid-Atlantic. Indeed, encountering such panicked declarations was such a persistent and pervasive feature of the newspaper reading experience that Samuel Miller's 1805 decision to use his status and standing to try to tackle this singular public health crisis was anything but original. His double-length pamphlet was actually a late addition to an already vast and growing collection of increasingly shrill public appeals to soul-sick people to choose life. Given its context, *The Guilt, Folly, and Sources of Suicide* was utterly unexceptional.[16]

Of course it was the context itself that was exceptional. How had it come to this? How had a private decision long attributed to the invisible hand of Satan become a primary index of the moral health of postwar society and a pliant tool in political speeches and social activism? What did the people of the newly United States see in the prospect of rising suicide rates that so alarmed them? Why had so much urban discourse become consumed by apocalyptic visions of a citizenry set on a course toward self-annihilation?

In the wake of the Revolution, suicide came to function as one of the most evocative and incendiary words in Americans' political vocabularies. To invoke the word in public discourse brought to mind not only the individual act of consciously putting oneself to death. It also telegraphed a variety of existential fears about the state of the union. Like freedom, slavery, democracy, tyranny, and disunion, suicide became a keyword in the new nation's lexicon because of its ability to embody complex ideas and provoke visceral emotional responses. In fact, the problems associated with deducing the precise intent of those who commit suicide are such that the act can be interpreted as submission or as protest, as dispossession or as mastery, as madness or as calculation. Its very capaciousness and opacity render suicide an enormously adaptable weapon in political combat. As they fought over the meaning of suicide, the early Republic's culture warriors used its finality and extremity to advance all manner of agendas—some conservative, others radical. In suicide they found a tool of political argument equally capable of unifying, validating, and mobilizing as it was of dividing, delegitimizing, and enraging.[17]

Because personal choices about how and when to die take place at the nexus of self and society, self-destruction has always been a matter of consuming political concern. The problem of suicide, as philosophers from Socrates to Sartre have long understood, strikes most directly at the core of questions about individual autonomy and collective organization, and it does so in ways that are agonizingly personal, pointed, and profound.

Should individual citizens have the freedom to do with their life and their liberty as they see fit? Or should obligations to serve community interests provide necessary restraint? Is it every man for himself, or are we all in this together?[18]

In the early United States, such questions were not abstract inquiries. On the contrary, they pressed down with great weight on the minds of every man and woman who ever paused to wonder whether the citizens of the new Republic had sufficient virtue, self-discipline, and care for one another to foster a stable and self-governing society. Determining the proper relationship between private will and public interest was the fundamental social and political challenge facing the people of the United States in the fragile, formative years after the Revolution. As a result, the meaning of suicide became a principal locus of contention.

The early American Republic was, after all, no ordinary political community. While every society, by definition, prizes mutual affinity (order) over unchecked personal autonomy (liberty), most champions of the republican experiment held fast to the belief that republics in particular are built on the promise of associative cooperation. They exist as a living expression of a renewable, sustainable social contract. "Every man in a republic is public property," Benjamin Rush reminded Philadelphians in an essay published in 1787 in support of the Constitution. "His time and youth—his manhood—his old age—nay more, life, all, belong to his country." Convinced that the fate of the new republican system of government hinged on the relationship between the self and society, men like Benjamin Rush and Samuel Miller could not help but regard the frequency of individual decisions to die as a sort of "moral thermometer" for the country's health. With more and more suicides clogging the arteries of the press than ever before, many citizens succumbed to the temptation to interpret such grim tidings as symptoms of impending national ruin and cultural collapse. As the editor of Boston's *People's Friend* had put it in 1807, each fresh case provided yet more "alarming proof of the increasing depravity and irreligion of the times."[19]

And these were extraordinary times. In the fifty years following the signing of the Declaration of Independence, the United States suffered through dramatic demographic changes and unprecedented economic expansion and restructuring. Simultaneously, the inheritors of the Revolu-

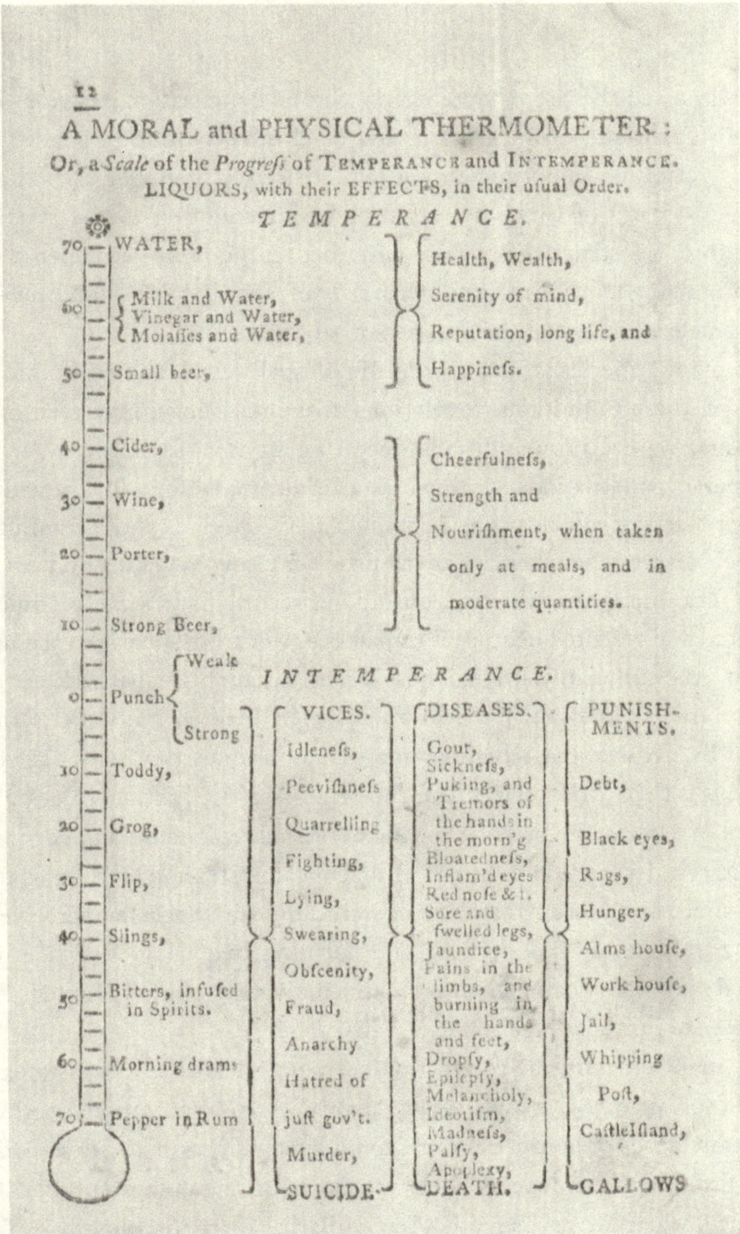

12

A MORAL and PHYSICAL THERMOMETER:

Or, a *Scale* of the *Progreſs* of TEMPERANCE and INTEMPERANCE.

LIQUORS, with their EFFECTS, in their uſual Order.

TEMPERANCE.

	Liquors	Effects
70	WATER,	Health, Wealth, Serenity of mind, Reputation, long life, and Happineſs.
60	Milk and Water, Vinegar and Water, Molaſſes and Water,	
50	Small beer,	
40	Cider,	Cheerfulneſs, Strength and Nouriſhment, when taken only at meals, and in moderate quantities.
30	Wine,	
20	Porter,	
10	Strong Beer,	

INTEMPERANCE.

	Liquors	VICES.	DISEASES.	PUNISHMENTS.
0	Punch { Weak / Strong	Idleneſs,	Gout,	
10	Toddy,	Peeviſhneſs	Sickneſs, Puking, and Tremors of the hands in the morn'g	Debt,
20	Grog,	Quarrelling	Bloatedneſs,	Black eyes,
30	Flip,	Fighting, Lying,	Inflam'd eyes Red noſe & f.	Rags,
40	Slings,	Swearing,	Sore and ſwelled legs, Jaundice,	Hunger, Alms houſe,
50	Bitters, infuſed in Spirits.	Obſcenity, Fraud,	Pains in the limbs, and burning in the hands and feet,	Work houſe, Jail,
60	Morning drams	Anarchy Hatred of	Dropſy, Epilepſy, Melancholy,	Whipping Poſt,
70	Pepper in Rum	juſt gov't. Murder,	Ideotiſm, Madneſs, Palſy, Apoplexy,	Caſtle Iſland,
		SUICIDE.	DEATH.	GALLOWS

Benjamin Rush's iconic illustration of the consequences of habitual drinking of distilled liquor placed "SUICIDE" at an extreme position along a spectrum of vices that ranged from "Idleness" and "Quarrelling" to "Anarchy" and "Hatred of just gov't." Benjamin Rush, *An Inquiry into the Effects of Spirituous Liquors on the Human Body. To Which Is Added a Moral and Physical Thermometer* (Boston: Thomas and Andrews, 1790). Courtesy of the Library Company of Philadelphia.

tion witnessed the rise of systematic electoral competition, religious disestablishment and disintegration, and a velvet revolution in gender and family relations. Important in and of themselves, together these broad changes—many of which appeared to be contributing to the startling spike in self-destructive behavior described in the press—signaled a vast and atomizing transformation, the arrival of what Ralph Waldo Emerson later labeled "the age of the first person singular."[20]

To many Americans in positions of political, social, and economic advantage, these tumultuous revolutions in the relationship between order and liberty were profoundly disconcerting signs of social decay, moral degeneracy, and national decline. As a result, many found it difficult to interpret acts of suicide in their communities, especially those committed by their direct dependents, as anything other than wrenching and irrevocable recalibrations of the relationship between self and society. "Suicide is feared and resented because it transfers power from society to the individual," the clinician and sociologist Robert Kastenbaum has written, and it "becomes a more salient threat when society believes it is under serious attack by divisive and rebellious forces. . . . It is not the death that disturbs. It is the affront, the threat, the act of assertion, the act of defiance, the act of self-empowerment." Setting to one side colonial-era understandings of self-destruction as a sign of diabolical possession or a sin against God, more and more Americans of status and standing now perceived a strong and binding link between the alarming frequency of suicides described in the early national press and the individualistic and disintegrative impulses of this budding capitalist society.[21]

For many citizens, the connection between suicide and the disintegration of social authority was deeply personal. Across revolutionary America, many heads of household came to understand acts of self-destruction committed by their dependents as attacks upon the domestic order. For instance, when Pennsylvania housewife Barbara Arndorff finally walked out on her husband, John, he tried to vindicate himself of her allegations of "ill usage," rape, and battery by playing the victim. "I think it not amiss to let the public know," John Arndorff wrote in Benjamin Franklin's *Pennsylvania Gazette* on February 28, 1771, "that she has at divers times abused me, without any provocation, and attempted to drown and hang herself." From John's jaundiced perspective, Barbara's attempts to destroy herself were no different from any of the other abuses and affronts he had suffered at her hands over the years. They were just another attempt to unman him. To try to put her in her place following these latest provocations, he defamed her in the press and steadfastly refused to pay for her support.[22]

In early national America, similar responses were surprisingly common when women in broken marriages attempted suicide. In 1795 John Kean, a Philadelphia bottler, packed his wife off to the city's poorhouse to punish her after she tried to drown herself. At her admission interview, Jane Kean told officials that she had thrown herself into the river because "her Husband [had] severely beaten her." By throwing his wife out of his house, John Kean, like John Arndorff before him, took highly visible public action to show that he would not stand to see his miserable wife humiliate him by taking her own life.[23]

Benjamin Rush likely felt something of the same furious mortification when on March 7, 1809, his eldest son tore a four-inch gash across his throat with a razor. It was the latest of "several attempts" John Rush had made "to destroy himself" since killing a friend and fellow naval officer in an angry and impetuous duel several months earlier. In fact, John had challenged three other sailors to duels during the course of his episodic and entirely undistinguished naval service. Fiercely independent, obstinate, and quick-tempered, John had spent his childhood in near-constant warfare with his strict parents and as an adult he had continued a pattern of studied defiance by openly indulging in all the vices against which his physician father so publicly railed. Removed from Princeton after tutors caught him playing cards on the Sabbath, John had refused Benjamin's offer of a job on his medical staff. Instead, he struck out on his own, enlisting in the fledgling U.S. Navy as a lieutenant. During a liquor-soaked stint at a base in New Orleans, he shot and killed a fellow gunboat commander, "the distress and remorse [of] which . . . deprived him of his reason" and led directly to his suicide attempt.[24]

John's wound was not fatal—the razor had missed the veins in his neck—and so although he remained "in a deep state of melancholy," the navy soon transferred him, against his will, to Benjamin's care. Back in his father's house once more, John, now thirty-two, staged one final domestic insurrection, enraging Benjamin by refusing "to speak or even to answer a question." After three days of noncompliance, Dr. Rush ordered that his prodigal son be confined to a basement room at the Pennsylvania Hospital where his staff of orderlies could compel him to cooperate. John remained there until he died, twenty-seven years later.[25]

While the enduring pathos of these agonizing acts of self-harm should not be disregarded, my focus here is on the bitter domestic reactions they provoked. Nothing, it seems, reminded violent, pitiless husbands and stern, overbearing fathers of the shrinking boundaries of their authority better than a suicide attempt. Indeed, while only a handful of social radicals in this period would grant that taking one's own life was an expression or appropriation of power, John Arndorff, John Kean, and Benjamin Rush came to understand that amidst the crumbling hierarchies of early national society, it marked power's limits.

For these reasons, suicide emerged as a potent means to connect public and private concerns in the young Republic. It functioned as a locus and crucible for arguments as to whether or not the individuals that uneasily comprised the newly United States embodied a sustainable blend of sense and sensibility, reason and passion, independence and self-restraint. Thus parents eager to restore their authority over increasingly autonomous offspring took to demonizing romantic suicides in sentimental novels. Physicians and ministers anxious to preserve and expand their professional authority established antisuicide groups committed to coercive intervention and long-term custodial supervision. Among the prosecutors, judges, and jailers on the front lines of the criminal justice system, inmate suicides emerged as subversive symbols of a series of broader challenges to judicial authority. And within denominational circles, mainstream faith groups fearful of losing market share tried to paint an upstart liberal sect as a permissive suicide cult that undermined agreed-upon understandings of the consequences of sin.

Such efforts figured certain species of self-destruction as unwelcome affronts to cherished social and political hierarchies. To this way of thinking, the suicides of adolescent novel readers, city bridge jumpers, convicted murderers, and zealous followers of liberal religion were signal proofs that the new nation suffered from a dangerous deficit of deference, maturity, responsibility, and self-control and a corresponding surplus of self-indulgence, rebelliousness, madness, and religious deviance. Yet on other occasions, partisans invoked suicide precisely because they wanted to challenge and undermine particular forms of embodied authority. Antigallows activists, for example, took to publicizing death-row suicides in order to expose the brutality of state-sanctioned executions. Universalists attempting to muscle their way into the religious mainstream did so by attacking the enthusiasm that sometimes drove attendees at evangelical camp meetings toward suicidal despair. Most daringly of all, militant abolitionists publicly and provocatively embraced slave suicides as libertarian protests against racial commodification.

Whether in the cause of restoring parental authority, professionalizing benevolence, defending law and order, debating the merits of denominational pluralism, or expanding civil rights, Americans animated by a range of special interests deployed the uniquely emotional grammar that talking about suicide made available. They did so in order to contest the limits of self-determination and thus to define, influence, revise, and transform the broad contours of early national and antebellum society. As they fought over the meaning of self-destruction—whose interests it threatened, what it represented, and whether it should be prevented or celebrated—parents, ministers, doctors, activists, novelists, and newspapermen struggling to create a viable political community out of the chaos and clamor that accompanied American independence used the pointed questions posed by self-murder as a means to wrestle into being their own distinct visions of a more perfect union.[26]

1

Suicide and the State of the Union

The first issue of the first newspaper ever printed in America featured a suicide on its front page. It described how a group of friends had discovered the body of an old man hanging from a rope normally used to tie up cows for milking. By the time they found him, Boston's *Publick Occurences* reported on September 25, 1690, "he was dead with his feet near touching the Ground." Weeks earlier, this unnamed man, a pious and sober figure by all accounts, had buried his wife. According to Benjamin Harris, the editor of *Publick Occurences*, "The Devil [then] took Advantage of the Melancholy which he thereupon fell into."[1]

While Harris was sensitive to the toxic blend of grief, loneliness, and penury that had poisoned this widower against life, the editor ascribed his death's larger meaning to the influence of Satan. This was standard procedure throughout British America prior to the Revolution, and especially in the New England colonies. In public at least, it was common practice to speak of the significance of individual acts of suicide in diabolical terms. Throughout the seventeenth century, ministers called upon to address local communities in the aftermath of violently premature deaths spoke with one voice. Unlike later commentators, they did not dwell on the challenges that annihilating the self might pose to natural law or the social compact. Suicide, they instead agreed, was a rebellion against God orchestrated by the Devil. Addressing a Boston congregation in 1682 following the death of William Taylor, a merchant who had hanged himself with his own bridle, Increase Mather warned those gathered that a wolf stalked among them, picking off those of weak faith or melancholic disposition. "DISTRESS *of Conscience* is that from which the *Devil* does many times, take occasion to *Tempt* Men unto the Sin of Self-murder," Mather explained. This was how Satan had ensnared poor William Taylor, and this was how he would prey on other wounded spirits. "Thus the Devil says, Murder, & Dy!—Stab thyself,—Shoot thyself,—Choak thyself,—& Dy!"[2]

In Mather's view, and in the view of a great many other colonial clergymen, every act of suicide tipped the scales in a divine struggle. The Devil attempts to "vex and molest the faithful Servants of GOD," Mather warned Boston residents, in order to drive a great wedge between the elect and their loving Father. "This first rebel, *is most highly gratify'd*, when he can prevail with any Person to destroy his own life," agreed fellow Bostonian Samuel Phillips in a sermon delivered and published almost a century later, in 1767. Indeed, while most of Phillips's contemporaries did not invoke the Devil quite as readily as Mather had in the seventeenth century, mid-eighteenth-century ministers continued to remind their audiences (as well as the readers of their published sermons) that suicide was, first and foremost, a mortal sin. It was, they insisted, a revolt against God. It defaced his image, dishonored his name, usurped his singular power over life and death, rejected his gift of life, denied his promise of salvation, and violated his sixth commandment (Thou Shalt Not Kill). No matter what the provocation, those who rushed unbidden into eternity in sound mind committed a sin so heinous that they would not enter the kingdom of heaven. Instead, they would suffer what the seventeenth-century English theologian John Sym had once referred to as a "second death farre exceeding the first in misery."[3]

The same understandings suffused popular belief throughout the colonial period. Evidence from townships in the Connecticut River valley suggests that ordinary men and women commonly interpreted suicide as a manifestation of spiritual confusion or lack of faith. In 1735 a merchant named Joseph Hawley dragged a razor across his throat at the height of Jonathan Edwards's conversion efforts in Northampton, Massachusetts. Dismayed townsfolk reflexively attributed his suicide to his growing conviction that he had no hope of being saved. As news of what had happened spread, the entire revival ground to a halt. Within days, people in and around Northampton reported hearing strange disembodied voices, encouraging them to do as Hawley—who was Jonathan Edwards's uncle—had done. "Cut your own throat, now is a good opportunity: *now, NOW!*" the devilish voices whispered.[4]

Many similar episodes punctuate the social history of the great awakenings. In fact, early eighteenth-century conversion narratives indicate that thoughts of killing oneself provoked by acute uncertainty about one's worthiness marked a key stage in the spiritual journeys of many ordinary people. "Satan comes upon me and says there is one way to know quick; destroy your self," recalled Nathan Cole, a Connecticut farmer and carpenter, after hearing George Whitefield preach in 1745. Even those who had successfully overcome the rituals of doubt and despair common to the evangelical conversion experience continued to regard the temptation to end their lives as a test of their faith. Another Connecticut farmworker, Hannah Heaton, confided to her diary that in 1751 her own hard-fought conversion was almost undone "when [her] little daughter dyed." Isolated from her parents after moving from Long Island to join her new husband in North Haven, Heaton's grief had threatened to overwhelm her. "Satans tone was go hang your self go hang your self," she later remembered, "and when I saw a convenient place I could hardly tell how to keep from it sometimes."[5]

This enduring conviction that suicide manifested a turn away from God helps explain why so many colonial legislatures responded to acts of self-destruction with the full force of the law. In Massachusetts a 1661 statute defined suicide as a "damnable Practice" and a marker of "how far Satan doth prevail." Accordingly, the law demanded that "every person" judged to have committed suicide in sound mind "shall be buried in some Common high-way . . . and a Cart-load of Stones laid upon the Grave as a Brand of Infamy." Such brutal bodily humiliation, which sometimes extended to driving a stake through the heart of the corpse to prevent the escape of evil spirits, reflected the Puritan conviction that suicide was no ordinary species of homicide but a diabolical offense akin to witchcraft.[6]

Other colonial legislatures were only slightly less draconian. While Pennsylvania's charter prevented its agents from making a legal distinction between willful suicide (felo-de-se, literally a "felon of himself") and other causes of death, justice officials in New Hampshire, Rhode Island, New Jersey, Maryland, Virginia, South Carolina, and North Carolina followed procedures derived from English Common Law that did just that. When a coroner's jury of inquest examined the corpse of someone who had died in suspicious circumstances and returned a verdict of felo-de-se, officials in these colonies typically moved to confiscate the goods and chattel of the deceased. What's more, with the cooperation of local ministers eager to deter such damnable practices, they frequently succeeded in preventing the burial of the body in hallowed ground. As a result, the potters' fields that served as makeshift boneyards for the unchurched and the poor often made room for the cadavers of suicides.[7]

Despite such statutory prescriptions, coroners and juries of inquest enjoyed a remarkable amount of discretion in the arbitration of the legal consequences of self-murder. Throughout the colonial period, the coroner and his jury of twelve local men often exercised their prerogative to shield from forfeiture and profane burial those they judged to be "lunatic, mad or distracted" (non compos mentis). Some decisions were straightforward. The presence of witnesses, the discovery of a note, or testimony that the subject had made a habit of threatening his or her own life were usually sufficient to convince a jury that a death had indeed been purposeful and was, therefore, punishable. Yet in other, more ambiguous cases, juries had to sift circumstantial evidence for clues and to consider the advice of the coroner in order to determine the fate of the deceased's body and estate. Given the personal relationships that often bound the farmers, tradesmen, and artisans who comprised most inquest juries to the grieving family and friends of the deceased, these impaneled officials faced tremendous pressure to return sympathetic verdicts, especially if survivors were well connected.[8]

Throughout the eighteenth century, but particularly in the years after 1750, more and more of the men called to serve on these unhappy tribunals began to buckle under the weight of such expectation, especially in Massachusetts, where the prescribed penalties for willful suicide were most severe. Indeed, a study of more than two hundred reports filed by Boston coroners between 1700 and 1799 reveals that juries were growing ever more reluctant to enforce the law. The percentage of verdicts of felo-de-se handed down by juries following suspect deaths fell dramatically from one decade to the next, from more than 80 percent of decisions before 1720 to no more than 20 percent of inquest verdicts after 1780. Instead, jurors attributed increasing numbers of likely suicides to accident, misfortune, misadventure, or, most commonly of all, mental derangement (non compos mentis). It is tempting to suggest that the spread of Enlightenment rationalism and the rise of "nervous medicine" account for this tidal shift in judgment. But that is not the whole story. In many cases, these petty officials and reluctant volunteers were simply submitting to rising pressure from increasingly acquisitive neighbors eager to assume ownership of their loved ones' property.[9]

The pace of decriminalization only accelerated after the Revolution as lawmakers in four states adopted new constitutions or statutes that outlawed forfeiture of property as a means to punish willful suicide. While their intent was to distinguish American criminal codes from English Common Law, efforts by legislators in New Jersey, Maryland, Virginia, and North Carolina implicitly acknowledged the fact that jurors across the country were growing ever more averse to imposing punitive verdicts that did harm to the guiltless relatives of suspected suicides. Arguing for the repeal of confiscation laws in Virginia in 1779, Thomas Jefferson reminded delegates that activist juries now regularly refused to impose the penalty of forfeiture on families left shattered by self-murder. "That men in general, too, disapprove of this severity," the thirty-six-year-old Virginian noted, "is apparent from the constant practice of juries finding the suicide in a state of insanity; because they have no other way of saving the forefeiture. Let it then be done away."[10]

As Jefferson's remarks suggest, even in the nine states in which legal deterrents against suicide still doggedly endured, enforcement was now increasingly unusual. In early national Massachusetts, where a few officeholders still jealously guarded the legal inheritance of the Puritan era, occasional attempts to enforce the old laws now met with a growing backlash, especially from young people convinced that roadside tombs were barbarous relics from a bygone age. When a jury in Newburyport handed down a rare verdict of "wilful self-murder" following a teenager's death in January 1788, twenty-one-year-old John Quincy Adams launched into a tirade denouncing the state's refusal to reform. "I cannot but think that laws against suicide are impolitic and cruel," Adams told friends the night Benjamin Hooper was buried.[11]

Despite this outburst, young Quincy had not been terribly surprised to learn that older townsmen had returned a felo-de-se verdict in this particular case. Benjamin Hooper was well known in Newburyport as the "dissipated and debauched" son of a hated Loyalist who had escaped to England during the war. As a result, when the inquest jury had convened to examine his body, it is likely that no one had risen to speak in favor of sparing him the final humiliation of a highway burial. Yet Hooper was in a shrinking minority. By the 1780s Loyalists and convicted criminals were the only members of society whom inquest juries still consistently found guilty of committing suicide in sound mind. As verdicts handed down by Paul Revere during his days as the Boston coroner in the late 1790s reveal, by the turn of the century even sailors, old slaves, and strangers stood a fair chance of being shielded from the law by compassionate jurors. And the more respectable the citizen, the more likely that a jury would return a verdict of "insanity" or "misfortune," regardless of the evidence. Thus when William Bant Sullivan, the son of the Bay State's powerful attorney general, shot himself in 1806, there was little question that the jury would find him insane. Although friends knew he was reeling from a recent romantic rejection, and although several others remembered that in all other respects the young man had been "in usual health," and although witnesses found a note he had penned describing his motives, the inquest verdict insisted his mind had been momentarily overthrown by madness. "A suicide in high life is [now] almost always acquitted as insane," an outraged editor of New York's *Oracle* later wrote, "whilst the poor wretch in low circumstances is as uniformly a *felo de se*."[12]

While this snippet of the *Oracle*'s blistering commentary dwelled upon the divisive privileges of status, the editor's larger complaint was that such brazenly selective regard for the law of the land did vastly more harm than good. With newspapers everywhere filled with disturbing claims that the number of suicides occurring across America each week had reached egregious proportions, volunteer jurors trying to do right by their friends and neighbors now found themselves the target of stinging censure. "Since suicide or self-murder is so common at the present day of immorality," Rev. Samuel Spring told his Newburyport congregation in 1804, "it is to be lamented that public authority does not carefully and uniformly mark the crime with those tokens of disgrace which men generally dread more than death itself." By Spring's reckoning, the only way to turn back the tide of self-destruction apparently engulfing his own town and the country at large was to deliver honest inquest verdicts that followed the letter of the law. Most suicidal people, Spring reasoned, "would rather omit the horrid act, than expose their bodies to be buried in the high-way." Samuel Miller made similar arguments to New Yorkers the following year, telling jurors there that their compassionate enthusiasm was likely contributing to the spike in recent suicides described in the press because "It tends to diminish, in the minds of those who embrace it, the *moral odium* which ought ever to be attached to the crime in question."[13]

By the time the editor of New York's *Oracle* joined this fray in September 1808, in a long essay bewailing news of three more suicides in that city, such criticism had become commonplace. Faulting jurors' generous use of non compos mentis verdicts as the product of "absurd" and misplaced conscience, the *Oracle* added its voice to a growing chorus of demands that juries honor the original intent of those antisuicide statutes that still remained on the books:

> The framers of our laws knew that suicide was as often committed by men in their senses, as by men who were insane; and in order to deter them from an act so dangerous to the community, they denounced the crime by imputing to it the highest guilt of Felony. But of what use is legislative precaution, if Juries from a false and criminal humanity almost uniformly determine otherwise?

The language here is telling. The *Oracle* did not harp on the succor compassionate jurors might give to Satan, nor did it pause to dwell on self-destruction as a damnable and defiant affront to God. Instead, the *Oracle*'s editor and publisher, J. J. Negrin, described suicide as "dangerous to the community," as a "crime" and "Felony" that disrupts the relationship between an individual and society. In *The Guilt, Folly, and Sources of Suicide* (1805), Samuel Miller said much the same. After acknowledging that self-destruction represented "a presumptuous attempt" to escape from divine control, Miller devoted himself to warning his readers of the damage it did to social relations. Suicide, he argued at some length, is "A SIN AGAINST SOCIETY" and a "Crime of the deepest dye." Individuals are bound to each other by friendship, labor, protection, and service. "And when such persons, regardless of all the obligations which bind them to society, abandon the post at which they are placed, they act a part which deserves to be stigmatized as selfish, unsocial, and base." Societies, he informed his readers, are not faceless abstract conceits; they are your flesh and blood: your family, friends, and neighbors. Can anyone in good conscience subject his nearest and dearest to so much unbidden grief, humiliation, and hardship? Suicide, Miller concluded, "is a practice which reverses all the doctrines of social benevolence, and sets up as a principle of action the detestable maxim, that private caprice and private enjoyment are to be regarded as more worthy objects of pursuit than public happiness."[14]

The moralistic outcry that accompanied decriminalization had exposed an important shift in the way Americans talked about self-destruction in public. Although they never abandoned the colonial-era conviction that the decision to forfeit life posed a radical challenge to divine authority, early national commentators were vastly more likely to interpret suicide as a challenge to community integrity and social order. In jeremiads denouncing the rampancy of self-destructive behavior in young America, men such as Miller and Negrin were apt to describe it in felonious (or otherwise secular) terms rather than in the language of sin and Satan. Indeed, in Negrin's estimation, jurors who refused to punish a person guilty of committing this crime were perjurers and "accessaries after the fact."[15]

On the heels of independence, more and more men of station and standing came to construe suicide as Miller and Negrin did—as the ultimate act of social alienation. That they did so at this formative moment in the early history of the United States testifies not simply to the instinctual opposition of ministers, some newspaper editors, and many heads of household to the gradual undoing of legal restraints put in place to deter suicide. It also bears witness to their dawning suspicion that de facto decriminalization and the calamitous wave of self-destruction apparently crashing down upon the country in its wake were part and parcel of an extraordinarily turbulent series of social upheavals coincident with, and partly catalyzed by, the American Revolution.

Initially, patriot elites had greeted news of the Treaty of Paris, signed in 1783, as the herald of a wonderful new dawn. After eight years of wearying struggle, sacrifice, and war, the colonists were now finally free of the long-standing constraints of imperial subordination. To punctuate the break with Britain, politicians in Philadelphia now proudly placed the spoils of the war into the hands of the American people, anointing every white man eligible to vote as an equal partner in a republican system of government, a political system never before tested on such a great scale. This fundamental change in the relationship of ordinary people to the state marked a radical redistribution of political sovereignty, a daring attempt to turn the ideas of the Enlightenment into vibrant reality. It was also an extraordinary vote of confidence, a measure of the founders' faith in the ability of their fellow countrymen to hold their own ambitions, vices, and appetites in check and to exercise wisdom, respect, comity, and self-restraint whenever called upon. If ordinary people could subordinate their interests to the common good in the war years, patriot leaders such as John Adams, James Madison, and Benjamin Rush reasoned, then why not in peacetime?[16]

Only as postwar euphoria started to thin in the late 1780s and early 1790s did this rapturous vision of a cohesive, organic state held together by individual virtue begin to flicker and fail. Boosters like Rush had hoped that the egalitarian spirit promoted by the republican revolution would thicken ties between different sections of society. Instead, the very opposite seemed to be unfolding before their very eyes. In the name of liberty, many men and women had begun claiming all manner of new rights and privileges at home, at work, at church, and at the polls, extending the guarantee of national self-government to include a dramatic expansion of individual autonomy. The ideology of independence had taken on a life of its own, alternately initiating or accelerating an array of upheavals at both the local and the national level. Now various social constituencies—young people, aspiring gentry, mechanics and artisans, western farmers, free blacks, the working poor, and women from all walks—began to exert their individual and collective independence from the customary ties that had bound them to the will of their fathers, husbands, ministers, masters, creditors, and other social superiors. As a result, men of status began to worry that the essentially conservative and reactionary political rebellion they had championed during the 1770s in hopes of restoring their economic liberty had since morphed into something much more radical: a genuine social revolution.

Mobility was the most obvious marker of this sweeping reorganization of American society. Even by colonial standards, the people of the newly United States were a young and restless lot. Between 1760 and 1830, the American population surged from two million people to more than twelve million. A postwar baby boom in the 1780s played an early and decisive role in this remarkable multiplication as confident young couples kept midwives like Maine's Martha Ballard running off their feet. Yet as these children came of age, reducing the median age of an American citizen to sixteen by 1800, the cold calculus of figuring out how so many young people might support themselves became a pressing problem. Driven from family farms by unsustainable inheritance practices, young Americans were forced to scatter. Cut off or cut free from the supposedly gentle patriarchy that organized life in the settled, rural communities most had grown up in, some trekked west to stake a claim on land in Ohio, Kentucky, and Tennessee. Many more headed east from rural hinterlands toward uncertain futures in busy port cities. As a result, the combined population of urban areas in the Northeast and the mid-Atlantic grew by 50 percent every ten years during the early national period. Despite the harsh, Malthusian effects of economic depressions, embargos, wars, and outbreaks of yellow fever, the number of people living in communities with more than twenty-five hundred inhabitants passed the million mark by the early 1820s.[17]

Many of these new arrivals in urban centers quickly fell on hard times. Though some newcomers found work on the docks or in the various industries associated with the thriving re-export business or the carrying trade, the numbers of those unable to find enough work to make ends meet skyrocketed. To make matters worse, the social safety nets that had sustained small numbers of charity cases in the early eighteenth century proved entirely unequal to the new challenges that rapidly growing port cities faced in the aftermath of the Revolution. Turned away by almshouses already packed with indigents and shorn of the support of family, many fresh arrivals were forced to take to the streets to plead for food. "The city and environs are greatly oppressed by numbers of beggars and vagrants, not only from various parts of this State, but from many others of the United States," the Board of Managers of the Philadelphia Almshouse complained in 1784. Confronted by this tidal wave of poverty, dismayed authorities in cities from Boston to Baltimore tightened residency requirements for public assistance programs and moved to criminalize destitution in hopes of controlling or driving out a population whose presence they were quickly beginning to associate not just with idleness but also with depravity and disorder.[18]

The slow death of slavery in the North over these same decades ensured that many of the migrants streaming into its cities in search of opportunity or charity were black. The gradual abolition of bound labor in states north of Maryland after 1775 and the influx of ever-increasing numbers of black fugitives from states further south and from the Caribbean combined to create blossoming communities of former slaves in the larger urban centers. In Philadelphia, for example, the free black population doubled in the 1780s and tripled in the 1790s. The massing of a black underclass along the docks and in the poorest parts of town made many white heads of household extremely nervous, none more so than the neighbors of one wealthy New Yorker whose house was raided by a mob of free blacks on August 10, 1801. The house owner in question was a former plantation mistress who had fled Saint Domingue five years earlier as a large and bloody slave revolt had consumed the French sugar colony. Fired by their admiration for the leader of that revolt, Toussaint L'Ouverture, a gang of 250 black émigrés had converged on the woman's residence with a plan to liberate the twenty slaves she had brought with her to Manhattan. While the rioters—many of whom had yet to secure any steady work in the city—were ultimately beaten back, their concerted effort to redistribute private property and reform the relationship between labor and capital by force of arms signaled a dangerous new seam of division and dissent in northern towns and cities.[19]

Whether fomented by whites or blacks, collective protests over terms of employment soon broke out everywhere. White workers, in particular, found ready cause to take to the streets to demonstrate against the decline of the traditional household economy and the insistent growth of outwork and piecework. By the 1780s and 1790s the powerful bonds of authority and reciprocal interest binding masters and their journeymen and apprentices were also beginning to unravel as employers began to hire labor for only the time it was needed. As a result, at the dawn of the nineteenth century, more and more young people found themselves working for wages in temporary jobs subject to the tumultuous cycles of boom and bust common to the new economy.[20]

In the urban areas where these upheavals were most pronounced, workers banded together to protest their declining status and job security. Between 1785 and 1810 journeymen shoemakers, printers, bakers, cabinetmakers, bricklayers, house carpenters, and sailors in New York City all experimented with collective bargaining. When those attempts proved maddeningly ineffective, many striking workers chose to riot. In Boston, city fathers raised to have confidence in a network of ties guaranteeing elite influence and lower-order loyalty, witnessed, among assorted other acts of violence, nine separate waves of assaults on tax collectors during the 1780s alone. In New York, officials responded to the threat of mobocracy with blunt force, violently suppressing riots that blew up in 1788, 1793, and 1799. Yet repression did nothing to ease the rising tensions between the haves and the have-nots. Even as per capita wealth in New York City doubled between 1790 and 1825, inequality grew faster. By the time Andrew Jackson took the White House in 1828, half of that city's noncorporate wealth was concentrated in the hands of just 4 percent of its inhabitants. While this mercantile elite clustered in enclaves close to Broadway, just blocks away the waterfront groaned with slums.[21]

Riven by inequality, faction, and violence, postrevolutionary society seemed to many wealthy, wary observers to be coming apart at the seams. The democratization of white male suffrage only made matters worse. While extending the franchise did succeed in making continued mob action seem counterproductive, the initiative ultimately proved divisive, bringing a flurry of agitated new voters to the polls impatient to politicize the concept of social superiority. Their unseating of the patrician John

Adams in the election of 1800 stunned elites who had assumed that their own elected representatives would govern in perpetuity as a sort of natural aristocracy. Instead, an inchoate alliance of urban mechanics and western farmers apparently unmoved by any feelings of fealty toward their social betters swept Thomas Jefferson to power.[22]

Demanding equality of respect and the right to govern themselves as they pleased, many members of the Jeffersonian coalition instinctively chafed at what remained of traditional patterns of deference and duty, and set themselves up in opposition to defenders of the old ways. Indeed, the most fundamental differences between these Democrat-Republicans and their Federalist rivals in the early national period stemmed not from foreign or fiscal policy but from deep-seated, self-interested disagreement about the virtues of dismantling social authority. Many Jeffersonians voiced unbridled optimism that the democratic forces unleashed by the Revolution would augur in an age of unprecedented equality, harmony, prosperity and self-possession. By contrast, their Federalist opponents could not take their eyes off of France. Anxiously following the bloody course of the revolutions there and in Saint Domingue, Federalists of John Adams's generation made nightmarish predictions about what a truly democratic future might hold. "There was never a democracy that did not commit suicide," the ailing former president warned in a letter to John Taylor in April 1814. To try to avert America's own descent into bloody terror, congressional Federalists and their supporters fought furiously to prevent the toppling of the social hierarchy atop which they still precariously perched.[23]

Few public figures were more animated in opposition to American Jacobinism than northern clergy. Yet their fears of encroaching deism and atheism paled in comparison to the beleaguered pessimism many established ministers displayed in the face of increasing competition from upstart sects. Once accustomed to automatic authority as ambassadors of God and stewards of the communal order, Anglican and Congregationalist ministers across New England and the mid-Atlantic watched with horror as one state legislature after another dismantled governmental support for established churches after the Revolution. No longer able to hide behind constitutional protections, the old orthodoxies quickly became the target of scorching criticism from their smaller rivals. In searing pamphlet attacks and vituperative public performances, strident young preachers representing minority religious movements ranging from Universalism to Methodism tried to stir distrust and disdain for the old guard by painting them as dangerously conservative, coercive, authoritarian, and antidemocratic.[24]

Such calculated anticlericalism paid them great dividends. Between 1775 and 1845 the number of denominations in America doubled as the Protestant faith fragmented and split apart. This centrifugal restructuring enlarged the reputations of new religious organizations that, their supporters hoped, might be better equipped to deal with the atomizing changes roiling early national society. But not everyone was so optimistic. Leaders of established churches, older ministers in particular, were thoroughly antagonized by the democratization of American Christianity. Writing in his diary in October 1810, William Bentley, the Harvard-trained divine who had given almost thirty years of his life to his congregation in Salem, Massachusetts, churlishly concluded that the rituals of evangelical revivalism now convulsing his little corner of the Bay State were not only responsible for every variety of civic unrest in the town over the past few months but also for the recent spike of suicides there:

> In our year past we have had five examples of suicide, Sheppard, Batchelor, Manning, Derby & Fisher, a greater number than ever has been known in the whole history of the settlement for 180 years as far as I can learn. And in this year we have had greater religious convulsions & more fury of sects than the settlement has witnessed since its establishment, and out of 300 new communicants not one has been bettered in his morals so far as I have known [or] observed. There have been more bankrupcies, flagrant vices, & enormities than ever before & in all these great professors have been the greatest offenders.

Walking the streets of Salem each day, Bentley was indignantly aware that the furious growth of new sects in the town had come at the expense of his own standing.[25]

Most gallingly of all, these erstwhile patriarchs found themselves marginalized at the exact moment when, they believed, their steadying influence might have been of most use. For years, ministers such as William Bentley in Salem and Samuel Miller in New York had been growing increasingly uncomfortable with the ungovernable behavior of the rising generation. Chief among their concerns was the growth of a permissive and eroticized sexual culture. Bastardy, prostitution, and all sorts of other illicit sexual activities were all on the rise in the postrevolutionary era, fostered in part by positive and playful portrayals of youthful sexuality in a print culture now increasingly dominated by secular authors. By 1799, for instance, the rate of bastard births among Philadelphians was twice what it had been in the decade before the Revolution. Likewise, as the spread of venereal disease throughout northern port cities during the same decade attests, brothels were thriving as never before; during the 1790s, Philadelphians kept at least sixteen bawdy houses in business.[26]

While married men and women often participated in this world of casual sexual relations, preachers and well-to-do parents of increasingly independent adolescents were particularly worried about the corrupting effect that the pursuit of so much personal pleasure was having on the young and single. Self-control seemed to be evaporating in the face of all manner of new temptations and diversions. Theaters and dance studios had sprung up to compete with libraries and lyceums. Liquor was everywhere. Horse races, cockfights, card parties, and balls now vied for time on many social calendars, while young people fortunate enough to have the means to do so tried to telegraph their aspirant cosmopolitanism by dressing in English gowns, donning French hairstyles, and reading the most fashionable and sentimental German novels they could get their hands on.[27]

In Boston, in 1785, one group of preening young adults indulged their cravings for cards, dancing, and wine with such ostentation that their behavior provoked a stinging backlash from conservative elders. One of their number, a haughty and ambitious young lawyer named Perez Morton, found himself rendered as "Mr. Importance," the living embodiment of all that was wrong with young America, in a scathing dramatic satire likely written by Mercy Otis Warren. Endorsing Warren's savage indictment of Morton's and other club members' overmannered affectations and conspicuous consumption, Boston's *Independent Chronicle* concluded that a single visit to their rented concert hall during one of their weekly assemblies could corrupt the republican character far more "than an evening spent in a back chamber of a tavern, among a group of wretches."[28]

Given his dilettante reputation, many Bostonians had little sympathy when Perez Morton found himself implicated in the suicide of his mistress three years later. According to an inquiry conducted by the Boston coroner, Morton had seduced his pretty wife's young sister, Frances Apthorp. She had become pregnant, had given birth in secret, and had taken poison when her father, a sober Presbyterian minister, discovered her disgrace. Overnight, newspapers decided that Morton—who had begged Apthorp to conceal his paternity—was the most despicable man in America, a verdict confirmed when he organized a private investigation into the cause of his sister-in-law's death transparently intended to clear his name. Throughout the fall of 1788, Boston papers lambasted Morton for his mendacity, accusing him of setting a dangerous precedent. "We may soon find it become very fashionable, in *particular instances*, to assemble a few private friends, in a private room, to review a matter after a legal decision by a Jury," the *Herald of Freedom* fumed. "This kind of review, may, in time, be considered among those who arrogantly stile themselves the polite circle, as the inquest of the 'better sort.' "[29]

In this and numerous other postwar blasts of frustration, concerned pillars of the community—many of them parents of teenage children on the cusp of adulthood—decried the corrosive effects of too much freedom on the character and conduct of this Joshua generation. As they did so, these aging parents were of course reminded of their own declining status not only within increasingly factious communities but also within the family unit itself. For decades, traditions of domestic subordination—children to their parents, wives to their husbands—had been slowly eroding. In their place more affectionate and egalitarian relationships had become the norm. Now, in the swirling uncertainty of the Revolution's aftermath, many heads of household were beginning to conclude that the trade-off had been hasty and ill advised. Armed only with the tools of tender affection and gentle persuasion, they now worried that their newly independent offspring had become ungovernable and unreachable and thus—like poor Frances Apthorp—might easily fall victim to crime, luxury, seduction, and sin. Benjamin Rush's brother, Jacob, a fifty-four-year-old judge and father to five daughters, distilled this generational anxiety in a collection of essays he published in 1803:

> It has long been my opinion, that the relaxation of domestic authority, is one of the most alarming symptoms both of the degeneracy, and dangerous situation of our country. Parents and masters seem to have abandoned all control over those that Providence has placed under their care and guardianship. They seem totally indifferent both as to the company and hours they keep, and the places they frequent.

From Boston to Baltimore, Judge Rush's peers echoed his assessment of the state of the nation, all the while adding to the list of symptoms of a breakdown of ethical unity. In Boston, Chief Justice William Cushing complained that young people "ha[d] shown themselves destitute of all morality," while in New Haven, Yale president Timothy Dwight lamented that "The profanation of the Sabbath, before unusual, profaneness of language, drunkenness, gambling, and lewdness were exceedingly increased" among his students. Further south, Philadelphia merchant Thomas Cope—another concerned parent—confided his fears to his diary in 1801: "Virtue is said to be the basis of a republic," Cope wrote. "If so, I fear ours is fast approximating toward its grave. . . . Moral virtues are giving place to gross depravity, licentiousness & corruption."[30]

In the view of parents, ministers, and magistrates like these, the country was on a road to ruin. The harmonious, self-regulating ideal that proud republicans like Benjamin Rush had anticipated after the war had failed to materialize. Instead, the taste for liberty had become contagious, sanctioning or hastening a string of wide-ranging social transformations that had undermined familiar mechanisms of public and private order and enshrined the individual as the prime unit in politics, economics, and religion. With few meaningful limits on personal freedom, young America struck conservatives such as Cushing, Dwight, and Cope as a chaotic and unruly place, a sprawling, dissolute, unrestrained popular democracy in the midst of unprecedented ethical declension. Patriarchy—as measured by the power of the state, the church, employers, and heads of household to exert their will over that of their dependents—was in disarray. Never before had the lines of authority seemed so confused and the future so uncertain.[31]

Many of these embattled father figures did not confine themselves to complaining about such marked declines in deference. Rather, they sprang into action. To concentrate and replenish their dwindling social capital, some of the more flexible Federalists joined with elite Democrat-Republicans such as Benjamin Rush to found new urban charities and other self-consciously voluntaristic advocacy groups, while many less pragmatic conservatives turned to more cynical means to preserve what remained of their power and preeminence. Such intransigents frequently seized the chance to exploit mounting fears about the spread of self-destruction throughout the new nation. They did so not only to warn their compatriots of the cataclysmic consequences of failing to repair this broken society and restore its moral covenant but also in order to prop up their own flagging social authority. To declare an emergency is, after all, to claim the power to declare an emergency.[32]

When those in Rev. Samuel Miller's line of work began decrying the decisions of activist coroners and juries, it was thus in great part because the cause at hand presented a golden opportunity for them to position themselves as selfless guardians of the nation's endangered moral health. Indeed, over time, Miller and his allies succeeded in turning their criticism of the relaxation of legal deterrents against suicide into a form of political theater that advocated the restoration of customary patterns of deference not only to ministers but also to parents and magistrates. Nor was this an isolated example. Whether castigating novelists for romanticizing fictional suicide or lashing out to punish anyone associated with inmates who attempted to kill themselves rather than face a state execution, various patriarchs consumed with apocalyptic visions of total cultural collapse tried to steer popular anger in reactionary directions.

The fact that many of the most socially conservative commentators also took to flaying newspaper editors for reporting every fresh act of self-destruction provides an object lesson in the uses of suicide politics in early national America. Initially at least, most patriot leaders had actively supported the dramatic expansion of the American newspaper industry after the outbreak of the Stamp Act controversy in 1765. Rapturous predictions that well-conducted newspapers would have "great influence in mending the morals and manners of a people" filled public discourse before, during, and immediately after the Revolution. Such encomiums joined with voracious public interest in the progress of the war, the Confederation crisis, and the rise of the first party system to ensure that this genre of secular reading quickly assumed a position of unparalleled prominence in the new nation. In 1760 only eighteen printers published newspapers in America; yet, by 1814, Philadelphia merchant Thomas Cope could report that "there are now published in the United States 294 weekly newspapers, 39 twice a week, 13 three times a week & 28 daily, making a total of 374." Newspapers had taken the country by storm. "If we have any striking traits of national character," the journalist and publisher Nathan Hale told readers of the Boston *Daily Advertiser* earlier that year, "their origin may be clearly discerned in our universal relish for newspaper reading."[33]

The rising appeal of newspapers reflected American editors' growing willingness to fill their columns with homegrown news and politics. News and opinion sourced from Europe had long dominated the colonial papers. But this had begun to change in the wake of the Stamp Act, and after independence the prominence of political and social news gathered from within the borders of the thirteen states became a matter of national pride. "What have the citizens of the United States to do with the duels, the elopements, the crim. cons. [*sic*], the kept mistresses, the murders, the suicides, the thefts, the forgeries, the boxing matches, the wagers for eating, drinking, and walking, &c. &c. of the people of Great Britain?" Benjamin Rush asked in an open letter to newspaper editors in 1788.[34]

Congress endorsed the same opinion in 1792 when it passed the Post Office Act. This federal statute mandated a national network of post offices, fixed the postage on newspapers sent to subscribers at one cent each, and declared that the customary exchanges of newspapers between editors through the country's mails could now be guaranteed and carried free. These provisions, intended to better bind citizens to their state representatives and the federal government, made every variety of domestic newsgathering dramatically cheaper, faster, and easier. According to Postmaster General Timothy Pickering, by 1794 many printers received three or four dozen exchange papers each day, all gratis. These daily deliveries encouraged American editors to fill their sheets with content cribbed and copied from an ever-widening circle of indigenous sources.[35]

For these reasons the Post Office Act was a major source of the early national suicide panic. It formalized and accelerated changes in news gathering that together ensured that turn-of-the-century newspapers were awash with news of hangings, shootings, and drownings committed within the United States. Regardless of whether or not the suicide rates in cities like Philadelphia or New York were actually rising—the tendency of coroners and jurors to attribute more and more suspicious deaths to a broad range of nonculpable causes such as insanity and accident makes it impossible to say for sure—the expansion of the exchange system saw to it that press coverage of suicide surged. The exchange system that now quickly brought news from across the country, tying citizens and readers together in a web of shared information and experience, had produced an unimagined consequence: the perception—likely unfounded, certainly exaggerated—that a suicide epidemic was laying waste to the Republic.[36]

Most of the elites unsettled by the apparently "alarming progress" of suicide in the new nation failed to recognize the inflammatory, distorting role played by the exchange system. Yet there were other reasons why many parents and ministers—several among whom had once expressed hope that the press might mend the morals of readers on the verge of turning from the world—were beginning to reconsider their prior optimism. The rise of hyper-partisan journalism and the passage of the Sedition Act during the 1790s convinced more and more subscribers that bulldog editors like John Fenno, William Cobbett, Philip Freneau, Benjamin Franklin Bache, and William Duane were, in the words of diarist Thomas Cope, as unlikely to disseminate "principles subversive to religion, morality & rational liberty" as they were to "give currency to opinions promotive of virtue, social order & moral harmony." As papers assumed the role of party organs in the 1790s, and as their political coverage became catalysts for conflict and faction, more and more armchair commentators concluded that other aspects of their reporting might also be dangerous.[37]

In a scolding letter "to the printers" published in 1801, the recently retired Federalist congressman Fisher Ames suggested that newspaper portrayals of violence might be responsible for dulling readers' moral senses. He singled out coverage of suicide, warning printers that "the spirit of imitation is contagious." A letter to the editor of the *Connecticut Gazette* in 1806 agreed. "I am fully convinced that the publishing of such accounts is one influential cause of an alarming increase of the crimes," a subscriber calling himself "A Friend to Virtue" cautioned. "If he reads a number of different papers, the same account is repeatedly presented to him (as almost every editor injudiciously copies such accounts) and his mind becomes familiarized to meditating on scenes, and acts, of horrid wickedness." Newspaper editors were not to blame for causing the recent rash of suicides, this correspondent explained, but their careless, ceaseless (and by now almost exclusively secular) reporting had certainly aggravated it.[38]

By this logic, early national newspapers were training manuals from which suggestible or heartsick readers could not help but learn. Their reporting taught subscribers that guns could misfire, allowing witnesses time to scramble to action; that jumping from a third-floor window was not likely to kill you; and that drowning oneself at sea was the best way to "prevent the operation of the law upon their carcases [*sic*] after their decease." Perhaps newspapers were even capable of dramatizing a learning curve in stories of those who made multiple attempts at suicide before finally completing. In 1791 *Claypoole's Daily Advertiser* reported the death of Daniel Pearson of New London, Connecticut. Pearson had made several prior attempts to hang himself, but his wife had repeatedly intervened. This time, the paper noted, he had learned from his mistakes, suspending himself by a bridle to a tree several hundred yards distant from his property. An item in a Pennsylvania paper in 1814 appeared to offer readers even more direct instruction. Describing how a young man had chosen too blunt an instrument to hack at his throat, the *Carlisle Gazette* reported that as he sat gasping for air, he "direct[ed] his friends, if they should think of suicide, to take some more effectual method than cutting one's throat with a dull knife." It mattered little that handwringers like Fisher Ames could muster scant proof that readers were making conscious use of newspapers as instructive manuals for suicide. After all, the power of the press was surely more deadly if ordinary readers were not aware that they were being slowly indoctrinated.[39]

After 1800 the growing belief that newspaper coverage might be contributing to an ongoing surge of self-destructive behavior led many conservatives to join Fisher Ames in calling for more selective reporting. "Man is an imitative animal," a letter sent to editors of two Federalist papers explained. "Examples are contagious, good or bad . . . Therefore, give the least possible notoriety to accounts of suicides." No doubt conscious of how such a blackout might affect their bottom line, most newspaper editors refused to abandon or curtail their coverage. Their readers, they protested, were more sophisticated than men like Ames gave them credit. Indeed, a writer for the *Middlesex Gazette* pointed out that such proposals would deprive readers of the necessary information to form "a tolerable estimate of the moral condition of a people." Censorship, he argued, would impede citizenship.[40]

Their failure to rein in newspaper reporting of self-destruction only served to remind many ministers and heads of household just how chaotic and ungovernable the new nation had become. Indeed, their growing conviction that the public prints posed a fatal threat to suggestible readers was rooted in the knowledge that the unprecedented expansion of the newspaper industry was part and parcel of a larger transformation in the ways ordinary men and women acquired information and ideas. Certainly, readers of newspapers after the Revolution were confronted with more news and narratives of suicide than they had been used to before. And as Samuel Miller knew from the letter he had received from a newspaper reader confined to debtors' prison, newspapers had quickly overwhelmed published sermons as the primary printed means by which Americans learned about suicide, its methods, and its motives. Efforts to curb news reporting should thus be seen as part of a rearguard effort to temper and tamp down the most liberal and secular inclinations of early national society and plead for at least a partial restoration of traditional order and orderliness—even if it meant censorship.[41]

Attacks upon the way newspaper editors conducted their business were but one of many means by which unsettled social conservatives attempted to leverage the stigma and apprehension surrounding suicide. Yet frightened reactionaries were not the only ones to try to advance their own interests by politicizing self-destruction. On the contrary, the factious and fragmented nature of postrevolutionary society ensured that contests over the social implications of certain suicides were never one-sided. The meaning and significance of self-destruction was, in fact, frequently challenged, most notably by liberal activists, some of whom were no less elite than their conservative adversaries. Over the course of the several critical decades following the break with Britain, these progressive reformers—several Democrat-Republicans and many Universalists conspicuous among them—succeeded in bending and twisting the emotionally charged vocabulary associated with suicide toward the purpose of creating a moral mandate for the destruction of arcane institutions. Committed to making the best of the fact that postwar America had become a laboratory of political democracy and personal freedom, these campaigners did not instinctively interpret the apparently swollen suicide rate as a predictor of the country's descent into anarchy. Rather, they instilled it with a radically altered meaning, embracing it as a politically useful reminder of the work still to be done to perfect the republican experiment and wielding it as an imperfect weapon in their own hard-fought struggle to challenge prevailing power structures and build an open, liberal society.[42]

As the United States teetered on the brink of disorder and disunion, such activists waged a series of paper wars upon slavery, the death penalty, and all manner of other inherited institutions they perceived as inhumane, authoritarian, and oppressive. To do so, these reformist groups—almost all of which were headquartered in northern cities where the challenges of balancing liberty and order were most viscerally apparent—seized the opportunity to turn certain suicides into moral capital. Over time, they centered much of their efforts on nurturing respect or empathy for debased individuals who chose death over tyranny. Whether lamenting that the brutality of public hangings in Jacksonian America drove condemned men to bash their brains out in their cells, or shouting in triumph as brave black fugitives cut their throats to escape antebellum slave catchers, this loose and ever-shifting coalition nursed support for institutional reforms they hoped might build a better world by representing certain acts of self-destruction as flawed yet potent rallying cries against the stifling of possessive individualism. For instance, as early as 1788 the author of an essay advocating "the Lawfulness of Divorce" for wives choked by marital bonds tried to tug at Philadelphia readers' heartstrings by calling to mind a recent newspaper report of a woman in the city "who destroyed herself" rather than endure another day with her husband. "If divorce was declared not only lawful by the legislature, but honorable by ministers and elders of religious bodies," this lobbyist argued, "it would probably remove one of the most melancholy misfortunes of the human being—suicide."[43]

Finding his stride, this anonymous pamphleteer spent the next several pages soberly explaining to city readers that the plight of wretched women trapped in loveless marriages with no prospect of escape save for suicide was no different than that of slaves abused by vicious masters. It was a calculated comparison and a canny means of reinforcing his claim that unbridled tyranny could lead dependents toward "the most melancholy misfortunes." After all, northern readers familiar with the Middle Passage were keenly aware of how commonly blacks aboard slave ships attempted to kill themselves to defy their debasement at the hands of white masters, and how insistently captains tried to prevent the self-destruction of their human cargo. Testimony from Anthony Benezet and Olaudah Equiano and reporting in Boston's *Independent Ledger*, the *Pennsylvania Gazette*, and a host of other popular newspapers had introduced thousands of revolutionary-era readers to the night watches and netting that crews used to stop slaves from jumping overboard, and the merciless trussings, floggings, and whippings they doled out to those they caught in the act.[44]

In these gruesome depositions, a device known as the *speculum oris* appears time and again. This ratcheted metal pincher was used to break jaws and force-feed men and women on board ship who attempted to starve themselves. It was thus the supreme symbol of the mortal struggle to prevent enslaved people from dispossessing their tormentors. In May 1792 *Dunlap's American Daily Advertiser* informed subscribers in Philadelphia and its environs how the device had recently been used aboard a slave ship. The crew of the *Elizabeth* had noticed that a young African man was refusing to take his daily ration. "He always kept his teeth so fast, that it was impossible to get any thing down," the ship's surgeon reported. To pry his mouth open, they had tried both a bolus knife and the *speculum oris*. "But the points were too obtuse to enter," and after nine days without food he passed away, feeble but resolute. Furious at the thought that his example could spread, the enraged captain ordered every black soul below decks to be whipped, though he knew that there was really nothing he or anyone else on board could do to prevent determined captives from killing themselves one way or another. "In the very act of chastisement," the surgeon, Isaac Wilson, later recalled, "they have looked up at him with a smile, and in their own language have said, 'presently we shall be no more.'"[45]

Between the Revolution and the Civil War, a broad spectrum of interest groups digested, synthesized, and appropriated acts of self-destruction as they labored to build a durable national community. Indeed, to understand

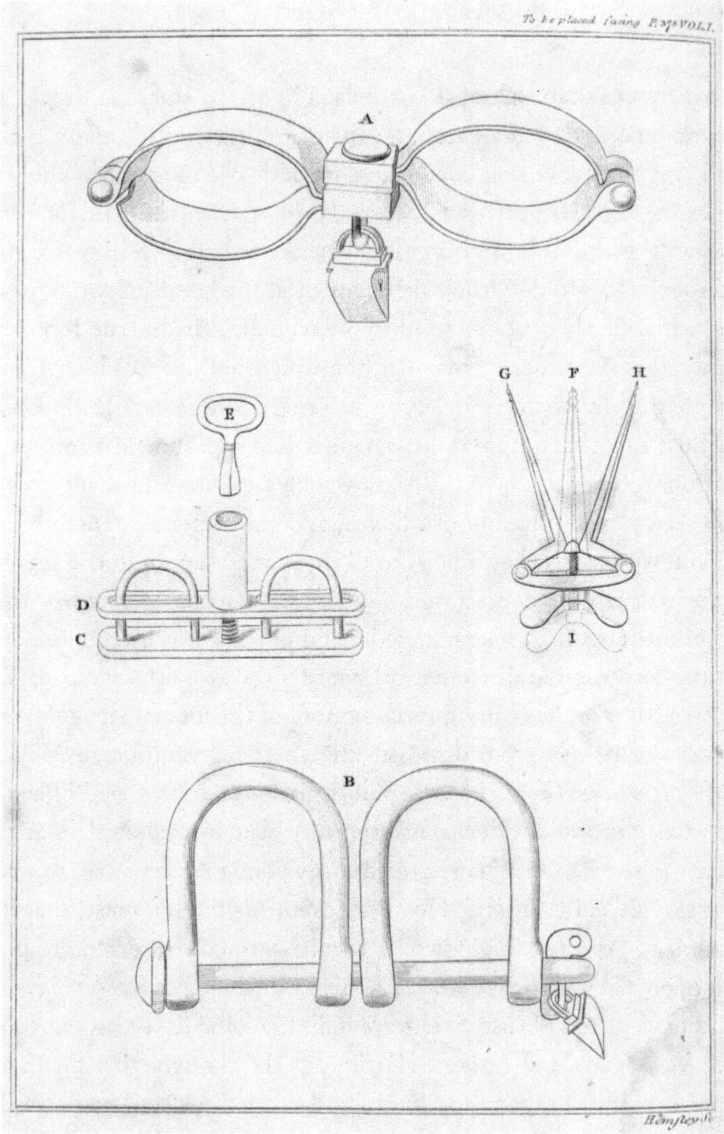

A speculum oris (center right). "On asking the seller of the instruments on what occasion it was used there, he replied that the slaves were frequently so sulky as to shut their mouths against all sustenance, and this with a determination to die; and that it was necessary their mouths should be forced open to throw in nutriment, that they who had purchased them might incur no loss by their death." Thomas Clarkson, *The History of the Rise, Progress and Accomplishment of the Abolition of the African Slave-Trade by the British Parliament* (London: Longman, 1808), quotation on page 302. A similar engraving accompanied the Philadelphia edition, also published in 1808. Courtesy of the American Antiquarian Society.

competing interpretations of the meaning of suicide in the early United States is to investigate larger struggles over power and social position in an environment in which the old markers of status and authority seemed to be giving way.

The politicization of self-destruction in this fragile, formative period in American history would prove to be revelatory, as fights over the significance of suicide allowed all manner of Americans to debate who owns the self in a republican system of government and to deliberate several of the most consequential questions about the kind of country the new nation was rapidly becoming and the kind of country it should strive to be: Should the public sphere ever be censored? What responsibilities do the well-to-do have toward their beggared neighbors? Does a republic have the right to execute its citizens? Is organized religion a threat to government and its people? Should slaves resist their masters or wait patiently to be rescued?

Answering these pointed questions requires us to track quarrels about the social and political implications of suicide in the early United States across a range of terrain, from the trenches of a campaign to brand all prose fictions as hypnotic cultivators of teenage suicide to the wharves and bridges where antidrowning groups staged dramatic, coercive rescues of those determined to die; from the fallout of a capital trial in which a prisoner was accused of talking his cellmate into killing himself to a series of muck-raking brawls between Protestant denominations aimed at tarring their opponents as suicide cults; and from the blood-soaked pages of abolitionist propaganda pamphlets to antebellum hand-wringing that allegorized the secession crisis as a form of national self-destruction.

Whether the setting is the jail or the plantation, the salon or the sitting room, the revival meeting or the asylum, the true subject here is power: the power of parents over children, of masters over slaves, of the state over inmates, of ministers over their followers, of authors over readers, and even of medical science over God. At one site after another, partisans found profit and purpose in interpreting self-destructive acts as potent subversions of these and other hierarchical relationships. In some cases, like the dozens of condemned criminals who took their lives before the hangman could reach them, justice officials took to harping on their dramatic suicides to try to seal their popular repudiation, figuring their self-inflicted deaths as despicable proof that the American people lacked the virtue, judgment, restraint, and reason to govern themselves. In other cases, like the fugitive slaves whose corpses would bloat the pages of the most radical antislavery pamphlets in the antebellum era, militant abolitionists learned to promote black suicides as righteous sacrifices on the altar of freedom, championing their choices as imperfect protests against draconian institutions that they hoped to sweep away.

2

The Sorrows of Young Readers

Setting down the novel for the final time, he raised the horse pistol to his temple and fired. Beachcombers found his young, "genteely dressed" body early the next morning, with the book and the gun lying together on the ground by its side. Three years earlier, in 1804, Alexander Hamilton's blood had pooled among the dirt and rocks on this same stretch of the New Jersey shore. Like Hamilton, this man was an immigrant, and, like Hamilton, he had been behaving strangely in the weeks before his death, telling friends that he was tired of life and ready to die. But this man had his own story, as the two letters tucked in his pocket and the novel found at his feet soon made clear. His name was Bertell, he was just twenty years old, and the first letter was his suicide note, addressed to whoever might find his body. It described how he had been cast aside by the young lady he loved, how the rejection had been too much for his heart to take, and how he had made up his mind that he could only find peace in death. In the second letter, addressed to a friend in Brooklyn, he had scribbled a hasty will, leaving two-thirds of his paltry estate to the girl who had broken his heart. The third text on the scene was the book that Bertell had been reading over and over these last few weeks. To readers of all the news stories that spread word of his suicide to Vermont, Virginia, and everywhere in between over the next few weeks, this well-thumbed and heavily underlined little volume was the most important clue as to why this young romantic had taken his own life. Bertell's copy of Goethe's *The Sorrows of Young Werther*, the most popular and yet most vilified sentimental novel in America, lay open at the page where Werther, pistols prepared, writes to the woman who has promised herself to another and takes his final leave: "They are loaded—the clock strikes twelve—I go. Charlotte! Farewell! Farewell!"[1]

Fiction, it seemed, could be fatal. Reading Goethe's inflammatory tale of how one adoring young man ended his anguish by pistol had led another to do the same. At least that was the conclusion many newspaper readers reached when printers splashed Bertell's story across their pages in July and August 1807. In fact, many of them had been expecting this. Bertell's suicide came as the inevitable proof of what protective parents and anxious ministers had been warning would happen ever since Goethe's overwrought romance first reached American shores in the mid-1780s, the latest in a postrevolutionary deluge of new narrative and literary forms aimed squarely at the rising generation.

By 1807, the growing fashion for fiction among the nation's youth had long since become the subject of heated debate among their elders and betters. Indeed, for years now, parents and preachers had claimed that stories like Werther's could steer suggestible young readers toward copycat suicide. People of standing and status—men and women who had initially embraced the hope that sentimental reading might instill virtue and sensibility in the country's future leaders—had come to cultivate a bitter suspicion of the sentimental novels and short stories popular among their sons and daughters. As more and more mothers, fathers, and ministers concluded that sentimental literature was a potent but surprisingly unreliable partner in the cause of moral education, many began to denounce such fiction as morally corrosive, dangerous nonsense that could do more harm than good. Seizing on the fact that *Werther* and a swath of early American novels that followed in its wake showcased the suicides of tremulous and tearful youths, critics of sentimental fiction pointed to suggestive (yet ultimately circumstantial) evidence that young readers like Bertell were being manipulated by the power of sympathy to follow in the fatal footsteps of their fictional heroes. Although many parents in particular ardently believed that novels posed an existential threat to their teenage children, their efforts to control the reading habits of the rising generation also betrayed their growing fears that the traditional order was crumbling around their ears. By attacking portrayals of young, self-absorbed romantics who seek solace in suicide, ministers and parents alike sought to deflate this secular genre's soaring popularity and to foreclose its socially subversive implications. In this oblique way, they sought to reassert parental authority over their increasingly independent dependents.

A reading revolution gripped America in the second half of the eighteenth century. Buoyed by economic growth and the related spread of academies aimed at the children of the burgeoning ranks of middling parents, literacy among young people was surging. In New England, where literacy rates were already high, young women coming of age after the Revolutionary War were finally closing the gender gap, achieving near parity with their male peers. Eager to put their reading skills to use, these young people gorged themselves on a diet of news and narrative imported from Europe. The Revolution notwithstanding, subscriptions to English literary periodicals quickly became status symbols among aspiring readers.[2]

The same combination of rising literacy and aspiration created a large American market for European novels. As early as 1760, almost thirty years before the first American novelist put ink to paper, works by European authors such as Richardson, Fielding, and Rousseau were elbowing their way to the center of the expanding colonial book trade. To keep up with accelerating supply and demand, more and more bookshops sprang up in towns and cities up and down the seaboard. In Philadelphia, the number of bookshops ballooned from just five in 1742 to more than thirty by 1780. Booksellers such as Robert Bell imported almost any European novel they could get their hands on, and several well-capitalized entrepreneurs also began reprinting these often-expensive imports in slightly cheaper local editions intended to try to reach, in Cathy N. Davidson's words, "those who were not educated at the prestige men's colleges, who were outside the established literary tradition, and who . . . for the most part read few books besides novels." Between 1789 and 1800, Bell and his domestic competitors reprinted more than 350 foreign titles, most of them novels.[3]

Despite such booming demand for novels across a growing spectrum of society, printing costs remained high and print runs remained low. Libraries bridged that gap. Between 1731 and 1800, wealthy gentlemen set up no less than 376 private lending libraries, more than two-thirds of which opened their doors in the 1790s. By contrast, shopkeepers, schoolteachers, tradesmen, and other middling strivers, along with their mothers, wives, and daughters, flocked to new circulating libraries, institutions open not only to the donors who coughed up the capital to rent a room and buy some books but also to anyone willing to pay a modest fee in return for using the collections.[4]

The catalogs of both social and circulating libraries offer further testimony to the surging demand for every sort of fiction in this period. About a quarter of all the books listed in circulating library catalogs in the 1780s were fiction, a share that jumped by another third over the next ten years and continued to climb in the first years of the nineteenth century. At the New York Society Library, the number of novels in its catalog—mostly European, but also a growing number of American works that imitated their plots, themes, and styles—rose from 41 titles in 1789 to 279 in 1800. No other category—history, philosophy, divinity, or medicine—came close.[5]

Readers could not get enough. At the Amicable Library in Philadelphia, the shelves groaned with no less than eight copies of *Clarissa*, though borrowing records suggest they were too much in demand to stay there very long. Elsewhere in the city, the records of Thomas Bradford's circulating library show that new novels flew fastest from the shelves and, judging by how quickly they were returned, were devoured as soon as they left the building. In fact, at the Library Company, the venerable Philadelphia institution founded by Franklin, librarians had to retire, replace, or rebind novels far more often than any other type of library book. Everyone wanted them. As an English visitor to one circulating library put it in 1803, "Novels are called for by the young and old; from the tender virgin of thirteen, whose little heart went pit-apit at the approach of the beau, to the experienced matron of three score, who could not read without spectacles." "This is a novel-reading age," concluded the editor of *New-York Magazine* in 1797. Few could disagree.[6]

Before it became clear that *Werther*—a novel that promoted romantic self-indulgence over familial duty—would become a best seller, this reading revolution was widely welcomed. The parents and preachers who traditionally felt responsible for the conduct of young people and the moral education of the lower orders embraced the new fashion for reading as a rare opportunity to wed instruction to recreation. They knew from their own experience that reading could shape ideas and behavior. Ever since the arrival of the first printing press in Cambridge, Massachusetts, in 1638, ministers had published edited versions of their best sermons, certain that their printed words had the power to shape the character of anyone exposed to them. Now, in the 1780s, as proud patriots fondly recalled (and too often mythologized) the function that the press and pamphlets like *Common Sense* had served in the Revolution, they had every reason to expect that proper reading could bring out the best in their unruly charges.

At first this postwar generation of parents and preachers greeted the new fashion for fiction as a godsend. Both groups believed their own moral authority was eroding rapidly in the wake of independence as all manner of ordinary Americans internalized revolutionary-era rhetoric about self-determination. For their part, parents such as Benjamin Rush—whose first son, John, was born in 1777—spent a lot of time worrying that their children were testing the boundaries of their authority like never before and that their offspring's impulsive decisions might lead to crippling consequences for their future happiness and for their family's reputation. Ministers too felt sidelined. Declining church attendance and intense public interest in deism in the 1780s and 1790s convinced many Congregationalists and Anglicans that their once-honored place in public life was under threat and that the country was entering a secular ice age. The proof was in their pocketbooks: to choose just one example, their once-popular execution sermons now competed with all sorts of salacious new genres such as trial reports, criminal biographies, and newspaper stories for readers' precious pennies. These upstart genres paid only lip service to the moral dimensions of crime and punishment, preferring instead to titillate readers with increasingly visceral descriptions of bodies in pain. Established clergy worried that as their own authority waned, the Republic itself might quickly become a new Sodom, a country consumed by the forces of atheism, dissipation, and selfish individualism.[7]

The rising appetite for fiction gave many of this station and generation hope that it would not come to this. If American authors might be co-opted to model restrained, moral behavior and to teach readers to listen to their elders and betters then perhaps the nation might yet endure. With rates of premarital pregnancy at record levels, many early supporters of the rise of the novel held out particular hope that fiction might smuggle lessons about female chastity and male self-discipline into the hearts and minds of adolescent readers by illustrating with riveting power the consequences of seduction. At the same time, advocates fantasized that novels and short stories could also be exploited to temper the selfishness that many associated with the rise of consumer society, by reminding better-off readers of their obligations to others less fortunate. In a very well-publicized lecture at the American Philosophical Society in 1786, Benjamin Rush hoped aloud that "a familiarity with scenes of distress from poverty and diseases" might heighten young people's regard for the growing army of indigents crowding city streets in the postwar years and singled out the literary arts as particularly potent tools if "properly directed." In fact, in Rush's mind, a carefully calibrated literature of sensibility might perhaps even usher in a new era of benevolence by training young men of feeling and young ladies of refinement to identify and sympathize with suffering wherever they found it. Sensibility might teach young readers to respond to the sight of a beggar by reaching into their pockets for coins. Better still, the doctor opined, it may even lead to more sustained acts of charity and selflessness along the lines of the new lifesaving rescue groups known as "humane societies, which are now established in many parts of Europe, and in some parts of America."[8]

Spurred on by boosters like Rush, many American authors and editors working in the 1780s and early 1790s gamely set about transforming sensibility into a national project. Between 1789 and 1796, the *Massachusetts Magazine* published more than one hundred stories, letters, and poems on the theme of seduction, while other newly established literary periodicals such as the *Columbian Magazine* and the *American Museum* stuffed their pages with examples of virtuous people in distress and fictionalized charitable acts as often as possible. Likewise, in the first American novel, the twenty-three-year-old invalid William Hill Brown's aptly titled *The Power of Sympathy* (1789), the protagonist,

Harrington, trumpets the moral value of feeling in an increasingly acquisitive society:

> Hail sensibility! Sweetener of the joys of life! Heaven has implanted thee in the breasts of his children—to soothe the sorrows of the afflicted—to mitigate the wounds of the stranger who falleth in our way. Thou regardest with an eye of pity, those whom wealth and ambition treat in terms of reproach. Away, ye seekers of power—ye boasts of wealth—ye are the levite and the Pharisee, who restrain the hand of charity from the indigent, and turn with indignation from the way-worn son of misery:—But Sensibility is the good Samaritan, who taketh him by the hand, and consoleth him, and poureth wine and oil into his wounds. Thou are a pleasant companion—a grateful friend—and a neighbour to those who are destitute of shelter.

Many of Brown's literary rivals went further, dramatizing the consoling, neighborly impulse engendered by true sensibility. For instance, in Susanna Rowson's *The Inquisitor; or, Invisible Rambler* (1794), the wanderer of the title is brought to tears by the deprivations suffered by the downtrodden men and women he meets on his travels. More important, his sympathy leads him to action: he shells out eighteen pounds to free a stranger from a crippling debt to an unscrupulous creditor; he risks his reputation to save a virtuous young girl from a house of ill repute; he talks another young woman out of her plans to elope with a cad who was only interested in her money; and he leads a prodigal daughter back to her parents to be reunited and redeemed. To fund all this good work, the rambler puts his own comfort on the line, dismissing his servants, parting with one of his carriages, and selling two of his horses.[9]

So far, so good. In a letter to his young cousin, Robert Skipwith, as the first wave of European novels washed up on American shores, Thomas Jefferson counseled him that "[t]he entertainments of fiction are useful as well as pleasant." "Everything is useful," the Virginian continued, "which contributes to fix in us the principles or practice of virtue. When an original act of charity or of gratitude, for instance, is presented either to our sight or imagination, we are deeply impressed with its beauty and feel a strong desire in ourselves of doing charitable and grateful acts also." By the mid-1780s, this view of the positive social utility of fiction, and of novels in particular, had become a commonplace, and evidence abounded that juvenile readers were responding. In fact, many young readers went so far as to borrow the names, personas, and third-person narration commonly found in novels purporting to model sensibility when writing in their own diaries or in private correspondence. Identifying with the plight of literary characters to the point of renaming themselves "Leander" or "Amanda," plenty of young readers, with hearts apparently as soft and malleable as wax, began to see the world through fiction's lens.[10]

Yet before the moral and social effects of reading so many didactic plots could be measured, *Werther* burst on the scene. Based loosely upon Rousseau's *Nouvelle Héloïse,* as well as on several painful events in the author's own life, Johann Wolfgang von Goethe's *The Sorrows of Young Werther* takes the form of a series of letters from a twenty-three-year-old artist to a faraway friend. Chronicling his emotional ups and downs over a year and a half, the letters speak directly and intimately to the reader and narrate the passionate Werther's story of love and loss during a sojourn in the bucolic fictional village of Walheim. There he meets and falls in love with Charlotte, the new fiancée and subsequent wife of Albert, a man several years her senior. Having promised her dying mother that she would marry Albert to provide security for her eight brothers and sisters, Charlotte flirts with Werther but ultimately cannot return his ever more insistent affections. Werther refuses to move on, and his growing obsession with Charlotte quickly starts to paralyze his mind and ravage his heart. Emotionally ill-equipped to break off his visits with her, he instead begins to harbor thoughts of death to relieve the torture inflicted upon him by Charlotte's duty to her mother and her siblings. Dressed in a blue frock-coat, yellow waistcoat, and breeches, Werther pens a suicide note—"Charlotte! Farewell!"—borrows two pistols from Albert, and shoots himself.[11]

In Europe the novel was phenomenally popular, a genuine literary sensation. First published in German in Leipzig in 1774, it was translated into French (1775), English (1779), Italian (1781), and Russian (1788) and reprinted again and again and again to satisfy swelling demand across the continent. Its effect on readers was palpable. A generation of young romantics took the character of Werther to their hearts. As historian

Georges Minois writes, "The youth of Europe learned his speeches as they learned Hamlet's." The novel's popularity spawned countless imitations and motivated the production of all manner of Werther collectibles, from gloves embroidered with the story's most dramatic tableaux to a perfume known as eau de Werther.[12]

Werther enjoyed equal success on the other side of the Atlantic and was one of the best-selling novels printed in the United States before the War of 1812. Many of the nineteen British editions issued before 1800 circulated in American cities, and local booksellers, such as Robert Bell in Philadelphia, produced eight editions of their own, in three different translations, between 1784 and 1809. Only Susanna Rowson's *Charlotte Temple* (1794), a novel concerning the seduction of a schoolgirl by a dashing British solider, was reprinted more often. Demand consistently outstripped supply. Indeed, according to newspaper advertisements trumpeting one American edition, copies of *Werther* "have much been called for, and for some time not to be got." At the height of the novel's popularity, between 1782 and 1809, booksellers placed more than five hundred notices in American newspapers to announce fresh supplies. *Werther* fever gripped America.[13]

The readers who most feverishly devoured this overwrought tale of the clash between familial duty and youthful passion were, by all accounts, the typical consumers of the sentimental plots that filled most other novels after the Revolution. A commentator in Charles Brockden Brown's *Literary Magazine* noted in 1806 that *The Sorrows of Young Werther* is "more read than any of its kind by the young." Many of them were boys making awkward steps toward manhood, like the sensitive young soul one British traveler came across in Georgetown in 1798 who "delighted in the perusal of the Sorrows of Werter [and] perfumed his handkerchief with lavender." Yet though the story was told from the point of view of a delicate young man of feeling, booksellers made the greatest efforts to target young female readers. *Werther* topped a widely circulated list of "novels for winter evenings" recommended "to the ladies," while other promotional pieces touted it as particularly suited to "the Entertainment of the Ladies." In her diary for Good Friday, 1784, twenty-one-year-old Anne Livingston of Philadelphia recorded her first encounter with the book: "After Tea Miss Cox & myself playd. by turns on the harpsichord while Emelia work'd. Then Emelia read to us the Sorrows of Werther while we work'd. It is a very affecting little history, & made Grace & myself sob & cry like Children, but there is certainly a luxury in some kind of sorrows, as well as bitterness in others."[14]

The luxurious sentimentalism of Goethe's novel left young readers eager for more. Its unprecedented popularity led to a flood of imitative works on a scale otherwise unseen on the American literary landscape until the arrival of *Uncle Tom's Cabin* in 1852. In addition to reading extracts of *Werther* published in American magazines, consumers could digest plays, poems, and even other novels that followed the famous story or featured its passionate hero. Among prose imitations, the most notable and opportunistic was English author William James's *The Letters of Charlotte*, a watered-down reimagining of Werther's story told from the female perspective. Tremendously popular in its day, it was first published in America as a companion to the 1789 Boston edition of *Werther*, and it subsequently enjoyed five solo printings. Poets too found Werther to be a compelling and profitable subject. Editors printed dozens of Werther poems in American newspapers throughout the 1780s and 1790s, and dozens more appeared in literary magazines. Dr. Joseph Ladd of Newport, Rhode Island, for instance, had four poems about Werther printed in the *American Museum* (1787), the *Massachusetts Magazine* (1791), and the *Philadelphia Repository* (1805). Some poets active in the early national period even chose "Werter" as their pseudonym, no doubt in hopes of associating their own often forgettable stanzas with this literary juggernaut. Playwrights too got in on the act: in 1797 audiences in Boston, New York, and Philadelphia were treated to the first American performances of a dramatic interpretation of the story. Originally published and performed in Dublin, the play was produced again in Charleston in 1803 and 1804 and returned once more to Boston in 1809.[15]

The popularity of *Werther* and its unashamedly self-absorbed and self-destructive central character forced parents such as Benjamin Rush in Philadelphia and preachers such as Samuel Miller in New York to confront the dawning realization that not all authors had signed on to their campaign to harness literature for the purposes of moral education. Quite the contrary. As European and American writers experimented with all the possibilities of sentimental fiction during the 1780s, plots and

In this illustration Charlotte weeps over the tomb of Werther. By such means, young readers in particular were encouraged to identify with Charlotte's grief following Werther's suicide. Johann Wolfgang von Goethe, *The Sorrows of Werther*, trans. Dr. Pratt (New York: Richard Scott, 1807). Courtesy of the University of Missouri–Kansas City Libraries, Dr. Kenneth J. LaBudde Department of Special Collections.

characters had begun to appear that seemed to complicate or even undermine the messages about living virtuously and acting charitably embedded in works like *Clarissa* or *The Inquisitor*. As *Werther* fever gripped young America, the very people who had once promoted the affirming power of novel-reading reached the reluctant conclusion that excessively sentimental narratives might actually skew young readers' delicate sensibilities to the point of perversion, encouraging them to wallow in exquisite fictional tragedies while ignoring those around them truly in need of their sympathy. Addressing the Young Ladies Academy in Philadelphia in 1787, at the very moment that *Werther* achieved cult status in America, Benjamin Rush voiced his distrust of a novel so sensational and stylized that it seemed to him to have replaced moral instruction with sentiments so cloyingly romantic and disparaging of social duty as to be downright damaging:

> The abortive sympathy which is excited by the recital of imaginary distress, blunts the heart to that which is real and, hence, we sometimes see instances of young ladies, who weep away a whole forenoon over the criminal sorrows of a fictitious Charlotte or Werther, turning with disdain at three o'clock from the sight of a beggar, who sollicits [*sic*] in feeble accents or signs, a small portion only of the crumbs which fall from their fathers' tables.

Rush did not bother to hide his disgust. A year earlier he had extolled the virtues of "properly directed" literature. But *Werther* was another matter entirely. Goethe, Rush told the governors of this pioneering female academy, had misused the much-trumpeted power of sympathetic identification to stir up affection for characters wholly undeserving of pathos. By doing so, this little novel seemed to have broken the link between sensibility and charity that Rush and other worried parents of disorderly teenage children had hoped the new fashion for fiction would foster.[16]

Werther had hit a nerve. After the doctor's comments appeared in the Philadelphia papers, a friend of his wrote to congratulate him for speaking out. "I have the honour of being of your opinion as to the effects of imaginary distress, as recited in novels particularly in the Sorrows of Werter," Susan Montgomery wrote. Further north, the editor of the *Massachusetts Magazine* appeared to endorse the same opinion when he reprinted an English review of the book in 1795 that denounced "the fiery spirit of enthusiasm and overflowing sensibility which pervades the Sorrows of Werter." Three years later, Philadelphia's *Weekly Magazine* applauded those among the new crop of novels that "produce only the most generous emotions," but then singled out Goethe's little book as a gooey yet sly and treacherous exception. "Werther is drawn with a richness," the essayist calling himself "Ubiquitarian" declared, "that, however pitiable the real character might be, the danger of a mistaken passion or an immoral indulgence of amorous affection is too great to be safely or prudently instructed to the consideration of minds not strongly formed."[17]

As copies of the novel continued to fly from the shelves of bookshops and libraries throughout the 1790s and on into the 1800s, more and more public figures climbed aboard Rush's anti-*Werther* bandwagon. To drive home their case against the book's unchecked sentimentality, most took to arguing that its tear-soaked pages encouraged tender-minded readers to follow in its idol's bloody footsteps. Playing on widespread fears that suicide was making alarming progress in the new nation, a gaggle of critics charged that by perverting the proper process of sympathetic identification so that a self-destructive and narcissistic young romantic became a literary hero, Goethe had produced a novel that seemed to condone and even valorize self-murder. In a frequently reprinted opinion piece published in 1806—the year before young Bertell shot himself on the New Jersey shore in apparent imitation of Wahlheim's most notorious resident—one female commentator lamented that artful writers could prostitute their talents "in the encouragement of the most atrocious crimes." Goethe could never compensate, the author continued, "for the injury that vague minds receive from those publications where SUICIDE is represented as heroism; nor can the writer of the Sorrows of Werther ever make atonement for the injury he has done to society." Goethe's offense, pundits agreed, was to transform the terrors of self-destruction into something soft and sweet and tempt "vague minds" to follow young Werther's example if ever their own romantic entanglements became too much to bear.[18]

Looking around, anxious parents found plenty of suggestive evidence that Goethe's sentimental rendering of romantic suicide might have already encouraged imitative acts. In the two decades before news of Bertell's 1807 death reached them, cosmopolitan Americans who subscribed to European magazines or London newspapers were learning of other suicides around the Atlantic world that were apparently the deadly consequence of reading *Werther*. In 1777 a young Swede shot himself, leaving a copy of *Werther* open by his side. A year later, when another Scandinavian drowned herself, having been abandoned by her lover, a copy of *Werther* was found in her pocket. In 1784 London's *Gentleman's Magazine*, a favorite import of city elites in the United States, reported the suicide of a Miss Glover. "The Sorrows of Werther were found under her pillow," the magazine noted, "a circumstance which deserves to be known, in order, if possible, to defeat the evil tendency of that pernicious work."[19]

Similar cases seemed to be proliferating all over Europe, particularly among young men who demonstrated their identification with Werther and his plight by dressing up in his distinctive uniform of blue tailcoat and yellow waistcoat before putting pistols to their temples. A facetious remark usually attributed to Madame de Stäel—whose *Reflections on Suicide* became the grist for similar criticism when it was published in Philadelphia in 1816—claimed that "Werter has caused more suicides than the most beautiful woman in the world." Lord Byron agreed, suggesting that *Werther* was responsible for more deaths than Napoleon himself. Across Europe, especially in regions where customary deference seemed to be eroding most quickly, few local authorities gave it the benefit of the doubt: councils in cities such as Leipzig and Copenhagen banned the sale of the book for fear it would catalyze suicide among young readers, and the bishop of Milan reportedly bought up every copy he could find. Such makeshift quarantine seemed like the only way to try to contain the contagious spread of "Wertherism."[20]

A suicide in Jamaica in 1784 provided Americans with their first warning that the ability of fiction to direct death might be just as powerful in the New World as in the Old World. On this occasion it was not *Werther* that was found at the scene but a little-known British play. In November a Charlestown, South Carolina, paper reported that a Kingston doctor named Thomas Pugh had recently discovered that his friend, a Mr. Clarke, was having a secret affair with the woman with whom Pugh was infatuated. The doctor's mind had quickly taken on "a most perturbed state," and on September 30 he had stabbed his rival to death before turning the knife on himself. The investigation in Kingston soon revealed that Pugh's destructive rage had been "heightened by reading the tragedy of the *Mysterious Husband*" the night before his rampage.[21]

British playwright Richard Cumberland's 1783 drama narrates a series of complicated romantic entanglements. It climaxes when Lord Davenant, the husband of the title, discovers his wife's infidelity and stabs himself. His last words heap blame on those who betrayed him, and he dies proclaiming that "misery like mine acquits the suicide." Thomas Pugh had apparently read the play carefully. An analysis of Davenant's dying speech and the widely reprinted transcription of Pugh's suicide note confirms claims made in the *South-Carolina Gazette and General Advertiser* that "several passages" resembling the former had found their way into the latter. Over the next two months, newspapers in eight other states picked up the story; many focused their coverage on the startling suggestion that reading a fictional account of adultery, discovery, and suicide had led this jealous doctor to imitate its bloody denouement.[22]

Only six weeks after word of Pugh's crime appeared in the mainland press, several of these same papers reported disturbing signs that *Werther*'s deadly influence had finally reached the United States. An item in some New England newspapers in early 1785 described the death of a gentleman-soldier whose hopeless passion for a woman who did not return his affections had driven him to search for "a passage from misfortune." His suicide note, as transcribed in the *New Hampshire Mercury* and reprinted in Boston's *Independent Ledger* soon afterward, bore marked similarities to that of Werther's. "The pistols are loaded," he wrote. "ADIEU, for the last time!—Love me after I am dead, as I did you while I was alive." Over the next few years, worried parents and grandparents invoked suggestive reports like this as evidence of an escalating *Werther* epidemic. In Boston, in 1789, one aging matriarch wrote to her sister-in-law of the recent increase in suicides in that city, a fact she had learned "from the newspaper." "Dont you think the Sorrow of Werther is a pernicious book," asked Margaret Mascarene Hutchinson. "I think [it] ought to be suppres'd. I have no patience when I hear anyone speak in favour of it, a book that justifys, so rash a deed as self-murder, horrid, horrid, I shudder while I write it." Others agreed. Writing in Philadelphia's *Weekly Magazine* in 1798, one female essayist tried to persuade booksellers such as Robert Bell to remove the book from their shelves for fear that more young readers might mistake its luxuriant sensibility for an encouragement to suicide. But the city's bookmen seemed to have ignored all this. *Werther* was too popular and profitable to suppress, and there were already thousands of copies in libraries and homes across the country.[23]

Werther could not be stopped. The book, the writer in the *Weekly Magazine* fretted, had already proved "the bane of more than one family" in Pennsylvania. By way of proof she offered a "short history . . . taken from real life" of Eleanor, a young woman in the grip of a depression brought on by a miserable marriage and an abortive affair. "In this unhappy state of her existence the novel of Werter was never absent from her bosom; her tears moistened its leaves daily and hourly; and she dwelt, with fond and sorrowful sympathy, over these passages between which and her situation she fancied a resemblance." When Eleanor's husband, Arthur, eventually returned from a long sea voyage, the essayist reported, he found his wife sitting weeping over *Werther*. After Eleanor tearfully confesses the cause of her anguish, Arthur, full of inarticulate anger, begins a hunt for her erstwhile lover. This purportedly unvarnished narrative ends as Arthur kills the other man in a duel and Eleanor collapses, "resolved not to survive him."[24]

News of the 1807 suicide of a twenty-year-old German immigrant named Bertell thus came as no surprise—just another exhibit in an ever more grim parade. Over the previous two decades, the conviction that reading Goethe's novel could lead to copycat deaths had become gospel in certain circles. In an anti-*Werther* diatribe that circulated in several newspapers in 1810, one Salem essayist claimed that its mortal effects had been felt in "hundreds of families" over the past few years. "Within the narrow circle of my own acquaintance," she confided, "I have known two young men who rushed unbidden into eternity, deluded by the sophistical arguments of Werther in favor or in vindication of suicide." Each was a textbook case of Wertherism:

> The bodies of each were found with the book carefully confined next [to] the heart; as if the self deceived victims imagined it would serve as their excuse at the awful bar of eternal justice. These young men both killed themselves for love, as it is called. Like Werther, each had seen a pretty girl, and decorated his goddess with a thousand imaginary charms, vowing, perhaps, from the first captivating glance, to be hers, or die. Difficulties arise, their hopes were defeated; so, taking a draught of Lethe from the sentimental stream of nonsense we have been viewing, they believed it no hazard to rush into the presence of the Judge of quick and dead.

Werther's poisonous promotion of unrestrained self-regard seemed to be infecting much of the fiction popular with young readers. To many parents' utter horror, two of the very first American novels, along with several widely read British imports, not only featured the suicides of their own self-centered and avowedly sentimental characters but depicted these tragic yet ecstatic climaxes as the fatal consequences of reading *Werther*.[25]

Its encomiums to sensibility notwithstanding, William Hill Brown's *The Power of Sympathy* (1789) placed the demonstration of the Werther effect at the heart of its convoluted plot. In a series of letters strikingly similar to Werther's, Harrington informs his priggish friend, Worthy, of his blossoming romance with Harriot. Yet when the two lovers learn that they are actually brother and sister, Harriot quickly succumbs to a spiral of despair and illness that claims her life. Harrington too revolts at the news that their relationship was incestuous. Trembling with grief and disgust, he resolves to suicide, defending the act in a series of Goethian arguments laid out in his last letters. While Worthy is busy writing the latest in a series of replies to Harrington to denounce suicide and chip away at all of the latter's excuses for it, he gets word that it is too late; Harrington has shot himself in his apartment. Arriving on the scene, Worthy sees the body for himself and reports that "A LETTER that he had written for me, laid unsealed upon the table, and *The Sorrows of Werter* was found lying by its side."[26]

No reader of *The Power of Sympathy* needed any explanation to understand the significance of the presence of Goethe's novel at the scene. Reading *Werther*, William Hill Brown strongly implied, had validated and perhaps strengthened Harrington's resolution to die; indeed, Brown left open the possibility that reading the novel had influenced Harrington's choice to use a pistol or may even have put the idea of suicide in his head in the first place. Certainly one can see Goethe's influence in the style and substance of the particular justifications that Harrington offers to Worthy for the rash act he intends to commit.[27]

Brown's literary dramatization of the feared connection between reading *Werther* and copycat suicide was hardly unique. By fictionalizing the "Werther effect"—the term modern sociologists use when debating the enduring claim that reading about suicide can influence the decision to commit it—Brown demonstrated just how pervasive such fears had become by 1789. Just four years later, the anonymous female author of

The Hapless Orphan (1793) offered further testimony. Like *The Power of Sympathy*, *The Hapless Orphan* is an epistolary novel of desire, disappointment, and multiple suicides. After her first suitor shoots himself, the young narrator, Caroline Francis, goes to stay with her friend, Lucy Wilkens, in Virginia. When Lucy's jealous new husband vanishes, she falls dangerously ill, her nerves shot to pieces, and soon dies. Wilkens, half senseless from being shot in the shoulder in a duel and now full of remorse for the way he treated his young bride, then returns and commits suicide to assuage his guilt. Amid later twists in the story, Caroline befriends Fanny and Frederick, a brother and sister who console her in the midst of all this violence. At the end of the novel, Fanny is shot and killed by Ashley, a young man whose affections she—like Werther's Charlotte—has persistently refused. Ashley had been reading *Werther* in the days and weeks before this murder and had taken to quoting passages to Fanny in which Werther "argues in favor of suicide" to show her the true measure of his love and devotion. After shooting Fanny, Ashley dispatches himself, leaving a suicide note confirming the novel's influence: "The Sorrows of Werther is now open upon my table: It animates my heart; it cheers my soul; it will sustain me through the scene which I am about to act." Several English novels that circulated in America at this time offered similar tableaux; *Werther*, it seems, was more than an instruction manual—it had become the ultimate literary accessory.[28]

Between 1780 and 1810, suicide spread through the pages of fashionable fiction like yellow fever. As rattled observers like Rush were acutely aware, texts featuring suicidal characters reading *Werther* represent only a fraction of the narratives in which an act of self-destruction plays a central role. The suicides of young men unlucky in love or young women ruined by seduction punctuate the plots of many of the most popular novels and short stories. Indeed, no less than fifteen (one-third) of the first forty-five novels written by Americans, all of them published before 1810, depict a character dying by his or her own hand. These fifteen novels together portray the suicides of ten women and fourteen men, and there are dozens more attempts at, thoughts of, and discussions about suicide in these and other early American novels.[29]

This crude body count takes no heed of differences in print runs, marketing and sales, or the likelihood of titles being reprinted. Nor does it differentiate between those works that appear to valorize suicide as an extreme romantic gesture akin to Werther's and those that portray acts of self-destruction with studied ambiguity, or as the just deserts of vice and villainy. But neither did many knee-jerk critics of sentimental fiction. Prominent people increasingly suspicious of the literary forms they had once championed did not usually pause to distinguish between the myriad moral valences authors attached to literary suicide. On the contrary, nervous witnesses to the disintegration of customary social restraints in early national society intuitively linked every portrayal of suicide in popular literature to *Werther* and thus to their larger concerns about community integrity and the preservation of their own status. Blinkered by the satisfying purity of indignation, observers such as Rush believed that all fiction had been poisoned by the fashion among a few writers for excessive sentimentality; to them, any literary portrayal of suicide was rendered suspect and assumed, until proven otherwise, to be dangerously romantic.

There were, to be sure, quite a lot of novels and short stories that fit this emerging stereotype. American fiction showcased numerous characters whose self-destructive violence seemed intended to elicit sympathy or pity among readers. The deaths of young women who had been seduced and then abandoned were often framed this way. In 1791 the author of a short piece in the *New-York Magazine* referred to a lady's decision to shoot herself after her reputation was ruined by scandal as an "Instance of Female Heroism." "If [a] suicide can meet compassion from an insulted God," proclaimed an approving narrator in a piece in the same magazine a few years later, "surely it must be the seduced female." Plenty of writers of long-form fiction seemed to have assumed as much. In a subplot of *The Power of Sympathy* that fictionalized Frances Apthorp's suicide following her affair with Perez Morton, the hapless Ophelia poisons herself after being duped and dumped by her sister's husband. As the drugs wrought their effect upon Ophelia, "her sensibility became more exquisite." Likewise, in Henry Brackenridge's *Modern Chivalry* (1792), readers were encouraged to share Captain Farrago's uncharacteristically emotional reaction to news of a similar suicide. The blustering hero "could not but shed tears" when he learned that a young woman disappointed in love had "suspended herself from the bed post with her garter." Five years later, James Butler generated pathos for the ruined girl at the center of *Fortune's Foot-ball* (1797) by sending the child to ask her parents' forgiveness before she rushed into eternity. "Pardon your retched [*sic*] daughter—who cannot, will not survive her disgrace!" she begged, her eyes shining with tears. Then, "to the astonishment of all present, [she] plunged a poniard to her breast, and expired instantly."[30]

By the first decade of the nineteenth century, these ordeals had become predictable set pieces. In Sukey Vickery's otherwise decidedly unsentimental novel *Emily Hamilton* (1803), a young woman swollen with shame "walked to the place [where] she had been accustomed to meet her seducer, and with a ribband he had given her, suspended herself from the branch of a tree on which he had engraved his name and her own." Two years later, in an affecting if by now formulaic episode in Caroline Thayer's *The Gamesters* (1805), a distraught father described his child's seduction and subsequent suicide. After giving birth to "a lovely infant, the fruit of an illicit commerce," young, despairing Celestia takes her own life. Her father discovers her "breathless remains" in her room accompanied by a suicide note explaining both to him and to the *Gamesters'* readers that she had surrendered to "a soft, angelic voice" that whispered to her of "another and a better world." Presented as the tragic consequence of a lapse of virtue, the suicides of these disgraced daughters were depicted as entirely deserving of the compassion that parents assumed their teenage children would lavish upon them.[31]

Cognizant that a healthy proportion of their readers were adolescent boys on the cusp of manhood, several authors depicted young men in similarly sentimental throes. In addition to those of Harrington and Ophelia, the third suicide in *The Power of Sympathy* is of Henry, a principled romantic who plunges "into the river—to close his sorrows with his life" after discovering that his beloved Fidelia has yielded to his rival. Likewise, in Susanna Rowson's supremely popular seduction novel, *Charlotte Temple* (1794), Charlotte's would-be suitor, Montraville, makes a dark threat when she refuses to elope to America with him: "'Cruel Charlotte,' said he, 'if you disappoint my ardent hopes, by all that is sacred, this hand shall put a period to my existence. I cannot—will not live without you.'" Four years later, the young hero of John Davis's *Ferdinand and Elizabeth* (1798) joins his lover in a suicide pact when the obstacles to their earthly union become insurmountable, while in *The Gamesters* (1805) the guilt-stricken Leander

Samuel Hill's engraving illustrating one of three suicides in the first American novel also served as its frontispiece. William Hill Brown, *The Power of Sympathy; or, The Triumph of Nature: Founded in Truth* (Boston: J. Thomas, 1789). Courtesy of the American Antiquarian Society.

Anderson throws himself into a stream after failing to act to stop a girl from being seduced by another man.[32]

Many of the most self-consciously sentimental novels and short stories even paired such tragic tableaux with direct instructions to readers apparently intended to guide their response. For example, before raising a pistol to his brow, Ashley tells readers of *The Hapless Orphan* (1793) that "the mind must be pusillanimous indeed, that could content to drag out [the] wretched life" of the unrequited lover. Similarly, in *Ferdinand and Elisabeth* (1798), the ardent young man of the title applauds his sweetheart's courage to abandon this life for the next: "Surely thy soul must be possessed of a finer spiritual essence than commonly falls on the share of a woman." The same year saw a jilted lover in Susanna Rowson's *Reuben and Rachel* (1798) use a final exchange to address the reader with a rhetorical question: "Why should we endure life," asks Eumea before drowning herself, "when the nights are passed in anguish, and every day is a day of sorrow?"[33]

These novels and the many (sometimes illustrated) short stories that asked similar questions and told similar tales together suggest an intimate connection between sentimentalism and suicide. As Goethe knew all too well, suicide was a defining element of the sentimental form, if not its apotheosis. "Death by suicide," the literary critic Herbert Ross Brown concluded in the early twentieth century, "was the supreme luxury of the sentimentalist." As the literary language calculated to cultivate sensibility, sentimental writing was designed to stir powerful reactions among readers to scenes of acute suffering. Depicting suicide offered the ultimate trial of a writer's skill, and a superlative opportunity for readers to test their developing powers of sympathy. When confronted by characters driven to commit heinous sins for romantic reasons, readers faced an exquisite dilemma. Was condemnation or pity the proper response? Only true sentimentalists would be able to muster a heart brimful of genuine sympathy. As a writer for the *Massachusetts Magazine* who signed himself "Werther" explained in 1790: "The heart of tenderness, while it abhors the crime, cannot but feel the most real sorrow for that distress which urged him on to the fatal deed." In essence, then, sentimental suicides provided the perfect stimuli for young readers to display their finer shades of feeling.[34]

The ubiquity of suicide in the works of American stylists straining to imitate Goethe was thus essentially demand driven. In fact, in an exasper-

American literary magazines published numerous short stories between 1780 and 1810 that culminated in the suicide of young women undone by seducers. Left: *Massachusetts Magazine* 6 (1794). Center: *New-York Magazine* 5 (1794). Right: *New-York Magazine* 2 (1791). Courtesy, respectively, of the American Antiquarian Society, the Library Company of Philadelphia, and the American Antiquarian Society.

ated aside in *The Inquisitor* (1794), Susanna Rowson, one of many writers whose own attitude toward sentimentalism oscillated between approbation and revulsion over the years, suggested that tender readers had come to expect a finely rendered suicide in every new romance. "Remember to mix a sufficient quantity of sighs, tears, swooning hysterics, and all the moving expressions of heart-rending woe," she sardonically advised authors hoping to profit from imitating Goethian forms. "If convenient, a suicide might not be amiss."[35]

Few other concerned observers of the rise of sentimental fiction shared Rowson's wry sense of humor. On the contrary: by the turn of the century, the presence of so many seemingly sympathetic depictions of suicide in early national literature had, in the minds of many wary critics, extended *Werther*'s reach and transformed all fiction into a blight on public health. In 1803 New York Presbyterian Samuel Miller complained that self-destruction now appeared so commonly in novels that the genre amounted to "an apology for suicide." His polemic remarks, which appeared in the central chapter of an otherwise temperate two-volume survey of recent progress in the arts and sciences, were frequently reprinted, usually with admiring commentary, in the pages of several of the more respectable magazines over the following years. Sensing strong demand among other friends of order for further chest-beating on the subject, Miller used the occasion of a suicide in the city two years later to publish *The Guilt, Folly, and Sources of Suicide* (1805), a sermon that elaborated his attacks on the mimetic power of novel reading:

> I cannot help remarking more explicitly, what was transiently hinted in another place, that the mischievous influence on popular opinions produced by many dramatic representations, and by licentious novels, may probably be considered as leading to many cases of the crime before us. Perhaps some will pronounce this a far-fetched and illiberal supposition. But let me ask such objectors, whether many of these compositions do not make virtue and religion contemptible and vice honourable, attractive, and triumphant? Do they not frequently put corrupt opinions into the mouth of some favorite hero, the splendour of whose character, in other respects, is made to embellish the most detestable sentiments, and the force of whose eloquence is employed to recommend the most criminal maxims? Do they not represent the most odious crimes that mortals can commit, and suicide among the rest, as venial faults, and sometimes as no faults at all?

Although self-destruction was only one "odious crime . . . among the rest," it was also the most extreme and irrevocable. Indeed, by Miller's reckoning, New Yorkers with an appetite for "licentious novels" were in great peril. "Is it far-fetched or illiberal to say that such compositions have a tendency favourable to suicide, and that those who habitually delight in and peruse them are in [*sic*] the high road of danger?" Convinced that *Werther* had already laid waste to young readers both in Europe and in America, plenty of distressed adults repeated similar arguments throughout the 1790s and 1800s. A piece in New York's *People's Friend* that appeared just weeks before news of Bertell's death reached that city's readers in 1807 bemoaned "the many instances of Suicide which have lately occurred" before blaming "those hot-beds of vice, the NOVEL SHOPS." Approving editors in Massachusetts and South Carolina reprinted the item when copies of the paper reached them two weeks later.[36]

Despite their indignant sincerity, these articles usually lacked any conclusive evidence that reading even the most sentimental account of a fictional suicide had led to a genuine case of copycat violence. Proof that any American fiction had equaled *Werther*'s destructive power was quite hard to come by. Rumors swirled in 1801 that the infamous Jason Fairbanks's attempt to cut his throat after murdering the young lady he was infatuated with had been influenced by his reading of "idle and romantic books." But no one seemed to know precisely which books he had read. Likewise, later news reports describing the death of seventeen-year-old Charlotte Tullibur in Gallipolis, Ohio, could not say which novels had been her downfall; they noted only that her suicide had been "occasioned by extreme sensibility, and romantic ideas, created by novel reading."[37]

It should not be surprising that many critics did not usually wait for evidence to catch up with their accusations. Decrying portrayals of fictional suicide was slowly—perhaps unconsciously—becoming a means to an end, a convenient and compelling opportunity to express deep disappointment that the reading revolution had run amok. The once-promising cult of sensibility that Rush, Rowson, and others had sponsored during the 1780s seemed in retrospect to have been hijacked by writers apparently unwilling to use their talents to give the nation's youth a timely moral education. Instead of shoring up parental authority and instilling fellow feeling in the rising generation, literature in America seemed to many post-*Werther* commentators to be going in a different, darker, and more dangerous direction. Too often these novels appeared to disparage familial duty in favor of youthful passion, apparently validating the loosening of traditional limits on individual behavior. Indeed, the most saccharine incarnations of the sentimental style seemed to be wreaking the opposite of their once-hoped-for effects, producing emotional epicures transfixed by the exquisite traumas of fictional figures yet utterly uninterested in pressing social problems.

As most critics had belatedly come to realize, sympathy was a force unto itself; once elicited and unleashed, it was too potent to be harnessed. While early champions of the novel had presumed that readers would have sufficient savvy to distinguish between characters whose positive example they were expected to emulate and those they were supposed to pity or condemn, characters like Werther confounded their expectations. In fact, novels that mimicked *Werther*'s use of epistolary devices only magnified the strength of fellow feeling between readers and the correspondent(s) whose choices they were supposed to denounce and reject. Furthermore, the fondness among American authors for tales that centered upon young women ruined by rakes required the genre to rely on the power of negative example to preserve its didactic credentials. But, in practice, delivering "sentimental pedagogy" through negative example proved easier said than done, not least because readers had to put themselves completely in the fallen woman's position in order to experience her anguish. Immersed in an intensive and intimate reading experience, consumers of novels that seemed to pervert the power of sympathy were hard to reach and to rescue.[38]

Novels or short stories that garbed acts of suicide in the language of sentiment only served to draw attention to this fundamental flaw in the campaign to use popular fiction to prod people toward acting right, exposing the disturbing lack of control that ministers and parents had over how young people interpreted fiction. *The Power of Sympathy* is, again, a case in point. The responses of the characters who discover Harrington's body at the climax of the novel perfectly illustrate the fears of those who had come to realize that sympathy was an ungovernable force. As if to model how readers should respond, the fictional spectators that gather in this final scene instinctively understand that Harrington has erred but refuse to condemn the young man's suicide because it is the product of the action of "violent passions" on his "too nice sensibility." While authors like William Hill Brown often used obsequious prefaces to insist that their work was intended to warn young readers of the "dangerous Consequences of SEDUCTION," critics of sentimental fiction increasingly concluded that the opposite was true.[39]

On these grounds, creeping cynicism about the power of reading soon became the conventional wisdom. In early 1787 the wealthy lawyer John Mifflin had kept his concerns private, confiding to his diary his fear that reading sentimental novels was having a "pernicious effect" on sensibility, "—that it incapacitates us to feel for anything but romantic distress—plain unadorned misery which is to be seen every day, passes unfelt and unheeded." This hushed skepticism spilled into the open over the next seven or eight years as *Werther* achieved cult status. Thus a 1790 poem published in the *Columbian Magazine* satirized the power of misplaced sensibility to cast aside familial duty in favor of luxurious self-regard by lampooning a young woman who ignored her dying father because she was distraught by the sight of a bruised flower. A few months later, in June 1792, a writer in the *Ladies Magazine* argued that even the most powerful pieces of literary sentimentalism could only generate transient acts of casual, momentary kindness. No romance writer, she argued, could foster true, lasting, Christian charity capable of ameliorating the acute social problems plaguing early national cities.[40]

Refusing to midwife a benevolent revolution, fiction seemed to its least forgiving critics to be bent on ensnaring its intoxicated young readers in enchanted worlds of tears, sighs and blushes—a world where their parents could not reach them. "Sentiment," Rev. John Bennett wrote in an open letter to young ladies published in the *American Museum* in 1792, "has triumphed over the vulgar shackles of conscience, and of every social and moral obligation." By way of illustration, the June 1794 issue of the *United States Magazine* described a young domestic, cut off from her family and alone in the city, who had "the misfortune" of living next door to a circulating library. "Her heart had been a thousand times melted and pierced and smitten and wounded" by her appetite for sentimental novels, leaving her vulnerable to anyone who would toss her a kindly word. Without sending word to her parents, "she ran away with a corporal quartered in the town, and has never been heard of since." Because conservatives believed that young women were more susceptible to the opiate of sentimental fiction (and more likely to be ruined by succumbing to the temptations of modern life), these tutting parables featured female characters disproportionately.[41]

The assault only intensified as the decade wore on. Word of the Reign of Terror in France reached American newspaper readers in the fall of 1793, illustrating to parents and preachers the political consequences of unchecked emotionalism. As a result, they redoubled their efforts to decry the dangers of sentimental reading. With each passing year, the number of literary magazines warning that reading novels and short stories might lead untutored minds both to mental and moral dissipation multiplied. Reprinting Samuel Taylor Coleridge's famous remarks on the chattel economy that underpinned polite culture, a 1796 issue of *The Watchman* described the hypocrisy of young female readers of sentimental fiction who had become slaves of feeling: "She sips a beverage sweetened with human blood, even while she is weeping over the refined sorrows of Werther." Indeed, *The Watchman*'s editor was keenly aware that the tears such readers shed for suicidal romantics like Werther infuriated many parents and guardians concerned about the corrosive effects of sentimental fiction more broadly. By century's end, that criticism showed no signs of abating. Once hailed as the answer to the social dislocations roiling the young Republic, novels seemed to have lost any shred of respectability. In the view of a writer whose work appeared in the *Lady's Magazine*, sentimental fiction had become "a species of writing which can scarcely be spoken of without being condemned."[42]

This storm of criticism about how popular fiction handled suicide is best understood as an expression of the anxious response of elites to the broader crisis of moral authority in the early Republic. Fighting for the survival of the traditional patterns of deference that supported their way of life, these jeremiahs reacted to the rise of the novel as if it manifested a fundamental challenge to their inherited privilege as the prime arbiters of good sense and appropriate sensibility. Because these early novels, many of which adopted sentimental postures, asserted the primacy of the individual reader's relationship to the text, they seemed to displace biblical and parental authority simultaneously. As such, novels like *Werther* became loci for apprehensions about the fragmentation of early national society.[43]

Yet sentimental literature did not fit smoothly into this proxy power struggle. The portrait of this body of writing painted in contemporary complaints about the wild and destructive influence of *Werther* and its literary kin manifested an extraordinary degree of paternalistic condescension to both authors and readers. To be sure, the sentimental language that framed several literary suicides did often blur the bright line between positive and negative example. Likewise, several authors were no doubt guilty of romanticizing suicide to appeal to young readers craving more of the luxuriously tender scenes that Goethe had spoiled them with. Even so, the fiction favored by young readers in the new nation was not nearly as subversive as its most paranoid critics made out. More often than not, suicide appears in novels and short stories published in America between 1780 and 1810 either as self-inflicted retribution for villainy or as something to be prevented or unambiguously censured.

Critics like Benjamin Rush, Samuel Miller, and John Bennett were either unaware or unwilling to admit that authors frequently described suicide as the well-deserved fate of literary villains—the scheming outsiders and immoral seducers who drove so many of these heart-melting plots. But it was nonetheless true. For instance, a short story by Thomas Bellamy that appeared in one of Boston's literary magazines in 1789 took pains to warn readers that conscience might one day catch up with callous young men. When the virtuous young lady he has ruined dies of shame, the once rakish Charles is suddenly struck down with guilt. Believing that he will be cast into hell for what he has done, he retreats to a cabin in the woods and fashions a wax effigy of the girl and prays to it for days. But doing so fails to deliver the solace he seeks, so Charles seizes a small dagger and plunges it into his chest. "May this unhappy man, with whom we have murdered many a guilty hour, prove an awful lesson!" the narrator concludes. Most other fiction writers avoided such direct addresses to readers, preferring to let their plots speak for themselves. In *Edgar Huntley* (1799), Charles Brockden Brown punishes Clithero, a homicidal sleepwalker, by forcing him to drown himself in the Delaware River to avoid being incarcerated in the newly renovated insane wing of the Pennsylvania Hospital for his crimes. Similarly, in Sally Wood's *Dorval* (1801) the eponymous speculator and murderer shoots himself in prison, while in George Watterston's *Glencarn; or, The Disappointments of Youth* (1810), Mrs. Richardson poisons herself after attempting to ruin the life of her husband's adoptive son. While each character thus escapes further punishment in the here and now by fleeing toward the hereafter, these authors each clearly frame the villain's suicide as a prelude to divine judgment and retribution.[44]

Perhaps in response to the chorus of criticism that sentimental fiction romanticized teenage self-destruction or perhaps in testimony to the fact that such blanket criticism was sometimes wide of the mark, American authors contrived to dramatize prevention as often as possible. "Despair;

or The History of Delia and Lorenzo," a short story published in *New-York Magazine* in 1791, typifies the blend of tragedy and coincidence writers required to do so. Delia, the daughter of a Philadelphia merchant, has been promised to her father's apprentice though she loves Lorenzo, a childhood friend now serving with General Washington. When word reaches her that Lorenzo has been killed in battle, Delia casts herself into the Schuylkill. "Rash deed!" exclaims the anonymous narrator. "But happy, happy circumstance! At a small distance, her ever faithful Lorenzo was crossing the river in a boat," rumors of his death apparently exaggerated.[45]

Such thrilling twists of fate were a staple of early national fiction. No fewer than three of the characters in the *History of Constantius and Pulchera* (1795) were saved from suicide by timely interventions, while in Susanna Rowson's *Trials of the Human Heart* (1795) the villainous Clara Moreton "conceive[s] the impious idea" to take her own life but is distracted from doing so when she hears "a rustling on the other side of the hedge." Similarly, Amelia, the ruined young woman at the center of a short story published in 1798, is prevented from swallowing laudanum when her father bursts into her room unannounced. In *The Gamesters* (1805) one of Leander Anderson's first attempts to drown himself stalls when "fancy gave him the resemblance of his father," while in *Kelroy*, a novel written by Benjamin Rush's niece, Rebecca, the suicide of the Wertherian protagonist is preempted by a fatal illness.[46]

Refusing to resort to such contrived plot devices to abort a suicide, one or two writers instead fictionalized the power of rational discussion to sap the resolve of people bent upon destroying themselves. The highwayman in James Butler's *Fortune's Foot-ball* (1797), for instance, listens while Charles and the appropriately named Mercutio "endeavoured both by moral and philosophical arguments to dissuade him from his desperate purpose—in which they happily succeeded." More conservative writers were not so coy and let characters articulate explicit antisuicide messages directly to the reader. In *The Coquette* (1794), Hannah Foster's alter ego, Julia Granby, comforts foolish Eliza Wharton after her most promising suitor forsakes her, telling her to resist any fatalistic daydreams. "I hope, said I, that you have formed no resolution against your own life. God forbid, rejoined she. My breath is in his hands, let him do what seemeth good in his sight." A few pages later, when Major Sanford's wife leaves him after discovering his affair with young Eliza, he briefly flirts with suicide before wrestling with his demons and resolving to live. "I would fly to death, and seek a refuge in the grave," the rake tells a correspondent, "but the forebodings of a retribution to come, I cannot away with!"[47]

A few authors went further, offering their work as custom-designed antidotes to the perceived toxicity of the Werther effect. The second American novel, Rev. Enos Hitchcock's *Memoirs of the Bloomsgrove Family* (1790), embodies the Providence clergyman's obvious dismay at the fashion for sentimental suicide in popular novels like *Werther* and *The Power of Sympathy.* Quoting Benjamin's Rush's much-reprinted indictment of Goethe's self-absorbed characters with undisguised admiration, Hitchcock describes his heroine, Rozella Bloomsgrove, as the antithesis of those "young ladies, who weep away a whole forenoon, over the criminal sorrows of a fictitious Charlotte or Werther, turning with disdain, at two o'clock, from the sight of a beggar." Hitchcock, a preacher with Federalist views and a veteran of the Continental Army, surely approved of a novel that appeared in the American market a decade later. Reprinted in Philadelphia in 1802 from a British original, *The Slave of Passion, or, the Fruits of Werther* attempted a thorough reworking of Goethe's story, an exercise the anonymous author hoped would "counteract the poison in Werther's Letters."[48]

The Slave of Passion loosely follows the outline of Goethe's narrative: a young man learns of the marriage of his intended and despairs, resolving to suicide. The protagonist, Charles, has been reading *Werther* and repeats the German's arguments to justify suicide almost verbatim in a letter to his friend, Henry. Unlike Goethe's Wilhelm (whose replies are assumed but unseen), or Worthy, in *The Power of Sympathy* (whose long-winded and intermittent replies lack focus or force), Henry writes back immediately, obliterating each and every argument that Charles, channeling Werther, has marshaled. After a moment of suspense, the plot veers drastically from the Goethian model when Charles writes back grateful and exultant to have been dragged from the metaphorical precipice by the arrival of Henry's last letter. With tragedy averted, a happy ending quickly follows as Charles learns that he has been misinformed of Maria's marriage. The novel closes as Charles and Maria prepare for their nuptials, the pair blissfully happy and their brush with *Werther* a distant memory.

The works of Charles Brockden Brown—as packed with scenes of self-destruction as any of this generation—demonstrate the often-confounding variety of portrayals of young men and women killing themselves to be found in early American fiction. Among the many suicides in Brown's multifaceted works, a handful seem straightforwardly sentimental. In *Arthur Mervyn* (1799), the sister of the title character is seduced by her schoolmaster, the "arch-villain" Colvill. "Young, artless, and beautiful," she takes her life to escape from "the upbraidings of her parents, from the contumelies of the world, from the goadings of remorse, and the anguish flowing from the perfidy and desertion of Colvill." Likewise, *Jane Talbot* (1801) confesses to her readers that "Often have I wished to slide obscurely and quietly into the grave. . . . Never felt I so enamored of that which seems to be the cure-all."[49]

Yet such sympathetic renderings of characters bent on destroying themselves were by no means typical of Brown's broad oeuvre. In the "Man at Home" sketches, first published in 1798, Brown's narrator recalls a young man forced to live with the consequences of an impulsive suicide attempt. For eighteen-year-old Henry Fairfax, the cause was the smallpox that claimed the life of his new bride. Battered by grief, this distraught young man had "sought out her grave, and shot himself at the foot of it." But his aim was not as true as his heart. Henry survived, though his head wound left him incapacitated, and he lived out his remaining years occupying "a cell in an hospital. Squalid, naked, and emaciated—what a monument of ruin and or rashness dost thou exhibit!" Later the same year, copies of *Wieland* began to appear in Philadelphia bookshops. Theodore Wieland ends that bloody and ambiguous story by murdering his family and then himself, fanatically convinced that God has ordered him to do so. Sometimes interpreted as a lampoon of high-strung sentimental fiction, this grisly tale presents Wieland's suicide as the product of his intoxicating delusion. Brown was undoubtedly fired by opposition to the unchecked emotional enthusiasm consuming France during the Reign of Terror and used the book's terrible denouement to warn of the dangers of decoupling skepticism from sensibility.[50]

Although critics of the nation's early literature chose to ignore such complexity, it was nonetheless present not only in Charles Brockden Brown's accumulated output but also within individual works by myriad other authors. In *The Hapless Orphan* (1793), young Ashley first enacts the Werther effect in textbook style, before the narrator, Caroline Francis, denounces the book as a plausible sanction for suicide. It seems as if a small minority of authors believed they could have their cake and eat it too, decrying *Werther* on one page while offering their own renderings of romantic suicide on the next. John Davis's *Ferdinand and Elizabeth* (1798) provides another case in point. Thirty pages before the star-crossed lovers of the title agree to a suicide pact, Ferdinand comes across a servant girl and asks her if she is a fan of "these love-inflicting volumes." "She replied with a coquettish air that she slept every night with the Sorrows of Werter under her pillow! I could hardly restrain my laughter, but discharging the bill, bade my novel-reading nymph farewell, whose susceptibility amused me."[51]

Such jarring juxtapositions make it tempting to view much of the invective leveled against romantic suicide by authors such as John Davis and William Hill Brown as cynical posturing. Certainly, the sanctimonious forewords attached to many sentimental novels, including *The Power of Sympathy* and later American editions of *Werther*, assuring readers that the tragic tales inside were meant as moral warnings, seem calculated. Likewise, authors such as Rebecca Rush, who exploited readers' expectations that a sensitive character was about to commit suicide, only to abort the act at the last possible moment, seemed to have hoped to satisfy the competing demands of young readers and their parents simultaneously.

As events in France in the mid-1790s engrossed the American imagination, it became more and more perilous for authors trying to walk this tightrope. In fact, by the turn of the century, it was all that struggling novelists could do to defend themselves against charges that their sensational designs smacked of Jacobinism. Charles Brockden Brown was one among several writers who tried to blunt some of the attacks on contemporary fiction as uniformly self-indulgent and politically corrosive. In a column he published in his *Literary Magazine* in 1805, Brown took on no less a figure than Samuel Miller, one of the most vocal scourges of sentimental writing—and who happened to be an old friend. Responding directly to passages of Miller's sermon impugning novel reading as a symptom of growing self-absorption and a leading cause of suicide, Brown argued that most of the literary diet consumed by ordinary Americans did not deserve such censure. "Suicide in truth, is very rarely to be found," he protested. "Wherever it occurs, so far as we remember, it is placed in such a light as to discourage rather than provoke imitation." Choosing Rousseau's *La Nouvelle Héloïse* as an example of a well-known novel in which a suicide was averted, Brown asserted that not all prose fiction was guilty as charged:

> The faults of Rousseau's famous novel are not few, but it really does not appear to us chargeable with promoting suicide. Some readers may suppose the preponderance of argument in the epistolary controversy contained in the work to be in favour of suicide, but readers of good sense can hardly fail, we think, of forming a different conclusion; and as to the intention of the author, something may surely be inferred from his having represented his hero as influenced by his friend's reasonings to lay aside his murderous purposes.

Offering a stout rebuttal to critics convinced they could discern authorial intention by scanning a book catalog or a title page, Brown here uses Rousseau's novel to anticipate the central insight of modern reader response criticism, namely, that meaning is made not at the site of production but at the point of consumption. Although he might have made similar claims about *Werther*, Brown avoided any mention of it; he did not want to push his luck.[52]

As the *Literary Magazine* found its feet, its editor slowly grew bolder, becoming something of an advocate for all those American novelists who rejected the Goethian fixation on overheated romantic fantasy and sentimental suicide. In a column for an 1806 issue, Brown wondered aloud how many novels critics like Miller, Bennett, and Rush had actually bothered to read before denouncing wholesale. (It was a fair point: in a preface to his excoriation of modern novels, Samuel Miller had confessed his ignorance of most of their contents.) Building up a head of steam, Brown charged parents and preachers with a patronizing disregard for their children's ability to discern the difference between positive and negative example. While critics of novels like *Werther* built their case on the assumption that typical readers had "vague minds" that could be easily corrupted, Charles Brockden Brown assumed that these same consumers had sufficient moral competence to undertake the task in hand. Even untutored adolescent readers, Brown scolded, could readily distinguish virtue from vice and deserved more credit. For his part, the editor continued:

> Neither can I refuse to teach a child to read, because he may possibly light upon something in the form of books trifling or pernicious. It would be just as wise to sew up his mouth, because he may possibly swallow a poisoned berry, or a brass pin: to break both his legs, because he may possibly walk under a penthouse when it is falling. As to prohibit him from reading every thing called a novel, because there are books under that denomination, which may possibly deprave the morals, or vitiate the taste.

By 1810 such blasts of common sense had become a regular refrain as a growing number of writers tried to distance and disassociate themselves from the excesses of sentimentalism.[53]

It was too late. Sensibility's reputation now lay in tatters. In its heyday, during the early 1780s, the aesthetics of sentiment had penetrated not just fiction but also advice books, sculpture, painting, poetry, and fashion, as all manner of moral pathfinders hailed the power of sensibility to secure the future of American democracy. However, as the eighteenth century gave way to the nineteenth, many of these same opinion makers embraced the dawning belief that the Republic's problems now extended far beyond those that a keenness of perception, delicacy of feeling, capacity for sympathetic identification, and ability to be stirred to profound responses by beauty and suffering might plausibly address. Throughout the late 1780s and 1790s, the expansion of the white male franchise, the growth of factory production and out-of-home labor, rising in-migration and immigration to the nation's largest cities, ethnic fragmentation, and the insistent and insidious spread of an overtly masculine doctrine of competition and profit seeking convinced more and more parents and preachers of the naïveté of a cultural program that touted affectionate ties as tools of successful nation building. As they groped for ways to understand and accommodate the increasingly capitalistic and individualistic culture ushered in with the new century without sliding into the anarchy engrossing revolutionary France, Americans grew ever more wary of the dangers of extreme sensibility.[54]

Caught amidst this reorientation, many of the authors who had experimented with the possibilities of sentimental literature found themselves the targets of attacks by ministers and patriarchs convinced that Werther and his literary cousins were not the cure but actually one of the causes of the nation's troubles. Eager to turn the page, writers coming into their own a generation later, after the War of 1812, seemed willing to do whatever was necessary to distance themselves from suspect sentimentality. Thus in John Neal's ruggedly masculine and fervently nationalistic novel *Keep Cool* (1817), Earnest pours scorn on the tropes of Neal's Eurocentric literary predecessors, telling his partner:

> "I may be romantick; but I would blow my brains out this very moment if I thought this was the sickening, sniveling romance of *novels*." His eyes flashed as he added in a lofty, affected tone, "mine, Percy, mine is a high souled romance—the poetry of extravagance. I would spill my heart's blood, to be serious."

Earnest's posture was a sign of the times. Library and bookstore records show that after 1810 both supply of and demand for novels filled with tears, sighs, and suicide noticeably slackened, a phenomenon likely shaped in part by three decades of warnings from parents and ministers that extremely sentimental fiction undercut the politically necessary restraints on individual behavior imposed by familial obligation and social conscience.[55]

In this new literary world, *Werther* was now a relic. While booksellers had paid for more than five hundred advertisements for the novel before 1809, over the next sixteen years less than 5 percent of that number turned up in newspapers, suggesting that the next generation of young readers had moved on to other things. Literary magazines stopped excerpting sensational moments in the now-familiar story, and the cottage industry in Werther paraphernalia sputtered and stalled. Summing up the novel's dramatic reversal of fortune, one Jacksonian minister remarked that even the most feebleminded of readers "would now regard it as a book too silly to cry over." "The book is sneered at," agreed Henry Wadsworth Longfellow in an 1835 journal entry. Soon enough, it became the subject of satires and parodies like L. A. Wilmer's "Sorrows of Skwerter" (1838).[56]

Antebellum youngsters who cracked open dusty copies, as Salem shipping heiress Clara Crowninshield did in 1836, found the main character's fatalistic affectation difficult to sympathize with:

> While he [Werther] was unhappy I could sympathize with him, but that a man should yield to and cherish such a morbid state of feeling excites my disgust rather than my sympathy, and I was infinitely more moved by his unhappiness in the beginning than by the shocking termination. At first I could sympathize with him, but thro' the dark valley which led him to the final catastrophe I could not follow him.

Nor would many female novelists still willingly follow Werther into his dark valley. In contrast to earlier work, the plots of such domestic fiction as Catherine Sedgwick's *A New England Tale* (1822) elevate female characters with intelligence and willpower over those unable to control the temptation to immerse themselves in unguarded sympathy for other people. Female novelists writing in the Jacksonian and antebellum eras worked especially hard to keep Werther at a safe distance, preferring instead to use the redeeming influence of evangelical heart religion to direct the sympathy of their heroines (and, by extension, their readers) toward worthy targets. Put another way, this latter-day cohort of cautiously sentimental writers avoided the pitfalls of trying to teach by negative example and confined themselves to modeling the transforming power of sympathy through positive portrayals.[57]

By the 1850s, sentimental fiction had been transformed, returning from the literary wilderness to serve as a powerful and respectable means to confront middle-class readers, particularly women, with the plights of people fundamentally different from themselves, most notably lower-class women, Indians, and the enslaved. As a result, by the middle of the nineteenth century it was rare indeed to find well-to-do characters committing suicide. Authors had no desire to be accused of inciting another wave of copycat deaths. Instead, writers such as Harriet Beecher Stowe seized on the suicides of enslaved blacks, noble savages, and desperate factory girls in hopes of turning their sentimentalized deaths to the cause of reforming an imperfect society.[58]

"So this is the little lady that started our big war." As Abraham Lincoln's apocryphal remark to the author of *Uncle Tom's Cabin* (1852) suggests, generations of Americans were brought up to believe in the power of sentimental reading, even if many ultimately concluded that it was an ungovernable and often destructive force. Standing helplessly on the sidelines of the reading revolution he had once supported, this is exactly the conclusion that Benjamin Rush reluctantly reached in the mid-1780s as he and many other like-minded parents of adolescent children displaced their growing disillusionment about the atomizing changes reshaping early national society onto Werther's slender shoulders.

Yet even as Rush washed his hands of sentimental novels, content to decry romantic reading as a contributing cause of many of the suicides that now glutted city papers, the doctor still refused to surrender the new nation to the dislocating forces that imperiled it. Unbowed and undaunted—perhaps even energized by his failure to nourish a literary movement that could serve a liberal agenda—Rush cut his losses and set out in a different direction, pouring money, time, and unbounded enthusiasm into a new project to model republican charity and attack the rising death toll head-on. Taking up his duties as the founding vice president of the Philadelphia Humane Society—the antidrowning charity that he had touted in 1786 as the associational embodiment of perfect sensibility—Rush shifted his focus, moving on from this depressing debate about the causes of so many recent suicides to the practical matter of figuring out how best to prevent them.

3

Saving Sinking Strangers

The man had been in the water about twelve minutes before they could get to him. No one had seen him jump from the Charles River Bridge, but everyone near the piers heard the splash as he hit the water. The man was about forty years old; he could not or would not swim and flailed only briefly before sinking below the surface. It took ferrymen and barrow boys those twelve long minutes to pile into two boats and row out to where he now floated, face down, apparently dead, with "nothing visible but his hair." With hands or hooks they pulled the body into one of the boats and returned to shore. Panting for breath, these unnamed rescuers carted the body more than three hundred feet to a grand brick house at the corner of Mason and Bow Streets, leaving wet tracks behind them. The house belonged to Richard Devens, a retired Boston lawyer and member of the Massachusetts Humane Society (MHS), a lifesaving group that Devens and others had recently set up to rescue and resuscitate men like this.[1]

Devens knew what to do. He sent a fleet-footed boy to fetch Josiah Bartlett, a young Charlestown doctor. A distant relation of his famous

New Hampshire namesake, Bartlett was another founding member of the MHS and had spent the past seven years studying what to do in emergencies like this. The doctor arrived to find that Devens and the other rescuers had started without him, just as the Humane Society's well-publicized protocols said they should. Bartlett found the unconscious stranger already stripped, wrapped in a blanket, and being rubbed to restore warmth, but to no obvious effect. When he examined the body, the "face was very much swoln, and the brain crowded. . . . Slight spasms of the breast were perceptible, but the circulations in the extremities had ceased." Wasting no time, the expert now took over from the amateurs, injecting warm water into the stranger's intestines to force a violent reaction, tipping liquor down his throat, and rubbing him with "woollens dipped in hot spirits." It seemed to work: the man's breathing began to recover, and as soon as he was able to swallow, Bartlett dosed him with an emetic to clear his stomach. Forty-five minutes passed before he was strong enough to speak, his breathing still difficult and his face apoplectic. It was three more hours before he was well enough to be carried in a carriage the mile to his home to begin his convalescence. It was September 5, 1793.[2]

The humane societies that sprung to life in several American cities in the last decades of the eighteenth century never made suicide prevention their exclusive concern. Cases like this one jostled for space in their records with tales of rescued children and shipwrecked seamen whose jeopardy was the product of mishap or misfortune. Yet preventing suicides consumed members' imaginations. Trying to turn the power of sympathy toward a legitimate target—the wave of self-destruction that newspaper reporting suggested was sweeping the country—activists like Devens and Bartlett in Boston and Benjamin Rush in Philadelphia enshrined the prevention of strangers' suicides at the center of their organizations' lifesaving missions. Indeed, even though they struggled to find many self-destructive people to save, the humane societies dotted along the Eastern Seaboard at the turn of the nineteenth century can be correctly understood as the early American antecedents of modern suicide prevention centers.

Preventing suicide is implicitly nonconsensual. Josiah Bartlett's triumph was to restore to life a man who had resolved to die, an intervention the doctor later justified by attributing his troubled patient's actions to passing madness. Seen in this light, the interventionist agendas of the professional elites who filled the ranks of early national humane societies reveal their response to one of the most fundamental dilemmas facing the constituents of the rapidly fragmenting new nation: What responsibilities did unrelated private individuals have to one another? Were citizens bound by a social contract in which each man was his brother's keeper, or did inalienable personal freedom trump mutual obligation? By preserving life, even against the will of those who had decided to die, men like Devens, Bartlett, and Rush made this seemingly abstract debate vivid and vital. Lives were quite literally at stake.

Across the Atlantic world, humane societies emerged at the end of the eighteenth century as the associational embodiment of sensibility, that social, outwardly directed mode of feeling that encourages people to recognize their connection to others and to be moved by every species of human suffering. Taking cues from Lockean psychology, the rising reputation of nervous medicine, and the theories of moral sentiment advanced by Scottish Enlightenment thinkers like Adam Smith, the cult of sensibility found its most imaginative and sometimes anarchic expression in popular literature. Yet unlike those sentimental novelists accused of fostering fellow feeling for distressed fictional characters wholly undeserving of pathos, the well-heeled humanitarian activists behind these pioneering lifesaving groups tried to channel the power of sympathy to extend a hand to those on all the lower rungs of American society and affirm a common destiny.[3]

In this respect, humane societies were emblematic of a broad surge of interest in private benevolence in this period. In New England alone, as many as two thousand new charities popped up between 1770 and 1820, most of them committed, in one way or another, to the critical care of those in urgent need and imminent danger. To Daniel Dana, an energetic young pastor in northern Massachusetts, this explosion of soup kitchens and neighborhood fire companies made it suddenly seem as if "every form of distress [now] finds its appropriate relief; every calamity, its remedy, or alleviation." Humane societies were in one sense the purest examples of this impulse because managers and members dedicated themselves to the preservation of complete strangers in the most extreme forms of distress.[4]

While activists in America were convinced that these new lifesaving charities could ameliorate aspects of social dislocation particular to the new Republic, their inspiration nevertheless came from Europe. In an address to members of the Boston association on its one-year anniversary in 1787, Rev. Dr. John Lathrop explained that the first humane society had been founded in Amsterdam twenty years earlier by a wealthy German resident who had been "struck with a variety of instances in which persons falling into the water were lost for want of proper treatment when brought on the shores." Pairing a tiered scale of cash rewards payable to any bystanders willing to risk their lives to save someone else with an array of astonishingly modern techniques, medical assistants for the Amsterdam Humane Society proved themselves able to rekindle the vital flame of more than 150 souls dragged from the city's famous canals in those early years, several suicides likely among them.[5]

As word spread of this humanitarian and scientific miracle, disciple groups quickly took root in Venice, Milan, Padua, Paris, Hamburg, Vienna, and several other European cities. William Hawes, a well-traveled and well-connected apothecary, set up a humane society in London in 1774 and quickly drew a wealthy merchant and medical elite to his cause. Over the next decade, the London society grew both its membership and its endowment at an astonishing rate; it gained royal patronage and soon ranked as one of the largest and most famous benevolent institutions in Britain. Knowing that they would be rewarded for their efforts, the society's surrogates plucked unprecedented numbers of people from the Thames's teeming waters throughout the 1770s and 1780s using antidrowning protocols that its doctors also adapted to treat those rendered senseless by poison, hanging, and all manner of other causes. By 1807 the recently renamed Royal Humane Society (RHS) had franchised its methods to a network of thirty-three affiliates across the British Isles and to others as far afield as Barbados, Jamaica, and Halifax, Nova Scotia.

Anxious to burnish their own humanitarian and cosmopolitan credentials, elites across the newly United States took the ideals of the humane society movement quickly to heart. During a visit to Boston in 1785, a blind Scottish doctor named Henry Moyes met for dinner with Rev. James Freeman, Dr. Aaron Dexter, and the lawyer and playwright Royall Tyler to pitch them the idea. Moyes, who had been tapped by managers of the London group for precisely this purpose, told his dining companions that a society similar to the RHS would surely thrive in their city. That spark was all it took. Within a few weeks, Freeman, Dexter, and Tyler had started soliciting subscribers and had persuaded Massachusetts governor James Bowdoin to serve as their honorary president. Wasting no time, the members of the Humane Society of the Commonwealth of Massachusetts, as they were formally known, held their first meeting at the Bunch of Grapes tavern on State Street on January 5, 1786, and soon began promoting their own rescue rewards scheme in local newspapers.[6]

Moyes traveled on to Pennsylvania and when the Philadelphia Humane Society (PHS) sprang to life a year later, in 1787, it became a second hub for what boosters like Benjamin Rush—who served as its first vice president and later as its leader—hoped would become a network of American franchises. Sure enough, over the next few years other humane societies announced their existence: in Baltimore (1790), Charleston (1793), Albany (1793), New York City (1794), Newburyport, Massachusetts (1802), Burlington, New Jersey (1806), and Wilmington, Delaware (1812). While several seem to have disappeared almost immediately, perhaps crowded out by competing philanthropic endeavors, some of these lifesaving groups laid down deep and lasting roots in local communities.[7]

The humane societies that survived to flourish during the early Republic—in Boston, Philadelphia, Baltimore, New York City, and Newburyport—did so because they were situated in crowded seaports where they appeared to be of most use and because they were able to attract active, respectable men to serve as leaders and a large base of wealthy and well-to-do subscribers. Drawn to the prospect of preserving life like moths to a flame, physicians and ministers flocked to urban humane societies, lending instant credibility and cache to these efforts and assuming important leadership roles. In Philadelphia, for instance, the PHS drew heavily on the ranks of the faculty of the university medical school, the Pennsylvania Hospital, and the College of Physicians. The situation was similar in Boston, where physicians such as Josiah Bartlett made up 15 percent (12 of 78) of the names on the first list of members and filled half of the first dozen posts as trustees and officers. Prominent local ministers made up the balance: in Newburyport, Massachusetts, six of the first ten elected officers of the Merrimack Humane Society were clergy.[8]

Other urban professionals soon gravitated around this nucleus of distinguished civic leaders. The mission and reputation of the Philadelphia Humane Society attracted not only Benjamin Rush, the most famous physician in America, but also well-known printers such as Mathew Carey and William and Thomas Bradford, the lawyer Horace Binney, the industrialist Thomas Dyott, Constitution signer Jared Ingersoll, and several Revolutionary War leaders such as Clement Biddle and Richard Bache. In Newburyport, captains, majors, and other military officeholders swelled the ranks of the society there. Such a genteel membership was typical of most respectable charities of the period; however, the MHS surpassed them all. Its rolls boasted six signers of the Declaration of Independence, including John Adams, who became an honorary member during the last years of his presidency. Samuel Adams, Paul Revere, Lemuel Shaw, Jedidiah Morse, James Bowdoin, Thomas Russell, and Josiah Quincy all supported the society at one time or another. Even lesser-known figures were likely to be professional men—well off, college educated, and members of several other civic organizations. The prospect of such exalted company was a magnet for up-and-coming merchants and the Boston society, easily the most active and illustrious of these American lifesaving groups, doubled the number of its subscribers again and again, with its membership peaking at more than six hundred in 1810.[9]

Subscription was no sinecure. As they struggled to mobilize, the humane societies hummed with activity and expectation. Corresponding secretaries communicated constantly with sister societies throughout the Atlantic world, exchanging information that helped managers refine, perfect, and promote their lifesaving techniques. Taking on the role of de facto medical boards, humane society doctors like Rush and Bartlett set about decrying some of the more violent folk methods of restoring a body to life such as hanging it by its heels, beating it, or running it back and forth in a cart. Instead, they agreed upon a series of procedures that drew heavily on the protocols pioneered in London and Amsterdam. "The Method," as it came to be called, emphasized re-warming to combat hypothermia and chest compressions and tracheotomies to restore respiration. The result was a medical protocol that seemed to work wonders when properly performed on likely candidates. In 1791 Dr. David Hosack estimated that residents of Philadelphia and Baltimore who had applied

"The Method" had succeeded in reviving three of every four people they tried to rescue.[10]

The effectiveness of "The Method" relied in great measure on specialized equipment and relentless publicity. Agents placed "boxes of useful medicines," typically emetics and smelling salts, alongside custom-designed grappling devices on the bridges, wharves, and ferries where they might be of greatest use. Both are clearly visible in the illustrated membership certificates distributed by the Philadelphia Humane Society in its early years. By 1799 that society had deposited at least eighteen sets of apparatus, accompanied by instructions printed on small pieces of stiff card, "in many places, the most advantageous on the Delaware and Schuylkill rivers." "Do Not Despair," these directives told anyone who needed them. To try to train potential first responders in their approved methods, managers also spent thousands of dollars on publicity campaigns. Donations from members paid for pocket pamphlets and cheap almanacs filled with directions on how to restore limp bodies to life. Managers even reproduced these same directions in the sort of versified forms they thought might appeal to the lower orders and pasted up large-print broadsides "in all the public parts" of the city.[11]

What explains why so many elite Americans sunk so much time and money into the humane society movement? Make no mistake, many simply wanted to help. Seizing upon a spectacularly powerful means to do good in their communities, members, enamored by the rhetoric of sensibility and distressed by the vicissitudes of life in bustling maritime cities, did their best to act altruistically. "It is scarcely necessary to say that the plan of this Society is totally void of all private interested views," the eminent physician Benjamin Waterhouse declared at an MHS gala in 1790. "None of its members receive any other recompence [*sic*] than the sublime joy of doing good." Yet the defensive tone of the doctor's claim suggests that others at least thought otherwise. Without undue cynicism, it seems fair to say that self-interest can never be entirely divorced from social action. Indeed, recognition of the ways in which this breathtaking brand of humanitarian activity advanced the interests of those who felt most threatened by the atomizing transformations reshaping early national society is plainly visible in the public addresses of speakers at several other humane society meetings and fund-raisers.[12]

In this illustration, which appeared on membership certificates printed for the Humane Society of Philadelphia, the clothes of first responders indicate their nonelite status. The arrival of the man on the shore, armed with a box of medicines and pointing the way for others to accompany him, prefigures the next stage in this dramatic rescue. Humane Society of Philadelphia. Membership Certificate, 1805. Courtesy of the Library Company of Philadelphia.

Look, for instance, at the sort of people who volunteered to serve in leadership roles. As founding members of most humane societies, Congregational ministers welcomed the respect and deference accorded to society leaders. Many marks of that esteem took tangible form: annual gatherings typically took place in their churches, and the societies often paid to publish their sermons. At festivals and celebrations, preachers savored the chance to lead their cities' favorite sons in fellowship and prayer before lecturing them about what Rev. Thomas Thacher called their "duty as men and as Christians." Buffeted by flagging attendance at regular weekly services, and an increasing cacophony of other voices competing for notice in the moral marketplace, men of the cloth found rare comfort in such company.[13]

In a similar fashion, university-trained doctors eager to augment their personal standing and their profession's rising reputation embraced the opportunity to differentiate themselves from folk healers. While humane society physicians often chafed at press criticism that their work amounted to "playing God," they delighted in the thought that they had developed the scientific acumen through which death might occasionally be cheated. Writing to colleagues in London in 1795, Benjamin Rush was exultant at what he thought he and other medical professionals working within humane societies across the Atlantic world had already achieved:

> In this age, MEDICAL PRACTITIONERS have done more:—their knowledge, their zeal, and philanthropy, HAVE PENETRATED THE DEEP AND GLOOMY ABYSS OF DEATH, AND ACQUIRED FRESH HONOURS IN HIS COLD EMBRACES. Witness,—the many hundred people who have lately been BROUGHT BACK TO LIFE by the ROYAL HUMANE SOCIETY, and other HUMANE SOCIETIES now established in many parts of EUROPE and in several parts of AMERICA.

Such pride was widespread among men of science connected with the humane society movement. In the Enlightenment paradigm, in which an afterlife seemed less certain and death more frightening, the prospect of stealing a soul from death's cold embrace was both audacious and exhilarating.[14]

As doctors like Rush and ministers like Thacher were acutely aware, doing good not only felt good, it also looked good. The business of benevolence was performative: participation allowed the ostentatious display of humanitarian concern and financial largesse for the purposes of concentrating authority and calibrating status. "What can tend more to exercise the virtues of pity, compassion, humanity, and benevolence," asked the Boston doctor John Warren in a letter to his RHS counterpart in 1789, "than repeated attempts to bestow life upon those who seem to be deprived of it?" While status-conscious adolescents announced their finer feelings by weeping over sentimental novels, parents of means could turn compassion into a verb by taking a hand in the unique lifesaving mission of the humane societies. Forget *Werther.* Real distress was all around. Here on the doorstep were drowning children, shipwrecked seamen, and flesh-and-blood men and women on the verge of suicide.[15]

Importantly, a great many figures within the movement also articulated their belief that their work had a broader social function. By extending their moral responsibility to the welfare of strangers, managers and members alike hoped to remind ordinary citizens of the ties of mutual obligation and aid that they believed had traditionally bound smaller, less factious communities together. "Such are our connexions, that our happiness greatly depends on one another," John Lathrop, a founding trustee, told the first cohort of subscribers of the Boston society in 1787. Most subsequent speakers said the same. When Lemuel Shaw, an aspiring lawyer who later became chief justice of the state's Supreme Judicial Court, rose to speak at a meeting of members twenty-four years later, in 1811, he sounded almost identical notes. The work of humane societies, Shaw declared, would convince any doubter

> that he is not an insulated and independent being, acting for himself alone, but the member of a widely extended family, the part of one great whole, a joint partaker in the common blessings of providence, aspiring to the same hopes, subject to the same wants, exposed to the same calamities, possessing the same powers, affections, and feelings, with his fellow man.

By reaching out to take the hands of perfect strangers and pull them to safety and a second chance at life, humane societies claimed the power to mitigate the antisocial effects of what Shaw obliquely referred to as "the union of men into large communities."[16]

Even though similar encomiums ricocheted throughout humane societies across the Atlantic world, what made the American franchises distinctive was the link that leaders drew between their work and the fate of the young Republic. In a republican system of government, the constitution of the New York Humane Society declared, each "life obtains a higher estimation, and assumes a more distinguished importance." Indeed, most managers believed that the United States Congress should bestow its particular favor on voluntary associations dedicated to saving lives and cultivating the conditions of coexistence. At Boston's Brattle Street church in

1799, Rev. Isaac Hurd pursued this line of reasoning further. "The Republic is like a Ship, in which we are all embarked, in which all our interests are included," Hurd explained, using an apt and evocative metaphor. "If we sink, we sink in a mass; if we prosperously sail, all shall enjoy the benefit of the voyage." A lecturer in Newburyport drove the point home. Standing before the members of the Merrimack Humane Society, Rev. Daniel Dana pledged that their work could be the country's literal salvation in this its time of greatest trial. Was it not possible, Dana asked, using the words of a hymn, that their next rescue "might be of some rare spirit detained on earth—some WASHINGTON perhaps—destined to 'save a sinking land.' "[17]

As Dana's allusion to the country's aristocratic first president attests, leaders of the American franchises were forthright in their hope that their charitable efforts might help remind ordinary citizens of the debt they owed to men of means and standing. With many of the customary ties of deference under strain, elites invested in voluntary benevolent societies as a means to reassert their position atop the social pyramid. Establishing a bureaucracy whereby committees of professional men decided which members of the lower orders deserved cash rewards for their vigilance and bravery was just the most obvious means by which the humane societies advanced the class interests of their constituents. In Boston the going rate was ten dollars for anyone who could convince the committee that he had risked his life to save his fellow man. Ever wary of fraudulent claims, members took their highly visible deliberations extremely seriously and set stringent standards as to what constituted deserving behavior:

> By signal exertion, the Trustees conceive, must be understood something more than bearly [*sic*] reaching out the hand, or throwing a rope from a wharf, or a boat, or even wading into the water to half a man's depth, and rescuing a man from drowning; for the principles of common humanity and sympathy are sufficient motives for such exertions, but it must include the endangering [of] his own life or incurring some damage by impairing the health, or injuring the apparel or other property.

By such expressions, these societies committed themselves to a peculiar interpretation of disinterestedness. While elites invested in people and programs designed to rescue anyone regardless of rank, race, or gender, they did so in ways that emphasized relations of power and an immutable hierarchy of authority and expertise. "Associational activity," one historian of philanthropy recently concluded, "was a response to burgeoning 'social confusion' about status." No one knew the truth of this better than the members themselves. When Rev. Thomas Barnard informed Boston philanthropists that by reaching out to those "endangered by disease, by sudden phrenzy of passion, and innumerable accidents . . . we are promoting the important interest of the civil community," it was clear whose interests were first and foremost in his mind.[18]

As the reverend's reference to men and women driven to drowning themselves by frenzied feelings they could neither fathom nor control suggests, preventing suicide was central to members' visions of how humane societies could rescue and rehabilitate the body politic. In fact the constitution of the New York Humane Society explicitly charged managers to devise a method to revive those persons who "either through melancholy, or distraction, attempt, by means of hanging, to destroy themselves." While the larger and more active Boston society lacked a written constitution, a succession of annual speakers confirmed that it was similarly committed to stemming the number of suicides in that city. In 1808, for instance, Dr. Thomas Danforth reminded members that "Perhaps, the subject of your resuscitation [has] sought in death, to terminate a wretched being." "Fulfill then your task," he charged. Likewise, at each yearly fund-raiser the members joined in a song that shone a lyrical spotlight on this part of their lifesaving mission. Following two opening verses celebrating the reanimating powers of first God, then physicians, the central stanza invoked the society's responsibility to prevent suicide:

> The self-destroying hand restrain,
> Soothe each desponding sigh!
> Teach man life's station to maintain;
> Nor heavenly power defy

The Merrimack Humane Society in nearby Newburyport used the same hymn at its own events.[19]

At almost every meeting, members rehearsed their reasons for restraining the hands of self-destroying souls. Echoing the rhetoric they would have heard in any number of pulpits in northern churches in the decades after the Revolution, speakers charged that rational acts of self-destruction were both unnatural and ungrateful, defiant dismissals of every individual's obligation to stay alive at all costs. "It is our duty to preserve our own life," John Lathrop told those assembled at the Massachusetts society's first meeting in 1787. At a fifteenth-anniversary meeting he hosted at his Congregational church in Roxbury in June 1802, Rev. Eliphalet Porter elaborated, eloquently explaining that the instinct for self-preservation was God-given and that, as the familiar verse put it, heavenly power should never be defied:

> Life, indeed, has its troubles, but it has its enjoyments too; and the last are more than the first. The dread of dissolution, so common to mankind, is not a principle arbitrarily implanted in the human breast by some superior malignant power who would condemn us to an useless and wretched state of existence, and has taken this method to prevent our untimely escape. Our attachment to life is the effect of the divine wisdom and goodness.

Do yourself no harm, St. Paul had told a despairing jailer in the Book of Acts. With impressive consistency, annual lecturers parroted the same Pauline instructions not only to their members but also to the wider community. In 1804 Dr. John Howard reminded readers of his published remarks that "the instinctive love of life prompts the irresistible effort to avoid the threatening danger." Two years later, in 1806, Rev. Thaddeus Mason Harris (who would publish a pamphlet entirely devoted to suicide prevention in 1812) told readers of a similar address that "Every man should nourish and cherish his own life, which, under all the inconveniences he falls or troubles he may meet, must be unspeakably valuable and dear."[20]

The most expansive articulations of this position revealed that many members considered the imperative to maintain "life's station" to encompass a social meaning. To leaders and rank and file alike, anyone who did not nourish and cherish his own life not only challenged God and nature but also seemed to shear the already fraying ties of fellow feeling and common interest that were supposed to bind citizens to one another in the new nation. "No being stands insulated, nor unconnected," Rev. Thomas Gray of Roxbury's third parish declared as he stood before an audience of society philanthropists in 1805. "No man liveth to himself alone. There are others, with whom his happiness is intimately involved. There are others, who are dear to him, as himself; and around whose heart every cord of his own is entwined. To a separation from such society he cannot feel indifferent." In a fragile new republic balanced on the brink of change, teetering between collective and individual models of the self, the temptation to interpret any suicide as an act of alienation was great. Animated by the prospect of restoring these people to their proper station while simultaneously asserting their own ability and social authority to do so, the status-conscious elites that funded and staffed the humane societies waded eagerly into the business of suicide prevention.[21]

They had reason to be confident: the lifesaving techniques the managers had designed, refined, and relentlessly promoted were effective against many of the most commonly used methods of suicide. According to newspaper coverage, about half of the reported suicides in early national America were attempted or completed by drowning, asphyxiation, or poisoning. The MHS had protocols to prevent all three. For example, the society's ubiquitous lifesaving directions told anyone who discovered a person hanging by their neck to take them down carefully and then bleed them immediately: "A few ounces of blood may be taken from the jugular vein, cupping-glasses applied to the head and neck, and bleeding at the temples. The other methods of treatment, the same as recommended for the apparently drowned." And make no mistake: a hanging was rarely an accident. In Salem, Rev. William Bentley recorded almost three hundred accidents in his voluminous thirty-five-year diary; not one was a hanging.[22]

Managers also promoted intervention to preserve the lives of people who had poisoned themselves, either purposefully or by abusing toxic opiates such as arsenic and laudanum. Humane society leaders reasoned that if men like Josiah Bartlett could reach them in time, perhaps they could be stopped. If self-poisoners could be caught before drugs were absorbed into the bloodstream, "The Method" explained how they could be made to vomit and saved from death. It was in the same spirit that in

March 1800 Boston's *Columbian Centinel* published a long article written by humane society managers that asked "Druggists, Chemists and Apothecaries" to limit the sale of arsenic to buyers accompanied by "two or more creditable persons" who could "testify to the vender [*sic*] the purpose for which its use is designed." Spurred by "the number of Cases that occur where the dreadful crime of SUICIDE is committed, by the taking of ARSENIC," these ambitious activists tried to drive men and women no longer interested in the ordinary act of survival out of the shadows and into the open by depriving them of this "secret and certain method of effecting their own destruction."[23]

Combining expertise and incentive, managers hoped their methods would mark a great leap forward in Western civilization's ongoing struggle to stop suicide. Most pressingly of all, they anticipated that they could turn back the tide of self-destruction that many humane society leaders, Benjamin Rush prime among them, believed was sweeping the new nation. A glance at newspapers and diaries from 1730 to 1830 reveals that before American humane societies organized to share money and resources to educate and encourage a great pool of would-be rescuers, successful interventions to prevent suicide had been few and far between. For the same reasons, most people who attempted suicide in the many early national towns and cities that remained unserved by humane societies survived solely because they did not cut deep enough, swallow enough poison, or jump from a high enough place to kill themselves. Rescues were rare indeed. For example, in August 1730, Benjamin Franklin told readers of the *Pennsylvania Gazette* that "a Servant Man belonging to one Tateham" had tried to hang himself from a tree in an orchard outside Camden, New Jersey. "But it seems the Rope broke in the Operation, and towards Morning he found himself alive upon the Ground to his no Small Surprize." Razors were no better. A year later, in September 1731, a rival Philadelphia paper informed its readers that "On Tuesday last, a young Man on board the Snow *Lovely Hannah*, cut his Throat very Deep, and fearing he had not done it effectually, jumpt overboard, but the Water being something Cold, so stagnated his Blood, that being taken up and proper means applied, he is like to Recover."[24]

These spoiled suicides often left the perpetrators scarred or paralyzed. An affecting item found in a Vermont paper described how a twenty-one-year-old man living in the Maine interior had tried to cut his throat by slashing at his jugular with a knife he had sharpened specially. The four cuts he made were deep but not deep enough to be immediately fatal, and after two hours lying bleeding in a deserted barn, he staggered to a brook and threw himself in. But it was too shallow and after a while he pulled himself out and "went into the house to his mother, dripping with water and blood." A few days later, a visitor to the property gave a local editor an account of the stricken man he found inside. It made for gruesome reading:

> The windpipe is cut entirely off, the gullet half off. He breathes at the wound. There he also receives nourishment. No large veins were cut. He is able to sit up and walk the room. I saw in him the most shocking sight I ever beheld. He gives no reason for his conduct, but that he tho't he should never be much in the world, and so had better be off, and such like reasons. He may live some days.

There were probably hundreds, if not thousands, of other unhappy men and women living out their days in similar agonies across the country.[25]

Most failed suicides, then, were not thwarted; they were botched. They did not fail because of a stranger's or a neighbor's intervention but because the methods chosen were not sufficiently lethal. Before city leaders in Boston, Philadelphia, Baltimore, Newburyport, and New York set up fledgling suicide prevention charities, it was rare to discover an attempt in time to prevent it. And in those occasional cases, there was an obvious pattern. Take, for example, the servant whose rope had broken. Franklin's report had not ended there but had followed the hapless young man as he tried again to end his life:

> At length having procured a better Rope, he hanged himself again in the Barn, and was there accidentally found by the Maid in the Afternoon. When he was cut down there appeared no sign of Life in Him, nor were any Means used to recover him; but by that Time the Coroner and his Inquest were got together, and come to View his Body, he was upon his Legs again, and is now living.

This despairing servant's life had been saved by a co-worker. Other news reports told similar tales. In 1732 the *American Weekly Mercury* reported on a ship's carpenter who cut his throat while the vessel lay at anchor in New York harbor and his shipmates were ashore. When two of the sailors returned early they found the carpenter "lying Bleeding not able to speak, but pointing to some Words he had wrote on the Deck. I forgive every Body, as I hope to be forgiven. I have done this my Self. He was immediately brought ashore; and by the Assistance of a Doctor, is in a fair Way of Living."[26]

At home, friends and family took the place of co-workers. In 1749 Rev. Ebenezer Parkman of Westborough, Massachusetts, confided to his diary that young William Rogers, the son of a friend, had tried to drown himself in the town pond the last evening, "but his Brother John went at that juncture to water his Horse, and prevented him. He got loose also a second Time and ran into the Pond Waste deep but his Brother got him out, and with help led him up to his Father's where he was watch'd all night." Female relations too were occasionally able to sound the alarm before it was too late, even if they lacked the brute strength to restrain their loved ones. For instance, a diary entry scribbled by the Philadelphia merchant Thomas Cope in November 1809 described how "the wife of a much valued friend" had sent for him the day before "on account of her husband having attempted his life by a dose of laudanum." Cope had rushed to the house, seen the husband's drug-addled delirium, and immediately called a doctor.[27]

Newspaper stories and diary entries like these suggest that parents, siblings, spouses, friends, and co-workers were vastly more likely to be confronted by someone attempting suicide than a perfect stranger. Because so many suicide attempts were made at home, or in secluded barns and outhouses, or at times of day and night when no one else was about, strangers seldom had the opportunity to intervene. That only happened on those rare occasions when men and women, burdened by the weight of the world, took their chance in plain sight. For example, when a man threw himself into a New Jersey creek in broad daylight one August day in 1730, the *American Weekly Mercury* reported that "some busy people" pulled him out "before he had quite finish'd his work." Likewise, five years later the same Philadelphia paper told readers that a young woman in that city had jumped into the dock and "would soon have been drown'd had not some Men came to take her out; which was done very much against her Will."[28]

Despite their rarity, cases like this filled humane society managers with hope. If more people could be encouraged to put their own lives on the line to save strangers from self-destruction, and if they had the right tools and training, then perhaps suicide's alarming progress could be stopped in its tracks. Working from this premise, members poured tens of thousands of dollars and hundreds of committee hours into the business of preventing suicide. And they had some limited success. The published records of the Humane Society of the Commonwealth of Massachusetts reveal that its surrogates restored 631 men, women, and children to life in its first three decades of operation, one every two weeks or so. More than one-third of those rescued between 1787 and 1817 (244) were children who had fallen into ponds or rivers or into other difficulties, and one-fifth (126) were sailors shipwrecked on the Massachusetts coast. Of the remaining 261 adults saved by the Boston Humane Society, the records described exactly seven as unmistakably suicidal.[29]

In fairness, the number of suicidal citizens that the Boston society saved from death was likely many more than seven. In more than a hundred of the entries that catalog the rescues of these 261 adults, there is insufficient information to determine whether accident or attempted suicide was the cause of their jeopardy. Managers like Josiah Bartlett occasionally went into great detail to describe the most noteworthy cases, but more often their logs of rescues and rewards wasted little ink. Typical entries to record how much each rescuer was paid were less than a single line long: "Aug. To Ward and Story, for saving a man," read one typically ambiguous item from 1793. Even slightly more elaborate descriptions left plenty of room for subsequent readers to speculate about what had prompted a person's distress: A cash payment went to James Brewer in July 1791 "for saving an unfortunate woman, near Griffin's wharf." Likewise, in April 1795 John Carman, Nathaniel Robbins, and Abiel Pierce split a five-dollar reward "for saving the life of Rhoda Hardy, who plunged into the water at West Boston bridge," while Daniel Tracy collected two dollars "for receiving the said Rhoda Hardy into his house and assisting in her recovery." Had she fallen or had she jumped? The record does not say.[30]

Whether seven, seventeen, or seventy of the souls saved by the early efforts of the Boston Humane Society's surrogates were suicides will never be known, though the low numbers of confirmed attempts indirectly support the view that the apparent spike in self-destructive behavior was largely an illusion of newspaper reporting. Even so, the limited information the managers recorded about those seven attempts at suicide is both striking and significant. Six of the seven attempts were made by men, a ratio almost exactly in line with gender patterns discernible in the newspaper reports of the day. By contrast, the methods these seven despairing souls chose to end their lives did not correlate closely with broader trend lines. While contemporary newspaper coverage suggests that across the country only about 15 percent of people who committed suicide did so by drowning, six of the seven souls the Boston society restored to life had been rescued from watery graves. For instance, in 1798 Joseph Eaton and Seth Nason took home four dollars after "saving a woman who had leaped from Treat's wharf." A decade later, in 1808, Bill Richardson received recognition and a larger cash reward for "taking several children out of the water near N. Mills, and preventing a young man from drowning himself." It made sense, of course, that in a busy port city desperate or disordered people might be more likely to try to drown themselves in dark waters than search for an isolated barn in which to sling a rope from a beam. What's more, the Boston society's lifesaving protocols were no match for a close-range pistol shot or a jump from a high roof, and so their logs never mentioned all the New Englanders who committed suicide by such lethal means.[31]

A careful reading of these often terse ledger entries makes it very clear how society philanthropists rationalized their drastic interventions to revive fellow citizens who had chosen to die. Confronted by the troubling possibility that some men and women at the end of their tether may have understood suicide as a final, awful assertion of their own battered selfhood, members of the American humane society movement justified their efforts to rescue such people by instead asserting a more comforting and enabling interpretation of the causes of self-destruction. They took the position that destroying oneself was so unnatural, ungodly, unpatriotic, and antisocial that no person could rationally intend to do it. While the managers did not dwell on the mental state of the woman who had leapt from Treat's wharf in 1798 or the man Bill Richardson saved in 1808, they summarily diagnosed four of the other five unambiguous attempts at suicide that they encountered as the product of temporary madness. In 1793 Josiah Bartlett had described the man who jumped from the Charles River Bridge as having suffered "a degree of insanity" for several days prior to his suicide attempt. Over the following years, his colleagues offered a slew of similar explanations. For instance, a list of cash payments dispersed in 1795 included one each to John Deluce and Daniel Spear "for their exertions in saving the life of a man who appeared deranged in his mind, in danger of being drowned at a distance from the shore." Similarly, in 1812, several Bostonians shared a three-dollar reward "for taking up an insane person who had jumped overboard," while four years later, in October 1816, John Gardner took home a cash award "for his exertions in preventing a Mr. Barrett from drowning himself in a fit of insanity."[32]

It is hardly surprising that managers saw derangement in despair so readily and reliably. After all, coroners' verdicts of inquest now habitually explained suicide as the result of nonculpable insanity. Such judgments represented growing compassion for the suffering of the deceased's family as well as a means to avoid statutory punishments in those states like Massachusetts where self-annihilation remained a criminal offense. At the same time, juries' expanding use of insanity verdicts to explain suicidal behavior marked the popularization of new medical theories that placed the moral and mental faculties side by side.

Falling into lockstep with these ongoing developments, the officers of the country's humane societies found it both intuitive and expedient to interpret each attempt at suicide they encountered as the product of a temporarily disordered psyche. The contention that people driven to hang themselves did so "either through melancholy or distraction" was enshrined in the constitution of the New York Humane Society, while further north, in Massachusetts, lecturers repeated the same equivalence at almost every annual meeting. Addressing the Boston members in 1804, Dr. John Howard told them that insanity and self-destruction went hand in hand. "Who is the distressed object that is thus snatched from a peaceful grave?" Howard asked. "May it not be some houseless wanderer, long since a burthen to himself and society, or perhaps some wretched maniac, to whose disordered sense existence has no charm?"[33]

Members' earnest conviction that most suicides were disordered maniacs gave them permission to intervene, legitimizing their efforts to revive people who had made the decision to die. Usually unconscious when rescuers reached them, men and women who attempted suicide were unable to grant or to refuse their consent to be revived, but managers made the calculation that in a rational person the will to live could be taken for granted. With insanity assumed, the interventionist dynamic would be vindicated just as soon as suicidal people could be restored to their right minds and made to see the damage they were doing to themselves, to their families, and to society at large. They would be thankful just as soon as they came to their senses.

Such reasoning did not always reflect reality. Newspaper coverage frequently demonstrated that men and women in apparently sound mind could decide to place themselves beyond the reach of help and harm. Those who took precautions so as not to be discovered, those who made careful preparations so as not to fail, and those whose foiled attempts only redoubled their resolve to try again are hard to pigeonhole as deranged maniacs. Likewise, those who left cogent suicide notes—like the ship's carpenter who scrawled "I forgive every Body, as I hope to be forgiven. I have done this my Self"—seemed coldly rational.[34]

The most powerful proof of this telling dissonance between the willingness of society officers to impute insanity and the clear-eyed nihilism of many early Americans who attempted to kill themselves comes from the Boston group's own records. One of the seven cases of thwarted suicide in their published ledgers offers incontrovertible evidence of the determination with which rational people could undertake to end their own lives. Unlike the unconscious persons dragged from rivers to receiving houses and revived by men like Josiah Bartlett, this would-be suicide had taken poison and was still conscious when the humane society doctor reached the scene.

The fact that he was still lucid when help finally arrived was little short of amazing. A. F., as the doctor called him in the case notes he wrote up two weeks later, had swallowed twenty grains of opium at three that afternoon, hoping such a massive overdose would end his life then and there. Even the most hardened addict could stomach no more than a grain of opium a day, and A. F. had taken twenty times that. But it hadn't worked; the world to come never came. So at four thirty, he tried again, choking down nine more grains. Convinced this time that "he had taken enough to effect his purpose," he beckoned two friends to his room "to take his leave of them." But he spoke too soon. His friends took one look at him and ran from the house to find Thomas Welsh, a Charlestown doctor and another founding member of the Boston Humane Society. He would know what to do.[35]

Welsh was not at home that Sunday afternoon, and it took them until six o'clock to track him down and rush him to the house. Still conscious when the doctor arrived, A. F. still had his wits about him and was not about to be rescued by a meddling stranger. "As soon as I had seen him and understood the state of the case," Welsh later recalled, "I proposed to administer to his relief; but he strenuously refused to take any thing, avowing his intention was to deprive himself of life."[36]

Now every minute mattered. The longer the delay, the more opium would digest and the more morphine would enter the bloodstream. Welsh had no time to argue, but with his combative patient refusing to swallow the emetic that could clear his stomach and save his life, he had no choice. So for several urgent minutes just after six in the evening on Sunday, February 21, 1795, these two men disputed the right to suicide. A. F. was adamant, "asserting that he was a free agent, and that, such, he had a right to free himself from the calamities which he suffered." His friends, the doctor, and this humane society that Welsh claimed to work for—none of them had any right to "compel him to take medicine against his will."[37]

But Thomas Welsh was not about to back down. Like Benjamin Rush, Welsh had seen action as an army surgeon during the Revolution, and, like Rush, he had parlayed his fervent postwar patriotism as well as a share of the profits from his thriving peacetime practice into this new charitable movement that asked every American to put his or her fellow citizens first. The guiding principle of each of the humane societies was simple: we are all in this together. The fledgling Republic that Welsh's wartime service had helped usher in was the political incarnation of the social compact, and, by the doctor's reckoning, the humane society was its apotheosis. Welsh shot back: "I maintained that he had, according to his own confession, attempted to commit a crime against society and to deprive it of one of its members; in consequence of which I should, if he persisted in his refusal of the medicine I intended to give him, compel him to take it."[38]

This is the clearest expression we have of the complex power dynamic that informed early national humane societies. Interdependence emerges first from the doctor's arguments. By taking your life, you are interfering with ours, Welsh tells his defiant patient. Control, however, quickly supersedes. You have no right to do this, Welsh tells him; your life is not your own; it is our property and we will stop you if we have to. Welsh couches this injunction in collective terms, invoking the social compact to explain the duty he felt "in common with every other individual" to prevent this tragedy. But as a doctor Welsh is, of course, uniquely positioned to enact his wishes by administering an emetic, and as a professional physician he expects deference to his authority and compliance to his will.[39]

Neither man would back down, and as seconds became minutes, the argument went on. It was only "at length" that Welsh got his way. Perhaps his arguments hit home, perhaps A. F. collapsed as some of the morphine finally metabolized, or perhaps the two men scuffled and swung at each other until one got the better of the other; Welsh's report did not say. Either way, Welsh saw an opportunity and seized it, administering the emetic. A few moments later, his newest patient was vomiting onto the floor, heaving up grain after grain of undigested opium until his stomach would surrender nothing more.[40]

Welsh's intervention saved this man's life. Yet the case report he later filed suggests that A. F. never thanked him. On the contrary, the two themes that emerge most plainly in the doctor's account are resistance and compulsion. One man's impassioned and strenuous struggle to make his own death is matched only by the fervent and coercive attempts of another man to keep him alive. Indeed, as their fraught meeting illustrates, these two Bostonians were diametrically opposed in their perception of who has the right to die and who has the right to preserve life at all costs. Despite the weight of elite opinion in support of a republican version of the social contract in which we are all our brother's keepers, this illuminating countertext suggests that many ordinary Americans were increasingly unimpressed and had instead embraced the individualist position that we answer to no one but ourselves. Talk of God and nature is conspicuously absent from Welsh's account.

So is any hint of insanity; Welsh did not dare call this man mad. The doctor's own son, Henry, suffered from lifelong "mental debility," so at least Welsh knew better than to attribute insanity to a man who could muster a powerful intellectual defense of suicide while morphine churned in his stomach. Most other humane society doctors showed less restraint. In every report that speculated upon a motive for a suicide attempt, they put it down to some passing mania. Time and again, the group's physicians justified their own coercive interventions by assuring themselves that they had their fellow citizens' best interests at heart.[41]

The same self-assurance continued to guide the most active humane societies as their mission evolved. After many years spent trying to encourage on-the-spot suicide prevention, the members of the Boston and Newburyport societies launched a new project: beginning around 1800 and gathering impressive momentum over the next twenty years, these two groups embarked upon a campaign to fund the construction of the first mental hospital in New England, a grand and imposing institution in which a professional staff could properly supervise, restrain, care for, and rehabilitate the suicidally insane.

America's first public asylum had opened in Williamsburg, Virginia, in 1770, and since 1796 Benjamin Rush had been treating a few mentally distressed and disturbed people—including his own son, John, admitted in 1810—in a private basement wing of the Pennsylvania Hospital. But in most early national cities, no such facilities yet existed. In Massachusetts the care of the insane was still largely provided by poorly equipped almshouses and jails, where inmates languished for years without medical treatment or therapy. This all changed once the New England humane societies announced their commitment to build a private asylum, a dream finally realized when the McLean Hospital opened in Charlestown in 1818. In fact, the fanfare surrounding its opening helped fuel a movement to fund and build other dedicated asylums for the medical treatment of the insane across the country. Within forty years, twenty-eight of the thirty-three states of the union had set up institutions modeled in some way or another upon McLean.[42]

In humane societies' members' minds, this was an idea whose time had come. Their anxiety about urbanization and immigration, their sincere commitment to philanthropic activity as a way to do good, and their increasing knowledge and admiration for European psychiatric treatments all coalesced around this campaign to privately finance the first mental hospital in New England. It is easy to see why. Asylums and other new carceral institutions popular with professional elites at the dawn of the nineteenth century represented, in the words of historian Steven Mintz, "an attempt to re-establish order in a society buffeted by the rise of a market economy, the disintegration of an older patriarchal and hierarchical order, and the growth of democratic individualism."[43]

More immediately, asylums like McLean began to proliferate in the early nineteenth century because physicians were developing a new interest in and understanding of the etiology of suicidal insanity. In the seventeenth century, most colonists had rested content in the belief that mania was simply God's will. More recently, a growing number of men of science had begun to embrace a different view. Enlightenment conceptions of the unity of the moral and mental faculties and growing consensus that environmental influences could produce biological effects now propelled iconoclasts like the French physician Philippe Pinel to conceive of insanity, in Benjamin Rush's later formulation, as "a disease of the mind."[44]

In France, Pinel translated this new understanding of insanity as the product of both nature and nurture into a revolutionary reform in institutional care. Without ceding any authority to his patients, Pinel's humanitarian and therapeutic approach freed lunatics from chained bondage and emphasized the need to create a new environment in which the subject could witness normal behavior and learn to emulate it. European asylums built according to the Pinelian ideal abandoned penal archetypes and instead resembled retreats. Opened in 1818, McLean was the first purpose-built asylum in the newly United States to try to incorporate these new ideas about suicidal insanity into every aspect of its treatment program.[45]

The impulses behind the founding of McLean Hospital were based in large part on the antisuicide agendas of the two Massachusetts humane societies. It was Jedidiah Morse, a prominent MHS leader, who first publicly suggested the idea of "the erection and endowment of a Hospital for Lunatics" in the Bay State. "There is no institution of this kind in New-England," the reactionary Congregationalist and geographer explained at the end of the twenty-page address he delivered to the Boston society in 1801. Before he had stood to speak, Morse had been leafing through a list of rescues that the Royal Humane Society had enclosed in a recently arrived packet of letters and pamphlets. Standing before the members assembled that day in a church in Charlestown, Morse was taken by one rescue in particular and relayed the details to his audience:

> The mother of eight children, a widow, was left to commit the dreadful crime of suicide. When found, she had been hanging half an hour, and had, when cut down, the strongest appearances of death. By the blessing of GOD on the means used, she was restored, first to life, and afterwards to peace of mind. In cases like this, which it appears have not infrequently happened, in England, this benevolent Society, with thankful hearts, might repeat and apply the following lines—"We snatch from death the victim of despair; / And give the means of penitence and prayer."

A few moments later, Morse proposed the lunatic hospital. It was thus in the context of remarks about preventing suicide and rehabilitating those who attempted it that the seed for what eventually became known as the McLean Hospital was first sown. Indeed, the essential link between the Boston Humane Society's life-preserving mission and the notion of funding a city asylum was the group's continuing interest in preventing suicide. While the day-to-day work of most American humane societies was split between attending to shipwrecked seamen, the victims of accidents, and would-be suicides, it is entirely clear which of these populations the Boston members had in mind as Morse asked them to expand their work to include the funding of a mental hospital to protect, care for, and reform the insane.[46]

Many privileged people who were not MHS members took up Morse's call in the years that followed, yet it was within the humane societies themselves that the issue commanded the greatest attention. The very next year, in 1802, Eliphalet Porter took up the proposal again, telling the gathered membership that institutions "which have for their object such as are lunatic and disordered in mind, cannot be displeasing" to God. "They must be highly approved by him in whom the maniacs, rushing frantic from the midst of the tombs, found a friend and benefactor, who restored them to the light and comforts of reason, and to a capacity for those of virtue and religion." When purse strings tightened during Jefferson's ill-conceived trade embargo in 1807, the managers fell briefly silent; yet even before the first green shoots of recovery appeared in Boston, Thomas Danforth took the stage at the society's next summer meeting and again lectured the membership on the need for a lunatic asylum in the city. Returning to the connections so many previous speakers had drawn between insanity and self-destruction, he argued that the society's ongoing antisuicide activities should be extended to include rehabilitative residential care for the furiously mad:

> Assist to raise some friendly dome, where lunacy may be secluded, from the wanton regards of impertinent and unfeeling curiosity. To rescue an individual from an untimely grave is oftentimes an act of instinctive bravery, or professional effort. But in accomplishing these objects, you may produce the most important benefits to community; the prevention of self murder.

Looking beyond short-term critical care, Danforth now asked his brethren to invest in long-term care for city residents who were a danger to themselves and perhaps to others. Indeed, because most members and managers were apt to explain local suicides as the product of passing madness, the leadership's growing insistence that subscribers fund the construction of "some friendly dome where lunacy may be secluded" can be understood as a direct extension of their ongoing agenda to prevent suicide in Boston and its environs.[47]

Danforth secured a few donations for the proposed asylum at that 1808 meeting, but the big money did not begin to pour in until Jefferson repealed the embargo in March 1809. Hoping to turn the rebounding wealth of the city's merchants toward the now seven-year-old project, Rev. John Bartlett, a chaplain of the city's almshouse and a distinguished figure within the MHS, approached members in the spring of 1810 with an ambitious plan to ally the proposal for a dedicated asylum with a new scheme to build a private general hospital similar to those already up and running in Philadelphia and New York. The sheer scale of the Bartlett plan quickly caught the imagination of the society's moneyed membership, and it soon became the cherished beneficiary of civic-minded donors across the region. To capitalize on this rush of postrecession enthusiasm for the project, Bartlett assembled a committee of leading Bostonians to draw up plans and coordinate fund-raising. He appointed as co-chair Dr. John Collins Warren, another member, trustee, and long-serving MHS officer. Warren moved quickly, sending out a circular outlining the case for these twin hospitals in August 1810 and securing a charter from the General Court a few months later. At the same time, he set up a committee charged to raise $100,000 in private donations. While the campaign's momentum was stalled by the War of 1812, it resumed again in earnest in 1816. In all, over a thousand people gave money, though the bulk of it came from a smaller group of individuals and a handful of organizations. Among these high-dollar donors, the New England humane societies and their members donated the lion's share.[48]

There were fourteen groups that contributed more than $100 each to the plans for an asylum for the city. Five businesses, four charities, three local governments, one church congregation, and one theater audience sent cash. Most of these group contributions were of a few hundred dollars; only three totaled more than one thousand. Of those, the two largest were from the coffers of the New England humane societies—$2,000 from the Merrimack Humane Society designated specifically "for the use of the Massachusetts Hospital for the Insane" in 1816 and $5,141 from the MHS "in further aid of those popular and beneficial Institutions—the GENERAL AND INSANE HOSPITALS" a year later. Together, these two outsized donations from the Bay State humane societies accounted for almost 60 percent of the total value of all group donations.[49]

The financial commitment to this project exhibited by the rank and file was no less striking—255 men made individual contributions of $100 or more to fund the new mental hospital; almost half (122) were MHS subscribers. While many of these donors were also members of other city charities, the concentration of donors on the humane society rolls was unparalleled. There was a clear correlation between membership and support for the asylum.[50]

Between them, these 122 humane society members contributed $56,103 to the cause, including $20,000 from William Phillips, a proud MHS member and benefactor of Andover and Exeter academies. Much of this money was likely raised at the asylum fund-raiser that the society held as part of its annual summer meeting in 1817. In fact, internal accounts show that the MHS even covered the cost of "printing subscription papers for [the] Hospital for Insane persons" during the financing campaign. Totaling up all the money raised by individual members and the institutional donations made by both the New England humane societies reveals the overwhelming support for an asylum among everyone involved in the movement. All together, they raised $63,244, more than half of the $115,000 pledged to this cause. No other organization could say the same. In fact, Bostonians sometimes confused the local humane societies with the asylum they bankrolled. Even before McLean finally opened to patients in 1818, newspapers had begun referring to the new building as the "Humane Hospital."[51]

"In this republican country," wrote Nathaniel Hawthorne in *The House of the Seven Gables*, "amid the fluctuating waves of our social life, somebody is always at the drowning point." The early national humane societies, in their heyday between 1786 and 1817, took the drowning point as the explicit focus of their extraordinary endeavor. While much of their daily business dealt with shipwrecked sailors and accident-prone children and adults, members and managers lavished disproportionate rhetoric and resources on the goal of preventing suicide during these three decades of direct activism.[52]

By trying to save the lives of those at the drowning point, humane societies rendered valuable service to those persons' families and friends, and also, their members ardently hoped, to society, to the state, and to their own embattled social authority. What service their singular efforts rendered to those who had leaped from city wharves and bridges of their own free will or to the determined man who had swallowed twenty grains of opium is more difficult to assess. Most managers preferred to see these cases as evidence of temporary insanity, a means by which they could justify the awkward fact that they sometimes intervened to preserve life against the wishes of those they sought to save. Deciding that they knew best, members threw themselves headlong into the business of suicide prevention as a means to protest the triumph of self-interest over well-ordered community.

When the New England humane societies swung their weight behind the proposals for an insane asylum put forward by Jedidiah Morse, Thomas Danforth, John Bartlett, and John Collins Warren, they opened a new front in their continuing campaign to curb self-destructive behavior in the early Republic. In the 1780s members and managers alike had worked together to craft a set of medical protocols and a system of cash rewards that they hoped might be especially effective at thwarting suicides. By passing the baton to the trustees of McLean Hospital in the 1810s, this second generation of society leaders signaled that they had reluctantly reached the conclusion that, at least as far as suicide prevention was concerned, a critical-care program that relied upon chance encounters and the bravery and vigilance of random strangers was vastly inferior to the emerging alternative. By putting up the money to build McLean, the model for the generation of psychiatric hospitals built in the years that followed, the New England societies thus took their antisuicide activism to the next level. Staffed by trained specialists and designed and operated to rehabilitate the suicidally insane, the "Humane Hospital" was a means by which the societies could institutionalize and professionalize the impulse to restrain the hands of fellow citizens who threatened to destroy themselves.

It proved to be a watershed moment. In May 1817 the MHS held a gala fund-raiser for the still-under-construction asylum. It would turn out to be the last time that the group would hold a public event, and the pamphlet featuring aging lawyer William Tudor's remarks that day became the last in an otherwise almost unbroken line of annual orations stretching back to 1787. Within a few years of McLean's opening, the Boston society assumed foundational status, abandoning a great part of its direct activism agenda and pledging much of its remaining resources to long-term care projects serviced by new medical and charitable institutions. The Merrimack Humane Society in nearby Newburyport went through a similar but more protracted change: it held its last public meeting in 1819 and disappeared from view in the 1820s.[53]

From a distance, the distinctive therapeutic regime promoted by boosters for the "Humane Hospital" compares favorably to the dangerous and sometimes violent practices that physicians elsewhere in early national America used to treat suicidal insanity. The McLean method relied on vigorous physical and mental exercise and set rehabilitation and eventual release as its twin goals. In contrast, in upstate New York, for example, one man calling himself a doctor spent the 1790s wandering from town to town looking for candidates for a course of electric shock therapy that he had designed to cure maniacs of the urge to do violence to themselves. In Galway, New York, Thomas Gale found a perfect subject: an incontrovertibly deranged man named Olcum who had tried to cut his throat. Understandably, Olcum proved to be a reluctant patient, and in the end his family had to drag him to Gale's machine, strapping him down "like a bullock to the slaughter." "I administered exceedingly heavy shocks upon him," Gale wrote in a description of the treatment he published in 1802. As the galvanic battery emptied its charge, Olcum "began to sweat freely; this he noticed himself, as something very extraordinary, for he said he had not sweated in any degree for thirteen years." Gale took the patient's sudden and profuse perspiration as proof that the shocks had restored the poor man's sanity and abruptly left town.[54]

Further south, even the vastly more respectable physicians that staffed Philadelphia's Pennsylvania Hospital still tended toward the use of extreme tactics to rehabilitate patients who had attempted suicide. In Benjamin Rush's influential *Diseases of the Mind* (1812), the first American medical textbook to explore suicidal insanity as a category of temporary psychological disorder, the Philadelphia Humane Society's founding vice president recalled some of the many times that he and hospital orderlies had intervened to prevent an inmate from taking his own life. "In the year 1803," Rush wrote, "I visited a young gentleman in our hospital, who became deranged from remorse of conscience in consequence of killing a friend in a duel." Now suicidal with guilt, the patient demanded a pistol to accomplish what his opponent had failed to. Rather than dissuade him, Rush thought it better to give the young man some practical advice. "I told him, the firing of a pistol would disturb the patients in the neighbouring cells, and that the wound made by it would probably cover his cell with blood." Instead, the good doctor offered to help the poor man die by "bleeding him to death, from a vein in his arm, and retaining the blood in a large bowl." The patient agreed immediately, and so Rush and the hospital's apothecary ostensibly proceeded to euthanize him. But as Rush had slyly anticipated, events took a different turn. "After losing nearly twenty ounces of blood, he fainted, became calm, and slept soundly the ensuing night." When the patient woke, not only was he too weak to try again, but his resolve had vanished. Rush's plan had turned the tables: "The next day when I visited him, he was still unhappy, not from despair and hatred of life, but from a dread of death; for he now complained only, that several persons in the hospital had conspired to kill him." The staff watched him closely over the next few weeks and when he no longer seemed like a threat to himself, Rush discharged him. Whether the great doctor employed a similar stratagem when treating his own son, John—who arrived at the hospital seven years later, in early 1810, following a duel and a suicide attempt each eerily similar to this one—Rush's otherwise expansive personal and professional papers do not say.[55]

Eschewing Gale's electric shock therapy and Rush's psychological ploys, doctors at the "Humane Hospital" in Charlestown developed their own rehabilitation regimen to treat patients who tried to harm themselves. According to its publicity, the hallmark of the McLean method was an orderly and disciplined routine built around daily physical exercise. In sworn testimony after two decades of inpatient care, the asylum's director, Luther Bell, claimed that "systematic, regular, employment in useful body labor . . . is one appliance of moral treatment, which has been proved immeasurably superior to all others." Hospital officials were supposed to maintain discipline and authority by constant supervision, and Bell went on record to say that patients were not regularly shackled or confined in isolation.[56]

Unless, that is, they were suicidal. A doctor visiting McLean in the late 1830s reported that, despite the director's claims to the contrary, attendants regularly used "mittens" and a "leather muff . . . to allay the vehemence of suicidal propensity." In an account of her own incarceration at the "Humane Hospital" in 1840, one ex-patient recalled how this anti-suicide protocol operated: after deciding to abandon the Methodist faith in which she was raised, Elizabeth Stone had chosen to embrace the Baptist Church. According to Stone's perhaps-embellished description of what happened next, her family had reacted to the news by paying a doctor at McLean not only to declare her insane but also to order that she be institutionalized. After only a few nights at the asylum, this frightened and betrayed twenty-nine-year-old tore her sheet into a strip and tried to hang herself from the hinge of the door of her room. She passed out before the makeshift noose broke. When she came to, attendants "had the leather muff put on" and kept her on suicide watch for the next several

View of McLean Hospital in Charlestown, c. 1825. Caleb H. Snow, *A History of Boston, the Metropolis of Massachusetts, from Its Origin to the Present Period, with Some Account of the Environs* (Boston: A. Bowen, 1825). Courtesy of the American Antiquarian Society.

days. "What they could wish to keep such a miserable suffering creature alive for, I did not know," Stone later wrote. While it would be incorrect to suggest that staff at McLean lacked compassion or humanity, it is noteworthy that those values found their expression in a form of coercive paternalism remarkably similar to the antisuicide interventions conceived and implemented by humane society doctors like Josiah Bartlett and Thomas Welsh at the turn of the century.[57]

After its opening, McLean quickly filled to capacity. Like Elizabeth Stone, its patients were increasingly likely to be the troubled relations of affluent families. Although it accepted charity cases from time to time, for the most part McLean came to function as an exclusive private clinic. So within a few years, the Massachusetts State Legislature stepped in, agreeing to fund and operate an insane asylum that would serve every member of the Commonwealth. When Worcester State Hospital opened in 1833, it siphoned dozens of the "lunatics and persons furiously mad" who had been confined to local jails into a long-term treatment center based on the

McLean model. In its first eight years, Worcester State admitted 139 patients whose apparent madness had manifested itself in attempts at suicide or talk of it. The leather muffs used on Elizabeth Stone were banned at the State Hospital, but attendants used "mittens and wristbands" to restrain anyone who looked like they might be a threat to themselves or to others.[58]

Worcester State Hospital was the first of its kind in the newly United States: a purpose-built, state-run insane asylum. Thanks to Horace Mann, Louis Dwight, and Dorothea Dix, the concept of treating insane persons from every class and background at taxpayers' expense soon caught on, and by the Civil War almost every state in the Union had built at least one public asylum. The opening of Worcester State thus heralds yet another phase in the history of organized attempts to prevent suicide in early America: saving persons they judged to be insane from self-harm was no longer the province of private philanthropists; it had finally become the state's business. Employing a rationale that echoed new thinking in legal circles about property rights, state governments now asserted something resembling eminent domain over the lives of those they thought might misuse the privilege of independent custodianship. Yet when it came to exerting the force of public authority to preserve the lives of those in the state's care, state mental hospitals were not breaking any new ground; the criminal justice system had been doing it for years.[59]

4

Wounds in the Belly of the State

Thousands trudged up Pancake Hill on a cold November morning in 1815 to watch Jonathan Jewett hang. Sick of his father's daily pleas that he find a job and mend his ways, Jewett, a free black man from Belchertown, Massachusetts, had stabbed the old man twice in the chest with a butcher's knife. When his case had reached trial in October, the crowd in the courthouse had cheered when the judge told him he would swing. Since then, Jewett's reported indifference to the fate that awaited him had made him infamous across New England, and now, with just hours to go, men and women jostled for position at the foot of the scaffold in Northampton. Everything was ready: the sheriff had already prepared the gallows, and a minister from Belchertown had finished drafting the execution sermon he would deliver to Jewett and an audience of more than ten thousand at eleven that morning. Last evening, the town jailer—a former tailor—had fitted Jewett for the white hood he would wear when the sheriff fastened the noose around his neck and had carried an empty coffin into his cell. It would be the condemned man's only company during his final hours.[1]

Sheriff Ebenezer Mattoon broke the news. With failing sight, the sixty-year-old clambered gingerly up the steps of the scaffold sometime before ten. When they saw the sheriff standing up there alone, a hush fell over the "large concourse of people" that had been gathering since sunrise on the blustery hilltop overlooking the town. Instead of delivering the prisoner for execution, Mattoon delivered confounding news: there would be no public hanging. Jewett had hanged himself in his cell in the early hours of the morning.[2]

Northampton's jailer, Cephas Clap, always put prisoners condemned to be executed on suicide watch, yet Jewett had somehow got his hands on enough sacking rope to make a noose to hang himself from the grate of the cell's low window while his guards slept. At three that morning, Jewett had let the rope take his weight. The sound of his choking had raised the alarm, but when Clap burst into the cell a few minutes later, he found Jewett hanging lifeless, "his knees resting on the floor and his head sunk about half a foot below the bottom of the window." The jailer cut him down and did his best to try to resuscitate him, using whatever he could remember of the lifesaving techniques that the Massachusetts Humane Society had been publicizing across the state. But it was no good. Jonathan Jewett was dead. After an inquest, Sheriff Mattoon sent the body back to Belchertown, where it was buried under a pile of stones by the side of the road.[3]

Rage, disgust, and disappointment filled Northampton in the days following Jewett's suicide, just as they did in every other town in which death-row prisoners killed themselves before they could be made to pay for their heinous crimes. Dozens of criminals facing death sentences took their own lives in American jails in the decades after the Revolution; justice was regularly thwarted, townsfolk's hopes of witnessing an engrossing public spectacle were regularly dashed, and families of the prisoners' victims were regularly denied the retribution to which many surely felt entitled. There was usually little that judges, juries, or jailers could do to prevent being made a mockery by wretched men who committed suicide to escape their sentences. They were beyond the reach of the law and the gallows.

But Jewett's death was different; Sheriff Mattoon and jailer Clap suspected that Jewett's hanging was not simply a suicide, but the product of prodding persuasion. George Bowen, a sometime laborer and full-time troublemaker locked in leg irons in the cell next door, had been calling to Jewett in the weeks before he killed himself, always with the same message. Do it. Do It. Hang yourself before they hang you, Bowen used to holler through the three-foot-thick wall that separated them. As Mattoon and Clap saw it, Bowen had driven their prisoner to suicide by force of will, snatching him from their custody just hours before they were to execute him for one of the most heinous crimes imaginable. Bowen's deadly influence had put this killer—this patricide—beyond the reach of justice, leaving crowds disappointed and these local officials humiliated. George Bowen should be made to pay. The attorney general agreed and petitioned the Bay State's highest court to hear the case. In September 1816, eleven months after Jonathan Jewett hanged himself in his solitary cell, the Supreme Judicial Court of the Commonwealth of Massachusetts met in Northampton to try George Bowen for a capital crime. He was charged with murdering a man he had never laid eyes on.[4]

What unfolded next reveals a great deal about early Americans' changing attitudes toward the death penalty and toward those men who committed suicide to escape it. The extraordinary trial that dominated the news in Northampton in the fall of 1816 was one of the most dramatic and absorbing manifestations of an already escalating fight about whether the states that constituted the new Republic had the authority to take the lives of their most malicious members. After the Revolution, civic-minded elites, disturbed by the leveling and centrifugal changes rocking early national society, were divided over this issue. Mainline clergy, many Federalists, and dozens of law-and-order officials maintained that public executions provided an essential bulwark against social disintegration, a stout warning from an otherwise weak state apparatus that individual autonomy should not exceed the bounds of collective interest. From the point of view of Mattoon, Clap, and Massachusetts attorney general Perez Morton, the cellblock suicides of condemned murderers such as Jonathan Jewett were species of both sedition and sabotage. Discovered just hours before the state could bring its most awesome power to bear, this family killer's flight from justice appeared to them as a stark symbol of a wider problem: the rising contempt among the most unruly members of the general population for all forms of embodied authority.

Other more liberal men of standing and status—including many Universalists, notably Benjamin Rush, Horace Greeley, and Charles Spear—took a very different view. They argued that finding a sustainable balance between liberty and order in the rapidly democratizing new Republic required its lawmakers to surrender the prerogative to execute sovereign citizens. In their view, embracing corporal or carceral solutions that preserved lives rather than destroying them would strengthen the grip of state power, not weaken it. As reformers such as Rush, Greeley, and Spear struggled to persuade legislators and the public at large to limit the use of the gallows, they seized upon the fate of inmates such as Jonathan Jewett to make their case. In fact, when the suicide of Richard Crowninshield, another high-profile prisoner on trial for murder, led to the execution of two legally nonculpable accomplices in Salem, Massachusetts, in 1830, liberal activists harped upon officials' shameless perversion of justice as proof that preserving the death penalty did vastly more harm than good. Over the following twenty years, antigallows reformers drove state executions to the brink of extinction by focusing the middle-class gaze on carefully mediated descriptions of inmate suicide. Refusing to validate any other explanation as to why pathological criminals might lay hands upon themselves, antebellum activists instead assembled a procession of prisoners so palpably terrorized and degraded by the prospect of their imminent execution that they tore themselves apart.

A few inches of ten-cent sacking cord ruined almost a month of preparations. Jonathan Jewett's suicide before dawn on the day he was scheduled to die prevented officials in Northampton and the thousands of people who crowded in from towns all around from acting out their roles on Execution Day. It was one of the most important days in the American secular calendar and had been at the center of ritual life since the 1620s. For the prisoner, the assembled masses, and the civil and religious officials assigned places in this municipal morality play, Execution Day was a uniquely powerful display of state authority and a public reaffirmation of the prescribed standards of individual conduct. Awesome yet familiar, the business of hanging a man in public was orchestrated down to the last detail. For instance, when two Irish Catholics were hanged for murder on Pancake Hill ten years earlier, in 1806, the Northampton newspapers described the proceedings as a series of carefully choreographed spectacles:

> At half past 10 o'clock they were conducted to the meeting-house by the High Sheriff, and his deputies, with a guard composed of a company of Artillery and a detachment of the militia. An appropriate and eloquent discourse was there delivered to a very crowded auditory, by the Rev. Cheverus of Boston, from 1. John 3. 15. *Whosoever hateth his brother is a murderer.* After the sermon the criminals were constantly attended by Mr. Cheverus, with whom, during the greater part of the time, they appeared to be engaged in prayer. At three o'clock sentence was executed by Major-General Mattoon, Sheriff of the county.

Execution Day was intended to impress and to intimidate. As Rev. Nathan Strong had told the throngs gathered in Hartford, Connecticut, to see Moses Dunbar hang for treason in 1777, "the power of government displayed in its most awful form is there." Displaying this awful species of government power served a didactic function, especially during the tense first decades following independence. Because the fledgling American Republic measured its strength and political integrity by the purity of men's hearts, it required a very public mechanism to punish those whose moral decrepitude or deviance threatened to become contagious. Thus Execution Days were advertised widely and well in advance and took place in natural amphitheaters so that entire communities could witness the state's response to those who abandoned virtue and whose foul crimes subverted civil harmony.[5]

Even the condemned man had a carefully circumscribed role to play in this distinctive drama. Prisoners such as Moses Dunbar and Jonathan Jewett were supposed to use the scaffold as a stage upon which to beg for forgiveness for their vicious attacks on community integrity. Indeed, final speeches, confessions, and dying words were a staple of the wildly popular street literature—some clerical in origin, but most now ever more likely to be sensational and secular—that usually accompanied public hangings in the early Republic. Staring death in the face, many prisoners seized the opportunity to bellow their cries of repentance into the wind. For example, a pamphlet describing the execution of Henry Mills in 1817 for the murder of his wife and children reported that "Kneeling down at the foot of the gallows, he continued in prayer for near half an hour, acknowledging his guilt, and the justice of his sentence, and fervently praying to God." By some measures, Mills's contrite performance was typical: in an influential survey of Execution Day behavior between the Revolution and the Civil War, the historian Louis Masur concluded that "evidence of criminals refusing to act as they were expected to act is rare." With a noose around his neck and the hangman looking on, a condemned man had little to gain by refusing to play his part.[6]

Yet for all the cathartic drama of Execution Day, not all Americans were content to play along. Over the three decades before news of the executions of Mills and Jewett hit the presses, a steadily growing number of postrevolutionary activists had begun to protest the extent to which the young country's criminal justice system had become reliant on the death penalty. Public executions took place remarkably regularly in early national America, not least because state legislatures had sanctioned the scaffold as a legal punishment for all manner of offenses, including arson, burglary, horse stealing, and counterfeiting. Even though some juries were reluctant to impose capital sentences for these nonviolent property crimes, they often had no legal alternative: only a handful of states had so far built prisons secure enough to hold criminals for extended periods. Consequently, between 1785 and 1815, courts in just three states—New York, New Jersey, and Massachusetts—executed no fewer than 182 people, two-thirds of whom had committed crimes other than murder.[7]

After the Constitutional Convention, foot soldiers of the republican revolution such as Philadelphia's Benjamin Rush quickly began to question whether so many public hangings were as good for the moral health of the new nation as many skittish Federalists and grim-faced conservative clergy claimed. Embracing elements of a larger transatlantic conversation about the purpose of punishment in enlightened society, Rush used a 1792 pamphlet to inform state officials that there were three simple yet potent reasons why the death penalty should be immediately abandoned: it did not deter criminals, it broke the Sixth Commandment, and it mistakenly implied a right to suicide. To the lawyers and legislators he was trying to persuade, the last of these three claims was the most startling. Channeling the Italian jurist Cesare Beccaria, the doctor explained that

This depiction of a penitent (possibly African American) murderer at the foot of the gallows circulated the year after Jonathan Jewett escaped a similar fate by taking his own life. *Narrative of the Pious Death of the Penitent Henry Mills* (Boston: H. Trumbell, 1817). Courtesy of the American Antiquarian Society.

"every man possesses an absolute power over his own liberty and property, but not over his own life":

> When he becomes a member of political society, he commits the disposal of his liberty and property to his fellow citizens; but as he has no right to dispose of his life, he cannot commit the power over it to any body of men. To take away life, therefore, for any crime, is a violation of the first political compact.

Here Rush refashions the age-old notion that only God has the right to extinguish a life into a form designed to appeal to his republican audience. He argues that because man has no God-given right to suicide, the power of life and death cannot be transferred or surrendered to the state. Other humane society managers such as Thomas Welsh and Josiah Bartlett would soon seize on this redoubtable reasoning as cause and cover for their coercive interventions to preserve the lives of those who had decided to die. But on this occasion at least, Rush had his sights set elsewhere. Convinced that the death penalty had no place in a modern system of government constituted by the people, Rush tried to persuade lawmakers that public hangings were evidence of the overreach of state power and unseemly relics of monarchical rule.[8]

Other activists echoed Rush's complaint that the death penalty was incompatible with the conditions of coexistence enshrined in the new Constitution. Indeed, a clutch of critics took to arguing that because capital punishment implied the legitimacy of suicide, its persistence hampered the efforts of parents, preachers, and private philanthropists to stem the tide of self-destruction apparently engulfing the new nation. "We are all taught to believe that we have no authority to put a period to our own existence," Robert James Turnbull wrote in a lengthy denunciation of public hangings published in Philadelphia in 1796. "If so, how can we undertake to deprive another of life?" To sanction the death penalty, Turnbull warned Pennsylvanians, was to sanction suicide. In New England a few years later, a Connecticut writer calling himself Philanthropos made an identical argument. And, in 1816, just a few months after Jonathan Jewett's Execution Day suicide in the Northampton jail, the anonymous author of a pamphlet impugning South Carolina's penal code declared that "The right of self murder will never be contended. If we cannot ourselves dispose of our lives, we surely cannot transfer the right to another—and if all the individuals of a society have not this sovereign dominion over their respective existences—the whole cannot collectively hold it, in any one instance, but by usurpation."[9]

This loose but vocal coalition of Universalists and Quakers found allies among lawmakers under pressure to refashion the criminal justice system into a form befitting an independent republic. Together they succeeded in forcing the rollback of a great many state laws governing the use of the death penalty. In 1794, just a few months after pamphlets by Rush and William Bradford, the new attorney general of the United States, began to circulate among Pennsylvania's legislators, the General Assembly there voted to limit the use of the death penalty to murder cases. Over the next twenty years, their counterparts in New York, New Jersey, Virginia, Kentucky, and Ohio followed suit. In New England, nervous Federalist politicians rebuffed similar attempts to reduce the number of capital crimes on the books but agreed to construct penitentiaries that could confine and perhaps rehabilitate criminals convicted of destroying private property. This gave judges more flexibility in sentencing and led to a dramatic decline in public hangings for crimes other than murder after 1800.[10]

State and local officeholders who made their living from Execution Day responded decisively to these statutory contractions. With their future livelihoods in doubt and their authority increasingly undermined by the declining use of the death penalty and the rise of untested carceral alternatives, those with a personal or an occupational stake in the preservation of the gallows did all they could to protect themselves from further humiliations. Across New England and the mid-Atlantic, front-line personnel intensified their efforts to exhibit the awesome efficiency of a public execution. Preventing the suicides of condemned men thus became imperative.

As jailers and sheriffs such as Northampton's Cephas Clap and Ebenezer Mattoon knew from their own experience, in towns across the country Execution Day was being regularly sabotaged by its principal players. For almost every weeping penitent who cowered before the gallows, there was an unrepentant murderer whose prescaffold suicide obstructed justice and thoroughly thwarted the purposes of Execution Day. For almost every Henry Mills there was a Jonathan Jewett. In fact, Henry Mills's idealized performance had never happened; it was too good to be true. Mills's story had been dreamed up to help parents teach their children "to regard their future welfare." Jonathan Jewett's actions were vastly more plausible. If newspaper coverage is to be credited, about a third of all the murderers whose bloody exploits made the papers tried to kill themselves, either before or after being apprehended.[11]

The persistence with which perpetrators of murder committed suicide was a cause of enormous outrage and frustration to the family members, neighbors, and law enforcement officials left to pick up the pieces. Regardless of whether an alleged murderer took his life at the scene of the crime or in the state's custody, a murder-suicide deprived the community of the customary slivers of closure, comfort, and consolation following a homicide that Execution Day was designed to provide. A glance at how residents of the Connecticut River valley dealt with the suicide of a man who had laid waste to five of his relatives illustrates the fury that crimes like Jewett's stoked. Suffering under a psychotic delusion that he and his family were not humans but machines, William Beadle, a once-respected merchant living in Wethersfield, Connecticut, in 1782, had used a knife and an ax to kill his wife, his son, and his three daughters, before turning a pistol on himself. Left seething by this domestic massacre, a jury of inquest in Wethersfield ignored evidence of Beadle's obvious insanity and instead made rare use of Connecticut's antisuicide statute to try to punish the dead man for these murders. James Dana, a fierce supporter of the death penalty, told those gathered in his Congregational church in nearby Wallingford that "the Jury of Inquest were of opinion, that he was of sound mind, and returned their verdict accordingly." Now Beadle's body could be disposed of in a manner befitting a monster.[12]

Convicted of committing willful self-destruction (felo-de-se), Beadle would not be buried right away. Instead his body would be put on public display "with the bloody knife fastened on the breast." Only when it had begun to rot would the corpse be thrown on a horse sled and "dragged to an obscure place, and buried with every mark of infamy." Yet even this rare and brutal treatment did not satisfy everyone. Refusing to wait for the Wethersfield sheriff to bury the body, a mob of townspeople, "almost frantic with rage," kidnapped the corpse and did it themselves, binding it with cords to a sled and dragging it to the banks of the Connecticut River. A local lawyer later recalled that when it arrived at the water's edge just after dusk on December 12, 1782, "the body was tumbled into a hole dug for the purpose, like the carcase of a beast." The way these Wethersfield residents responded to this family massacre (both as jurors and as members of this extralegal mob) suggests not only the fierce reaction of early Americans to brutal murders in their midst but also their frustration that the law could do little to punish men such as Beadle—

men who killed members of their families and then themselves in quick succession.[13]

The only people more blood-boiling were men such as Jonathan Jewett—murderers who waited until the very eve of their execution to rob expectant survivors of the hope of retribution. Yet suicides like Jewett's were quite common. Between 1780 and 1820, dozens of alleged murderers attempted to take their lives in American jails. In fact, from the moment of capture to the day of execution, those suspected or convicted of murder found opportunities for suicide wherever they could. A small sample of stories culled from New England papers in this period makes the point. For example, in 1790, John Fotheringam of Falmouth, Maine, stabbed himself in the stomach the day after being imprisoned in the Portland jail for killing his wife, Betsey. Down in Cambridge, Thomas Daniels, a career criminal facing charges of robbery and murder, hanged himself in his cell before he reached trial. (In an act of retaliation, the coroner turned his body over to local surgeons to practice dissection.) And in April 1814, a hatter from Rutland, Vermont, who had been sentenced to die for battering and strangling a merchant to death, made a makeshift noose from the lining of his jacket and swung from the jail's ceiling just six hours before his execution.[14]

Although many of these men likely killed themselves for personal reasons that the extant sources make difficult to fathom (perhaps to staunch their engulfing guilt or, perhaps, like William Beadle, to fulfill frenzied death wishes), newspaper reports tended to interpret each such suicide as an externally directed protest against the state's prerogative to execute its citizens. As Rush and other antigallows reformers worked to legislate Execution Day out of existence, newspaper coverage of inmates who took their own lives presented these deaths to a ravenous reading public as allied acts of sabotage. In a typical story from 1786, a writer for Boston's *Independent Ledger* told his readers that it was "the dread of impending punishment" that drove Michael Moseley to take poison in a city jail. Likewise, in Maine, Portland's *Eastern Argus* reported that before he cut his throat Joseph Whiteford had barked to the jailer and his fellow inmates "that he never would be carried to the gallows to be made a spectacle of for thousands of people." Early national readers became so familiar with the notion that killers behind bars chose suicide as a way to cheat the hangman, obstruct justice, and avoid public disgrace that the New Jersey playwright William Dunlap dramatized it in his 1803 play *Ribbemont.* Awaiting trial for killing a scheming servant who had tried to frame him for murder, Theodore Ribbemont tells his father that the prospect of being hanged for all to see does not bear thinking:

Is that hope then cut off . . . a death of infamy!
Shewn to the gaping crowd a gazing stock! . . .
The unblemish'd honor of our glorious name
Shall not be stain'd by such a scene as this!
Oh, death! how welcome wouldst thou be to me
In any other shape . . . aye, suicide . . .
I have no wish for life
[. . . If] no other means of death I find,
I'll dash my madd'ning brain against the walls
And cheat these erring ministers of justice.[15]

Such dramatically satisfying simplifications of the complex motives behind inmate suicide seemed credible because readers immersed in unrelenting newspaper coverage of self-destruction and the sheriffs, judges, and jailers on the front lines of the criminal justice system were well aware of the degree of resolve, preparation, and ingenuity required to take one's own life while in custody. Local presses carried news of a steady stream of condemned men who had persuaded friends on the outside to smuggle in a few grains of opium. In Baltimore, Jacob Hertich gulped down six ounces of laudanum that a visitor had quietly pressed into his hand before surreptitiously throwing the empty vial through the casement into the yard. As Hertich knew all too well, inmates bent on suicide had to prepare for the possibility that their attempt might be prevented by other prisoners or by the jail workers paid to watch over them until they could be brought to trial or dragged to the scaffold. Thus when his cell mate screamed for help after watching him cut his throat with a razor, William Hultz lunged at him with the blade to try to shut him up. Other determined prisoners opted for subterfuge: on his rounds on a winter morning in 1790, Mr. Motley, a jailer in Maine, found an inmate who had been sentenced to be executed for murdering his wife reclining on his bed with his breakfast untouched. The man gave no reply when Motley asked him what was wrong. It was only when a second visitor saw blood dripping from the bed to the floor that they discovered that he had been carefully concealing "a wound in his belly about two inches above his navel—from which bloody matter was issuing." A surgeon later removed a seven-inch blade from the dead man's abdomen. No one could say how he had got hold of it.[16]

Given the frequency of death-row suicides and the considerable publicity that each fresh case commanded in the newspapers, jailers guarding condemned men such as Jonathan Jewett were acutely aware that they posed a special kind of flight risk. At George Bowen's trial, the Northampton jailer, Cephas Clap, testified that he had been expecting Jewett to try to kill himself and so had been careful to "keep all the means out of his way with which he could accomplish such a purpose." Clap had good reason to be on such high alert. News had recently reached Northampton that a sheriff and his deputies a hundred miles away had lately been outwitted by an inmate who hanged himself on the very morning he was to be executed. In the aftermath, the local press had made mincemeat of the jail staff for failing to stop him.[17]

The inmate in question, James Anthony, had been scheduled to swing on April 14, 1814, for murdering a merchant in southern Vermont. So, on the afternoon prior, the Rutland sheriff had instructed his subordinate, Jedediah Hammond, "to keep the prisoner safely, so that he might see him alive in the morning." Hammond dutifully kept watch all night. At dawn, Anthony made his move, telling Hammond that he was planning to write his final confession and persuading the exhausted deputy to fetch his relatives to visit him one final time. Hammond was naturally suspicious, so before leaving he scoured the cell, taking from the prisoner "his handkerchief, and every thing, as he thought, that he could injure himself with." It was only then, after Hammond left the building, that Anthony frantically went to work, tearing his pillowcase and the linings of his hat and coat sleeves into strips and splitting a board from a stool. He tied the crude noose he had made around the board and jammed it between the stone walls of a ceiling ventilation shaft. When Hammond returned, Anthony's body was already rigid. The Rutland sheriff was incandescent with rage and, according to one account of what happened next, refused to abandon the execution. With thousands of people gathered in a nearby meadow expecting to witness the public hanging of James Anthony, jail staff carried his dead body out to the gallows and strung it up.[18]

Deputy Hammond's fatal oversight excepted, diligent and experienced jailers probably prevented numerous felons from committing suicide before justice could be served. But men such as James Anthony and Jonathan Jewett were the ones who made the papers. Each time they did, the press roasted the sheriff and the staff of the jail in question for failing in the most basic responsibilities of custodial oversight. Hammond himself was accused of gross negligence and threatened with charges of accessory to murder.[19]

It was easy to understand the fervency of public outrage: suicides committed in America's jails as prisoners awaited trial, sentence, or execution humiliated everyone with a stake in punishing the perpetrators of capital crimes. Local justice officials felt this most acutely because suicides like Anthony's and Jewett's occurred under their very noses and in the midst of the process they had set in motion to deliver retribution. So it was natural that judges, attorneys, sheriffs, and jailers, especially those who could remember newspaper coverage of the flamboyant courtroom suicides of political prisoners during the Tribunals in Paris in the 1790s, would construe jail suicides not as inwardly directed expressions of insanity or depression but as acts of sabotage directed at them. To Clap and Mattoon, Northampton's jailer and sheriff, Jewett's suicide could only be interpreted as an unmistakable refusal to abide by the rules of social compact that bound citizens—even murderers—by a supposedly mutual code of laws and consequences. With the future of the death penalty hanging in the balance, everyone with a personal interest in the successful operation of criminal justice and capital punishment in the early Republic felt each new cell-block suicide like a wound in the belly.[20]

While every New Englander likely understood the basic impulse behind the attorney general's decision to try George Bowen for his role in Jewett's flight from justice, almost from the outset there was a palpable sense that authorities in Northampton were grasping at straws. The title of a lengthy pamphlet published that fall said it all: *Report of the Trial of George Bowen; for the Murder of Jonathan Jewett, Who Committed Suicide.* Its author, Frederick Packard, was a twenty-year-old law student who watched these strange proceedings play out from the benches set out for spectators at Northampton's new courthouse. His reporting fed local and national interest in the controversial charges and his pamphlet found readers not only throughout New England but as far afield as Pennsylvania, Virginia, and Washington, D.C. Closer to home, the *Dedham Gazette* reported that the trial "was of a novel nature, and has excited much public curiosity," while other newspapers covered the story under the byline "Singular Trial."[21]

Whereas Clap and Mattoon had been the ones to press their higher-ups to try Bowen for Jewett's suicide, it fell to Attorney General Perez Morton to make the case before the Commonwealth's highest court at a special session on September 19, 1816. As a younger man, Morton had found himself in Bowen's shoes, facing very public accusations that his seduction of his wife's pretty young sister, Frances Apthorp, had contributed to her subsequent suicide. Morton—or "Mr. Importance," as he had once been known—had spent the intervening years trying to put his scandalous past behind him, and now, at age sixty-six and at the peak of his profession, this vain and corpulent man may have felt some self-righteous pleasure in assuming the role of accuser in this particular case.[22]

Rising to address two associate justices and the newly minted chief justice, Isaac Parker, Morton charged that George Bowen "did counsel, advise and urge Jewett to disappoint the Law, the Sheriff and the mob, and that his persuasions were effectual—that Jewett hung himself, in the course of the night preceding the day appointed for his execution." Even though Jewett had evidently been alone in his cell at the time of his death, Morton told the court that his neighbor's incessant encouragements turned this seeming suicide into a premeditated murder. When one man "advises another [to] kill a third, and he does it," the attorney general argued, that man shares principal responsibility and thus should face the death sentence. In 1801 a judge at the trial of Jason Fairbanks for his role in the apparent suicide of his sweetheart had used similar reasoning to propose that persuading someone to kill herself be considered an offense punishable by death. But, as Morton, a veteran prosecutor, knew all too well, the court's ruling that it was Fairbanks himself who had stabbed Elizabeth Fales to death had made that argument moot. Now, as the attorney general explained the charges he had brought against George Bowen, he seized the chance to finally set the precedent that the state should not shelter a killer whose weapon was words. Bowen pleaded not guilty.[23]

Predictably, both sets of lawyers spent much of the ensuing trial defining the extent and consequence of Bowen's conversations with Jewett. However, what is most striking about what unfolded before the Supreme Judicial Court that autumn day is the assumption, shared by both the prosecution and the defense, that Jewett's death had been intended as a form of protest. While the two sides clashed on the question of culpability—was it Bowen or Jewett who had intended "to disappoint the Law, the Sheriff, and the mob?"—they spoke in unison about the nature of the crime that had occurred. At every opportunity in the course of this trial, these lawyers told the court that whoever was responsible for Jonathan Jewett's death had mounted an odious attack on the Commonwealth of Massachusetts and its citizens, on the staff of the Northampton jail, and on the integrity of the death penalty itself.[24]

Over the next several hours, the attorney general called a small battery of witnesses. Each would testify that he had heard George Bowen offer deadly counsel to Jonathan Jewett. Just as importantly, each would depict the defendant as a man hell-bent on disappointing the law, the sheriff, and the mob. Cephas Clap, the tailor turned jailer who had been the last person to see Jewett alive, was the first witness to be sworn in. Clap claimed to have heard everything and told the jury about all the shouted exchanges the two inmates had made through the three-foot wall that separated them:

> While Jewett was in confinement both before and after his sentence, I frequently heard them conversing. Bowen would say to Jewett—"If you are sentenced you will be hung—If that should be your case will you go there"—(meaning the place of execution). I have heard him say to Jewett, "if you let them hang you, you are a d—d fool. I had rather hang myself twice than be hung once." Bowen would say "will you do it?" Jewett would reply "it can't be done"—Bowen says "it can. I would make a string of my bed-tick and hang myself to these grates in five minutes."

Acutely aware of what this suicide seemed to say about his own job performance, Clap claimed he had urged Jewett to ignore this talk: "I told him it was as bad to take his own life as to take another man's, and he would then have two murders to answer for." But Bowen never let up. According to Clap, he had even tried to poison Jewett's mind against the court-appointed clergymen who visited his cell in hopes of hearing his confession. "Bowen told him what they said was all d—d nonsense, and he had better not be influenced by it," the jailer recalled. In Clap's mind, Bowen's guilt was overwhelming. He had told Jewett to commit suicide to avoid a public hanging; he had suggested the method that this feckless fellow would later use to do so; and he had mocked the ministers whose task it was to prepare the condemned man for the scaffold.[25]

Clap's deputy, John Partridge, said much the same, giving evidence that he had heard Bowen try to talk Jewett toward suicide "Frequently. Every Day." Partridge even remembered how Bowen had once told Jewett that "he was a d—d fool to let old Mattoon come to hang him for he could die but one death." Bowen's cell mate, Isaac Mitchell, gave similar testimony, telling jurors that other prisoners had christened him the "Speaker of the House" because of the time he spent yelling at Jewett that "he never would go upon the hill (meaning the place of execution) to have the boys make fun of him." Mitchell, in jail for passing counterfeit bills, also swore that when he had heard Jewett choking on the night he hanged himself and had made to raise the alarm, Bowen had hissed at him to hold his tongue. "What in h-ll do you care for a d-n-d negro" the defendant had snapped. There was more: in a powerful piece of testimony that reminded the court that at the time of Jewett's death Bowen had been in the Northampton jail on charges of "petit larceny . . . disrespect for the sheriff and occasional turbulence," Mitchell reported that when the jailer discovered Jewett's stiffening body, Bowen had rattled his leg irons and bellowed out: "I am as glad as if I had a hundred dollars, now Clap and old Mattoon have lost their fees; and I have saved the County two hundred dollars." Expressing his challenge to the state's power over him in his glee at the prospect of denying these local officeholders their pay, Bowen appeared, in the prosecution's evidence at least, to be a rebel against the Commonwealth, a man bent on depriving the state of the opportunity to exert its most precious prerogative. Jewett was just a pawn. His race and his predicament made him expendable.[26]

When Attorney General Perez Morton ceded the floor to the defense team, Isaac Bates and his colleague, Jonathan Lyman, called three witnesses of their own. Dismissing their client, George Bowen, as a mischief maker of questionable influence, the two young lawyers made their case for his innocence by assembling testimony that it was Jewett who had mounted a conscious and cynical attack on the institution about to exert its fatal authority over him. The witnesses that Lyman and Bates led before the jury that afternoon were each asked to dwell on moments when Jewett had hinted of his intention and intimated its meaning. First came Nathan Tanner, a local builder who had been making some long-overdue repairs to the jail. Tanner remembered Jonathan Jewett as a shrewd and calculating figure who had announced plans to cheat anyone expecting a "fine frolick" on Pancake Hill long before George Bowen came along. "He told me once, he believed he should prosecute the plan of the man in Vermont, who destroyed himself in prison," Tanner recalled, referring to James Anthony's widely reported suicide. "[Jewett] would invite people to come and see him hung," he continued, "and when they were gone, he would say to me, 'those men will be disappointed.' "[27]

Another workman who had done jobs at the jail the previous fall also recalled Jewett's bravado. Undermining the prosecution's suggestion that Jewett was a timid and reluctant puppet in thrall to the angry mastermind next door, Shubael Wilder testified that three days before Jewett was found dead in his cell, he had heard the prisoner boast that "he would not go to the place of execution." In fact, Jewett had told him that he would scramble up onto the window ledge of the cell and from there throw himself "headlong on the floor" to avoid execution. " 'You will see what my courage will do,' " he had crowed. Elihu Sanford, a friend from home who had visited Jewett in jail before Bowen had arrived in the neighboring cell, continued in this vein, testifying that the deceased had asked him to smuggle in a pouch of tobacco laced with poison. Sanford had refused, but Jewett seemed undaunted. "General Mattoon never shall hang me," he predicted.[28]

Newspapers described the defense team's closing arguments as "ingenious and eloquent." Isaac Bates, who would one day represent Massachusetts in the United States Senate, and Jonathan Lyman, who was known locally as a lyrical Fourth of July speech-maker, each addressed the jury, building their defense of George Bowen around three core propositions. First, Bates explained the consequences of the attorney general's insistence that the defendant, George Bowen, face the death penalty. To try to deliver a death sentence, Perez Morton had had to argue that Bowen was the principal cause of Jonathan Jewett's death. Yet legal precedents limited the definition of principals to those who had been physically present when a crime was committed, and a parade of witnesses had testified that Bowen had been shackled in leg irons behind a thick stone wall on the night Jewett murdered himself. Any claim to the contrary was simply fantastic. Bates told the jury that the attorney general had overreached and that "If punishable at all, [Bowen] is punishable as an accessory and not as a principal."[29]

Second, Lyman reminded the jury that a coroner's inquest had already pronounced Jewett's death a felo-de-se. Statutes detailing how to punish those responsible for a homicide had no relevance to a case in which the principal had killed himself rather than a third party. Murder and suicide "are in law different offences," Lyman said, and produced the text of an 1805 Massachusetts statute to prove it. Laws governing murder had no traction or jurisdiction in this case and, despite one judge's musings at Jason Fairbanks's trial in 1801, there were no actual legal precedents for prosecuting a man suspected of persuading another man to kill himself. "This is a novel case," Lyman said. "No precedent parallel to this has been cited within the history of the criminal jurisprudence of our own country." Whatever Bowen had said, the law could not touch him.[30]

Despite the potency of these two legal arguments, Lyman and Bates both realized that they might not be enough to deter a jury of local men still outraged by Jewett's flight from justice from punishing Bowen as a convenient scapegoat. So to redirect this still-simmering resentment, each man embraced the prosecution's premise that Jewett's death was intended to "disappoint the Law, the Sheriff, and the mob," yet then pivoted to argue that it was Jewett, not Bowen, who had set out to defraud Mattoon and the mob of their due. Building on the sworn testimony of the defense witnesses, Jonathan Lyman told the jury that a man in Jewett's position required no encouragement to consider suicide:

> A ferocious and unnatural parricide, he was reprobate beyond hope; conscious that his days were numbered and that the sword of justice must soon fall, unrelenting and unrepentant, he executed the long settled purpose of his soul, and by his last act evinced a consistency in wickedness which distances all competition.

Jonathan Jewett knew that retribution for his crimes was imminent. Twelve hours before his scheduled death, with all realistic hope of reprieve long vanished and his coffin placed next to his bed, how could he not consider an early escape?[31]

Bates went further. Without betraying any sympathy for a man who had killed his own father in a fit of misdirected rage, Bates argued that anyone faced with public execution would likely have mounted the same bold challenge as Jewett. Turning to face the twelve jurors, he asked whether watching each Execution Day procession ever gave them pause for thought:

> When you have heard "the note of preparation" for the punishment of a capital offense, and surveyed the procession as it passed along, have you never thought how you could bear the shame and ignominy of a public execution? I confess to you I have; and I have thought that a "Cato would open to himself a passage." And I do affirm, that a man must be senseless as a block, or well imbued with the principles of our religion, and immoveably established in its doctrines, or like Cato, he would do it. So natural is this, so much a matter of course, that even the gaoler, Mr. Clap, tells you, that they are always careful to remove from the cells of capital offenders every thing with which they might destroy life.

Adopting a position that embedded a cautious yet an unmistakable criticism of capital punishment, Bowen's lawyers argued that, backed into this corner, it was not surprising that Jewett should lash out against the system that demanded his death. Such sabotage was to be expected.[32]

Watching the case slipping away from him, Attorney General Perez Morton used his closing argument to focus the court's attention back on the man in the dock. He wisely refused to be drawn into a debate about the legality of the charges. Instead he asked jurors to look at the facts and trust their instincts. His witnesses had sworn that after incessant encouragements and advice on how to do it, Jewett had followed Bowen's instructions to the letter—even choosing the method that his neighbor had suggested. How, then, could reasonable men deny a link between cause and effect? "Is there a particle of doubt in your minds," he asked the jury incredulously, "that the prisoner advised [Jewett] to kill himself?" Bowen's guilt was obvious.[33]

Before the jury retired, Chief Justice Isaac Parker summed up the case. Parker's rapid rise through the ranks of the Commonwealth's judiciary was due in part to his reputation for sound judgment and impartiality. But to the dismay of Bates and Lyman, his summation left jurors in no doubt that he expected them to find George Bowen guilty as charged. Parker, the Federalist judge who had imposed the death penalty on Jewett for the murder of his father a year ago, seemed downright eager to see someone pay for evading that sentence. That morning, Perez Morton had told the court that "a man is under the protection of the law until he dies by the law." The chief justice now completed that thought, telling the jury that "justice was thirsting for its sacrifice." In Parker's view, it was entirely just that George Bowen should forfeit his life because he had encouraged the suicide of "a culprit within a few hours of death, by the sentence of the law." "Gentlemen," he went on, "the community has an interest in the public execution of criminals—it is interested in the awful and effectual warning and to take such a one out of the reach of the law is no trivial offence." On the contrary; as the figureheads and guardians of that "community," both Parker and Morton felt it like a fist to the stomach, a bodily challenge to the terms of dominance and dependence upon which they had built their frequently intertwined legal careers.[34]

Softening his tone, the chief justice also suggested that Jewett's suicide had preempted the possibility that Governor Caleb Strong might have pardoned him at the last minute. Every Execution Day, Parker argued, was pregnant with opportunities in which the "Government may interpose its clemency, and rescue the miserable offender from anticipated punishment." In truth, this was a convenient bit of puffery: reprieves were portioned out sparingly in the early Republic, and unrepentant family killers with no close ties to those in power did not stand a chance. Bringing his remarks to a close, the chief justice tried to brush aside the defense team's protests that the court had no jurisdiction over deaths previously ruled to be self-inflicted and also informed the jury that it mattered little if Jewett had thought about killing himself before Bowen began calling to him. "If you find the prisoner encouraged and kept in view motives previously existing in Jewett's mind, and suggested others to augment their influence," Parker concluded, then Bowen must be executed for murder.[35]

The jurors retired at eight o'clock. They had been asked to decide the fate of a man brought up on charges never before seen in an American courtroom. Of course this was not the first time that one person had encouraged another to commit suicide: three decades earlier, newspapers in Boston had accused Perez Morton himself of doing little short of that. But the fact that Jewett's death had occurred just hours before his scheduled execution had made Bowen's shouted advice the Commonwealth's business. Already sentenced to be hanged for a "ferocious and unnatural" parricide that many probably perceived as an assault upon the foundations of family government and civil society, Jewett's suicide manifested a second attack, this time on "the Law, the Sheriff and the mob." As the Northampton *Repertory* reported, "It appeared to be a cool, deliberate act, resorted to for the purpose of thwarting the design of punishment, and defrauding justice of its due." The *Salem Gazette* concurred, noting that Jewett's death served "to wrest from the arm of Justice his forfeited life."[36]

As the Commonwealth's chief legal officer, Attorney General Perez Morton prosecuted this case precisely because the deceased was a prisoner, a man in the state's care under sentence to be executed. His death was no ordinary act of self-destruction. While we will never know to what extent, if at all, George Bowen or Jonathan Jewett conceived of the latter's suicide as a means to undermine the state's ability to enact the death penalty, what should concern us is how vigorously both counsels strained to make such arguments. Conscious of broader attempts to limit states' use of capital punishment, each counsel prioritized persuading the jury not simply of Bowen's guilt or innocence but that the words and actions of either the defendant or the deceased constituted conscious and purposeful attacks on the ability of the criminal justice system to fulfill its function.

In the midst of overwhelming agreement about the damage done by Jewett's predawn death, the jury's job was to decide whether Bowen too should die. If they could lay their own still-bristling bitterness to one side and focus on the legality of the charges against the defendant, their task seemed straightforward: Bowen had committed no crime. As Bates and Lyman had damningly demonstrated, Morton had zealously misrepresented the statutes governing homicide and exaggerated their jurisdiction. Not only was there no legal precedent for holding someone principally responsible who was not physically present for a murder when it was committed, but murder statutes had no relevance to cases in which a coroner had returned a verdict of suicide.

At ten o'clock the foreman, Elisha Graves, delivered the jury's decision. As the Boston papers reported the trial's thrilling denouement, "the jury . . . notwithstanding a charge from the court, which was strongly against the prisoner, brought in a verdict of Not Guilty." George Bowen was released.[37]

Morton and Parker were furious. Their attempt to punish Bowen for Jewett's suicide had failed in dramatic fashion. In fact, the great publicity generated by the Commonwealth's peculiar charges had probably only made matters worse. At the trial, Lyman and Bates had reminded everyone that Jewett had read about James Anthony's death-row suicide in the newspapers; might Jewett's posthumous fame now stir similar copycat acts? When Thomas Daniels looped his handkerchief over a slim limb of wood he had wedged into his cell's ceiling in the Cambridge jail three years later, in 1819, many observers surely wondered whether he had read about James Anthony and Jonathan Jewett doing similar things.[38]

If Morton and Parker had hoped that Bowen's trial might have served as some sort of deterrent against inmate suicide, it did not seem to have worked. Thomas Daniels was one of several murderers in New England to choose suicide as a means to evade the hangman's reckoning in the years that followed Bowen's acquittal. In Connecticut, in 1825, seventy-three-year-old Adonijah Bailey hanged himself just two weeks before his execution date. Two years later, Charles Marchant, a sailor who had been sentenced to die for killing the captain and mate of the schooner *Fairy*, was found in his cell in Boston "suspended, by means of a strip torn from his blanket, and a handkerchief about his neck, from the grate which lighted his room." He was followed a few months later by Robert Bush, a troubled and intemperate barrel-maker living not far from Northampton, who had shot his estranged wife. In an intervention that would have thrilled humane society managers, a doctor had foiled Bush's first attempt to kill himself by forcing the distraught man to vomit up the thirty grains of opium he had swallowed. Weeks later, just two days before the date scheduled for his execution, Bush tried again, this time swallowing a crude mixture of opium and tobacco similar to the blend Jonathan Jewett had attempted to smuggle into the Northampton jail. By the time the jailer discovered him, Bush was dead.[39]

Given their positions atop the Commonwealth's legal hierarchy, Morton and Parker were surely stung every time another condemned man in the state's custody committed suicide. Yet both men remained unbowed. Despite the embarrassing outcome of Bowen's trial, they and their local subordinates continued to search for ways to prevent inmate suicide from derailing justice in Massachusetts. In 1830 the perfect opportunity fell into their laps; a case came before the Supreme Judicial Court that gave the chief justice and the attorney general a second chance to confront the specter of jail suicide head on. In some ways the new case was a replay of the first. For the second time in fifteen years, Perez Morton and Isaac Parker would wade into controversy surrounding the cell-block hanging of a defendant charged with the murder of an old man. Once more they would tell a packed courtroom that an inmate had committed suicide to thwart the expectations of the Commonwealth and to sabotage the death penalty. Once again both men would try to bend the law to secure a capital conviction. But this time they would win.

On an April morning in 1830, a servant rushed from one of the grandest houses in one of the grandest streets in Salem crying murder. His employer, eighty-two-year-old Captain Joseph White, had not risen at his usual early hour, and when the servant had gone to rouse him, he had found White dead in his bed. His skull had been crushed by a savage beating with some kind of club, and there were thirteen stab wounds in the old man's chest. Nothing else in the richly furnished house seemed to have been touched.[40]

Captain White's murder shocked genteel Salem to its core. The region had endured its fair share of homicides in recent years, but never before had elites here in this Federalist stronghold seen one of their own killed in his bed as he slept. Trust vanished overnight. Everyone was terrified; no one went out after dark. Over in Cambridge the young Oliver Wendell Holmes wrote to a friend that "we have to look in our closets and under our beds, and strut about with sword canes and pistols. Poor old Mr. White was stabbed in the dark, and since then the very air has been redolent of assassination." In Salem, members of the great families took to arming themselves; storekeepers quickly sold out of pistols and knives and had to order more from Boston.[41]

White had no obvious enemies. He was widowed and childless and had long ago announced his plans to distribute the million-dollar fortune he had made from commercial shipping and occasional smuggling. His grandniece, Mary Beckford, would receive a percentage after his death, while his nephew, Stephen White, would inherit the lion's share. With no clear suspects, his nephew, a state senator who had made his own small pile on the quarterdeck before turning to politics, announced a reward for information about his uncle's assassin. The town council pledged to match it and, in a move that showed a startling disregard for privacy, empowered a Committee of Vigilance to search every home and interrogate anyone. Yet weeks of searches turned up nothing. For all of April, Captain White's murderer walked free. On May 2, out of little more than desperation, the committee arrested Dick and George Crowninshield, the black sheep scions of one of Salem's most distinguished families.[42]

The Crowninshields had made their money the same way Captain White had: Crowninshield wharf stood alongside White's, and the family was rumored to have made close to $20 million from privateering over the years. As a result, the elder Crowninshields—several of whom had taken leading roles in the Massachusetts humane society movement—guarded the family's reputation vigorously. So when a young member of their clan, Richard Crowninshield, had married a New York City hotel maid at the turn of the century, they had swiftly disinherited him. Richard's sons, Dick and George Crowninshield, took after their father and seemed intent on besting his shortcomings. Expelled from one boarding school for plotting to burn it down and robbing the next of several hundred dollars, they washed up back in Salem in the 1820s. George opened a whorehouse, while Dick embarked upon a life of petty crime in which he embroiled his brother from time to time. Dick tried his hand first as a jewel thief, then as a grave robber, and finally as a gambler. He also raped a neighbor's daughter but talked his way out of the charges. Charming, well mannered, and utterly immoral, by age twenty-six Dick Crowninshield was living in Salem as "the admitted leader of all the rascals in Essex County."[43]

Although they seemed like likely suspects, both Dick and his brother George had solid alibis for the night of April 6, 1830, and after a few weeks there were still no grounds on which to continue to hold them. Then, in mid-May, a strange series of events exposed a blackmail plot by another of the town's lowlifes to extort money from Joe Knapp, a twenty-four-year-old ship captain who had often worked for Captain White and who had recently married the old man's grandniece. It turned out that Captain White had thought Knapp was a fortune hunter and so had tried to block the marriage by threatening to draw up a new will to deny Mary Beckford the small share of his estate he had previously promised. The Committee of Vigilance now learned that Joe Knapp had paid Dick Crowninshield $1,000 to kill Captain White before he could do the paperwork. Taken to jail, Knapp now came clean in hopes of gaining immunity. On the night of the murder, Knapp confessed, Dick Crowninshield had slipped away from his friends by feigning stomach trouble after dinner. He rode into town, and then clubbed and stabbed White while he slept. Knapp's eighteen-year-old brother, Frank, who had once shared a New York City jail cell with both of the Crowninshield brothers, had kept watch out on the moon-washed street behind the mansion while Dick was inside.[44]

Four men—Dick and George Crowninshield and Joe and Frank Knapp—were now behind bars. There was not yet any evidence that George had been involved in the plot, and Joe's confession had made it clear that Dick was the only conspirator to have entered White's Essex Street house. Nevertheless, Attorney General Perez Morton laid plans to try each of these four young men for murder before the Supreme Judicial Court in July and to seek the death sentence for them all.[45]

Perhaps Morton should have anticipated what happened next. On the afternoon of June 15, the Salem jailer, Nehemiah Brown, found Dick Crowninshield dead in his second-floor cell. Like James Anthony, Jonathan Jewett, Thomas Daniels, Adonijah Bailey, and Charles Marchant before him, Crowninshield had made a halter from clothes and sheets. He had tied it to the bars in the cell window and then crouched until his neck took his weight. Brown found him swinging. His knees were almost scraping the ground and his head lolled grotesquely. The jailer cut down the body and when doctors arrived they used the charge from a "galvanic battery" to try to restore a pulse. But the blood remained still. The coroner ruled the cause of death as willful suicide.[46]

Before his death, Dick Crowninshield had been reading local newspapers in his cell and so was well aware that Joe Knapp, confined on the

An unnamed illustrator imagined Dick Crowninshield murdering Joseph White. This image circulated in the popular pamphlet literature surrounding the trial. *Most Important Testimony Adduced on the Trial of John Francis Knapp, for the Murder of Capt. Joseph White, of Salem* (Providence: H. H. Brown, 1830). Courtesy of the American Antiquarian Society.

floor below, had spilled the beans and sealed his fate. Expecting a death sentence, Crowninshield committed suicide to disappoint the thousands in Salem who bayed for his blood. During his imprisonment he had told his sister Sarah that public executions were so unjust and brutal that not even "the savages of the Western wilds, who never saw a Christian, would inflict [them] upon their greatest enemy." And in a letter to his brother George written just hours before he hanged himself, Crowninshield explained that townspeople's reactions to Captain White's murder had convinced him that no jury would show him mercy: "[I] perceive my case to be hopeless, therefore I have come to the determination to deprive them of the pleasure of beholding me publicly executed, as after I am condemned they will not give me the opportunity." Crowninshield knew full well that as soon as Chief Justice Isaac Parker sentenced him to die, he would be placed on suicide watch. He had to act now.[47]

There was another reason Dick Crowninshield would not wait. He had been thinking it through and had realized that by taking his life now, before his trial even began, he might be able to protect his brother from whatever trumped-up charges Morton might come up with to secure a fourth capital conviction. In the days before he hanged himself in his cell, Crowninshield spent many hours with the family's lawyer, Franklin Dexter, going over and over the legal definition of principal and accessory in murder cases. Dexter had explained to him that a principal was usually the person who committed the murder, an accessory was any person in on the plan, and that in Massachusetts the prosecution of a suspected accessory to murder requires the prior conviction of a principal for the same crime. Joe Knapp had sworn that Dick was the only defendant to have set foot in the White mansion on the night of the murder. If he lived to see it, Dick would be charged and then convicted as the principal, and only then would his brother George and the Knapps be tried as accessories. Was there any way that an accessory could face death if no principal could be convicted, Crowninshield asked Dexter. No, came the answer. When a case like that came to trial, it would have to be dismissed.[48]

Townsfolk in Salem could not believe his audacity. When news of Dick Crowninshield's suicide broke, dozens of people demanded to see the body for themselves. So for one day and one night Nehemiah Brown opened his jail while people from across Essex County paraded through to see the corpse of the Salem murderer before it was taken away to be unceremoniously disposed of. In the days that followed, their disbelief quickly gave way to the familiar outrage felt by communities confronted by the jail suicides of known murderers. "The fiend has since robbed justice of its victim," one pamphleteer lamented to his readers. He hanged himself so "that he might avoid the ignominy of a public execution," the author of a broadside agreed.[49]

A few sharp minds soon realized that Dick's daring suicide was even more potent. With no principal to be tried and convicted, the cases against the Knapp brothers and George Crowninshield now seemed inadmissible. Joe Knapp, the man who had allegedly conceived and paid for the White murder, and his brother, Frank, the man who had stood watch while it happened, would both walk free. So too would George. Stephen White was so angry that he used his position as a state senator to try to convene the Massachusetts legislature in an emergency session to overturn the law that barred the trial of accessories without the prior conviction of a principal. But with the Supreme Judicial Court scheduled to hear these cases in just a few short weeks, there was no time for the legislature to oblige.[50]

With the law of principals still firmly intact, Attorney General Perez Morton made a brazen decision. He refused to let this latest jail suicide sabotage the highest-profile capital trials the new nation had yet seen and announced that they would continue. With the true perpetrator dead by his own hand, Morton would instead try Frank Knapp as principal in the murder, with his brother Joe and George Crowninshield as accessories. Just days earlier, Joe Knapp had withdrawn his confession because Morton had refused to protect him and his brother from prosecution. So the attorney general would have to build from scratch the linchpin case against Frank Knapp. To stand a chance of securing the death penalty for anyone involved in White's murder, Morton would not only have to establish that Frank Knapp had kept watch outside the White mansion while Dick Crowninshield was inside but also that his actions led directly to the captain's death. He had to prove beyond all reasonable doubt that if it was not for Knapp's lookout, the old man would still be alive. It was all or nothing.

As soon as the attorney general announced his plan, whispers began that he wasn't up to the job. Morton had just turned eighty, just two years younger than the aged merchant prince whose murder lay at the center of these proceedings. He had served as the Commonwealth's chief legal officer for longer than any of his predecessors and had recently become the oldest alumnus at Harvard's annual commencement procession. The prospect of a long and intricate series of trials to get the capital convictions that he and the Commonwealth clearly craved must have left him feeling his age. So Morton was probably relieved when Stephen White used his connections within the rapidly crumbling Federalist Party to lure Daniel Webster to Salem to help the attorney general pull off the extraordinary legal acrobatics he had promised. In 1830 Webster was beginning a career in the United States Senate and enjoying his growing reputation as the "American Cicero." But he was also deeply in debt and so jumped at the invitation and the fee of $1,000—the same amount Joe Knapp had promised Dick Crowninshield to murder Captain White.[51]

At the arraignment that July, Perez Morton indicted the surviving prisoners. Addressing the four justices arrayed on the bench, Morton charged "that Richard Crowninshield and J. F. Knapp made an assault upon White, that Richard murdered him with a bludgeon and that J. F. Knapp was present, aiding and abetting, that Richard killed himself so that he could not be further proceeded against, and that George and Joseph were accessories before the fact." Chief Justice Isaac Parker nodded his approval and made a brief speech bemoaning the necessity of observing the law of principals in a case like this. Turning to the charges now before the court, Parker then tried to lower the legal hurdles Morton and Webster needed to clear by offering perhaps the most expansive definition of who might constitute a principal ever heard from the bench of an American courtroom:

> It is not required that the abettor shall be actually upon the spot when the murder is committed, or even in sight of the more immediate perpetrator, or of the victim, to make him a principal. If he be at a distance, co-operating in the act, watching to prevent relief, or to give alarm, or to assist his confederate in escape, having knowledge of the purpose and object of the assassin—this, in the eye of the law, is being present, aiding and abetting, so as to make him a principal.

Parker's reading of the law of principals required Morton and Webster to do little more than place Frank Knapp in the vicinity of the scene to secure his conviction. If they could convince the jury of that, then Parker left them in no doubt that Knapp and the two men charged with being accessories to this murder would pay with their lives. With the law now calibrated to his liking, Parker sent the prisoners back to their cells to await the first trial the following week. It proved to be his final order. Two days before Frank Knapp was next scheduled to appear before him, the sixty-two-year-old chief justice died of a stroke while at home in Boston.[52]

When Associate Justice Samuel Putnam finally called Frank Knapp's trial to order on August 3, the courtroom was crammed to bursting. Those lucky enough to make it inside saw Perez Morton coax testimony from a motley crew of supposed eyewitnesses who could offer only dim recollections of having seen a man similar to Frank's description loitering near the

White mansion on the night of the murder. When cross-examined by defense attorney Franklin Dexter and his assistant, Robert Rantoul Jr., none of the witnesses could say for sure that they had seen Frank's face and they disagreed about his clothes.[53]

When Daniel Webster rose to deliver the prosecution's closing statement, he had his work cut out for him. Dexter and Rantoul had sown considerable doubt in jurors' minds about Frank Knapp's role as a killer's accomplice. Acutely aware that without Joe Knapp's confession the evidence against his brother was conjectural, Webster spent eight hours over the best part of two days talking not about the defendant but about the murder itself. He gambled that if he could stoke jurors' fury that a helpless old man had been killed in his bed by an assassin who had committed suicide to flee from justice, that these twelve local men would convict Frank Knapp as a proxy for Dick Crowninshield. Relishing the occasion, Webster retold the facts of the murder in outrageous detail and made Dick's suicide the emotional focus of the entire proceedings. In what became a famous passage of this often-reprinted speech, Webster told jurors that Dick's suicide was the ultimate proof of the guilt of these conspirators: "The guilty soul cannot keep its secret. . . . It *must* be confessed. It WILL be confessed. There is no refuge from confession, but suicide. And suicide is confession." This was powerful stuff, and it threw the jury into disarray. When they returned from their deliberations, the foreman sheepishly announced a hung jury: they could not agree whether or not Frank Knapp was the guilty principal. The case would have to be tried again.[54]

The news sent the press into paroxysms. Ever since Dick Crowninshield had hanged himself in June 1830, public interest in the fallout of the Salem murder had been growing and growing. New York papers had sent reporters such as the young James Gordon Bennett north to cover it, and the streets of Boston and other northeastern cities were awash with broadsides breathlessly relaying each new twist. Never before had anything like this received so much attention. Indeed, the press interest in White's murder and Crowninshield's suicide might usefully be compared to the furor following a presidential assassination in modern times. Opportunistic publishers rushed at least five different reports of Frank Knapp's trial into print, and tell-all memoirs from minor figures in the case found hungry readers. Local ministers, whose predecessors might have once expected to satisfy prurient interest in a story like this by rushing a condemnatory sermon into print, could not compete. So insistent and invasive was the secular press coverage of the events that Perez Morton complained to the judges present that justice might easily be perverted by so much untoward attention—a claim similar to one he had made in 1788, when Boston papers had accused him of driving his mistress to taking poison.[55]

Despite Morton's protests, press interest continued to escalate, and the courtroom was packed again when Frank Knapp's retrial began before a new jury on August 14. Amazingly, there were few differences between this and the first trial; both sides called the same witnesses and asked them the same questions. Yet having seen the three surviving suspects escape conviction as a result of the first hung jury, almost all of the returning eyewitnesses were now suddenly more certain that they had seen Frank Knapp outside the White mansion that night. "[I] can't swear positively" became "[I] have no doubt." "I judge it was Frank" was revised to "I can swear positively," and "My belief is" became "I've no doubt." Dexter and Rantoul were caught off guard by these unexpected reversals and fumbled their response. They failed to put forward any compelling counterexplanation of who the mysterious figure outside White's mansion might have been, or what innocent purpose Frank Knapp had been pursuing if he had been on that corner. "From the figures [these two attorneys] made, it is problematical whether they will ever rise above the mediocrity of the profession," scorned James Gordon Bennett in the pages of New York's *Courier and Enquirer*.[56]

Webster saw his opportunity. In a closing statement, he cast this new jury's decision as a matter of their own survival and neatly disarmed any skeptics troubled by the prosecution's barely concealed attempt to pervert the law of principals to get these convictions. "Whenever a jury, through whimsical and ill-founded scruples, suffer the guilty to escape," goaded the histrionic attorney, "they make themselves answerable for the augmented danger of the innocent." Dick Crowninshield, a man who had spent his adult life shirking punishment for ever more vicious and flagrant violations of common ethical standards, had already slipped through justice's fingers; Frank Knapp could not be allowed to do the same.[57]

The new jury deliberated for six hours before announcing the guilty verdict. Perez Morton immediately moved that Frank Knapp face the death penalty. On August 21 Judge Putnam, the associate justice who had shared the bench with Isaac Parker during George Bowen's trial fifteen years earlier, granted the request. Knapp would languish in the Salem jail for five weeks while the preparations were made. He used the time to write letters protesting that his trial as principal was unlawful. Beyond the walls of the jail, national interest in the Salem murder was now finally beginning to cool. The local press reported Knapp's shifting state of mind regularly as his execution date approached, but papers in New York printed fewer and fewer stories. "Many people have become sick of hearing of the Salem murder," James Gordon Bennett wrote. Having watched as Morton and Webster triumphantly secured the death penalty for Dick Crowninshield's lookout, it is likely that some readers were beginning to feel remorse or revulsion at the thought that the court had let the attorney general and his team bend the law so shamelessly to send Knapp to the gallows. On September 28, 1830, the Salem sheriff hanged Frank Knapp in the grubby park outside the town jail. Four thousand people, far fewer than had been expected, watched him die.[58]

Six weeks later, amid rumors that he was trying to starve himself, Joe Knapp entered the defendant's dock. With his brother Frank already convicted and executed as the principal, it was an easy matter for Morton and Webster to demonstrate that Joe Knapp had been the brains behind the plan to kill his wife's rich and bullying great-uncle. He was executed as an accessory on the same spot as his brother. Even accounting for the cold winter weather, the crowd that had gathered to watch was small and strangely subdued. It seemed as if even the people of Salem had had enough.[59]

After Webster's triumphant speech securing the all-important conviction of Frank Knapp as proxy principal, Franklin Dexter, the lead attorney for the defendants, had told the jury that they would one day regret letting the court overreach its authority. "The time will come when this trial will be coolly and impartially examined," Dexter had warned. "It is on record forever. The murmurs of applause that will follow a verdict of guilty from the multitude that now surrounds you will soon subside and another and more enduring voice will then inquire whether you have been faithful to the law and to your oaths and consciences." He was right about the applause: the hanging of Frank Knapp helped salve the intense anger that had followed the suicide of the real principal, Dick Crowninshield. But Dexter was also right about the tug on the collective conscience that followed in its aftermath. Thankfully for George Crowninshield, by the time he stood trial in November, even the prosecutors had lost their appetite for blood. Having secured not one but two capital convictions, Daniel Webster had already done enough. He took no part in the proceedings against George, and not even Perez Morton could summon much vigor to press the case. Without any evidence connecting George Crowninshield to the murder of Joseph White, he was easily exonerated and swiftly released.[60]

Twelve weeks later, on February 19, 1831, the Massachusetts legislature voted to abolish the law of principals.[61]

The execution of the two Knapp brothers reignited the campaign to abolish the death penalty. Having successfully lobbied several turn-of-the-century legislatures to slash the number of capital offenses and build state-of-the-art penitentiaries to give judges better alternatives to sanguinary punishment, the movement had lost focus and momentum after the death of its most prominent spokesman, Benjamin Rush, in 1813. The hanging of Joe and Frank Knapp changed all that. After justice miscarried in Salem, Robert Rantoul Jr. took up the doctor's fallen standard and led the charge. Rantoul's father had campaigned with Rush decades earlier, but it was the son's experience as Franklin Dexter's assistant defending the Knapp brothers that transformed Rantoul's inherited antipathy toward the death penalty into his life's work. Rantoul was just twenty-seven years old when he watched Morton and Webster twist the law of principals beyond all recognition to send two of his three clients to their deaths. Within five years, Rantoul, a Unitarian, had won election to the Massachusetts House of Representatives as a Democrat and soon set about using his platform there to lead a growing coalition of fellow liberals galvanized by what they had seen in Salem to obliterate the death penalty in the Bay State once and for all.[62]

The tactics adopted by this new generation offered further testimony to the profound impact of the Salem trials on men such as Robert Rantoul. In Rush's day, opponents of capital punishment had stood by while men such as Morton and Parker pointed to jail suicides as dangerous acts of social sabotage. But no longer. In the wake of Salem, antigallows activists set about trying to reframe popular understanding of the relationship between self-destruction and the scaffold. To do so they turned news of every subsequent cell-block suicide into a powerful indictment of the death penalty itself.

Initially at least, the revived campaign sounded familiar notes. Repeating the Rushian rhetoric that had been so pervasive in his father's day, Rantoul and many of the Unitarians, Universalists, and Quakers allied with him reminded lawmakers that God alone has the power to take a life. A few days after Dick Crowninshield hanged himself in the Salem jail, Rev. A. C. Thomas stood up before a Universalist congregation in Philadelphia to ask a simple question: "Has a man a right to destroy his own life? If the negative be established, all that is said relative to the right of human laws to inflict the punishment of death must go for naught." Over the next decade, fellow activists would ask the same question to legislators in almost every northern state. It was a smart and timely way to harness universal condemnation of Dick Crowninshield's preemptive death—and of self-murder in principle—and redirect it against the gallows itself. "Suicide, in all countries, and at all times, both by the moral sense of the people and all the laws of the land, has been considered a crime against nature and society," a crusading committee chairman in the Albany legislature declared in a report on capital punishment published in 1832. "If man does not possess the right, how can he delegate it?" Five years later, Robert Rantoul hit the same talking points in his own committee's report recommending abolition: "Has a man a right to commit suicide?" he asked his Whig Party opponents in the Massachusetts Senate. "Every Christian must answer no. A man holds his life as a tenant at will." As position papers like this began to multiply in the wake of the Salem trials, the old argument that capital punishment could only rest upon the sanction of suicide even filtered down to become a recurring feature in clemency petitions written by the condemned themselves.[63]

Defenders of the death penalty soon began to challenge this repeated claim as a specious oversimplification of the nuances of social contract theory, a move that forced reformers to try a different tack. To persuade law-and-order conservatives to abandon the state's most devastating legal weapon required liberals to pair their legalistic arguments with new, emotive pleas that could humanize their cause. Thus antigallows campaigners writing in the shadow of the Salem trials began to focus their energies on publicizing the brutalizing effects they believed public executions wrought on the increasingly coarse crowds of commoners that still often cheered them on. This too was a familiar gambit, a new version of the old argument made by parents and preachers suspicious of the rise of the novel a generation earlier. Adapting that reactionary reasoning for their own progressive purposes, Rantoul and his allies now told lawmakers that without the moderating presence of respectable citizens, the ignorant mobs that turned out on most antebellum Execution Days lacked sufficient moral sense to appreciate a public hanging as a ritual affirmation of civic identity.[64]

Antigallows activists now began to claim—typically without evidence—that suicides by rope were actually liable to increase sharply among those who saw the state repeatedly hang men by their necks. "Often, very often has it happened, that an execution has been followed on the next day, or within a few weeks, by suicides among those who witnessed the scene," Rantoul informed the Massachusetts legislature in 1835. Across the state line, another Democratic Party operative, the journalist and congressman John O'Sullivan, told elected officials in Albany the same:

> Who can reckon the number of minds, distributed at any given moment throughout the community, which, just trembling on the uncertain base of reason . . . are ripe and ready to add another prey to the many victims whom despair has lured to self-destruction, and need but a hint or suggestion of example to secure their insane imitation!

Playing upon legislators' sense of themselves as capable protectors of community integrity, O'Sullivan told lawmakers they had to act now to abolish the gallows. There was no time to lose: dozens of "ripe" minds had already been nudged toward suicide by public executions. "Self-destruction seems sometimes almost to rage as an epidemic," he remarked before reminding politicians gathered in the state capital of a local tragedy that had filled the papers there a week earlier: "Two or three days after [a recent public] execution," he recalled, "a fine boy of about sixteen years of age, the delight of highly respectable and estimable parents, hung himself from the bannisters of the stairs in his father's house, in Albany." To O'Sullivan at least, the link between cause and effect was obvious—no other interpretation of the cause of this young man's tragic death had merit. If a "fine boy" blessed with dutiful parents and a decent moral compass could be led fatally astray by witnessing a recent hanging, then think of the effect upon the unwashed masses who still swarmed to these events in such great numbers.[65]

With the lives of so many suggestible citizens apparently on the line, lawmakers had to be seen to act. But many Whigs, in particular, relied on the political support of those clergy and justice officials in their districts who remained staunch defenders of the death penalty. Thus when state legislatures began to respond to growing pressure from Democratic reformers such as Rantoul and O'Sullivan to outlaw the gallows, most only took half measures. Maine effectively abolished capital punishment in 1837, but elsewhere lawmakers dampened criticism of public executions simply by moving them to jail yards and other secluded sites where, theoretically at least, only a few carefully chosen observers could witness the moment of death. Pennsylvania led the way (1834), and New York (1835), Massachusetts (1836), and the other New England states followed. Advocates of capital punishment, such as Presbyterian firebrand George Cheever, privately cheered these bans on public executions because they silenced reformers' shrill claims that use of the gallows increased suicides and other crimes among susceptible spectators without ceding ground on the larger issue of its legitimacy. Rantoul and his allies had been outflanked. In New York, Universalist newspaper editor Horace Greeley lamented that by privatizing legal executions, recent legislation had "subtracted much of the force" from the campaign for complete abolition.[66]

It was not until the suicide of another high-profile inmate a few years later that frustrated advocates of total abolition found a means to restart their campaign. On November 18, 1842, the day he was to be hanged for killing a printer with a hatchet, John C. Colt stabbed himself in his cell in New York City. Squads of newspapermen, including James Gordon Bennett, now the editor of the *New York Herald*, had covered his trial earlier that year and had found plenty to write about. After all, the thirty-year-old defendant was the brother of Samuel Colt, the famous Connecticut revolver maker, and the family fortune had paid for wily lawyers to fight the overwhelming evidence that, rather than pay a gambling debt, Colt had bludgeoned a man to death and then jammed his body into a crate and onto a ship bound for New Orleans. In the course of a two-week trial that Colt's attorneys crammed with theatrics and time-wasting ballistic tests, they settled on a plea of self-defense, while his friends bombarded the press with testimony to his gentle character. Appealing to the court of public opinion, they painted a compelling portrait of a young man from good stock who had been consumed by the city itself. Alone in the metropolis, the weaknesses in Colt's character had become fatal flaws as he had been sucked ever deeper into a life of gambling, forgery, and burglary. New York ate men like John C. Colt for breakfast, liberal papers such as Horace Greeley's *Tribune* told their readers during his trial.[67]

Despite growing agreement in the press that Colt was no monster, just an ordinary man who had made appalling choices in awful circumstances, the jury proved unsympathetic and found him guilty as charged. Judge William Kent sentenced him to death. On the day set for Colt's execution, the city itself seemed to pause as readers scoured the newspapers for details of his final reckoning. James Gordon Bennett's *New York Herald* printed several special editions throughout the day to relay breaking news from their informant on the inside. And at four o'clock Bennett got the scoop of his career: John Colt had killed himself. "Going into the cell, there lay Colt on his back stretched out at full length on the bed, quite dead, but not cold. A clasp knife, like a small dirk knife, with a broken handle, was sticking in his heart," the *Herald* breathlessly reported. "Thank God! Thank God!" his brother Samuel cried when he heard the news.[68]

While few people following the events that day shared the extent of Samuel Colt's relief and satisfaction, only the rough crowd that had gathered outside the prison to catch a glimpse of his brother's hanging seemed bitter and disappointed. In contrast, several of the papers that had tried to stir up some sympathy for Colt among their middle-class readers during his trial offered up the condemned man's suicide as mortal proof that capital punishment was too blunt a weapon to confront the endemic problems of city living. Horace Greeley, the socially radical editor of the *Tribune*, was the first to speak up. Following logic unthinkable in the wake of earlier cell-block suicides like Jonathan Jewett's or James Anthony's, Greeley now rushed into print with a long opinion piece that began by decrying the corrosive social effects of capital punishment:

> Not from compassion to criminals but from regard to the community—whose sympathies and whose feelings are so unhealthily excited by public executions—whose abhorrence of crime and reverence for law are confused and disturbed by these deeds of legal butchery—we demand the abolition of the Punishment of Death.

If Colt had been sentenced to a life of solitary confinement, Greeley argued, he would never have committed suicide, and justice would surely have been better served.[69]

Other liberal activists sidelined on this issue since lawmakers had banned executions in public followed Greeley's lead and returned to the fray in the months that followed. Each of them used Colt's suicide as bloody evidence that capital punishment was a barbaric torture that drove the very people it was supposed to punish to kill themselves. In the December 1842 issue of the *Democratic Review*, a high-brow literary magazine that often published antigallows poetry, editor John O'Sullivan used Colt's self-inflicted wounds to draw a purposefully provocative comparison between the psychic horrors of an impending execution and the mythic excesses of widow-burning rituals on the Indian subcontinent:

> Well, it is now all over. . . . For that act of a mad moment—even if it were not one of justifiable self-defence—the soul of its wretched author has been wrung with long tortures, a thousand-fold keener than all the physical pangs which make the demoniac ecstasy of the Indian sacrifice. He has been gradually hemmed in—pressed closer and closer up to the very verge of the eternal and immeasurable chasm—and has at last been plunged off into that dread darkness from which no ray nor echo returns to reveal to us the perhaps infinite consequences of our awful act. All this has been done, and it is to be hoped that those whose doing it has been are now satisfied.

Here O'Sullivan walked a fine line. To condemn capital punishment in this way required him to describe the emotional distress this felon felt at the thought of his imminent execution, without being seen to condone a convicted murderer who chose to avoid lawful punishment by committing a second homicide. To do so, O'Sullivan had to direct his readers to focus single-mindedly on the intrinsically oppressive effects of receiving a death sentence. Hitting a note not heard since Isaac Bates's closing statement in George Bowen's trial in 1816, O'Sullivan portrayed Colt's decision to preempt the hangman as a rational response to the certainty that he was about to die:

> We regret sincerely the mode of his death, though it is impossible to see in it, under the circumstances, any ground for harsh severity of condemnation. In its proper sense, of the guilty abbreviation of the natural term of life, the word suicide is scarcely, perhaps, applicable to the act. It was adopted by him only at the last moment, when the last shadow of a shade of chance had departed, and when it was a simple choice of modes of death.

In hands as skilled as these, Colt's suicide was a powerful new weapon for the cause, and other activists soon scrambled to find similar stories of inmates driven to suicide to add further fuel to their rejuvenated campaign.[70]

They were spoiled for choice: when Charles Spear, a publicity-savvy Universalist minister and publisher, set up a new weekly newspaper called *The Hangman* to press the case against the gallows, he stuffed its pages with numerous reports of scheduled executions foiled by inmates who took their own lives. In one of its first issues in May 1845, *The Hangman* published the suicide note of a South Carolina man sentenced to death for the murder of his stepmother. It was addressed to the sheriff: "Dear Sir,—I have saved you the trouble. AMBROSE H. JONES. I am innocent of the charge." A week later, Spear reported that a Hoboken woman had hanged herself from the stovepipe of a county jail after robbing and killing her brother. "Did she do wrong?" he asked, before slyly reminding readers of earlier reformers' insistence that the state's death-dealing powers implied a right to suicide. "Was it not as right and proper for this murderess to hang herself, as it would have been for the hangman to do the deed?" Almost every new issue contained similar stories of inmate suicide, each one annotated with this sort of commentary. "No fact is more notorious in this country, than the attempt of the criminal to be his own executioner," the editor told *The Hangman*'s several thousand readers by way of explanation.[71]

Charles Spear leavened this grim diet of death with powerful pleas that lawmakers replace all capital convictions with corporal punishment and

"An Innocent Man Preparing for Execution." Following John Colt's suicide in New York's Tombs in 1842, antigallows authors took to reminding their readers of the psychological torments that drove condemned men to take their lives. G. W. Quinby, *The Gallows, The Prison and the Poor-House: A Plea for Humanity* (Cincinnati: G. W. Quinby, 1856). Courtesy of the American Antiquarian Society.

reformative incarceration. Surveying the use of the lash in Russia, he told *The Hangman*'s hardy readership that "so far as I know, no Russian has yet committed suicide in order to escape it." Likewise, in January 1846, Spear circulated a questionnaire "To the Wardens of State Prisons throughout the Union" in hopes of gathering data to prove his conviction that most long-term prisoners were rarely visited by the torment and terror that seemed to drive so many death-row inmates to tear their sheets into strips.[72]

In Rush's day most Americans would have refused to consider the psychological distress wrought on the condemned man as a justification for abolishing the gallows. Yet in the wake of Colt's suicide, activists succeeded in exploiting plunging middle-class tolerance for the spectacles of bodies in pain. "It is becoming quite common for humane persons now to sympathize deeply with the prisoner," Spear told readers of *The Hangman* in October 1845. "Formerly it was not so. We are beginning to understand that though he has erred, yet he is to be forgiven, and may be reclaimed." This was a sign of the times. Indeed, rising sensitivity to the suffering of others was one of the defining characteristics of middle-class life in the first half of the nineteenth century. Representing the suicides of indigents, factory workers, natives, and slaves in order to prick middle-class consciences and reform the social and political institutions that oppressed them thus became a central component of most antebellum reform efforts.[73]

Profound changes in patterns of religious belief and practice not only signaled but also shaped this continuing moral realignment. Indeed, the preponderance of Universalists among the ranks of antigallows activists was significant. The stunning growth of Universalism during the Jacksonian era had led many converts to this upstart liberal denomination to announce their hope that every sinner might one day be welcomed in heaven. Prominent Universalists such as Charles Spear and Horace Greeley had thus become very interested in the causes of criminality and tended to stress environmental determinism over innate depravity.

In the aftermath of the Colt case, Spear, Greeley, and their allies paired emerging discomfort that the death penalty was driving so many condemned men to suicide with their other arguments for abolition. In a battery of purposefully provocative pamphlets and reports, antigallows reformers positioned their newest line of attack alongside two by-now-familiar claims: first, that civil government exceeded its authority each time it usurped God's singular right to deprive man of life, and, second, that executions always corrupted the sensibilities of those who observed them. This tripartite offensive—each element of which placed the relationship between self-destruction and the scaffold at its heart—slowly made converts to the cause, enough to fill the ranks of several state organizations not just in New York, Massachusetts, and Pennsylvania but also in Ohio, Indiana, Iowa, Tennessee, Louisiana, and Alabama.[74]

By the mid-1840s the antigallows movement was at the height of its powers. While its size and reach never equaled those of allied campaigns against slavery and hard liquor, and although its leaders suffered relentless attacks on their character and motives, death penalty reformers had nevertheless succeeded in finally seizing control of the terms of the debate. For decades, officials at every level of the criminal justice system had invoked inmate suicides as dangerous challenges to the state's prerogative to punish by death—and hence as symbolic attacks on the legitimacy of every other tie that bound their society together. Now the shoe was on the other foot. George Cheever, the fierce Presbyterian opponent of death-penalty abolition, spent the ten years after Colt's death disputing campaigners' repeated claims that such suicides demonstrated the self-defeating barbarity of state executions. In stump speeches, pamphlets, and even in a series of feisty debates between himself and John O'Sullivan at the Broadway Tabernacle in 1842, Cheever found himself forced to take the line that the suicides of condemned men manifested welcome proof of the deterrent value of capital punishment:

> But you object that it *leads* to suicide. We answer, that it places suicide itself as a terrific consequence of crime, a terrific form of vengeance uprising behind the shade of the murdered man to the murderer's own view. It places the crime of murder on one side—a public execution or suicide on the other, with no possible alternative.

Most petitions, votes, and referendums pressing for total abolition were still falling short, but the gap was closing. Fewer and fewer respectable people still regarded executions as unimpeachable mechanisms for the display of righteous state power. Over time, middle-class sympathies had slowly drifted away from the judges, jurors, and jail staff willing to go to extraordinary, sometimes quixotic, lengths to prevent cell-block suicides.[75]

Now the wind was blowing in the other direction. Activists driven to speak out either by what had happened in Salem in 1830 or by John Colt's death ten years later, in 1842, now found a ready audience for their argument that the brutality of the death penalty could be measured in the number of suicides it generated. Several decades of efforts to pare back the authority of the criminal justice system to a point that might better balance the competing interests of liberty and order in a republican system of government seemed on the verge of bearing fruit. Finally, in 1847, Michigan became the first modern jurisdiction to outlaw all state executions. Wisconsin and Rhode Island followed suit soon afterward. "It will not be long before capital punishment will be banished from every State of this great and glorious Union," Tobias Purrington, a Democrat in the Maine Senate, boasted in a report to that body published in 1852.[76]

As it turned out, Purrington's prediction would prove to be spectacularly wrong. After these few precious victories, more pressing priorities quickly overwhelmed legislators in other states. Already by 1847 the growing conflict with Mexico had begun to distract the campaign's hard-won legislative allies from the task at hand. The fighting in the West also gave political cover for defenders of the death penalty to force through a slate of expedient half measures that postponed executions for a year after sentencing. Then, in the tense peace that followed the end of hostilities with Mexico in 1848, escalating disputes about slavery and sectionalism quickly suffocated this and every other reform agenda. When the Civil War finally came, it stifled any hope of further antigallows legislation for the duration.[77]

This string of setbacks reflected the ferocity with which defenders of the death penalty responded once they saw that public sympathies were beginning to swing toward the reformers' cause. Over the twenty years following the Salem trials of 1830, Cheever and other gallows supporters had ratcheted up a smear campaign that plumbed new lows in public discourse. Tarring Universalist leaders of the movement such as Spear and Greeley as dissolute apologists for murder and suicide, they warned that the end of capital punishment would lead to anarchy, mob justice, and widespread lynching. In fact, Congregational and Presbyterian defenders of the death penalty succeeded in putting the entire Universalist social agenda on trial during the 1830s and 1840s. Linking arms with Methodist recruiters eager to stop the spread of this hopeful new gospel of universal salvation, this unlikely coalition eventually succeeded in branding Universalism as little more than a suicide cult slavishly followed by deists and deviants who could not tell right from wrong.

5

The Threshold of Heaven

In some ways the saddest suicides were those that seemed to slip by unnoted. Despite prevailing panics regarding the proclivities of novel-reading teenagers and condemned criminals, no one paid much heed when a lonely old man named George Richards killed himself in March 1814. Details of his death were sparse and hard to come by. Most newspaper readers learned only that this poor, apparently deranged ex-clergyman had hanged himself in a basement ward of the Pennsylvania Hospital. Other than that, his death went almost unheeded. While a few old friends mourned his passing, no one else gave a second thought to the suicide of a former preacher who had lost his pulpit, then his wife and his sight, and then finally his mind.[1]

At one time George Richards had been one of the most important religious leaders in America. A prolific if prosaic hymnodist, Richards had written the first Universalist songbook and had also helped draft this new denomination's profession of faith in 1803. He had led a thriving Universalist society in Portsmouth, New Hampshire, for more than a decade before a dispute over salary forced him from his meetinghouse in 1809. Relocating to Philadelphia, he took over a new pastorate there before resigning after just three years, citing difficulties with his congregation. A few months later he was dead, struck down by sorrow and confusion. His friends held a low-key memorial service and then left him to rest in peace in the city's recently opened Universalist cemetery.[2]

Less than two decades later, everything had changed. When a Universalist minister named Alfred Bassett cut his throat in Dedham, Massachusetts, in 1831, local Congregational and Baptist leaders made it a cause célèbre, seizing on the news as damning proof that Universalism was a suicide cult. Stripping Bassett's death of its context and complexity, rivals of this upstart new church spent the better part of the 1820s, 1830s, and 1840s invoking his suicide and hundreds of others as evidence that Universalism's distinctive promise of salvation for all removed every moral barrier to self-murder and indeed sanctioned it as a shortcut to heaven.[3]

Universalists fought tooth and nail to defend themselves and tried similar tactics to stain their orthodox and evangelical competitors with the same bloody stigma. In doing so, a small army of Universalist preachers, newspaper editors, and pamphleteers took particular aim at the hysterical soul storms sometimes stirred at the revival meetings that had become so popular among other faith groups. With crocodile tears, Universalists wailed that the emotional excesses of these signature expressions of heart religion were plunging thousands of evangelical Methodists, Baptists, Presbyterians, and Congregationalists each year into paroxysms of religious despair that too often ended in suicide.

Placing the focus on this unfamiliar dimension of the often-told story of the democratization of American Christianity allows us to trace the course of a long and tense argument about the power and purpose of faith in the newly United States. Their no-holds-barred fight to cast each other as nurseries of self-destruction—that most extreme embodiment of social disaffection—reveals the extent to which Universalists and their rivals approached the unmistakable social and political problems manifest in the tumult of the early Republic from fundamentally different positions. For their part, Universalists embraced the bustling, confounding, and irksome diversity of life in the new nation and insisted upon the liberal, democratic, and decidedly populist creed that we are all brothers in this life and heaven bound in the next. Widespread recognition of common fellowship and destiny, they argued, would not only act as a new check on self-indulgent or self-destructive behavior but would also be sufficient to tamp down other individualistic impulses, curb escalating violence, exploitation, and inequality, inspire majestic acts of benevolence, and bind us all together. Under the Universalist banner, the American people might finally reject the last vestiges of authoritarian social control and instead build a sustainable political community upon the bonds of brotherhood.[4]

By contrast, they painted their competitors in this cutthroat religious marketplace as dangerously reactionary. Demonstrating their own raw ambition for members and market share, Universalists conveniently elided major differences in Calvinist and Arminian beliefs about sin and the prospect of salvation and refused to recognize the degree to which many evangelical leaders were suspicious of traditional sources of religious authority. Instead, Universalists argued that any faith predicated upon the prospect of selective (partial) salvation was fundamentally invested in a vision of the world in which judgment and punishment were central pillars. While terror and fear might well subdue and suppress the egalitarian urges of the unschooled and unsophisticated, Universalists spent the best part of thirty years trying to persuade men and women searching for faith that partialist dogma was an alienating and often lethal form of tyranny.

The Universalist Church came late to America. While the Methodist, Baptist, and Presbyterian denominations had emerged as challengers to established Congregational and Episcopalian orthodoxies long before the Revolution, John Murray settled the first Universalist congregation, a humble group of eighteen souls, in Gloucester, Massachusetts, in 1779. A disaffected English Methodist, Murray had been barred from George Whitefield's London tabernacle when he began preaching the ancient doctrine of universal salvation and so had upped sticks to New England. Three hundred miles away, in Philadelphia, Elhanan Winchester, an ex-Baptist minister and the son of a shoemaker, established his own Universalist society there two years later, in 1781.[5]

Uniting under the 1803 profession of faith that George Richards had brokered, the fledgling Universalist denomination soon numbered several high-profile patriots among its early converts, including Judith Sargent

Murray and Benjamin Rush. The latter had been raised by Presbyterian teachers who had insisted that only certain souls deserved to be saved. Yet after the Revolution, Rush had begun to question that doctrine and turned to Universalism as a faith system more closely aligned with the values of the great republican experiment he had come to champion. The central credo of the denomination—that salvation was an inalienable right granted to all by a benevolent creator—spoke powerfully to Rush and many other young republicans committed to finding a new balance between liberty and order. As Rush informed Jeremy Belknap, the Congregational clergyman, in 1791, "A belief in God's universal love to all his creatures . . . is a polar truth. It leads to truths upon all subjects, but especially upon the subject of government. It establishes the equality of all men."[6]

While obviously resonant in the context of the founding of this sprawling, muddling republic, the belief in God's universal love for all his creatures has a long history. Universalist writers often invoked St. Paul as their biblical inspiration and noted that all sorts of colonial sects had subscribed to one form of Universalism or another. Even stalwarts of New England's Congregational establishment, such as Charles Chauncy—Boston's "Old Brick"—had published occasional works arguing for universal salvation over the years. Indeed, as Universalists were quick to point out, their elegantly simple and forgiving doctrine was nothing more provocative than an attempt to apply reason to the inconsistencies they saw within Calvinist salvation theories. How, they asked, could a Calvinist God be benevolent when He damned those not among the elect to endless misery after their deaths? How could a merciful God be the author of a system of partial, partisan redemption? The Universalist preacher Alfred Bassett put this apparent contradiction in Congregational and Presbyterian theology in its starkest terms in a sermon he delivered over and over to audiences in and around Boston in the three years before his suicide: "Now the question to be settled is this, which must we believe without any qualification: The declaration that God will not cast off forever; or the one which says the wicked shall be turned into hell?" Proposing a vastly more optimistic and inclusive version of Calvinist predestination, one in which everyone now numbered among the elect, Universalists offered a gospel of comfort that banished the anguish of uncertainty that the doctrine of eternal punishment burned into men's hearts. "The idea that the Lord will not cast off forever," Bassett told Bostonians, "is full of consolation, and hope to the soul weary with the troubles, misfortunes, and trials of this woefraught world."[7]

Under the leadership of Hosea Ballou, another charismatic ex-Baptist, the Universalists quickly formalized the major tenets of their controversial faith. Rejecting anything that seemed to them arbitrary, illogical, or superstitious, they built a doctrinal system that proposed a unitarian understanding of the personality of God, denied that man's sins were original and eternal, and proclaimed that God's love would triumph over all. The only thing that Universalists disagreed about was whether wrongdoers would have to perform some limited penance in the afterlife before the gates of heaven opened to them. At first Ballou suggested that some type of limited future punishment was likely, a period of temporary purgation lasting perhaps fifty thousand years. But he soon backed away from that position and began to sympathize with those in his church convinced that God exacted all necessary punishment for this life's most heinous sins—rape, adultery, murder, and even, strikingly, suicide—through the rule of law and the weight of conscience. While leading figures within the church would argue privately about this subject until the 1850s, in public they initially tried to project a united front, speaking in one voice of their shared belief that their God would not punish finite sins with infinite torment.[8]

It was a powerful message well suited to the times. Aping the methods already mastered by Methodists and Baptists, dozens of rough-and-ready Universalist preachers traveled far and wide on horseback spreading their populist vision of a heavenly community of love and fellowship in which all markers of earthly status melt away. As a result, that vision found favor not only with cosmopolitan intellectuals like Benjamin Rush but also among journeymen and mechanics working long days for low pay in urban centers such as Boston and Philadelphia, struggling farmers and tradesmen in small northeastern towns who were suspicious of the affectations associated with evangelical revivalism, and disputatious free thinkers across the country who were spoiling for a fight. Much like the factious young Republic itself, the Universalist tent strained to contain a teeming, colliding jumble of people and interests. To be sure, the evangelical Baptists and Methodists were the ones who made the most hay from the breaking of church-state ties after the Revolution, but the Universalists offered daily proof that there was room too for a liberal, rationalist alternative.[9]

In fact Universalism thrived on such contrasts; the church's leading disputants strutted through the pages of the early American press like prizefighters and took every opportunity to drag their larger and better-funded rivals into bare-knuckle public brawls on all sorts of subjects. In 1839 the Vermont Congregationalist Andrew Royce, himself no shrinking violet when defending his own besieged church, offered exasperated testimony to the quarrelsome character of the expanding Universalist media machine:

> The spirit of their religious papers, generally, is one of unceasing and bitter warfare upon other denominations. They abound in profane jesting, calumnious insinuation and open slander, written as it were "with a serpent's fang, leaving deadly poison in every line." The most scurrilous political partizan papers of our land do not contain more of brutish and personal attack upon those who differ from them, than many of these papers contain.

As Royce was painfully aware, Universalists had at first concentrated most of their fire on the Congregational establishment. In 1793, for example, an early disciple named Joseph Young attacked the God of New England orthodoxy as tyrannical and depraved: "[He] has brought millions of beings into a state of existence out of a state of non-existence, in which case they were incapable of offending him, or suffering any inconvenience whatever, *knowing*, and having predetermined that they should be *punished in hell flames* to the *endless ages of eternity!*" Similar snipes, picks, and pokes at Universalism's closest theological cousin continued for decades, only drawing down slightly when Congregationalism's declining popularity began to tumble steeply in the 1840s.[10]

By then Universalists had found a far better foil. The rapid rise of evangelical denominations in the decades after the Revolution had been nothing short of spectacular: by 1811 more than one million Americans were attending revival meetings each year. The evangelical message—that individuals could play a part in securing their own salvation—seemed tailor-made to speak to the concerns of a shopkeeper class struggling to take control of its own destiny in a society buffeted by a perfect storm of social transformations. And unlike the sometimes chilly rationalism of Universalist doctrine, evangelicals placed compelling, soul-stirring rituals of conversion and revival at the heart of their faith.[11]

For Universalists eager for free publicity and the chance to define their brand of liberal Christianity on a national stage, there was no bigger target than evangelical religion. To believers in universal salvation committed to thinking their way coolly and carefully toward God and the rewards of heaven, the passionate extremes and convoluted theology of revivalism could not have been more offensive. Beginning around 1820, Universalists began to rip into revivalism at every opportunity. In Rhode Island, Jacob Freize called it madness, asking his Pawtucket congregation how anyone could believe that "his salvation depends entirely on God and partly on himself?" No one in their right mind would swallow such nonsense; that was why, Freize went on, the folk who came to revival meetings had to be "driven out of their senses, before they could consent to such preposterous absurdities." Some of his colleagues went further, calling revivalism priest-craft pure and simple and denouncing the disheveled firebrands who went from town to town whipping up vulnerable people into frenzies of existential despair about the state of their souls. In the incendiary language Universalists used to indict evangelicalism and to contrast it with their own clear-headed faith, they habitually libeled revival leaders as corrupt seducers who preyed (sometimes sexually) on "weak and credulous females."[12]

Universalist leaders were not afraid to make enemies. In fact their recruitment strategy depended upon their ability to snatch away the marginal members of other faiths, notably Congregationalism in New England and Methodism in New York and further afield. So as revivalists moved west in the 1820s and 1830s to target settlers of new states and territories, so too did the Universalists, punching and kicking their evangelical rivals as they went, in hopes of catching anyone shaken loose. By the early 1830s, plenty of people had forsaken their old faiths and put their lot in with the Universalists; the denomination boasted a small army of nearly three hundred itinerant preachers as well as statewide organizations from Alabama to Michigan. By some counts there were now almost half a million men and women who identified as Universalists, making theirs the fastest-growing major denomination in America.[13]

So bright did their prospects appear that in 1832 Thomas Whittemore, an irascible former bootmaker who now edited a widely read Universalist newspaper, suggested that all believers should celebrate a day of thanksgiving "in view of the rapid spread of the doctrine of Universalism, and the consequent happy change in the moral condition of society." This aggressive and self-confident new movement had burst onto the scene as if from nowhere and seemed poised to eclipse rival churches that had been around a lot longer. By 1832 Universalism was the sixth largest denomination in America, more sizable than the Unitarian Church and fast on the flagging heels of the Episcopalians. Looking over its own shoulder in 1834, one Congregational newspaper offered the snarling tribute that Universalism had become "the reigning heresy of the day."[14]

As such acid-tongued assessments suggest, Universalism's clawing rise did not go uncontested. Quite the opposite: as the church found traction at the expense of others across the theological spectrum, those rivals hit back decisively, denouncing Universalism as a naïve yet scurrilous heresy. As leaders from the Congregational, Episcopalian, Presbyterian, Methodist, Baptist, and even Unitarian churches frequently told their own members, the doctrine of universal salvation imagined a universe in which the fashion for equality trampled basic fairness. In a shot across the bows in 1826, the Congregational pastor Joel Hawes told New Yorkers that "[t]he doctrine of universal salvation is inconsistent with the character of God as a rewarder. . . . What is bestowed indiscriminately on all, is reward to none." By promising heaven to all, Universalists seemed to invert everything that most Americans understood about the way that religion and morality were supposed to work.[15]

More immediately, the perversity of the Universalist view of the hereafter seemed, in the eyes of its denominational competitors at least, to have dangerous social implications in the here and now. Because Universalist theology appeared to leave the relationship between God's mercy and his justice completely unbalanced, it apparently excused even the most monstrous sinners of their crimes. Even those Universalists who trusted in the prospect of some finite period of future punishment after death seemed dangerously permissive. "To say that punishment was limited," one historian of American religion has explained, "was not much different than saying that there was really no punishment at all." And no punishment meant no incentive not to sin or break the law. The doctrine of universal salvation "sweeps away every barrier to crime, and when reduced to practice forms a thoroughly depraved character," Congregational clergyman William Sprague told an audience in western Massachusetts in 1826. Other attacks frequently exploited this angle, characterizing Universalism as a faith system in which followers were left morally adrift by an emasculated God unhappily tethered to a "feminine sort of goodness" that "constrains him . . . to keep all sinners from pain." In a scathing piece aimed at shoring up Methodist support in New York in 1832, Wilbur Fisk offered a definition of universal salvation that dripped with contempt for such chamomile convictions:

> The plain language of this doctrine is, You ought not to be wicked, it is true; but if you are, God will love you just as well. Nay, it is impossible for you, however rebellious you may be, to forfeit his love. Heaven shall be yours; fear not. In the midst of all your blasphemies, and all your uncleanness, and all your excesses; yea, in your extortions, your robberies, your murders, rejoice and be exceeding glad, for heaven, with all its weight in glory, is yours.

In the wake of some of the most dramatic social upheavals in American history, it was easy for men like Fisk to represent the Universalist message as a recipe for mayhem and lawlessness entirely unsuited to the chaos of the times. The implicit contrast was obvious: a belief in eternal judgment was the safest way to steer errant individuals back toward virtuous conduct and preserve whatever was left of the social order.[16]

Other critics of Universalism were even less circumspect. Appealing directly to middling heads of household concerned about rising crime and crumbling respect for authority in the new Republic, Rhode Island Congregationalist James Davis portrayed the Universalist Church as a refuge for criminals; a faith too fey and feeble to curb the selfish wickedness of its growing membership:

> If this doctrine of Universal Salvation is true, men are encouraged to continue in sin. Remove from the human mind all fear of future

> retribution and punishment, and you encourage them to remain in rebellion. . . . He says to the murderer, slay your victim, you shall be safe after death. He says to the thief, go on in your depredations, you shall be safe after death. He says to the whoremonger, go on in your sacrifice of female innocence, after death you shall be safe. He says to the traitor of his country, go on in your career, you shall be safe after death. He says to the liar, the adulterer, and the incendiary—the drunkard, the swindler, and the pirate—go on in your work, you have nothing to fear after death! What a doctrine is this!

To try to make all this stick, the new church's many rivals took to identifying dozens of high-profile criminals, including Dick Crowninshield, the Salem murderer, as closet Universalists. With crusading zeal, they charged that the country's jails and prisons were bulging at the seams with unrepentant delinquents, scoundrels, and perverts convinced that God would one day have to forgive them.[17]

Yet Universalist leaders gave as good as they got. They invested early and heavily in the tools of print communication, setting up more than 130 newspapers, several of which attracted more than five thousand subscribers a month. They mounted an impressive rapid response operation and never let an accusation made against them in the press go unchallenged. "If a paragraph appears in any periodical reflecting, in the least degree, on them or their doctrines, it is made the basis of a labored and spirited defence," wrote New York Presbyterian Edwin Hatfield in the introduction to his own book-length takedown of Universalism. Sure enough, within weeks, Universalists answered Hatfield's 340-page screed with an equally shrill blast only twenty pages shorter.[18]

Even though they were fighting on several fronts, Universalist leaders seemed to have ready-made answers to almost all the criticism hurled at them. Most importantly, they refused to accept the premise of claims that their theology lacked the teeth to discourage believers from corruption, crime, and all manner of other assaults on the fragile social order. On the contrary, spokesmen argued both in public and in private that the promise that all would be saved created powerful new bonds of brotherhood that would check every selfish and atomizing impulse. "These principles," Benjamin Rush had written to a friend back in 1787, "have bound me to the whole human race; these are the principles which animate me in all my labors for my fellow creatures." "Who, believing and realizing this, can be unkind?" agreed *Trumpet* editor Thomas Whittemore a half century later. "Who can be entirely engrossed in his own welfare?" True moral compliance, Universalists never tired of explaining to anyone who would listen, need not be predicated on the threat of future punishment but should derive instead from a social conscience—or sensibility—grounded in benevolence and an enlightened concern for one's fellow man. Righteousness should be its own reward.[19]

As if to prove the point, many prominent members of the church self-consciously devoted themselves to various worthy social causes. "[T]here is no duty of our holy religion that is more earnestly enjoined, and to the performance of which there is attached a most lasting reward, than that of Benevolence," Henry Bacon explained at a fund-raiser for the Universalist Female Charitable Institute in Cambridge, Massachusetts, in 1836. Steadfast in the belief that actions spoke louder than words, princes of the church such as Benjamin Rush and Charles Spear led the charge against the death penalty—a cause in perfect sync with their faith's challenge to traditional understandings of the purpose of punishment—while other Universalists took major roles in campaigns promoting temperance, abolition, prison reform, and public education.[20]

That still left all those supposed Universalist criminals to account for. When he learned that several Boston papers had repeated rumors that Dick Crowninshield had been a believer, Thomas Whittemore, the fierce and unyielding editor of the *Trumpet*, told readers that nothing made him more furious than all the recent attempts to "represent all murderers and other vicious characters as believers of Universalism." Whittemore would not stand for it and instructed his fellow editors to hit back at anyone who accused his church of sheltering or nurturing such monsters. Indeed, several of his colleagues already had. For instance, a few years earlier, in 1824, the Universalist *Gospel Advocate* had tried to shift the burden of proof by surveying the religious demography of the new prison in Auburn, New York:

> Let facts speak. The State Prison in this city contained, a few days since, 623 criminals, of various faith and religion; but, NOT ONE

> UNIVERSALIST AMONG THEM ALL!! The Editor of this paper went through the various departments of this gigantic reservoir of depravity . . . and heard, from the lips of the delinquents, their confession, that they believed in the endless misery of the wicked.

Whittemore had been thrilled with the piece and encouraged subsequent investigations at Sing Sing and other large penitentiaries in New York and New England over the next two decades. Unsurprisingly, each one produced similar findings; an 1838 probe even claimed to have turned up "seven preachers of endless misery" doing time in a prison in Charlestown.[21]

This characteristically bold offense served to distract attention from several crippling weaknesses in the Universalist defense. For one thing, they were having real trouble undermining allegations that the nation's worst criminals were members of their church. Persistent claims that most murders were committed by men confident of their place in heaven dogged the movement as it tried to muscle its way into the mainstream. With so many of these monsters dead either by their own hands or at the hands of the state, it was usually impossible for Universalists to disprove a connection after the fact. So, instead, church leaders like Hosea Ballou cried foul, protesting that jealous rivals had twisted the true tenets of the denomination's central doctrine, misrepresenting it as a morally spineless creed that dismantled the most fundamental barriers to lawlessness by removing all punishment for sin.

It did not. As Ballou tried to explain time and again, universal salvation simply confined punishment to a finite period. Of course he refused to be drawn, at least at first, on whether Universalists viewed death as the beginning or the end of this temporary period of punishment. This was a costly but necessary concession to the factions within his church that had not yet agreed on a position on that subject. Throughout the first few decades of the nineteenth century, the highest echelons of the Universalist leadership were almost evenly divided. On the one side stood Ultra-Universalists like *Trumpet* editor Thomas Whittemore who believed sufficient punishment for sin was exacted by earthly laws and human conscience in this life and that salvation followed immediately on the heels of death. On the other stood Restorationists like the volatile Massachusetts clergyman Jacob Wood who believed in a form of purgatory in the world to come prefacing eternal salvation. Hamstrung by these differences, defenders of the faith dodged and wheeled each time rivals painted Universalism as a particularly insipid brand of atheism. All they could do was repeat the only language that both Ultras and Restorationists could agree on: sinners will face punishment, either in this world or the next.

As Universalist spokesmen trod gingerly around the subject of limited punishment, opponents smelled opportunity. Beginning around 1820, as the Universalist Church's appealing message and talent for self-promotion catapulted it into the national spotlight, Old Lights joined with New Lights and even Unitarians to launch what soon became a coordinated campaign to divide Ultras and Restorationists for good. They chose the perfect wedge. In 1819 the editors of *Kaleidoscope*, an opinion-setting Unitarian magazine, dared Universalists to answer a simple question: Was Judas in heaven? After betraying Christ and then hanging himself soon afterward, had Judas been made to pay—either for his treachery or for his suicide? The church's usual gladiators could not ignore the challenge, nor could they agree on a common response. Yet instead of biting their tongue, members of both the immediatist and eventualist factions spoke out, each with their own explanation as to whether or when Judas faced judgment. They had taken the bait.[22]

The Judas question quickly turned what had once been little more than an internal dispute over a seemingly minor doctrinal issue into a full-fledged fight within the Universalist society. Restorationists, led by Jacob Wood, rushed into print to argue that Judas had of course faced punishment after his death for both his disloyalty and his self-murder, though Wood refused to be drawn on "how long or great the condemnation of Judas may be." Instead, he turned his fire on the Ultra belief that all punishment was confined to the terms of this life and that death was the threshold of heaven. Wood could see why rivals had asked about Iscariot and showed no qualms in joining them to demand that Ultras answer pointed questions about him. Because Judas had hanged himself so soon after betraying Christ, when did Ultras think his punishment for his treachery had occurred? And what of the fact that his precipitous death had been self-inflicted? Was this not a second crime? Would Judas never be held accountable for it? "[T]he doctrine of immediate universal salvation gives force to the temptations of sin," Wood concluded, referring to Judas's suicide as a case in point. Ultraism, he warned, could too easily be misrepresented as moral cowardice because it seemed to promise that a man like Iscariot "may end his sorrows by suicide, and instantly reach the pure abodes of heavenly felicity."[23]

Opponents of Universalism embraced this damning logic with gusto over the next three decades, amplifying Wood's internecine critique of Ultraism so that it reached a broad national audience. In a popular American Tract Society pamphlet, Congregational minister Joel Hawes told New Yorkers that the doctrine of immediate universal salvation "represents God as often treating wicked men far better than he does the righteous." If Ultra-Universalists were to be believed, Hawes wrote, wicked men like Judas may commit suicide and then be "taken directly to heaven; while the righteous are left to linger out, in this vale of tears, the full term of their earthly being, and arrive late at the kingdom."[24]

The Ultraists had been ambushed. Caught off guard, immediatist spokesmen blurted two hasty responses to the Judas question, neither of which silenced their critics. In one early answer to the *Kaleidoscope*, an Ultraist editorial in the *Christian Messenger* wondered aloud whether the scriptures actually condemned self-destruction, arguing that the ambivalence in the language used to describe biblical suicides made moot the question of whether Judas would face postmortem punishment for taking his own life. Congregationalists like Hawes sounded positively exuberant when they relayed this line of reasoning to their membership; to them it was incriminating proof that Universalism placed no moral obstacles in the way of desperate or despicable men who had determined to die. Immediatist leaders soon saw their strategic mistake and had to quickly backtrack, retreating to a narrower exegetical response to the Judas question. Drawing on new scholarship, Ultra-Universalist magazine columnists now argued that the Greek words used to describe Iscariot's death in particular referred not to suicide but to rapid mortal decay. While the received translation of the book of Matthew was that Judas "hanged himself," a piece in the 1820 *Christian Messenger* suggested that a more accurate translation showed that Judas "died with anguish," the subject of a swift physical or moral decline brought on by his remorse, but not necessarily volitional or suicidal in intent. The same author noted that a passage in the book of Acts that also describes Judas's death does not mention suicide, but merely that he died when his bowels fell out. It was as if his death was also his punishment.[25]

While Ultras spent the early 1820s quibbling about scripture to try to reject the premise of the Judas question, rival churches expanded their attacks. Refusing to let Ultras hide behind the Bible's petticoats, they left Iscariot behind and instead began to demand that Universalist leaders explain when and where ordinary Americans who committed suicide would face punishment. To exploit what now appeared to be a growing schism within Universalism, Calvinist and Arminian pamphleteers and newspaper editors began publishing numerous accounts of the suicides of supposed Universalists, holding up each desolate act as an accusation that the doctrine of immediate universal salvation was a gutless sham unwilling to punish self-murder and incapable of imposing meaningful order upon the individual members of a blighted society many believed was now spinning out of control. Ultra-Universalism, men like Hawes began to chant in the 1820s, made promises of unconditional salvation after death that turned this upstart new faith into little more than a suicide cult.

After ten years of marriage, Harriet Leonard had had enough. She and her husband Samuel had been married only two months when something had changed in him. Ever since, he had become impossible to live with, shouting at her and their ever-growing brood of children almost daily and threatening Harriet with a beating whenever she talked back. Unable to divorce him, Harriet turned to the Congregational Church close to her home in western Massachusetts for strength and for fellowship. But her newfound faith only made Samuel madder. According to an account written by the minister of Harriet's church in Springfield, her husband hated it when she left the house to go to worship. When she returned, he would often "snatch the Bible from her hands, and cast it across the room, with great violence, in token of his displeasure." He treated his seven children no better, and "if he saw them reading the Bible, or any other serious book, he would often profanely rebuke them, and bid them substitute a Universalist magazine." Why Samuel Leonard was so angry, miserable, and bitter at heart goes unrecorded, but his symptoms of deep depression soon gave way to thoughts of suicide. He made four attempts to kill himself, by poison and by rope, before Harriet finally plucked up the courage to leave him on December 13, 1825, promising her children that they would join her within days. The next morning Samuel appeared at her parents' door with news that their baby daughter was sick. Harriet dutifully followed him home, where he beat her head in with an ax before cutting his own throat. "His daughter of eleven years of age," Harriet's minister said, "lay upon the bed, and witnessed the whole transaction."[26]

For anyone hoping to use the suicides of ordinary Americans to paint Universalism into a theological corner, this tragic tale had all the necessary elements. William Sprague, the Congregational minister Harriet had risked so much to hear each week, certainly wasted no time. In a memorial sermon he preached and published with the ostensible purpose of celebrating Harriet's life and character, Sprague pointed a righteous finger at the Universalist Church and demanded that it be held responsible for this bloody violence. Anyone who believes that salvation is universal and guaranteed, Sprague explained, "cuts himself off from an appeal to the immutable distinction between right and wrong." Without the dread of infinite future punishment common to all respectable faiths, how were Universalists like Samuel Leonard to distinguish virtue from vice, and what incentive had they to retreat from sin? "There is nothing more likely," Sprague went on, "to constitute the foundation, or to accelerate the progress, of a grossly depraved habit, than a belief in the doctrine of universal salvation."[27]

Although his congregation and his readers had to take on trust Sprague's claims that Samuel kept Universalist books and magazines in his house, the minister was unequivocal: this domestic massacre was deadly proof that Universalism lacked the punitive apparatus necessary to deter its members from the most heinous sins imaginable. "Why is it," he asked, "that the doctrine of which I am speaking, makes so conspicuous a figure, in the annals of suicide?" Like any preacher worth his salt, Sprague was ready with the answer: "A God, who desires so much the happiness of his creatures, that he can save the most abandoned of them, in their sins, will not be offended if, by a self-destroying act, they shorten a little the path to Heaven." "Why not a little pain," he sardonically concluded, "in order to stop the vital current, when, the moment the work is done, the glories of heaven are bursting upon the soul?" Of course, Restorationists like Jacob Wood had never suggested that heaven bursts upon the soul at the moment of death. Yet Sprague was not interested in nuance. In fact, it served his purposes well to conflate Universalism as a whole with the immediatist faction within it and to ignore the subtlety of Restorationist notions of limited future punishment entirely.[28]

Sprague was not alone in trying to forge a link between Universalism and the "alarming progress" of suicide in the early United States; indeed, his voice was soon lost among a growing chorus proclaiming that universal salvation was so morally frail that it effectively encouraged people to take their own lives by failing to punish them for doing so. Ever since a Unitarian antagonist had pressed Ultras and Restorationists on the state of Judas Iscariot's eternal soul in 1819, similarly awkward questions had become mantra. By 1826, Methodists, Baptists, Congregationalists, and Presbyterians—in short, all the faiths slowly ceding ground to the rapidly advancing Universalist movement—were already hard at work on print campaigns designed to stigmatize the Universalist Church as a cradle of self-destructive thought and action. A sampling of their printed attacks published between 1820 and 1850 suggests that more than three-quarters used the suicide question as ammunition.[29]

It was a canny maneuver. For one thing, many segments of society were already accustomed to interpreting individual acts of self-destruction as embodied examples of the deficit of deference rending the social fabric of the new nation. For that reason, most Americans still considered it heresy to suggest that suicide—in the abstract at least—was anything less than the blackest of crimes. Abolitionists had recently embarked on a campaign of their own to cultivate northern sympathy for southern slaves driven to suicide by the prospect of the lash or the auction block. But in the 1820s most middling people still found it immensely difficult to privilege their complicated and conflicted feelings for particular individuals driven to take their own lives over their bone-deep conviction that the act itself was beyond the pale. The uproar following immediatists' tentative claims that the Bible might not condemn self-murder proved the same point. Thomas Upham, a Congregationalist who taught philosophy at Bowdoin College, said as much in 1836, opining that the idea that no man has a right to suicide is "a principle, upon which writers on moral philosophy, and mankind generally, are more universally agreed than almost any other." Indeed, in recent years, that positive certainty had served as the moral authority not only for humane society interventions to prevent suicide but also for calls to abolish the use of capital punishment.[30]

Suicides like Leonard's thus made perfect cudgels to clobber Ultra-Universalists about their belief that no future punishment occurred after death. Immediatists like the *Trumpet*'s volcanic editor Thomas Whittemore were used to explaining that men who committed crimes like murder, rape, or adultery spent the rest of their lives consumed by guilt and in fear that the law might catch up with them. Their lives were a kind of hell, these Ultras typically argued. But if believers committed not murder, rape, or adultery but suicide, every opportunity for earthly repentance surely vanished. "How can that man be said to receive in this life, either a disciplinary or a satisfactory punishment for the most heinous crime, in the very perpetration of which he dies instantaneously?" Presbyterian William McCalla asked his Ultra-Universalist opponent Abner Kneeland during a heated debate in a Philadelphia church hall in 1824. "Does the law of God," Methodist minister Timothy Merritt asked New Yorkers a few years later, "cease to condemn this last, murderous act, by which a man throws himself out of the world, and away from the place and means of repentance?"[31]

McCalla and Merritt had no interest in waiting for an answer. Their purpose was to define Universalism as a dangerously tolerant liberal fantasy that could condemn Jacksonian America to more bloody chaos. Poor Samuel Leonard was the perfect mark. In fact, attacks on Universalism published after 1820 gave readers the distinct impression that every domestic massacre in living memory had been committed by a follower of that faith. Merritt himself reintroduced American readers to William Beadle, the Connecticut merchant who had killed his wife, his children, and then himself in 1782, in the midst of a delusion that many at the time had attributed to deism. Only as Merritt now saw it, modern Universalism was the direct descendant of Beadle's deism. In the same vein, in 1825 Adam Empie told fellow North Carolina Episcopalians that Ultras' well-known devotion to rational deduction created the logical incentive for anyone who believed in immediate universal salvation to slay his family and then himself:

> [S]uppose all are fully persuaded of the Universalist doctrine, what could hinder those who were in a state of suffering, from committing

> suicide, and taking a short cut to heaven! In numberless instances, what could prevent a destitute, afflicted father of a family from murdering himself, after, in the plentitude of his mercy, he had murdered his wife and children! Would it not be natural for all the children of penury and sorrow to reason thus?

Moderate Universalists who had yet to pick a side in the church's internal debate about the consequences of sin thought this sort of reasoning was anything but natural. So as the blows rained down on the Ultraist position throughout the 1820s, its support among the rank-and-file members of the denomination nosedived. Restorationists like Jacob Wood, who ascribed to a belief in some limited form of postmortem punishment, seemed on the verge of carrying the day. That is, until Hosea Ballou waded into the fray.[32]

In 1832 Ballou published a treatise that declared immediate universal salvation the official position of the Universalist Church. His decision showed a stark disregard for tactical concerns and underlined his reputation for bold, independent thinking. Earlier in his career, Ballou had expressed support for the Restorationist view that sinners were likely to face some limited punishment after death. But throughout the recent controversy, he had remained silent. Now, in a spectacular reversal of his youthful endorsement of Restorationism, Ballou subscribed himself and his church to the Ultraist belief that punishment was confined to the period of one's life. Officially at least, Universalism and Ultraism were now one and the same. This caused an uproar within the church. A small group of New England Restorationists, led by David Pickering of Providence, went so far as to secede to form their own association. The more moderate majority expressed gaping disbelief that Ballou would wed their growing church to a doctrine so extreme it had proven almost impossible to defend over the previous decade.[33]

Ballou's decision was an extraordinary gift to Congregational and Methodist leaders. Attacks on Universalism as a dangerously lax form of magical thinking quickly surged to an all-time high following this 1832 declaration, and the vast majority now took up the cry that Universalism and suicide went hand in hand. Just weeks after Ballou announced his decision, Methodist itinerant Timothy Merritt reminded his readers that under Ultra-Universalism self-murderers "commit one of the greatest crimes, and yet do not remain a moment in the world to suffer for it." The last gloves were now off, and before the year was out, a Congregationalist minister from Malden, Massachusetts, put out the most scathing assault yet seen. In twenty sarcasm-drenched pages in a pamphlet that stormed through four editions in six years, Alexander Wilson McClure told readers that the "*great duty of Universalists as Universalists* is THE COMMISSION OF SUICIDE." With faux sincerity and ill-disguised scorn, McClure's *Lectures on Ultra-Universalism* urged anyone of that faith who found themselves overwhelmed by life's troubles to "[plunge] the knife into the faithful heart of your wife, then drive it up to the hilt into the bosom of each of the little ones whom you love too well to part with, and finally turn it with steady and pious hand, against your own manly breast."[34]

By McClure's count, there were in fact twelve reasons for devout Universalists to lift knives to their throats right away: to be happy, to escape misery, to be holy, to be consistent, to people heaven, to deny oneself, to honor heaven, to follow the example of "Saint Judas," to fulfill the scriptures, to please God, to show faith by works, and "to gain the confidence of the public." As he explained each one, McClure appended ghoulish suggestions for appropriate ways to die. For instance, after urging Universalists to commit suicide to escape from the misery of daily life, and to populate heaven, and to demonstrate their faithfulness, McClure described three different means to do so quickly and cleanly:

> How CAN ye escape the damnation of hell? With the utmost coolness and composure, they reply by putting their hands in their pockets, taking out their knives, and cutting their throats:—while the benevolent Jesus stands astonished and rejoiced to see how completely they have escaped the damnation of hell! . . .
>
> Go, then, my Universalist friend,—hasten to add one more accession to their joys. Choose some one of the many ways of emigrating to that land of promise. What say you to taking laudanum; and so sleeping the sleep of death? What say you to drowning?—water is the mirror of heaven, and the symbol of its purity:—go by water, then on your pilgrimage to increase the population of that holy land. . . .

> Since faith without works is dead, put life into your faith by putting a bullet into your skull, or two or three inches of cold iron into your heart, or a dose of poison into your bowels. Thus will the brightness of your hopes and the excellence of your system of truth become luminously and transcendently manifest.

"The way is plain—brethren," McClure smirked, "GO HANG. Amen."[35]

This was satire to be sure, but the message was unmistakable. As McClure admitted in a come-clean preface, he was using ridicule of the immediatist position to make believers "ashamed of the absurdities of their doctrine, and then they will be open to the approaches of common sense and scripture." Trying to lead by example, McClure told everyone else struggling to hold the line against the advance of Universalism across the new nation to take a page from his book:

> Push them with the suicide-argument, and they are down. Let not this powerful instrument of their confusion remain unemployed. As often as they would dispute with you, drive it down their throats: and they will soon be glad to let you alone; and if they have any conscience and honesty, they will let alone their doctrines too.

Judging by the frequency with which others repeated the essence of his attacks over the next few years, a lot of his colleagues took notice.[36]

Charges that the weakness of Universalist theology effectively encouraged suicide became so ubiquitous in American religious literature in the wake of Ballou's declaration that McClure was soon not the only critic bold enough to experiment with extremes of tone and form. Among the tide of denominational tracts, pamphlets, and newspapers that tried to drown Ballou's young church in blood in the 1830s and 1840s, Edwin Hatfield's 1841 diatribe, *Universalism as It Is*, also stands out. Attempting to equate his own campaign against immediate universal salvation with the moral suasion activities of Garrisonian antislavers, Hatfield offered a careful takeoff of the title and contents of Theodore Dwight Weld's *American Slavery as It Is* (1839). Indeed, Weld's arcade of images of black men and women driven to kill themselves by the horrors of the plantation system and the domestic slave trade elegantly anticipated the savage scenes Hatfield tried to conjure as he tore into Universalism. "It has always been a difficult matter for men of this sort to dispose of the suicide," he intoned at the book's conclusion. "In this case the crime is not consummated until life is extinct. The individual is then, if in conscious existence, in the future state. It is evident that he cannot be punished in this life, and if punished at all, must be in the life to come."[37]

As the link between Universalism and self-destruction became a stock in trade, one Methodist leader even ventured a poem on the same subject. Writing for an Ohio readership in 1846, Alexander Hall ended a nine-stanza assault on the doctrine of immediate universal salvation with two verses that raised the suicide question:

> How happy is the sinner's state,
> When he from earth is driven;
> He knows it is his certain fate,
> To go strait up to heaven!
>
> There's Judas too, another Jew,
> Whom some suppose accurs'd;
> "Yet with a chord, he beat his Lord,
> And got to heaven first!"

It was a none-too-subtle reminder that since taking the *Kaleidoscope*'s bait back in 1819, Universalists had still not satisfactorily explained how and when Judas paid for his treachery.[38]

As these attacks became ever more audacious, they also became increasingly pointed and personal. No longer content to rely on flimsy claims that a belief in immediate universal salvation had failed to stop laypeople like Samuel Leonard and Dick Crowninshield from committing suicide, critics active in the 1830s and 1840s began to fixate on the deaths of Universalist leaders they said had scrambled, in Alexander Hall's words, "to heaven on a rope ladder." "Several popular preachers of Universalism have left the world by their own hands," Matthew Hale Smith, a disgruntled and disillusioned ex-Universalist, announced in one of several book-length exposés of his former faith. What could be more damning, Smith reasoned, than the suicides of those most committed to and publicly associated with the doctrine of immediate universal salvation? For proof, Smith exhumed the memory of George Richards, explaining his long-overlooked 1814 suicide as the result of Ultraist error. In fact, Richards had been an articulate defender of Restorationism during his life, and no one at the time ever suggested that his death was the product of anything other than the loss of his wife and the ailing state of his body and mind. But Smith had no use for the truth and slotted Richards easily into a prime position on what he believed was an incriminating inventory of Universalist clergy who, by taking their own lives, had contributed to the suicide epidemic apparently consuming the young Republic.[39]

On one of the coldest days of 1831, the name of another well-known figure in the church was added to that list. The *Dedham Advocate* broke the news: "The Rev. ALFRED V. BASSETT, Pastor of the Universalist Society in this town, committed suicide on Monday night, December 26, by cutting his throat with a razor!" Bassett had had strong ties to the Universalist leadership; Thomas Whittemore, the redoubtable editor of the Boston *Trumpet* and second only to Hosea Ballou in the church's loose hierarchy, had been his mentor and had preached Bassett's ordination sermon in Dedham just eighteen months earlier. Since then the young preacher had built a reputation as a hard-nosed promoter of the comforts of universal salvation and had been at the center of Universalist recruitment efforts in and around Boston. Now he was gone.[40]

Acutely aware of how Bassett's suicide played into the bloody narrative that now seemed in danger of defining Universalism, Thomas Whittemore himself gave the eulogy at the funeral. When he arrived, he found the Universalist meetinghouse in Dedham packed with more than the usual number of people; members of the local Congregational and Baptist churches had invited themselves in to see how Whittemore would answer the question that hung in the air like a shroud. He did not disappoint: "I see two or three who are whispering, 'it was his doctrine that drove him to this. Here we see the dreadful effects of the sentiments he has defended.'" Whittemore would have none of it:

> No one who ever believed this sentiment will suppose it can make a man sick of life; and those who believe it know the influence of it better than those who do not. The deceased was heard to say, but a short

> time before his death, that he should prefer to suffer the heaviest lots of human ills, while blessed with the consolations of Universalism, rather than possess all the earth could afford, and believe in the horrid doctrines of the Calvinistic creed.

Bassett, he said, "had every thing earth could afford to render him happy." The blessings of family, friends, money, and reputation had all been his. Until the twenty-five-year-old's health had taken its recent turn, Alfred Bassett had enjoyed the daily fruits of divine favor; he had been living proof of a benevolent Creator.[41]

So why had Bassett cut his throat? The *Dedham Gazette* had reported that "Mr. Bassett had been unwell several days with the prevailing influenza, and complained of a pain in his head, from which it is supposed that a fever on his brain produced that derangement of mind which caused him to commit the fatal deed." This was the only explanation Thomas Whittemore would entertain. "The event of his death," Whittemore declared on the same spot where Bassett himself had stood the week before, "must be attributed to an alienation of mind, which his complicated diseases had produced." Whittemore had spoken to his protégé often over the last few months and had noticed all sorts of signs that he was not himself. "Once or twice of late, in my intercourse with him," the editor now recalled, "I had perceived that his conversation and statements slightly approached the marvelous; and I distinctly recollect telling him, a few weeks since, that he was insane, although all I meant by it at the time was that his language was extravagant." The influenza that had seized Bassett a week ago had only clouded his head more, Whittemore explained, and after last Sunday's service he had had some kind of fit that had left him mixed up and rattled. Whittemore could not say precisely why the young preacher had cut his throat, but "that he was not possessed of reason when the fatal act was done, is as certain, in my apprehension, as inference can make any thing." It was a compelling performance that balanced pathos with pugnacity. Whittemore made a strong case for the lunacy defense and avoided the larger questions of if, when, and how men who cut their throats faced judgment and retribution for doing so, insisting instead that Bassett's madness removed responsibility. His poor soul deserved pity, not punishment.[42]

Thomas Whittemore's forthright defense of Universalism was one example of what was quickly becoming a full-scale fight-back against the now-commonplace claim that the church's central doctrine was a major source of the "alarmingly frequent" number of suicides in the early United States. As early as 1820, Hosea Ballou had accused rivals who beat this particular drum of distracting the American people from the fact of his denomination's "now rapid progress." Similarly, when an 1824 issue of a Congregational paper reported the suicides of two young men in Boston under the headline "Universalism Favorable to Self-Murder," the sharp-eyed editor of the Universalist *Gospel Herald* had immediately shot back with a reply that combined ridicule with menace: "Supposing we were to publish the account of the treason of Benedict Arnold, and head the article 'Calvinism Favorable to Treason!' "[43]

Universalist polemicists did not wait long to make good on this threat. When Silas Bradley, a believer living in Potsdam, New York, cut his throat and bled to death in 1826, Jonathan Wallace, the local Universalist pastor, scrambled a sermon into print that tried to turn the tragedy to his church's advantage. He began by hitting the usual preemptory talking points, telling Potsdammers that his church was growing fast, not hemorrhaging slowly, one suicide at a time. But Wallace was not finished. "Facts are stubborn things," he said, and by his count the weight of evidence from all the self-inflicted deaths reported in the papers over the last few years pointed to Congregationalism, Methodism, and Baptism as more significant sources of suicidal ideation, not just here at home but throughout the Atlantic world. In what would soon become a hallmark of Universalist agitprop, Wallace went on to list the names of almost thirty members of those churches, including those of several deacons, who had recently taken their own lives. If this was to be a numbers game, the Universalists were determined to win it. "One hundred to one of the cases of suicide which occur in the world, are by believers in endless misery," the Potsdam pastor announced.[44]

Universalist bulldogs snarled similar retorts over and over again throughout the 1820s and beyond. In Massachusetts, writers for the *Universalist Magazine* and the (Universalist) *Evangelical Repository* responded to the libelous claims that Congregational clergy like William Sprague had made against their faith after Samuel Leonard's suicide by putting out a list of "the names, places of residence, &c. of sixteen members of CALVINISTIC CHURCHES, who have committed similar deeds, in the same region." The list included one reverend, one deacon, and Sprague's own aunt "who hung herself with a skein of yarn." With barely a morsel of evidence, editors described each of these tragic deaths as the direct and unambiguous consequence of the Calvinist belief that only some would be saved. "We have not the least doubt," the *Repository* explained in April 1826, "but that many of these unhappy victims are led to these fatal crimes by the soul-paralyzing, reason-destroying doctrine of endless reprobation and misery." In contrast to their own sunny soteriology, Universalists took to framing Congregationalism and Presbyterianism as gloomy faiths that offered little hope to earnest believers convinced that they were not among the elect. The (Universalist) *Gospel Herald* pointed to another clutch of recent deaths that seemed to serve this point before drawing the lesson: "Let Calvinists no longer condemn Universalists as believing a doctrine which makes 'a conspicuous figure in the annals of suicide,' for they, who judge, do the same thing, and more abundantly."[45]

In the course of this campaign, Universalist writers singled out the suicides of ministers of rival faiths for special scrutiny. Because clergy were so closely identified with the doctrines they espoused, Universalist editors and pamphleteers found it all too tempting to argue that their dogma had been a factor in their deaths. For instance, when Daniel Lovejoy, a Congregational minister from Albion, New York, hanged himself in his barn in 1833, Thomas Whittemore told readers of the *Trumpet* that local papers had it wrong. "The papers state that he was partially deranged; but do not add, what we believe was the fact, that his derangement was none other than the effect of religious melancholy." "He doubted his being one of the elect," Whittemore went on, "and this consideration preyed fatally upon his mind." Apparently Whittemore saw no contradiction between this analysis and the skillful way he had bracketed the influence of his own faith's doctrines upon Alfred Bassett just a few months earlier.[46]

Reports of Calvinist ministers killing themselves became a staple in Universalist newspapers in the 1820s and 1830s, but the suicides of their wives made for even better copy. Thus when word reached them of the drowning of the unnamed spouse of a Presbyterian clergyman in Manlius, New York, several Universalist papers, including Manhattan's *Gospel Herald* and the

Philadelphia Universalist Magazine, turned it into a major story. Each described her as "another VICTIM to the gloomy, heart-rending, and LIFE DESTROYING doctrine of eternal, cruel, and unmerciful sufferings." And they had a letter to prove it—a firsthand account of this poor woman's final weeks purportedly written by a close friend of the family. "For about three months she had been in a very melancholy and even despairing state of mind," the letter began. Despite years of dutiful service as the exemplary wife of a respected minister, she had suddenly lost hope of heaven and had told friends that she feared her God had intentionally and irretrievably consigned her to perdition. "From that time she seemed to lose her hold on earth," and when she began to make dark threats, her family hid razors and knives from her. On one tumultuous night she found the stash, slashed at her throat, and ran to a bridge before jumping from it into the river below.[47]

The Universalist papers portrayed the relationship between this woman and her clergyman husband as central to understanding her suicide. In an overt and certainly quixotic attempt to try to exoticize Presbyterianism, editors drew a parallel to the Hindu practice of widow-burning in order to imply that this poor woman's death was the result of dogged and misplaced allegiance to her husband and his faith. "It is believed that the victims who have fallen under this God-dishonoring doctrine, within a few years (since "Revivals" have become so frequent,) far exceed the number who have died on the funeral pile, as three to one," the *Gospel Herald* editorialized. The delight some Universalist editors seemed to take in reporting stories like this was almost palpable. In fact, when Richard Storrs awoke to find his wife Harriet hanging from a beam at their Braintree, Massachusetts, home in July 1834, Thomas Whittemore described it as the Congregational minister's just deserts:

> While we mingle our sorrows with those of Mr. Storrs on this occasion, it becomes our duty to call to his recollection the many hard things he has said against the doctrine of universal grace. . . . How many times has he declared that the doctrine of Universalism leads to suicide? Was this dreadful case, in his own family, caused by a belief in Universalism? What great sorrow was it that prostrated the noble mind of his amiable wife, and drove her to the commission of suicide? It certainly was not Universalism that caused it. We pray

> that this affliction may be sanctified to his good,—that it may lead him to review his past course, and to inquire, very seriously, whether the charge which he has brought against Universalism, of leading to suicide, is not altogether groundless.

Using lines drawn from a leading Congregational newspaper's account of Harriet Storrs's death, Whittemore told his subscribers that the cause of her suicide was not in doubt:

> For several months past, "her soul has been full of trouble," for she thought that God had "laid her in the lowest pit, in darkness, in the deeps, that his wrath was lying hard upon her," "that she was cast out of his sight, and should never be again permitted to look towards his holy temple." "She longed for death," and it has come.

"O dreadful effect of orthodoxy!" wailed Whittemore with ill-disguised satisfaction.[48]

These partisan scare stories derived much of their narrative power from the suggestion that these devoted young women had been somehow indoctrinated by their charismatic and overbearing husbands. The mention of widow-burning hinted at all this and more. Thus when Universalists looked beyond ministers and their wives for other examples of cultish suicides within the Congregational and Presbyterian churches, they often alighted on laywomen who had developed close relationships with local preachers. Under headlines like "Another Sacrifice Offered to Moloch" or "Horrible Effects of the Doctrine of Endless Misery," Universalist editors turned their pages into a graveyard for dead Calvinist women. "Again a victim has been immolated on superstition's fatal altar," a writer calling himself Philanthropist declared after a woman from Rockingham, North Carolina, cut her throat in 1820. She was "under the conviction that she was an object of Divine wrath and would not be saved," he explained. A year later, an item published in several Universalist papers told readers that it was the ministers themselves who had the blood of these young women on their hands:

> Go to their houses of terror—hear them tell of lakes of fire, gulfs of flame, and the agonizing groans of the damned! Groans rung from

> their bleeding bosoms by hellish torture and never-dying pangs! While they are listening to those dire tales of wo, look at their sad countenances and pale faces, which indicate their fearful apprehensions. View the tender female going to the house of terror! On her way thither she is cheerful as the lark—modest, artless, and lovely—on her cheek is imprinted the vermilion of the rose—with nimble step, lightly she treads the ground, and the smile of innocence bespeaks the inward peace and calmness of her mind. She returns pale, dejected, and forlorn; her bosom rent with sighs, and her eyes red with weeping.

The sheer volume of reports of women like this—women who returned home from church meetings to search for knives or razors—made this cycle of cause and effect seem deadly and real. "Let the young, and female in particular," Thomas Whittemore warned in 1828, "be cautious how they become ensnared." Even children were not safe. Harping on the notion that Calvinist "priests" clouded the judgment of the most vulnerable members of their flock, some Universalist papers told parents that Sunday schools had become breeding grounds for juvenile self-murderers convinced that they were "beyond the reach of mercy." When a young pupil at Deacon Warren's academy in Woburn, Massachusetts, committed suicide in 1829, Thomas Whittemore used the pages of the *Trumpet* to sound this alarm. "Who knows," he asked in a mocking yet chilling editorial, "but your child may be the next victim."[49]

Universalist agitators active in the 1820s and 1830s claimed to have found more victims of this powerful and dangerous doctrine than they knew what to do with. In 1835 Russell Streeter, a savvy propagandist from Maine, told readers of one of his rollicking diatribes against Calvinism that "though the examples of its deleterious influence are numerous, I have no wish to retort, or wound the tender sensibilities of surviving relations and friends, by recording the names of the hundreds of victims of that system of despair, which have come within my knowledge." While his colleagues never tired of naming names, Streeter was more interested in talking about the scale of the scourge he saw ravaging the ranks of the various Calvinist churches. "I believe it may be said with truth, that nine-tenths of the suicides among the religious part of the community, may be traced to the doctrine in question," he wrote. "Its influence must be injurious to people of weak nerves and exquisite moral sensibilities." Anyone reading the rest of the Universalist press would have reached the same conclusion. A survey of fifteen Universalist weekly newspapers published between 1820 and 1840 reveals literally hundreds of stories of "partialists" killing themselves. In the vast majority, the editors ascribed the motive for the suicide to anxiety and depression "respecting a future state of existence."[50]

Under siege on all sides, Universalists did not concentrate their heavy artillery solely on their orthodox critics. In fact, as Methodist operatives like Wilbur Fisk, Timothy Merritt, and Alexander Hall took aim at the doctrine of immediate universal salvation, Universalists trained more and more firepower on their rapidly growing evangelical rivals. Without adjusting their arguments, they accused Methodism and Baptism of promoting the same partialist, limitarian doctrines as Congregationalism and Presbyterianism. In Universalist eyes, it made no difference whether the elect were chosen before birth or earned their salvation through conversion. The error was the same.[51]

The only distinction worth drawing between Old Lights and New Lights pertained to practice, not principle. As Universalists never tired of warning, the peculiar camp meetings that came to define the public profile of Methodism in the early nineteenth century only served to intensify the encouragements to despair, derangement, and suicide already embedded in doctrines of selective salvation. What would happen, Universalists asked on page after page of promotional books and pamphlets, to attendees who left these overemotional recruitment meetings uncertain whether their faith in Christ was true enough and sure enough to whisk them to heaven when their time came? Bewilderment, stupefaction, anxiety, and insanity were just some of the milder consequences Universalists began to impute to attendance at revivals. It was no surprise, a columnist in the *Gospel Herald* declared, that "the present violent and boisterous method of conversion, where threats of endless misery, instead of persuasion, are resorted to, produced mental distraction." Referring to the hospital in Charlestown that members of the Massachusetts Humane Society had founded and funded, Thomas Whittemore told readers of the *Trumpet* that "[t]hree quarters of the cases of insanity that have come under the care of that institution, have been produced by religious excitement and fear."[52]

Perhaps those patients should count themselves lucky. If the frantic displays regularly witnessed at camp meeting were to be taken at face value—as genuine crises of faith—then might not the women and men who succumbed to them be a danger to themselves? Universalists answered their own question with a resounding yes, and as revivals caught fire across New England, New York, Pennsylvania, and the western states in the 1820s and 1830s, they turned this claim into the central front in their war on evangelicalism. In fact, in a prescient item published in most Universalist papers in 1822, editors had asked readers to send in "information of all cases of suicide and insanity which shall be evidently produced either by the terrific system of doctrines, or by the terrific style of preaching prevalent in this country." They got plenty of responses, some more credible than others, and by the 1830s their newspapers were awash with such stories. They often appeared in small clusters of twos and threes to buttress the idea that waves of self-destruction followed in the wake of most revival tours. Much longer tallies ranging from seven to twenty-seven names at a time even surfaced now and again.[53]

Many of these pieces originated in the *Trumpet*, Thomas Whittemore's best-selling Boston weekly. In fact, between 1828 (when Whittemore assumed editorial control) and 1839, the *Trumpet* printed more than fifty articles describing men and women who killed themselves after attending revival meetings, most of which were then picked up by sister papers and broadcast farther. As one furious evangelical writer observed in 1832, four years into Whittemore's tenure, "It is a matter of prodigious notoriety, that these meetings drive great numbers of those who attend them into desperation and self-destruction. When does the brazen 'Trumpet' twang its weekly blast, without swelling this keynote?" Whittemore did not disagree. "The number of those that have committed suicide, since the commencement of what are falsely termed revivals of religion, is almost innumerable," he marveled in 1835. "If I were to tell you the aggregate numbers of those who have committed suicide under the influence of partialism, within two years past, I should astonish you—I will say an hundred."[54]

While Whittemore often succumbed to the temptation to editorialize, the most affecting items in this grim parade were often those given over to simple, allegedly impartial reporting. For instance, on October 29, 1831, the *Trumpet* informed readers that a woman had recently been fished from the river in Portsmouth, New Hampshire, the town George Richards had once served as minister. Her rescuers said she had leaped into the current as if she hoped never to rise again. According to the *Trumpet*, she had spent the last few days "at a four days meeting held by the members of her church, and had been much excited during its continuance. She is of a credulous disposition, and any tale of mystery and superlative horror is devoured by her with avidity." The sly parallel drawn here between the credulous consumers of evangelical preaching and young female readers brought low by gothic novel reading was likely intentional. In fact, the gender of the protagonist in this brief report and the unmistakable emphasis on her gullibility and emotional vulnerability were important defining features of this poisonous new genre of reportage.[55]

Longer, less economical versions of this archetype added poignant texture. With room to draw their central (typically young and female) characters more clearly, extended pieces usually noted the deceased's previously cheerful disposition and her strong ties to family and community. They also made sure to linger upon the prolonged mental anguish and alienation that their subjects purportedly experienced after attending revival meetings. And when despair inevitably gave way to suicide, these accounts always wallowed in the sorrow that ensued, lingering voyeuristically on the "bereaved children and friends of the deceased" who survived to grieve. They often concluded with a direct address to readers to remind them that "Universalism presents the only cure for such evils."[56]

By 1832 these dismal tales were already so ubiquitous that one Universalist writer compiled an anthology, a stand-alone four-page list of "113 Victims to the Doctrine of Endless Misery!" Each of the poor souls listed there, its author Lewis Andrews promised, were "duped followers" who attended "'Four Days,' 'Protracted,' and other 'Meetings.'" While a few were now sequestered at asylums like Charlestown's "Humane Hospital" or incarcerated in prison on murder charges, most (75 out of 113) had succumbed to the "horrid epidemic" of suicide because evangelical preachers had convinced them that they were damned for eternity. In secular newspapers, reports of suicides committed by males typically outnumbered those of females by wide margins. In this regard, then, the fact that Andrews had collated reports of no less than forty-one women driven to drown themselves or cut their throats after going to these revival meetings was striking indeed. Andrews claimed this was just the tip of the iceberg: "We presume we have not recorded more than one hundredth part of the cases of insanity, murder, and suicide which have actually taken place in the United States, within a very few years, from the operations of fanaticism, and the false and dishonoring dogmas of an 'endless hell' and 'implacable Jehovah.' "[57]

Controversialists like Andrews and Whittemore were fixated on the perceived connection between self-destruction and evangelical revival for two reasons. For one thing, even if many of the stories that they and their fellow Universalist editors printed were made up or the facts stretched to suit their purpose, they fit the bloody pattern established during a wave of revivals in the previous century. Some well-read subscribers to the *Trumpet* were surely aware that Jonathan Edwards's Northampton revival had been brought to a screeching halt in 1735 when two members of his congregation, one of whom was Edwards's own uncle, cut their throats in despair for the state of their souls. Scattered reports over the years had also suggested that the evangelical preaching of Gilbert Tennent and George Whitefield had born similarly bitter fruit.[58]

In an increasingly crowded religious marketplace, seizing on the sometimes hysterical and occasionally self-destructive consequences of evangelical revivalism also allowed Universalists to highlight contrasts of belief and practice. In part this was born of necessity. Baptists and even some Congregationalists and Presbyterians who initially condemned the theatrical extravagances of camp meetings soon developed their own "four-day" or "protracted" meetings in awkward imitation of the Methodist model. By contrast, Universalists never experimented with any kind of outdoor mass meeting. It was not an option. Their theology was entirely unsuited to a ritual that relied on provoking a fear of hell before a gathered audience. Universal salvation, as its devotees found themselves constantly explaining, was a religion of hope and happiness, and promises made to all, not some. Revival meetings, then, embodied the doctrinal distance that separated liberal and evangelical religion. "These revivals," a writer published in the *Trumpet* sneered in 1831, "have nothing to do with the head, but with the heart; or in other words the judgement becomes the tool, the mere suppliant observer of the passions."[59]

Letting the passions reign, Universalists argued, could be dangerous, and perhaps deadly—not only for individual adherents but also for the country itself. After all, Universalists had built a national church on the promise that their brand of cool-headed rationalism could usher in a new era of fellowship and fraternity that would salve the burning rancor produced by postrevolutionary social dislocations. But to deliver on this vision, they had first to dethrone and discredit their immediate opposition. Stocking their pages with the death scenes of overwrought victims of revivalism, Universalist leaders thus took aim at all the faith groups that encouraged would-be converts to elevate their own interests above all others and to indulge in every possible emotional excess if divine assurance was not immediately forthcoming.

Revivalist leaders did their best to dismiss all this as desperate hyperbole. In 1833 William Sprague, one of the ministers at the center of the recent battle over the meaning of Samuel Leonard's suicide, strode into print with a vigorous defense of evangelical preaching and recruitment methods that tried to set the record straight. Sprague was a learned student of religious history and knew well enough that individual journeys toward salvation had long been associated with the temptation to kill oneself when the convert became convinced of his or her own sinfulness. For centuries, sincere strivers from Michael Wigglesworth to Olaudah Equiano had experienced pangs of self-destructive hopelessness as a final test of faith in the moments before God had reached out to rescue their souls. So while Sprague did not deny that a few attendees at early nineteenth-century revival meetings might not have had the spiritual strength to climb from the pit of their despair, he asked his readers to use their common sense to interpret the fantastic scenes of evangelical genocide that populated so many Universalist publications:

> When you hear of instances of suicide in revivals, remember that such instances occur in other scenes of life, and other departments of

> action; and if you are not prepared to make commerce, and learning, and politics, and virtuous attachment, responsible for this awful calamity, because it is sometimes connected with them, then do not attempt to cast this responsibility upon religion, or revivals of religion, because here too individuals are sometimes left to this most fearful visitation. I have said that some such cases as the objection supposes occur; but I maintain that the number is, by the enemies of revivals, greatly overrated.

Most other evangelicals took similar stances, arguing—in language that echoed how sentimental novelists and partisan newspaper editors had responded to similar charges earlier in the century—that on balance revival meetings did vastly more good than harm. "See, how many they translate from sin to purity, from woe to blessedness, from earth to heaven," Alexander McClure protested in 1835. Tellingly, however, responses like these suggest that Universalist attempts to link revivalism to hysterical suicide—and, by extension, to the larger problems of disorder and moral confusion buffeting young America—seemed to be gaining traction. As Sprague himself had to admit, it had become "a subject of general notoriety and conversation."[60]

But so too had claims that Universalist doctrines offered a short path to heaven. Regardless of the success of their attacks on Congregationalism and Methodism, Universalists were still struggling to explain their own beliefs about if, when, and how a person who commits suicide faces judgment and punishment. An episode in 1836 captured the essence of their continuing dilemma. The sad occasion was the suicide of Loriman Stevens, a stockholder in a Congregational church in South Boston. According to its minister, Rev. J. H. Fairchild, Stevens had displayed Universalist sympathies in the weeks and months before he cut his throat. When the local Universalist pastor, Benjamin Whittemore, got word that Fairchild had "charged Universalism with having a direct tendency to promote suicide," he retaliated with a sermon of his own.[61]

Like his brother Thomas, Benjamin Whittemore refused to be browbeaten with the suicide question and defended the immediatist position the church had assumed in 1832 as best he could. "Universalism Against Suicide," he roared on the published sermon's title page, before launching into a spirited rendition of the church's now-familiar assurances that its doctrines promoted obedience and self-preservation:

> How must the reasonable person act who believes this? He will glory in the goodness of God; he will be reconciled to his dispensations; he will be happy. Yes, says one, but he must commit self-murder, if he does not believe in future punishment. Why must he do this? O, to get rid of trouble. But the opposer forgets that this man believes he realizes no trouble but what is for his best good. He has no desire to quit this world, so long as it is God's good pleasure that he should remain in it.

Despite its polish, this was a boilerplate answer that ducked the real question: What punishment do men like Loriman Stevens face for murdering themselves? Following Hosea Ballou's immediatist declaration four years earlier, Universalists could no longer shelter behind the Restorationist position that suicides suffer meaningful retribution after death. Instead, Ballou's lieutenants now typically offered one of three responses to the suicide question. For his part, Benjamin Whittemore chose scripture as his shield. Cycling through the biblical descriptions of the suicides of Saul, his armor-bearer, Ahithophel, and Judas, he bravely returned to the old argument that these stories offered evidence that people who cut their throats or hanged themselves had committed no sin and thus faced no future punishment.[62]

In the aftermath of Ballou's 1832 decision to lash Universalism to the doctrine of immediate universal salvation, a decision he refused to reconsider or regret, most other defenders of the church chose one of two alternate responses. The first was to argue that killing oneself was its own punishment. "The man who has determined on self-immolation, is a suicide the very moment he has formed the resolution," a writer in the *Universalist Review* ventured in 1838. If most churchgoing Americans were right and suicide was in fact a sin, then that sin was committed at the moment of decision. A person's punishment consisted not only of the agonizing and guilt-stricken interval between resolution and commission but also of the pain of death itself. While clearly consistent with immediatist dogma, this explanation met with widespread ridicule beyond the Universalist

Church. For one thing, it created a delicious logical fallacy whereby God was the author of both sin and punishment. That made no sense. Sin and punishment could not have the same author, nor could intent and action be so conveniently separated. If sins naturally created their own punishments, Methodist Timothy Merritt asked mischievously, did that mean that adulterers felt the pain of retribution as they cavorted in bed with their lovers?[63]

Because scriptural arguments about self-destruction smacked of secularized apostasy, and because sin-as-punishment arguments could be easily caricatured as nonsensical, immediatists like Thomas Whittemore learned to hedge those positions against a third response to the suicide question. Expanding the claim Whittemore had made at Alfred Bassett's funeral in 1832, disciples like the Maine preacher Russell Streeter increasingly claimed that it was insanity and not theology that had driven a handful of their many followers to early graves:

> That a few of the many cases of suicide which take place, occur among those professing Universalism, is readily admitted, but so far from being induced by their doctrine, the deed is done in a moment of deep depression, despair, or derangement. It is because they have lost sight of the cheering sun of their profession that they do an act, so entirely at war with its theory and precepts.

Suicide, a Universalist writer agreed in 1841, is "prima facie evidence of alienation of mind." "In case of insanity," another church member wrote in 1847, "no doctrine of religion will avail to prevent suicide." While this explanation could not be rolled out each and every time, its logic was both fashionable and convenient. By the 1830s, medical and legal authorities working in recently opened state asylums now customarily interpreted confounding madness as the product of uncontrollable biological phenomena. Without fear of contradiction, Universalists thus asserted that evidence of insanity rendered suicide unpunishable; it was hardly a sin if committed in an altered state.[64]

As these unreconciled replies suggest, there was no disguising the disarray within the church on the best way to respond to the suicide question. "Various devices have been sought out and adopted to meet this exigency," Edwin Hatfield gleefully told readers of *Universalism as It Is* in 1841. Three years later, in 1844, when the Universalist leadership issued their members with the first edition of a handbook of talking points, they were still dithering. *The Universalist's Book of Reference: Containing All the Principal Facts and Arguments, and Scripture Texts, Pro and Con, on the Great Controversy between Limitarians and Universalists* devoted several paragraphs to the business of trying to explain how and when a person committing suicide would be punished under the doctrine of immediate universal salvation. "Self-murder! We know of no such crime," author Everet Guild began. "Murder implies malice aforethought. But the Bible informs us that 'no man ever hated his own flesh.' The crime of self-murder is therefore impossible." But Guild did not stop there. Instead, he flung out several other rebuttals, hoping one would stick. Chief among these was the old immediatist chestnut that no one in their right mind "ever coolly and deliberately, in the sober exercise of his judgement, put a period to his own existence." But Guild did not know when to stop. Turning from solitary maniacs to consider how murder-suicides like Samuel Leonard and William Beadle fit into this tangled exculpatory schema, Guild threw up his hands: "We frankly confess that this is, to all appearance, one of the greatest difficulties, in the way of our theory, which can possibly be stated. We admit it to be a very plausible objection." Thank God, Guild concluded, that such cases were no more frequent than "one to an hundred thousand."[65]

Hosea Ballou passed away in 1852, just as the second edition of Guild's handbook was going to press. While the church mourned the loss of its charismatic figurehead, in one sense his death was a blessing. With Ballou gone, rank-and-file Universalists could finally speak their mind about the immediatist doctrines his policies had forced them to defend these past twenty years. Despite Ballou's 1832 declaration, most members of the various state conventions had never discarded their personal beliefs in some period of limited future punishment. They had merely kept quiet. After his death, this long-silent majority hurriedly rededicated their church to this Restorationist position. The decades of ridicule they had all endured because of Ultras' muddled responses to the suicide question was likely a major contributing factor in this dramatic realignment.[66]

This sideways step allowed important triage, but it came too late to save this once-brash denomination from death by a thousand cuts. Ever since a Unitarian magazine had asked Ultras and Restorationists about the future state of Judas Iscariot in 1819, their rivals across the theological spectrum had talked of little else. After Ballou committed the church to defending the immediatist belief that all punishment was confined to this plane of existence, the chorus of critics demanding that Universalists explain how and when self-murderers face retribution became almost deafening. While Ultras had quickly found ways to turn some of this scrutiny back onto their opponents' faith in partial salvation and eternal suffering, they had failed to offer a consistent or intuitive response to the suicide question. "We would not now wish to be understood as justifying the act of suicide. Very far from it," Everet Guild protested as he nitpicked scriptural accounts of Judas's death. But that was exactly what it sounded like when rivals relayed responses like this to their readerships in the battleground states.[67]

By the time the Restorationist majority finally overpowered the Ultraist camp in the 1850s, bringing an end to accusations that universal salvation delivered each new Iscariot promptly and directly to heaven, the damage to Universalism's credibility had already been done and the church's momentum had evaporated. To be sure, there were other important structural and tactical reasons Universalism's surging growth began to stall in the 1830s and 1840s, but the fact that the church failed to shake the stigma of being labeled a suicide cult permanently tarnished its uplifting message of salvation for all. In 1832, when Thomas Whittemore made plans for a day of celebration and thanksgiving, the church had seemed to be on the cusp of greatness. But, by the late 1840s, its growth was no longer outstripping national population increases, and, by the 1860s, this once-strident denomination had shrunk from sixth largest to twelfth. By then negotiations to merge with the Unitarians and start afresh were already well under way.[68]

All those who had worked with such unsurpassed concentration to define this upstart liberal church as a new and toxic strain of infidelity could breathe a small sigh of relief. For evangelical denominations in particular the bitter fight with the Universalists had helped them position themselves more safely and securely within the religious mainstream. Methodist ministers like Timothy Merritt had spilt barrels of ink to argue the case that only faiths capable of stirring fear and awe were strong enough to provide a moral framework in which the chaotic, colliding, and dislocating impulses peculiar to American democracy could safely thrive. A weak and watery liberal theology that could not restrain its followers from committing even the most outrageous crimes must be shunned if the competing interests of liberty and order were ever to find equilibrium. Sins must be punished. Actions must have consequences.[69]

Yet no side emerged entirely unscathed in this knock-down, drag-out fight over the power and purpose of religious belief. Over the course of a single generation, Ballou, Whittemore, and dozens of other publicity-savvy Universalist leaders had turned their fledgling church into a major antagonist of organized revivalism. In fact, as Universalists flooded the country with their dire warnings about the mortal perils of heart religion, interest in revivals had slowly started to wane. Beginning in the late 1830s, the number of camp meetings, protracted meetings, and four-day meetings held each year began to tumble, gradually at first and then precipitously, forcing evangelical denominations to look to other means to sustain themselves. Historians have offered several explanations for this decline including the knock-on effects of the economic depression that began in the late 1830s, the retreating frontier, growing urbanization, and the development of permanent congregations in areas previously unserved by full-time clergy. However, given the monumental campaign launched by Universalists to link revival meetings to images of howling young women slashing at their throats, heed must be paid to their role in bringing these signature outdoor assemblies to the verge of extinction.[70]

In this existential battle for the people's trust—a war of words made possible by increasingly democratized access to the tools of print publishing—all sides had leveraged the public's still-instinctive reflex to condemn acts of suicide in order to advance their agendas. Most of these antagonists grounded their arguments on the enduring belief that suicide remained beyond the pale, a politically potent and socially divisive decision unsanctioned by God, society, or natural law. Yet green shoots of dissent were also apparent here and there. A few of the most liberal Universalists—Everet Guild and Benjamin Whittemore notable among them—had tentatively advanced the claim that the scriptural injunction not to kill might not apply to suicide at all. Several more had asserted that insanity insulated troubled souls like George Richards and Alfred Bassett from judgment. Most notably, many critics of Methodist camp meetings had tried to stir sympathy for young women driven to drown or hang themselves by arguing that they had been unable to escape the overbearing pressure on them to rid themselves of sin and embrace their personal savior.

While everyone involved in this scrabble for members and market share stopped far short of condoning a single act of self-destruction, even such limited exceptions to the blanket condemnation of suicide familiar to previous generations seemed to signal that attitudes toward suicide were shifting slightly, not just within preaching circles but perhaps across society at large. More and more it seemed as if circumstance shaped the way the reading public responded to individual decisions to die. This was a vein of possibility that antislavery activists had already begun to mine. Between the Revolution and the Civil War, three distinct generations of abolitionists made extraordinary efforts to highlight the savage indignities of chattel slavery by forcing the specter of slave suicide into the national spotlight.

6

The Problem of Slave Resistance

Pinning his master to the ground, Quashi sat astride his chest and drew a blade from his belt. His master had chased him across this stone-strewn field and when Quashi had tripped and fallen, they had struggled for what seemed like hours, "wrestl[ing] for mastery." At last the stout black overseer got the better of his white owner, "the elevation of his mind add[ing] vigour to his arm." His pinioned young master now guessed his fate and "lay in dreadful expectation, helpless and shrinking into himself." His bloody murder would be swift retribution for pursuing his once-favored slave here, to whip him for a crime Quashi, arm poised to strike, still claimed he had not committed:

> Master, I was bred up with you from a child; I was your play-mate when a boy; I have loved you as myself; your interest has been my study; I am innocent of the cause of your suspicion; had I been guilty, my attachment to you might have pleaded for me. Yet you have condemned me to a punishment of which I must ever have borne the disgraceful marks, thus only can I avoid them.

With his master's bulging eyes locked on his, the slave brought down the blade. But his owner was not its target. Instead, Quashi plunged its cutting edge into his own flesh, tearing a wide gash across his throat "with all his strength." He died without a groan, his body slumping across his childhood playmate's chest, "bathing him in his blood."[1]

Although the original events had purportedly taken place on the tiny Caribbean sugar island of St. Kitts, accounts of Quashi's final moments achieved the greatest resonance within the continental United States. When reports started turning up in American newspapers and literary magazines in the late 1780s and early 1790s, they typically took homiletic form. Editors stripped Quashi's story of any distracting reminders of its island setting and centered it instead upon the unconquerable nobility of a black man brought low by plantation despotism. To excuse and explain his suicide, each reprise larded the tale's bare outline with a thick layer of testimony to Quashi's lifelong dignity and sense of honor. Born into slavery, Quashi had risen to the position of overseer by virtue of his unimpeachable character, and as an adult, the *New-York Journal* reported in 1788, he displayed uncommon "tenderness," "respect," and "affection" for his master. Until now this ostentatious diligence and dedication had ensured that Quashi's skin remained "unraised by the whip." According to the *Massachusetts Spy*, he had long "dreaded this mortal wound to his honour." So when his master had promised him an unwarranted thrashing, Quashi had fled to the huts in the fields safe in the knowledge that his fellow slaves had "too great a regard for him" to betray his hiding place. When the two men finally met, the American papers framed Quashi's dramatic yet reluctant suicide astride his tormentor as a stern rebuke to the revolutionary-era assumption that African slaves lacked the natural virtue to stand firm against tyranny. Far from it. "Such greatness of mind!" mourned an antislavery columnist in Philadelphia's *Independent Gazetteer* in a typical eulogy.[2]

In these repeated retellings, activist writers and editors represented Quashi's suicide as part and parcel of his struggle for mastery. Wrestling in the dirt with his owner, Quashi is seen violently asserting his selfhood and his manhood by depriving his master of his labor and depriving himself of his life. The account, one of the most frequently reprinted descriptions of a slave apparently choosing liberty through death to populate the press at the turn of the century, stands in stark contrast to the way that abolitionists of the 1820s and 1830s interpreted the meaning of subsequent suicides committed by enslaved people. To try to stir evangelical readers to immediate intervention to destroy the peculiar institution, Benjamin Lundy, William Lloyd Garrison, and Lydia Maria Child each reimagined slaves' self-inflicted deaths as acts of utter humiliation—final and peculiarly feminine capitulations to the inescapable, toxic hegemony of the Slave Power. It was not until militant black abolitionists like Henry Highland Garnet and Joshua Bowen Smith muscled their way onto the national stage in the 1840s and 1850s that men who dispossessed their owners by behaving like Quashi were restored to something approaching heroic status.

These shifting calculations about the political palatability of representing slave resistance in polemical writing reveal the extent to which debates about agency, power, and consent—and thus about self-destruction—lay at the heart of the new nation's struggle over the future of slavery. Was a slave's suicide an act of principled yet costly resistance to tyranny that challenged the hypocrisy of the revolutionary settlement? Or was it a measure of abject victimhood that begged for humanitarian intervention? That representations of black suicide oscillated so dramatically between these opposing interpretive frameworks testifies to abolitionists' persistent need to match their message to their changing audiences and transforming mission. Ultimately these shifting portrayals reflect deep differences within the movement between moderates and militants and between whites and blacks as to who had the power to bring slavery to its knees: white evangelicals who might be moved by displays of slave suffering, or black slaves with the courage to fight and die for their freedom.

Many textbook histories of the abolition of slavery in the United States still begin with William Lloyd Garrison. However, by anointing Garrison's "immediatist outburst" in a Boston newspaper on January 1, 1831, as the founding text of an insurgent evangelical movement notorious for courting publicity and controversy wherever it went, this chronology obscures more than it reveals. For more than a century prior to Garrison's ferocious pledge to be "as harsh as truth," whites and blacks from Massachusetts to Pennsylvania (not to mention across the Atlantic, in Britain) had been engaged in various acts of consciousness-raising and rabble-rousing. Long before the *Liberator*'s editor demanded to be heard, Quakers such as John Woolman and Anthony Benezet were raising their voices to decry the international slave trade and the mendacity and greed of those who reaped its rewards. Often choosing to focus on the brutalizing experience of slavery during the Middle Passage, these colonial critics habitually dwelt upon stories of saltwater slaves who "in a desperate Resolution starved themselves to death."[3]

In the 1770s and 1780s some of these disparate antislavery stalwarts began to work together. The world's first organization dedicated to the abolition of slavery started meeting regularly in Philadelphia in 1784. Founded before the Revolution, but dormant during the war, the Pennsylvania Abolition Society (PAS) was jolted back to life by the suicides of two members of the city's free black community who had been seized by kidnappers planning to send them to slave auctions farther south. As Anthony Benezet recalled in a letter to a Quaker friend, each man had begged his captors to be released but had been either ignored or mocked. With no hope for a reprieve, one of the men, a free "French Negro," hanged himself before he could be hustled aboard ship. The other waited with desperate patience for the vessel on which he had been stowed to depart, before throwing himself from its deck to drown in the waters of the Delaware River.[4]

Over the following years, PAS members—including Benjamin Rush and several other prominent Universalists—dedicated themselves to preventing similar suicides by offering legal aid to free blacks in the city kidnapped or seized on suspicion of being runaways. Soon joined by sister organizations such as the New York Manumission Society, the PAS also took up legislative tools to advocate for gradual abolition. Most of this careful, reasoned work occurred behind the scenes and, because members were mindful of being accused of Jacobin excess, typically eschewed the rhetorical pyrotechnics and aggressive emotional enthusiasm many Garrisonians would embrace in later years.[5]

Not all early national antislavery activity was confined within white-led associational frameworks. Scholars have recently begun to credit leaders of the free black churches like Philadelphia's Richard Allen for their outspoken protests against revolutionary-era fugitive slave laws. Yet while their disruptive voices rang loud and clear when it came to protecting the free black community, the most vocal criticism of the international slave trade and the plantation system it supported came not from the PAS itself, nor from this impressive network of "black founders," but from a group of white ministers, poets, and ex-slavers working on the fringes of organized antislavery. Showing great debt to contemporary British attempts to mobilize public opinion against the international slave trade, this diffuse group of writers—most active in the late 1780s and early 1790s before the bloody violence of the revolution in Saint Domingue stunned many of them into silence—was the first to try to saturate the press with accounts of slavery designed to elicit outrage and action among ordinary readers. Long before the arrival of the *Liberator* or Theodore Dwight Weld's *American Slavery as It Is* (1839), middle-class consumers of early national print culture found themselves bombarded by often anonymously authored tales of righteous slaves bedeviled by cruel kidnappers, vicious ship captains, and tyrannical masters.[6]

The popularity of a British import set the tone. Based on a report that had appeared in several London papers, Thomas Day and John Bicknell's 1773 elegiac poem "The Dying Negro" is a suicide note in verse written from the point of view of a black servant whose master plans to depart the British capital to return to the Caribbean. Knowing he is bound for fieldwork, the unnamed plaintiff stabs himself as the ship leaves its dock in the Thames. Day and Bicknell evidently intended "The Dying Negro" as a means to impugn the feeble enforcement of Lord Mansfield's recent ruling that no slave could be made to leave Britain against his or her will. To press home this point, the poem draws attention to this black Briton's recent Christian baptism and describes his violent suicide as an attempt to escape a life blistered by unmerited abuse and injury:

I ask no lazy pleasures to possess,
No long eternity of happiness;—
But if unstain'd by voluntary guilt,
At your great call this being I have spilt,
For all the wrongs which innocent I share,
For all I've suffer'd, and for all I dare;
O lead me to that spot, that sacred shore,
Where souls are free, and men oppress no more!

Extremely successful in England, "The Dying Negro" also found a broad readership in North America. A version of the first edition nosed its way into Isaiah Thomas's *Royal American Magazine* in February 1774 and into the *Pennsylvania Magazine* in January 1776, the same month its editor, Tom Paine, published *Common Sense.* Over the next thirty years it became, alongside Quashi's story, one of the most frequently reprinted depictions of slave suicide in the American press, pitching up in the *Universal Asylum and Columbian Magazine* in May 1790, the *Massachusetts Magazine* in January 1791, and, in excerpted form, in Olaudah Equiano's *Interesting Narrative* when the first American edition of that startling memoir reached subscribers in Connecticut, New York, New Jersey, and Pennsylvania later that year. Pamphlet editions of the poem freighted the shelves of booksellers and circulating libraries throughout the 1790s, and the poem's unflinching portrayal of virtuous manhood under attack remained the subject of discussion in the public prints as late as 1805. Unambiguously antislavery and unabashedly sentimental, the popularity of "The Dying Negro" in northern literary circles helped establish the figure of the self-destructive slave as a moral problem demanding acknowledgment and action.[7]

Evidently influenced by Day and Bicknell's sorrowful masterpiece, early national writers embraced the subject of slave suicide. It proved to be a timely tactic, a means to render slaves' torments in forms that catered to novel readers' ghoulish fascination with mortality and their sweet tooth for sentimental narratives. To be sure, a few anonymous poets likely took to the topic solely to serve their art, using the egregious suffering of slaves to fire the romantic imagination. However, in the instances where authorship can be ascertained, there is overwhelming evidence that most of those who sentimentalized slave suicide in this early period were not romantic opportunists but were instead wholeheartedly committed to an antislavery agenda. Take Thomas Branagan, the author of *Avenia* (1805), an epic poem that imagined the headlong plunge to her death of an Angolan slave raped and beaten by her West Indian master. Branagan was an American John Newton, a former planter and slave trader since drawn to Christ. Now haunted by the barbarities he had seen and so often sanctioned, Branagan moved to Philadelphia in 1798 to "bear testimony against slavery, from the press." He had little talent for romantic poetry but forced himself into

DYING NEGRO,

A

POEM.

To you this unpolluted blood I pour,
To you that Spirit which ye gave restore

The THIRD EDITION, Corrected and Enlarged.

LONDON:

Printed for W. Flexney, opposite Gray's-Inn-Gate, Holborn; J. Wilkie, in St. Paul's Church-Yard; and J. Robson, in New Bond-Street.

M.DCC.LXXV.

[PRICE ONE SHILLING AND SIX-PENCE.]

An illustration that accompanied several British editions of "The Dying Negro" used the protagonist's classical posture to suggest that the act of self-immolation is deliberate, rational, and righteous, perhaps even divinely sanctioned. While the newspaper report on which the poem was based specified shooting as the cause of death, Day and Bicknell found greater pathos in the dagger. Thomas Day, *The Dying Negro, a Poetical Epistle* (London: W. Flexney, 1773). Courtesy of the Library of Congress.

rhyme because, he reasoned, "many will read a performance in poetry; who could not be induced to peruse the same materials, however well arranged and digested in prose." Branagan was unembarrassed by the workmanlike quality of his verse and promoted it relentlessly. When Thomas Jefferson was first deliberating whether to sign a bill being proposed in the United States Senate that would prohibit the further importation of slaves, he received a letter from Branagan requesting that the president subscribe for a copy of *Avenia*. Jefferson did not write back.[8]

Like Branagan's magnum opus, the appearance of a great many other early national portrayals of black suicide appears to have been timed to put moral pressure on federal lawmakers debating the future of the international slave trade. Borrowing inspiration from English sources, many such pieces took the horrors of the Middle Passage as their theme, quickly turning saltwater suicides into major motifs. Whether in verse or in prose, activists including Hartford lawyer Zephaniah Swift, New Haven preacher Jonathan Edwards, and Rhode Island provocateur William Patten dwelt upon the dread, despair, and distress that sometimes seemed to drive blameless Africans to "plunge themselves into the ocean, and terminate at once their lives and their misfortunes." While some of these writers preferred to talk in the aggregate of the "thousands" of slaves whose self-inflicted deaths bore witness to the trade's unprovoked inhumanity, most found stories of individual suffering and suicide more powerful. In 1792 *Dunlap's American Daily Advertiser* introduced Philadelphia readers to no less than seven separate stories of recent suicides aboard ship, while a great many papers in other cities recounted the purportedly true tale of another slave who "plung'd in the deep hoping death would have found me" before being "snatch'd" from the waves and bundled back below decks.[9]

Whether intended to stir public support for the federal abolition of the slave trade or for gradualist schemes to exterminate racial bondage in northern states like New York, a great many depictions of slaves dead by their own hands tended to strike the same notes. Between the first American appearance of "The Dying Negro" in 1774 and the ban on further imports of African slaves eventually endorsed by Congress and signed by President Jefferson on March 2, 1807, poets and prose writers offered up myriad portrayals of slave suicide that rejected century-old beliefs that such deaths manifested little more than inborn African sullenness and obstinacy and instead repeatedly emphasized the just cause and classical virtue of their protagonists.[10]

Most early national readers still considered taking one's own life to be an alarming affront to God, to nature, and to society at large. Hence in this burgeoning moral suasion literature, much of which rested on documentary sources of decidedly dubious provenance, no slave was permitted to commit suicide without extreme provocation. A short piece that made the rounds of the New England papers in 1789 imagined the fate of a West Indian slave reminiscent of Quashi's. "Tortured for a slight offence, of which he was not even guilty," the unnamed man had climbed to the roof of his master's house and then leaped to his death. Likewise, in the *Preliminary Essay* (1804) that Thomas Branagan wrote to promote *Avenia*, he reported having once seen Antiguan slaves "scourged in the cruellist manner. One slave, to escape the fury of his cruel master, plunged into a copper of boiling sugar, and immediately expired."[11]

While fresh converts to Christ like Branagan took pains to embed pleas to Christian conscience and charity in the margins of these stark stories, the figures at their center were typically secular. In this regard, the recent baptism of the desperate black Briton known to American readers as "The Dying Negro" marked him out as a rare and noticeably foreign exception. For the most part, early national activists writing amidst a tumultuous period of reformation and realignment in American Christianity preferred their protagonists to demonstrate strengths of character that could stand independent of any discernible denominational faith. Instead they offered up a corpus of tales in keeping with the new Republic's fetish for classicism. Eschewing the imagery of Christian martyrdom, antislavery advocates framed slave suicide as the last act of an Aristotelian hero, the nobility of spirit of the wronged black protagonist offering the most affecting testimony to slavery's disgrace. Thus the anonymous author of "The Gally Slave," an elegy printed in the *New York Packet* on May 29, 1786, offered poetic praise for a "proud" ship-bound slave who "despairing, tempts the dang'rous leap, / To search for freedom in the spacious deep." Around the same time, papers from New Hampshire to Pennsylvania could be found celebrating the "superior" deportment of two slaves who executed a suicide pact in Santa Cruz. Likewise, in 1792, the final moments of Fidlao, an African king "in whose soul, although uncultivated by science, humanity and every social virtue flourished," appeared in no less than ten different sheets. Defeated in battle by a rival leader in league with American slave traders, Fidlao sees that all is lost and "thrust[s] a dagger into his breast" so that he will not have to endure the indignity of capture and enslavement.[12]

When we add Quashi's often-reprinted story to this catalog of distressed righteousness, the insistence of claims that slaves commit suicide to protect their dignity and protest their treatment becomes unmistakable. This was no coincidence. Many of these items appear to have been carefully conceived. Whether entirely fictional or embellished from fact, Quashi's story and others like it were each constructed in such a way as to figure slave suicide as a pointed commentary on the republican obsession with natural virtue. In this regard, depictions of the deaths of men like Quashi served not only to indict the commerce and exploitation of human beings but also to challenge the widespread belief that blacks were unfit for freedom, an enabling understanding that had ensured that African Americans remained excluded from any formal role in postrevolutionary politics.[13]

As activists like Branagan, Swift, Edwards, and Patten knew all too well, early national political discourse was full of insidious assumptions about who deserved freedom and who did not. Revolutionary-era claims that the colonists had fought bravely to resist enslavement by the British had bequeathed the new nation a powerful language to normalize the perpetuation of race slavery. Spread by schoolbooks, reading manuals such as the *Columbian Orator*, and hagiographical sketches of patriots like George Washington, the understanding that liberty rested on principled resistance to tyranny achieved common currency after the war. Patrick Henry's cry of "Liberty or Death" captured the essence of this mythological view of the Revolution. This liberal-republican view of the nation's founding implicitly validated planters' arguments that their black slaves had consented to their own exploitation by failing to fight to the death to resist it. Thus they deserved no better. Because the revolutionary generation had enshrined consent as the basis for the political legitimacy of every social institution, the founders had also sanctioned a pervasive ideology in which principled resistance to the death was the only measure of institutional illegitimacy.[14]

This view was so widely held among the reading populace that early national antislavery activists—even the few ex-slave authors among them—rarely challenged its logic. Instead, they strove to construct stories in which exceptional bondsmen proved their worth playing by Patrick Henry's rules. Promulgating a vision of a pure-hearted black man willing to sacrifice his life to preserve his dignity and manifest his virtue, each reprinting of Quashi's fatal struggle for mastery reminded white readers that some slaves did, in fact, deserve their freedom.

These initially cautious attempts at cultural reprogramming grew ever more audacious with time. On July 4, 1791, Dr. George Buchanan rose to speak at a public meeting of the Society for Promoting the Abolition of Slavery in Baltimore. Grandson of a city father, former student of Benjamin Rush, and sometime promoter of the humane society movement, Buchanan used his platform to conjure for his approving audience (and later for readers of the pamphlet that carried his remarks further afield) a vision of the Middle Passage that equated the shipboard suicides of African slaves with acts of courage and statesmanship committed by ancient republicans such as Cato and Seneca. "Like a noble Senator of old," Buchanan declared, "death is their choice in preference to lingering out their lives in ignominious slavery—and often do we see them meet it with a smile." Delivered on Independence Day, Buchanan's remarks made calculated swipes not only at the insidiousness of revolutionary rhetoric but also at Thomas Jefferson: slave owner, drafter of the Declaration, and author of a recently published indictment of the debased character of New World slaves, *Notes on the State of Virginia* (1787).[15]

Buchanan was hardly alone in alluding to classical suicide to attack the Virginian's maddening brand of racism. A few years later, in his *Observations upon Certain Passages in Mr. Jefferson's Notes on Virginia* (1804), Clement Clarke Moore, a New York linguist, challenged the new president to revise his dismissive view of bondsmen's supposedly natural incapacity for virtue in light of the news that another proud island slave had recently jumped into a boiler of melting sugar to escape an unwarranted whipping. This was, Moore assured his readers, an indisputable example of a black man's "nobleness of spirit, and delicate sense of honour":

> Let it not be imagined that this anecdote is related without a just abhorrence of the crime of suicide. But if Roman Cato has been extolled for ages, because he could not endure to survive the liberty of his country, surely a poor untaught slave, whose only glory was an

> unbroken skin, showed equal magnanimity when he chose to die in torment, rather than live and bear about him what he thought an indelible disgrace.

By framing slave suicides like this one as potent political gestures worthy of approbation, activists such as Buchanan and Moore offered the reading public a reason to question Jeffersonian prejudice and to reconsider the widely held view that self-destruction was, by definition, an act committed by only the most selfish and self-indulgent. Furthermore, by elevating enslaved African men to the heights of moral aristocracy, they positioned their advocacy in opposition to those who argued that the only prospects for the dismantling of slavery in America lay in the repatriation of blacks back to Africa. Rejecting the bigotry that undergirded such exclusionary schemes, many early national writers who injected Roman nobility into stories of slave suicide seemed to gesture toward a postslavery politics in which men named Cato, Caesar, and Pompey might one day play the roles to which their slave names had mockingly referred.[16]

Forceful, ubiquitous, and radical in its social and political implications, the figure of the virtuous slave drawing a knife across his own throat with all his strength assumed a central place in this first flowering of activist discourse. Yet such provocative defiance of prevailing ideas about the relationship between slavery and citizenship had striking limits. While Jefferson and his critics argued ferociously as to whether black men had the moral capacity to participate in political decision making, the debate did not yet extend to their sisters, mothers, wives, or widows. Thus the vast majority of portrayals of noble slaves taking their own lives in early national print culture represented male protagonists. In the few instances when suicidal female slaves found their way into the pages of newspapers and literary magazines in this period, activists still reflexively interpreted their fatal actions as hysterical impulses bereft of righteousness or reason. For example, an eleven-stanza poem that turned up in papers from Newburyport, Massachusetts, to Philadelphia around the turn of the century described the final plunge of a "raving mother" driven mad when her son is seized and sold to a slave ship captain.[17]

Activists' attempts to forge a link in the public imagination between black male suicide and virtuous resistance to the ignominies of commodification reached a zenith in 1803 when Philadelphia booksellers began promoting a sensational new pamphlet. Telling the arresting story of yet another slave's self-inflicted slaughter in the city of brotherly love, *Reflections on Slavery* called to mind the two deaths that Anthony Benezet had once credited as a catalyst for the revival of the Pennsylvania Abolition Society. In a brief dedication to that organization, the pamphlet's enigmatic author, writing under the telling pen name Humanitas, begged PAS members to divert funds earmarked for lobbying legislators to develop a print campaign that would "excite abhorrence" for slavery in as many lay readers as possible. Then came the details of the suicide, an expansive retelling of a news story that had swept through the pages of papers from Philadelphia to Vermont the previous fall.[18]

Twenty-seven-year-old Romain, his wife, and their young child had only had a few hours' rest at Howell's Inn on Second Street when they were hustled from their cots and shepherded back toward the coach in which they had arrived. En route to the West Indies from Trenton, New Jersey, Romain and his family traveled under the prodding supervision of a hired constable and an associate of their French owner. Monsieur Salaignac had sought safety on the mainland for himself and his most valuable slaves during the violence in Saint Domingue a decade earlier. Now he was planning to start over on a neighboring Caribbean island. Romain and his wife could remember "from fatal experience" that Salaignac's plantation regime "was calculated to produce nothing but misery and wretchedness," and at some point on this journey they had resolved to save their youngster from the same suffering. So when the constable was briefly distracted by the arrival of the carriage in front of the inn that morning, Romain's wife took a chance and darted out into the street with her child. They disappeared into the dawn bustle before the constable could catch them. Angry and humiliated, Romain's French escort bellowed at him to get into the carriage. But Romain refused. "Determined to be free, he adopted his dernier [last] resort, took a pruning knife from his pocket, and dreading a spark of life should remain, whereby he might be restored, he three times cut his throat across, and fell dead on the pavement."[19]

In a long, muscular commentary Humanitas condemned the laws that allowed men like Salaignac to transport their human cargoes in and out of the country "as [one] would a peice [*sic*] of furniture." To do so, he painted a picture of the character of the dead man that emphasized not only

Romain's loving care for his absconded wife and child but also his classical manhood. Though unlettered and "benumbed by oppression," Romain had possessed a "noble soul" and "virtue sufficient to prove to the world—that he felt the injustice and degradation with which he was treated." By suicide, the pamphleteer explained, Romain had "emancipat[ed] himself from the grasp of avarice and inhumanity." He would brook no dissent on this point and went so far as to model the reaction he expected from readers in his description of the crowd that had gathered at the scene:

> The moment the act was committed, the sensibility of the citizens, who viewed the breathless corse [*sic*] and blood-stained pavement, were excited; and mingled expressions of horror and compassion were mutually exchanged: and an universal sentiment of detestation, seemed to prevail against a system productive of such consequences. Many of those who witnessed the lifeless monument of oppression, remembering their own arduous struggles for Liberty, seemed to say, "In vain have we rejected the tyranny of kings, while we permit in our country a domestic despotism, which involves in its nature most of the vices and miseries we have endeavoured to avoid: for domestic slavery is repugnant to the principles of Christianity."

This language was as bold and ambitious as anything seen so far. Deftly exploiting a rich vein of patriotic self-regard, Humanitas here flattered readers' pride while simultaneously using the fact of Romain's suicide to condemn their continued indifference to the racial tyranny under their noses. Configuring this bloody violence as a lonely, principled strike for liberty, Humanitas challenged readers to recognize in Romain's self-destruction the hypocrisy of the postrevolutionary polity. To top it all, he illustrated the pamphlet with a haunting and intricate woodcut, perhaps the first image of a slave committing suicide to be published in North America.[20]

Despite such deliberate and crafty appeals, it is difficult to gauge what effect this reading diet had upon northeastern constituents and their elected representatives. One careful study recently concluded that the passage of New York's gradual emancipation law in 1799 was likely substantially aided by precisely this sort of material. In addition, a debate

This urban street scene brought home the realities of the rising interstate commerce in slaves to northern readers. Humanitas, *Reflections on Slavery* (Philadelphia: R. Cochran, 1803). Courtesy of the American Antiquarian Society.

about a prospective ban on imports of Africans in the House of Representatives in 1806 took suggestive notice of some saltwater slaves who "commit suicide through terror or despair." And it is certainly true that the notion that a slave's suicide could mark him out postmortem as a person of elevated moral stature amounted to a bold step forward in the way the urban reading public confronted the subaltern subject after the Revolution. Indeed, men like Quashi may be considered cousins to the dishonored and doomed native chiefs who peopled the pages and stages of Jacksonian America thirty years later during the period of Indian removal, only to hurl themselves nobly from high cliffs at each work's tragic denouement.[21]

Yet the influence of stories like Quashi's can be easily overstated. For one thing, the bloody insurrection that consumed Saint Domingue between 1791 and 1804 likely limited any possible gains in American public sympathy for blacks willing to use violence to resist their enslavement. For another, we must keep in mind the highly circumscribed goals of these early national advocates. Almost to a man—if any female activists contributed to this output, they did so anonymously—they refused to contemplate anything more radical than gradual abolition. Condemning the revolutionary bloodshed in Haiti and the chaos and violence of Gabriel Prosser's recent rebellion in Virginia, most stopped far short of suggesting that bondsmen imitate en masse the fatal protests men like Quashi enacted in poetry and prose. "The moment you act improperly, and rebel against the authority of those whom you should serve, and whom you are bound to obey, that moment will your friends foresake you, and you will ever remain as you are now," Humanitas warned plantation slaves in the wake of Romain's suicide. "Deserve freedom, and you will be free."[22]

Antislavery activism fell into something of a lull after the congressional ban on the importation of slaves took effect on January 1, 1808. Gradual abolition legislation was by now on the books in every state north of the Ohio River and the Mason-Dixon line, and the horrors of the Middle Passage had been legislated out of legal existence. But slavery is a many-headed monster, too profitable to be strangled by the stroke of a pen. Planters adapted quickly to the new realities imposed by the federal ban, organizing to orchestrate a new domestic trade that could redistribute enslaved persons from estates in surplus in the Upper South to new plantations along the Mississippi Valley and the Gulf Coast. Between 1808 and 1860 one million Chesapeake slaves made the trek south and west to outposts of the new Cotton Kingdom in Kentucky, Tennessee, Arkansas, Louisiana, Alabama, and Mississippi. To accomplish this forced migration, small-town jails replaced Gambian barracoons as holding pens for captives in transit; steamships grunting along the Mississippi replaced slave ships plowing across the Atlantic; and coffles of slaves slouching southward became common sights on country roads everywhere from Baltimore to Natchez.[23]

It took a while for antislavery activists to realize the limits of what they had accomplished. Because it was confined wholly within the southern states, the rapid escalation of the domestic slave trade after 1808 was not immediately obvious to northern observers. Arriving in Washington, D.C., in 1816 in hopes of observing Congress in session, one Philadelphia physician literally stopped in his tracks when he caught sight of a procession of slaves bound together in pairs by ropes and chains and trudging across Capitol Hill. As Jesse Torrey discovered when he questioned the drivers of this miserable convoy, these Maryland slaves had been parted from their families and sold to new masters in Georgia. His visit to the House of Representatives forgotten, Torrey turned on his heels and hurried back to his lodging. He made inquiries with guests at his boardinghouse and soon learned from them that "several hundred people, including not legal slaves only, but many kidnapped freemen and youth bound to serve for a term of years, and unlawfully sold as slaves for life, are annually collected at Washington (as if it were an emporium of slavery) for transportation to the slave regions."[24]

Reasoning that his fellow Philadelphians, and northerners further afield, probably shared his ignorance of the scale and perversity of this "*uncontrolled slave trade*, between the middle and southerly states," the doctor decided that it was his duty to enlighten them. Over sixty-two pages, Jesse Torrey's *A Portraiture of Domestic Slavery in the United States* (1817) declared a new front in the war against American slavery. As befits a whistle-blower, he kept things clear and simple, letting the facts speak for themselves. To condemn the illegal kidnappings and legal breakups of families that were, to his mind, the twin hallmarks of this new Middle Passage, Torrey eschewed the poetic forms that many antislavery predecessors like Branagan had favored, imitating instead the documentarian instincts that Humanitas had displayed in Philadelphia only a decade earlier. To try to create for his readers the sense of witnessing the trade's daily barbarities firsthand, Torrey stocked his pages with a series of carefully sourced descriptions of "such deeds as are likely to shock the feelings and sympathy of the friends of humanity." The intention, he explained, was to convince northern readers to pressure "the state or general governments" to support a colonization plan that would eventually choke off the supply for the domestic trade.[25]

In addition to evidence of kidnappings, beatings, and murders committed by buyers, traders, drivers, and their accomplices, a plurality of the dozen or so atrocities documented with clinical precision in Torrey's catalog of horrors described how members of slave families had killed themselves after being "dragged asunder, never to behold each other" again. While he had copied several of these accounts from newspapers in and around the federal city, the doctor spilled the most ink reporting the details of the failed suicide of a slave woman he had interviewed himself. Tipped off by a lodger at his Washington boardinghouse, Torrey had learned that a black woman in another coffle of slaves destined for Georgia had jumped out of the third-floor window of a brick tavern on F Street. The fall had broken her back and both of her arms, leaving her close to death. Soon Torrey was by her deathbed, offering his services first as doctor but then as an amanuensis:

> I inquired of her, whether she was asleep when she sprang from the window. She replied, "*No, no more than I am now.*" Asking her what was the cause of her doing such a frantic act as that, she replied, "*They brought me away with two of my children, and would'nt let me see my husband—they did'nt sell my husband, and I did'nt want to go;—I was so confus'd and 'istracted, that I did'nt know hardly what I was about—but I did'nt want to go, and I jumped out of the window.*"

This pitiful tale of a wife snatched from her husband only to be driven to distraction and self-harm formed the crux of Torrey's indictment of the domestic slave trade. Like Thomas Branagan and Humanitas before him, Torrey sidestepped all questions of whether suicide violated a duty to God or to natural law and maintained a focus on the social and political implications of this poor woman's death. Yet, in one important respect, the doctor's portrayal marked a turning point. In a striking shift from revolutionary-era activists' understanding of suicide as the singular prerogative of men of exceptional character, Torrey instead placed a wife and mother's desperate last act front and center. He made no claims as to this poor woman's virtue, nor did he fete her as an extraordinary champion of liberty. On the contrary, he seemed to suggest that any feeling person in the same position would have done the same.[26]

Intended as a clarion call, Torrey's pamphlet was widely ignored. The doctor could find no literary magazine or newspaper in Philadelphia, his hometown, willing to review it, and no evidence survives to suggest that booksellers there either stocked or promoted it. Torrey soon conceded its failure in the mid-Atlantic market and traveled north to peddle it in person around progressive pockets of Massachusetts. Yet by year's end he admitted that he had sold no more than "one hundred and fifty books in

A caption reads: "but I did not want to go, and I jump'd out of the window." The author himself designed the strange, ghostly image of the woman falling to earth that accompanied the text in the original 1817 pamphlet and its 1822 London reprint. Jesse Torrey, *A Portraiture of Domestic Slavery* (Philadelphia: John Bioren, 1817). Courtesy of the Library Company of Philadelphia.

Boston, at one dollar each." And despite his documentarian instincts, rumors swirled that "in his philanthropic zeal," he had made up many of the outrages he had described.[27]

The pamphlet's limp sales reflected most northerners' lack of appetite for renewing the campaign against slavery in the aftermath of the costly War of 1812. As the threats of secession made by Federalist delegates to the Hartford Convention in 1814 and 1815 demonstrated, plenty of New Englanders did not consider the domestic slave trade to be their concern. Thus the problem of slave suicide was not theirs to solve. "We are not slave-holders here in New-England," a writer for the *Independent American* snarled. "Why does he inundate our towns and villages with his trash?"

> If he wishes to excite the sympathy of the public and relieve the slaves from their burdens (which we have no doubt are heavy enough), why does he not direct his Quixotic career to Virginia or Georgia? Will our pity for the blacks melt their chains? Will our tears, if the Doctor's book extort any, persuade the driver to lay down his cudgel, or the owner to relinquish his claim to their services?

Although roundly snubbed by the general public, Torrey's 1816 pamphlet did in fact find its way to the hands of at least three young readers who seem to have studied its contents with care. In later life, Benjamin Lundy, William Lloyd Garrison, and Lydia Maria Child each wrote admiringly of Torrey's pioneering effort to document sufferings pressed upon slaves by the internal traffic.[28]

Lundy in particular seems to have studied the doctor's grisly exposé closely. There are powerful resonances between *The Genius of Universal Emancipation*, the apostolic antislavery paper he founded in 1821, and the pamphlet he once applauded for its unflinching "description of the cruelties and misery as [Torrey] there witnessed them, produced by the internal slave trade." In fact, one of the signature features of Lundy's eclectic newspaper was a graphically delineated special section known as the Black List that trafficked in news of verifiable recent atrocities peculiar to American slavery. These occasional columns, which were usually sandwiched between correspondence from fledgling antislavery societies the editor was trying to coax into life, included several accounts of slaves driven to suicide after being torn from their families and sold south. A Black List entry for August 1821, which drew on a brief report that had first appeared in a Maryland paper, set the tone:

> "A few days ago, a negro woman near Snow Hill, in this state, on being informed that she was sold, first cut the throat of her child, and then her own, by which both of them immediately died." Is there no blame to be attached to the murderous conduct of the villain who can thus with impunity drive the victims of rapacious power to the commission of such a horrid deed? Methinks I now see the creature smiling with the most perfect indifference at a relation of the fatal transaction, apparently no further concerned about it than what the idea of his loss in property suggests. O my country! truly dost thou nurse within thy bosom a scorpion which it is to be feared will yet sting thee to death.

For Lundy, a Quaker, slave suicide was a peculiar species of sin. Its guilt did not rest on the trembling shoulders of women like this one but upon the conduct of all those "villain[s]" who bought and sold people as though they were mules. Nor was the wickedness of such men a matter of private conscience. "O my country!" Lundy wailed, reminding readers that the specter of slave suicide would haunt every corner of the nation until this vicious traffic was annihilated.[29]

Whether the scene was a Maryland plantation, a Richmond jail, a steamer bound for Natchez, or a whipping post in New Orleans, the portrayals of slave self-destruction that peppered the Black List intermittently throughout the 1820s and 1830s marked a striking departure from earlier antislavery writing about suicide. Following Torrey's example, Lundy largely rejected the impulse to frame these deaths as freely chosen acts that betokened exceptional character. Instead he went in the opposite direction, muting black agency by completely absolving distressed mothers from responsibility or guilt for their actions and ascribing their suicides to the overwrought grief inevitably produced by the breakup of families. In Lundy's reckoning, the blame for each senseless loss of life was shared between "the wretch who induced the death of the inoffensive black" and the slave system itself. "Who is guilty of the murder in this case," the Quaker editor queried his readers after another of these reports, "the poor ignorant negro, driven to desperation by the frightful prospect of being sent down the river . . . or the government, which sanctions this 'infernal traffic in human blood?' "[30]

By the time William Lloyd Garrison published the first issue of *The Liberator* in January 1831, the Black List had become an irregular feature of the *Genius.* Lundy's scattered readers thus frequently confronted empathetically rendered images of slave mothers surrendering to suicide after being torn from the people they held most dear. Although Lundy's paper never achieved a mass circulation, surviving on a shoestring budget and buffeted by the itinerancy of its frail but restless editor, it nonetheless served as an important model for some of the motifs central to the far broader moral suasion campaign William Lloyd Garrison spearheaded in the 1830s. In fact, Garrison himself got his start writing copy for the *Genius*'s Black List when Lundy brought the paper to Baltimore in the late 1820s.[31]

Garrison did not stay long in Lundy's shadow. He did not share his mentor's enthusiasm for the ideas of the American Colonization Society, and he was suspicious of the southern legislatures with whom Lundy was always trying to negotiate. Powerfully affected by David Walker's *Appeal to the Colored Citizens of the World* (1829), Garrison instead proposed nothing less than immediate and unmitigated emancipation. Hopeful that the recent surge of evangelical awakenings across the Northeast could be harnessed for this purpose, and with an eye toward the progress of a bill before Parliament to emancipate every slave in the British colonies, Garrison reckoned that there would never be a better time to persuade the American public that drastic action to destroy every vestige of domestic slavery was both imperative and achievable.[32]

Garrison wasted no time. In 1833 he partnered with Manhattan silk importer Arthur Tappan to found the American Anti-Slavery Society (AASS), the first abolition society dedicated to the cause of immediate emancipation. Within a matter of months, Garrison had put his partner's considerable capital to work to launch a massive print campaign designed to flood the nation—the North and the South—with material that challenged slaveholders' moral authority. The scale of this campaign was entirely unprecedented. Within a few years there were, according to one society official, "upwards of a hundred" antislavery papers, including Garrison's *Liberator*, in circulation. Most were given away or sold to subscribers at deeply discounted rates, ensuring that they reached readerships far in excess of the *Genius of Universal Emancipation*. Beyond newspapers, the AASS and its growing network of regional affiliates assembled songbooks, hymnals, poetry collections, broadsides, tracts, circulars, prints, annual almanacs, all manner of stand-alone pamphlets, and even embroidered handkerchiefs, candy wrappers, and printed envelopes to do the work of moral suasion. By 1837 the AASS was mailing more than one million pieces of antislavery literature around the country each year in hopes of changing the hearts and minds of middle-class men and women not yet committed to immediate abolition. "Those who can be induced to *Read*, will most assuredly be abolitionized, and THOROUGHLY converted," a publisher's note inside one Garrisonian pamphlet promised.[33]

With a convert's zeal, Garrison spent the 1830s encouraging his growing throng of supporters to embrace the use of witness testimony to put American slavery on trial. To rebut proslavery depictions of well-cared-for black laborers too brutish and dull to feel pain, grief, and sorrow, the AASS poured its resources into doggedly detailing the bitter truth of slavery for detached and disinterested readers. In fact, Theodore Dwight Weld's *American Slavery as It Is* (1839), a catalog of cruelty that sold more than one hundred thousand copies in its first year, promised readers the "testimony of a thousand witnesses." Reflecting the central yet circumscribed role that black activists played in this proselytizing campaign, testimony provided by ex-slaves featured prominently in Weld's account and across every other genre of abolitionist writing during the 1830s. Indeed, the emergence of ex-slave narratives prefaced by well-credentialed white abolitionists in this period can be best understood as a contribution to this sort of evidentiary journalism. "Slavery is one of those monsters of darkness to whom the light of truth is death," Frederick Douglass, the author of no less than three autobiographies, later explained on a visit to London.[34]

Whether the witnesses were black or white, the overwhelming theme of this extraordinary flood of ink was the veritable agony of the slave experience. Reflecting lessons learned from Lundy and perhaps Torrey and

Humanitas too, Garrison and his disciples perfected a style of writing and reporting best described as "humanitarian realism." This tactic was carefully chosen to tie the cause at hand to emerging public sensibilities. Gruesome bodily tribulation became the primary staple of moral suasion literature in the 1830s as writers discovered that the gains made by evangelical and liberal faiths in many northern states over the past two decades had brought with them a tender-minded revulsion for bodily violence. Depictions of the instruments of physical cruelty, graphic illustrations of their use, and distressing elaborations of the emotional and spiritual scars borne by suffering black servants came to dominate accounts. So voyeuristic, fetishistic, and ubiquitous were these descriptions that southerners quickly complained that abolitionists were exaggerating the extent of slavery's cruelties.[35]

But Garrisonians refused to relent, holding firm to the belief that their strategy would turn neutrals into partisans. "All honest minds revolt at the spectacle of slavish oppressions," the lawyer and activist Charles Olcott explained in a memorandum to aspiring abolitionist authors in Ohio. "They instinctively take sides with the injured party, and long to punish the aggressor." As the lack of any discernible gender bias in Olcott's language suggests, the society's efforts included considerable outreach to women as well as men. Given the demographics of evangelical Christianity and the much-trumpeted successes other reform movements were having persuading female supporters to cajole their fathers, brothers, husbands, and sons to embrace causes such as temperance, to have done otherwise would have beggared reason. Although many abolition societies did not admit women as full voting members during the 1830s, they encouraged and sometimes sponsored writing by Lydia Maria Child, Abigail Mott, and Elizabeth Chandler and worked hard to feminize the image of the American slave.[36]

Governed by these imperatives, abolitionists pushed proud Caribbean Catos like Quashi to one side. In their place authors paraded a procession of suffering slaves—a majority of whom were female. Desperate and distracted wives or mothers, torn from their children or otherwise abused, now took center stage. Rather than wrestle their owners for mastery, these wounded women knelt in submission, beckoning good Christian readers to rush in and rescue others like them. Out went the encomiums to black virtue. In came language that served to strip enslaved people of their dignity in order to flatter evangelical readers' self-image as compassionate humanitarians. Selecting testimony that fit this new script, activists churned out countless reports of tender plants prostrated and put to grief by the institution's inescapable agonies, encouraging white readers everywhere to imagine themselves as these afflicted victims' last best hope.[37]

Depictions of women driven to suicide loom predictably large in this pageant of humiliated humanity. In fact, so many of these harrowed subjects surrendered to heaven that the image of a female slave lying dead by her own hand became one of the preeminent icons of Garrisonian antislavery writing. This iconic status derived in great measure from the fact that three of the most generic scenes in abolitionist print culture encompassed the possibility of the subject's suicide. Whenever white activists or ex-slave authors described black women and men subjected to unwarranted beatings, or sold away from their loved ones, or cornered or captured having tried to flee, the outcome was often the self-inflicted death of the slave. Oblivion, these Garrisonians lamented, was the only certain respite from such exquisite tragedy.[38]

A long statement from a sworn eyewitness that appeared in an 1832 issue of *The Liberator* offers an example of how suicide often punctuated the first of these pitiful set pieces. Reporting the testimony of Tennessee Presbyterian John Rankin, the Boston paper introduced northern readers to six young African girls recently arrived on a Georgia plantation. Set to labor in the fields, the adolescents were confronted by a vicious cycle of work and punishment designed to break their will and maximize productivity. On the owner's orders, the overseer had assigned them "a certain portion of labor during each day of the week, and in case they should fail to perform it, he was commanded to give them a considerable number of lashes each, and add the remainder of the task to the next day's labor." The girls were soon defeated by this unrelenting system—they could never meet the daily production targets, and so the number of lashes promised them grew each day. On the third morning they could take no more and resigned themselves to suicide. "This appeared to be the only means of escaping the most terrible cruelty," Rankin noted with obvious sympathy. When dinner was called, all six girls lingered behind, and while the other slaves gratefully left the fields, they ducked into a thicket and one by one hanged themselves. "Who can estimate the sum of similar cruelties that are practised upon the poor Africans, by the many thousand tyrants, who, from the slaveholding states, have literally received license for tyrannical exercise?" Garrison asked in a postscript that accompanied Rankin's report in most subsequent reprintings.[39]

Visions of equally outrageous beatings, whippings, and hamstringings in and around other plantations in the Deep South were common sights in the torrent of testimony that poured forth from the society's presses in the 1830s. Yet they were easily overshadowed by a far greater number of descriptions of Chesapeake slaves taking their own lives to avoid transportation to the Cotton Kingdom in the first place. "It is an awful thing to a Virginia slave to be sold for the Alabama and Mississippi country," James Williams, an ex-slave, wrote in his 1838 autobiography. "I have known some of them to die of grief, and others to commit suicide, on account of it." To testify to this awful truth, and to compel comfortable middle-class men and women to consider the "license for tyrannical exercise" given to slaveholders by the Constitution, Garrisonian newspaper editors and pamphleteers glutted their pages with bloody proof that the plantation regime in the Deep South was so intolerably vicious that slaves in the Upper South would retreat to the grave so as not to succumb to it.[40]

This reporting became so prevalent in the moral suasion literature after 1833 that in a single issue of New York's *American Anti-Slavery Reporter*, the editors published no less than four different accounts of men and women yielding to the temptation to commit suicide after becoming ensnared in the domestic slave trade. In one, an African youth living in Philadelphia "cut his throat, almost mortally, merely from the apprehension, as he said, of being sold." Another detailed how a cook on an Eastern Shore estate had reacted to news that she had been sold to a cotton planter in Georgia. In a climax exceptional in the wake of Nat Turner's 1831 revolt for its impolitic depiction of outwardly directed slave violence, the cook stabbed her owner with a carving knife before turning the blade on herself and falling lifeless "on her master's corpse."[41]

Though every Chesapeake slave dreaded the day that his or her turn might come, families divided in these sales felt the terror of long-distance migration most acutely. "There is nothing in slavery, perhaps, more painful, than the unavoidable separation of parents and children," the ex-slave William Grimes once mournfully remarked. Judging by the zeal with which Garrisonians turned the division of dozens of families into wrenching journalistic spectacles that might muster support for immediate emancipation, it seems that they could not have agreed more. In 1834, for example, Lydia Maria Child brought New York readers news that the mother of three little boys on a Missouri plantation had decapitated her children with an ax when she learned they would be sold to a slave trader from Texas. "She then put an end to her own existence." Child told this story time and again in various pamphlets aimed at different segments of the reading public over the next few years. In a version adapted for young readers in Massachusetts, she used an imagined dialogue between a girl named Caroline and her uncle to ventriloquize her belief that the distraught mother should not be blamed for these murders or for her own suicide:

> CAR. My mother loves me, too, but she wouldn't kill me.
>
> MR S. You ought to thank God that your mother is not a slave. . . . You can judge from this what slavery is. The mother, who had tried it, preferred death.
>
> CAR. Is it not wicked to kill?
>
> MR S. Yes; but this poor woman had not been allowed to read the Bible, and learn that it was wicked. She did what she thought was best for herself and children.

Here Child embeds an ambitious agenda within an intimate exchange. By forcing young readers to wonder whether their own mothers would copy this frantically protective black woman's response to a threat against her children, she skillfully shifts the burden of blame for these deaths, dividing it between the devils who are willing to break up families for profit and implicitly complicit northerners who turn away.[42]

Whether the setting was a Missouri plantation, a boardinghouse in the District of Columbia, or a Mississippi steamer, abolitionists never tired of showing readers the emotional dislocations wrought by the domestic slave trade. Throughout the 1830s a steady stream of activists in places like Boston,

Newburyport, and New York reprinted Jesse Torrey's conscience-stirring account of the woman who had jumped from a Washington window after being torn from her husband. "Did not the heart of that poor slave suffer acutely?" Child herself asked in a brief commentary she appended to one 1838 retelling. A prominent passage in a best-selling antislavery book published the following year hit similar notes. Citing Rankin as its source, Weld's *American Slavery as It Is* (1839) gave an account of a woman who made repeated attempts to leap from a steamboat puffing down the Mississippi after having been "carried off from all she counted dear on earth."[43]

In addition to cataloging the fatal consequences produced by fierce plantation discipline and the division and sale of slave families, Garrisonians wrung equal pathos from the suicides of thwarted runaways. The Boston minister and antislavery almanac editor Nathaniel Southard presented a typical example of this third archetype in a pamphlet the AASS published in New York in 1838. The entry began with a transcription of a news item that had first appeared in two southern papers:

> The negro woman (Lucy), confined in our jail as a runaway, put an end to her existence on the 28th ult. by hanging herself. Her master came to this place the day on which it occurred, and going to the jail, was recognized by the woman as her master. He had left the jail but a short time when it was discovered that the woman had destroyed herself. We have never known an instance where so much firmness was exhibited by any person, as was by this negro. The place from which she suspended herself was not high enough to prevent her feet from touching the floor, and it was only by drawing her legs up and remaining in that position, that she succeeded in her determined purpose.

While the southern papers emphasized Lucy's "firmness" and cast her hanging as an insolent yet "determined" challenge to those entitled to enslave and imprison her, Southard led readers of his pamphlet *Why Work for the Slave?* in the opposite direction. In a coda, Southard reoriented responsibility for her suicide, apportioning liability to the southern slave owners and traders who drove her to her death, and, by implication, to every northerner not already committed to immediate abolition. "Lucy," he lamented, "was, in effect, murdered by slavery. She cannot now describe to us the horrors from which she tried to escape, nor speak of the apprehension and despair which impelled her, thus, to seek the 'king of terrors' as a shelter from American slavery." Of course, there was no need for Lucy to speak. Southard spoke for her. In his account, the desperate actions she had been "impelled" to spoke volumes. She had had no choice.[44]

Southard's willful interpretation of the broader meaning of this slave's suicide was no aberration. Throughout the 1830s, abolitionist presses turned out account after account of the last moments of failed fugitives, framing each self-destructive act as inevitable capitulation to the pervasive power of the slave system. The effect was to strip runaways of the desperate courage many had surely mustered and to turn proud souls into submissive ciphers whose plights pleaded for compassionate intervention. Even male slaves, a group that revolutionary-era activists had worked hard to associate with honor and virtue, were brought low by this treatment.[45]

Among the many frustrated fugitives eulogized in Garrisonian outreach literature, none was more pathetically rendered than Paul, a Congolese man found hiding in a Carolina swamp having fled his master. According to Charles Ball, the author of a popular ex-slave narrative first published in Lewistown, Pennsylvania, in 1836, the man he discovered in the swamp that day was walking wounded; his back "was seamed and ridged with scars of the whip." So beaten had he been that "the natural colour of the skin had disappeared and was succeeded by a streaked and speckled appearance of dusky white and pale flesh colour, scarcely any of the original black remaining." Captured and transported to the Americas five years earlier, Paul had had to leave his aged mother and his wife and four children in Africa. Ever since he had been at the mercy of a drunk and violent owner "whose temper was so savage, that his chief delight appeared to consist in whipping and torturing his slaves." This master had formed a particular dislike for Paul, forcing him to flee to the swamp where Paul had lived on the meager meat of frogs and tortoises for more than three weeks. Still wearing the iron collar with dangling bells in which his tormentor had encased him as punishment for previous escapes, Paul had been afraid to travel much or search for food in daylight, "lest the sound of his bells be heard by someone."[46]

Paul's thoughts had long since turned to suicide, and Charles Ball reported to readers of his autobiography that on their first meeting Paul "reasoned with me upon the propriety of destroying a life which was doomed to continual distress." Ball did all he could to ease his companion's burdens: he lit a fire, helped Paul to food, and implored him to "bear his misfortunes as well as he could" before promising to come again the following Sunday with tools to release him from his fetters. But when he returned, the ravens and buzzards were circling ominously. Ball soon discovered why: "The lifeless, and putrid body of the unhappy Paul, hung suspended by a cord, made of twisted hickory bark, passed in the form of a halter round the neck, and firmly bound to a limb of the tree."[47]

Stories like Paul's saturated abolitionist output throughout the 1830s. Intended to appall and affront respectable readers' delicate sensibilities while simultaneously playing upon the Old Testament story of the suffering servant (Isaiah 53), the endless recycling of so many reports of slaves compelled to suicide by the crushing weight of their peculiar burdens served as a potent shorthand for all the sins of slavery and came to define the moral suasion campaign at the moment it achieved a national profile. In this effort, these Garrisonian immediatists demonstrated extraordinary message discipline. Like Robert Rantoul and his fellow antigallows campaigners, these antislavery reformers found little purpose in casting suicide as something unnatural or personally damning. They also distanced

Citing Charles Ball's memoir as his source, Nathaniel Southard included this simple woodcut alongside an abridged version of Paul's story in his popular abolitionist almanac. Nathaniel Southard, ed., *American Anti-Slavery Almanac for 1838* (Boston: Webster and Southard, 1837). Courtesy of the American Antiquarian Society.

themselves from revolutionary-era associations between self-destruction and principled resistance to tyranny. Instead Garrison and his acolytes offered a remarkably consistent vision of subaltern suicide as the inexorable product of a culture of oppression—what Durkheim later termed "fatalistic" suicide. Regardless of the specifics of setting or the particular provocations that actually drove each black person toward his or her seemingly inevitable self-destruction, activists repeated the same indictment over and over again. "Such is the system of slavery!" the New York editor of *The Slave's Friend* concluded after relaying the story of a New Orleans fugitive who drowned himself rather than be carried back to face his master.[48]

Paul's biographer said the same. Addressing the many readers of *Slavery in the United States* (1836) directly, Charles Ball made the case for exculpating men like Paul. "Surely," he asked,

> if any thing can justify a man in taking his life into his own hands, and terminating his existence, no one can attach blame to the slaves on many of the cotton plantations of the south, when they cut short their breath, and the agonies of the present being, by a single stroke. What is life worth, amidst hunger, nakedness and excessive toil, under the continually uplifted lash?

Slavery, this ex-slave author argued, was a special case, and when men and women ensnared in it take their own lives they should be exempt from the moral and religious reprobation they would meet with had they been free. When he had been sold south years earlier—"[I] was told that I would be able to get another wife in Georgia"—Ball himself had often thought of hanging himself, a fact he now believed said more about his circumstances than about his character. "Such an act, done by a man in my situation," Ball wrote, looking back, "could not be a violation of the precepts of religion, nor of the laws of God."[49]

In retrospect, the publication of Charles Ball's affecting and wide-ranging autobiography in 1836 marked the apotheosis of organized moral suasion. By the time Weld's *American Slavery as It Is* appeared in 1839, Garrison's grand biracial coalition had begun to splinter. After the financial crash of 1837 wiped out much of most abolition societies' assets, operations came to a temporary halt. The pause paralyzed the movement, giving rise to second-guessing within the leadership as to whether their vast investment in moral suasion was paying off.

By many measures the Garrisonian campaign—which had used depictions of slave suicide so consistently and unsparingly to prick white conscience—had been an unprecedented success. More than one thousand local antislavery associations were now up and running, including several dozen devoted to female activists. Newspapers such as *The Liberator* and *The Emancipator* were selling well in New England and New York; so were ex-slave narratives like Ball's. Abolition had found a reading public, many of whom seemed ready to become more actively involved. In fact, by the end of the 1830s, petitions signed by more than a million northern men and women had reached Congress. Efforts to harness the power of print to dissolve racial prejudice and incite humanitarian support for immediate emancipation had finally forced debate about the prohibition of the domestic trade and the immediate abolition of plantation slavery onto the national agenda, overcoming the restrained, embarrassed character of earlier antislavery writing.[50]

Yet for all their shrill urgency and strategic savvy, abolitionists remained marginalized. Their nearly decade-long national crusade to shock comfortable middle-class readers out of their apathy had elicited a powerful backlash. Society meeting rooms had been torched by proslavery thugs, both Garrison and Tappan had been hanged in effigy, and a mob had martyred Elijah Lovejoy, an abolitionist printer in Illinois. While few could deny that the moral suasion campaign had seized the nation's attention—"I want no better evidence of it than the rabid violence of our enemies," the activist poet John Greenleaf Whittier wrote—the effect was abrasive, polarizing, and often counterproductive. The leadership's early hopes of reaching out to southerners through the mails had been easily blocked by partisan postmasters, while in the North, only 109,000 of the region's many millions of inhabitants claimed membership in antislavery societies by 1838.[51]

In 1840, after three years of increasingly angry recrimination within the society, the AASS split in two. A majority of its leaders, including Lewis Tappan and corresponding secretary James Birney, concluded that moral suasion was a utopian delusion that woefully underestimated the political influence of the slavocracy. They abandoned the persuasive print campaign that had defined organized abolition for the better part of a decade and turned instead to direct political action in the shape of the American and Foreign Anti-Slavery Society and the Liberty Party.[52]

A minority of perfectionists, including Garrison himself, remained behind to carry on their program of moral education. As their depictions of black suicide over the previous decade attest, these die-hard Garrisonians were under no illusion about how far the tentacles of the Slave Power reached. Quite the contrary—those who stayed by Garrison's side after the schism did so precisely because of their distrust of a political system that they had long regarded as constitutionally proslavery and thus fundamentally corrupt.

In one sense the split of 1840 had scant effect on the function of black suicide in antislavery persuasive writing. Whether allied with the remnant of the AASS or operating independently, activists still committed to moral suasion resumed their work in earnest after the schism. The only marked change was the appearance of novels that attempted to fictionalize the most affecting aspects of documentary testimony—a neat inversion of the debt to fictional tropes evident in many popular slave narratives of the time. Harriet Beecher Stowe's *Uncle Tom's Cabin* (1852), which found examples for many of the atrocities it described in Weld's *American Slavery as It Is*, epitomized the way literary abolitionists of this generation invoked slaves' suicides to remind white, northern readers of their moral and social responsibilities. In a dramatic set piece aboard a steamer bound for New Orleans, the slave trader Haley sells a black infant to a fellow passenger. Later, as Tom looks on, the child's distraught mother learns of her loss and then hurls herself from the deck, drowning in the swirling waters below. "The poor bleeding heart was still at last," Stowe wrote by way of benediction. Similar episodes, likewise calibrated to appeal to the maternal instincts of evangelical female readers and by so doing rehabilitate the reputation of sentimental fiction more generally, popped up in many other books, plays, newspapers, and pamphlets authored by white abolitionists between 1840 and the eve of the Civil War.[53]

Yet when we examine the full spectrum of portrayals of slave suicide emanating from abolitionist presses during the 1840s and 1850s, it is clear that this Stovian brand of humanitarian realism did not reign unopposed.

THE POOR BLEEDING HEART.

"At midnight Tom waked with a sudden start. Something black passed quickly by him to the side of the boat, and he heard a splash in the water."—Page 111.

Clenched hands, elevated above her head, telegraph this woman's desperate mental state as she reaches out in pleading prayer both to the heavens and to readers for help. "Poor Bleeding Heart" read the caption accompanying George Cruikshank's famous illustration. Harriet Beecher Stowe, *Uncle Tom's Cabin* (London: J. Cassell, 1852). Courtesy of the American Antiquarian Society.

In fact, a dramatic reversal in the way these last acts were understood and represented in abolition's public sphere was already under way, a shift indicative of the emergence of an important new force in American antislavery activity.[54]

The moment of the schism had coincided with the arrival in the North of several talented and vocal fugitives such as Frederick Douglass, Henry Highland Garnet, and William Wells Brown and the political maturity of free-born black activists like Joshua Bowen Smith and Martin Delany. These men were among the activists most dissatisfied by the slow pace of progress achieved by nonviolent moral suasion. Accordingly, these iconoclasts struck out in their own direction, turning their backs on the fight for the hearts and minds of white, northern readers. Heartened by rising numbers of fugitives arriving in cities like Boston, and two successful shipboard revolts (*Amistad* in 1839 and *Creole* in 1841), this new generation of free black leaders tried to reach out to southern slaves to urge them to assert their manhood and free themselves from bondage. They broke with the national movement's age-old commitment to pacifism and began openly encouraging bondsmen to seize their freedom and dispossess their masters—or die in the attempt. Henry Highland Garnet, a fugitive turned preacher settled in Troy, New York, justified this radical new message in a speech ostensibly addressed "to the Slaves of the United States of America," delivered at a convention of "colored citizens" that was held in Buffalo in 1843:

> NEITHER GOD, NOR ANGELS, OR JUST MEN, COMMAND YOU TO SUFFER FOR A SINGLE MOMENT. THEREFORE IT IS YOUR SOLEMN AND IMPERATIVE DUTY TO USE EVERY MEANS, BOTH MORAL, INTELLECTUAL, AND PHYSICAL, THAT PROMISES SUCCESS. If a band of heathen men should attempt to enslave a race of Christians, and to place their children under the influence of some false religion, surely, Heaven would frown upon the men who would not resist such aggression, even to death.

Brushing aside the previous decades of patronizing instructions to slaves to wait to be rescued, Garnet instead challenged them to take responsibility for their own emancipation and fight for their freedom, "even to death."[55]

Reaching back to the rhetoric long used to justify planters' exploitation of black life and labor, Garnet and the other members of this small but largely uncoordinated band of militants set about turning Patrick Henry into the hero of their own revolution. "LIBERTY OR DEATH. Oh what a sentence was that!" Garnet cried:

> Brethren, arise, arise! Strike for your lives and liberties. Now is the day and the hour. Let every slave throughout the land do this, and the days of slavery are numbered. You cannot be more oppressed than you have been—you cannot suffer greater cruelties than you have already. *Rather die freemen than live to be slaves.*

Importantly, Garnet, who was trying to secure votes to endorse his motion to appeal to slaves to use violence, did not differentiate between southern blacks who took their own lives or those killed while trying to flee or to raze the plantation. "What kind of resistance you had better make, you must decide by the circumstances that surround you," he advised. To Garnet, the distinctions were merely contextual. Flight, insurrection, and suicide were, despite polar opposite outcomes, coequal testimonies to slaves' capacity to sacrifice everything in the pursuit of freedom.[56]

Although Frederick Douglass would vote against Garnet's 1843 motion to appeal to southern slaves to use violence, his published writings suggest a growing sympathy for Garnet's position. When Douglass's first autobiography appeared in 1845, it redefined the rules for ex-slave writing, draining the genre of the pathos that authors such as Charles Ball had cultivated throughout the 1830s. Instead, Douglass instilled a new breed of masculine heroics that placed the slave's challenge to the master's economic and paternalistic authority at the heart of an egocentric narrative. Douglass's various autobiographies are thus rife with scenes in which the author and other male slaves put their lives on the line to protest their subjection and strike out on their own. "We did more than Patrick Henry, when he resolved upon liberty or death," Douglass wrote as he described an early attempt to flee his owner's estate. "With us it was a doubtful liberty at most, and almost certain death if we failed. For my part I should prefer death to hopeless bondage." He larded his account of his fight with Covey—a display of machismo unthinkable in ex-slave writing a decade earlier—with similar bravado and signaled his obvious approval when a fellow rebel slave committed an indirect form of suicide rather than be recaptured. Facing a lashing from an overseer for some prior infraction,

Demby had fled to the safety of a creek and stood there shoulder-deep, refusing to come out:

> Mr. Gore told him that he would give him three calls, and that, if he did not come out at the third call, he would shoot him. The first call was given. Demby made no response, but stood his ground. The second and third calls were given with the same result. Mr. Gore then, without consultation or deliberation with any one, not even giving Demby an additional call, raised his musket to his face, taking aim at his standing victim, and in an instant poor Demby was no more. His mangled body sank out of sight, and blood and brains marked the water where he had stood.

Standing his ground even as his life was threatened, Demby, like Douglass, preferred the certainty of death to the certainty of taking his punishment and remaining a slave.[57]

Douglass elaborated upon this uncompromising credo in an item he and coeditor Martin Delany published in the *North Star* in 1848. The occasion was the suicide of Stephen Redden, a free black man who had been convicted for trying to deliver "certain pictures of an abolition character" to plantation slaves in Maryland. Sentenced to more than ten years behind bars for his crime, Redden took his own life soon after the judge passed down the verdict. Casting Redden as a latter-day Cato, Douglass lauded him for taking his life "in the spirit of Roman chivalry." Then, with the sort of admiration for a jail suicide that would have turned Massachusetts attorney general Perez Morton beet-red with rage, Douglass explained that Redden had "preferred death to imprisonment" and had "chosen to die by his own hand!" Seeing no daylight between this free black man and the slaves he was jailed for trying to stir, Douglass figured Redden's suicide as a potent challenge to the domestic despotism inherent within the slave system:

> If there was meaning, beyond the mere sound of a rhetorical imprecation, in the exclamation of Patrick Henry, "Give me Liberty, or give me Death!" then we cannot help sympathizing with a poor, friendless individual, of a downtrodden race, arraigned in a slaveholding community, before a slaveholding judge and a slaveholding jury, without money to employ counsel, and convicted under laws of

GORE SHOOTING DENBY.

Refusing to return to shore, Demby (or Denby in some editions) waits for the overseer to shoot. This illustration appeared in many editions of Douglass's third autobiography. Frederick Douglass, *Life and Times of Frederick Douglass* (Hartford: Park Pub., 1881). Courtesy of the American Antiquarian Society.

which he was in all probability totally ignorant . . . —ay, even in that act of suicide which has hurried his soul into the presence of its God!

In the minds of Douglass, Garnet, and a growing number of other radical abolitionists, then, slave suicide had once again acquired a heroic dimension. They rejected the still-popular framing of similar deaths as fatalistic and pathetic testaments to slavery's hegemonic power. Instead they reconstituted the act as a triumphant and absolute form of withholding—a devastating assertion of self-mastery.[58]

In the wake of the passage of the Fugitive Slave Act on September 18, 1850, more and more black leaders began to speak of suicide as a robust and existential defense against the tyranny of the Slave Power. At an emergency meeting in Boston's Belknap Street Church two weeks later, on October 5, Joshua Bowen Smith, a free-born black member of the city's new Committee of Vigilance, told the anxious ex-slaves gathered there that if he was ever in their situation and a slave catcher came calling, "he should not be taken alive." After quoting Patrick Henry, he advised every man present "to arm himself with a revolver" and prepare to defend his liberty by dying for it. Three weeks later, the men gathered at a meeting in Philadelphia made an almost identical promise to themselves: "Resolved, That we endorse, to the full, the sentiment of the Revolutionary Patriot of Virginia, and should the awful alternative be presented to us, will act fully up to it—'Give me Liberty or give me Death.'"[59]

Many of these men seemed to have kept their promises. In fact, on December 5, two months to the day after Bowen Smith's address to Boston's fugitives, two slave catchers arrived in the city and knocked on the door of Lewis Hayden, demanding to know if he was sheltering William Craft. Hayden and Craft were runaway slaves, and both had barricaded themselves inside hoping that this day would never come. Hayden appeared at the threshold carrying a lighted torch and yelled to the men in the street that he had rigged the house with gunpowder and would blow everyone up rather than surrender. The slave catchers slunk away, vowing to return. Nine months later, a similarly self-destructive ultimatum rang in the ears of the marshals who laid siege to a group of runaway slaves holed up at a farmhouse in Christiana, just west of Philadelphia. When the marshals threatened to burn down the building to flush out their prey, William Parker, the self-appointed spokesman of the fugitives huddled inside, hollered back: "You can burn us, but you can't take us; before I give up, you will see my ashes scattered on the earth." While the arrival of an armed posse of local free blacks and their ensuing firefight with the marshals made Parker's promise moot, the sequence of events at Christiana in September 1851 demonstrates that reactions to the Fugitive Slave Act served to invest black suicide with a defiant, revolutionary aura not accorded to it since the turn of the century.[60]

As dark threats like those made by Parker and Hayden multiplied, they became familiar moments in press accounts of northern fugitives struggling to protect their freedom. In fact, when Anthony Burns, a quiet twenty-three-year-old Baptist living in Boston, was arrested under the powers of the Fugitive Slave Act in 1854, some city residents fully expected him to pull a pistol or draw a knife across his throat rather than be dragged back to slavery. " 'I cry for shame that he will not kill himself!' " one inconsolable young black woman reportedly wailed as she watched Burns shuffle resignedly toward the steamer that would return him to his Virginian master. " 'Oh! why is he not man enough to kill himself!' "[61]

This emerging conviction—that black men "man enough" to kill themselves were striking a decisive blow against slavery—was wrapped up in a broader attempt to reconstitute African American masculinity in antebellum America. By contrast, black leaders rarely voiced enthusiasm for the idea that slave women had the courage and virtue to mount the same revolutionary opposition. Such racialized sexism reflected an assumption shared by many within the abolition movement—that black women lacked the capacity for self-determination and self-government. For decades now, moral suasionists from Lydia Maria Child to Harriet Beecher Stowe had painted almost every black wife's or mother's suicide as a humiliating submission to a culture of oppression—the act of a victim, not of a rebel. Indeed, this understanding remained largely unquestioned until the spring of 1856, when abolitionist papers began to buzz with news of the trial of the fugitive ex-slave Margaret Garner, who had displayed terrible determination to prevent recapture by slitting the throat of one of her beloved daughters before attempting to kill her other children and then herself.[62]

In this respect, then, William Wells Brown's novel *Clotel; or, The President's Daughter* (1853), published three years prior to Garner's forthright and fatal defense of her family, marks an important early challenge to this gendered double standard. *Clotel*—often hailed as the first novel by an African American author and written in response to *Uncle Tom's Cabin*—culminates as the titular female fugitive races to the banks of the Potomac River, pursued by slave catchers. Bereft of a revolver but otherwise in lockstep with Joshua Bowen Smith's advice, Clotel leaps from a bridge as the catchers close in and drowns in the waters below. The chapter—titled "Death Is Freedom"—ends with a few verses of poetry that follow the bloated corpse of Jefferson's illegitimate mixed-race daughter as it is swept downstream and eventually disgorged on the banks of George Washington's Mount Vernon estate. Clotel's body washes up within sight of the revolutionary hero's tomb, leaving readers to consider the juxtaposition:

> That bond-woman's corse [*sic*]—let Potomac's proud wave
> Go bear it along *by our Washington's grave*,
> And heave it high up on that hallowed strand,
> *To tell of the freedom he won for our land.*
> A weak woman's corse [*sic*], by freemen chased down;
> Hurrah for our country! hurrah!
> To freedom she leaped, through drowning and death—
> Hurrah for our country! hurrah!'

Brown's blunt suggestion that a female slave's suicide could equal a patriot's wartime sacrifices found little favor among other black activists. Nor did its caustic, sarcastic encomiums to national pride—"Hurrah for our country!"—sit well with the white reading public, who largely shunned the novel until it was reissued during the Civil War.[63]

Regardless of the gender of the slave in question, there were, at first, very few antebellum whites willing to revisit the revolutionary-era proposition that the suicides of enslaved people could echo the patriotic struggles of the nation's founders. Only slowly, as proslavery interests in Congress achieved a string of legislative victories in the 1840s and 1850s, did one white abolitionist after another begin to entertain that possibility. Ironically, the most famous pacifist in America was in the vanguard. Stung by criticism that his long-standing objection to violence was hamstringing a proper response to anti-abolitionist riots

Arms raised and spread, as if in triumph and thanks, Clotel escapes imminent capture by darting over the railing at the last possible second. This illustration, titled "The Death of Clotel," was a standard feature in several editions of Brown's novel. William Wells Brown, *Clotel; or, The President's Daughter* (London: Partridge & Oakey, 1853). Courtesy of the Library Company of Philadelphia.

and lynchings, William Lloyd Garrison briefly set aside his conscientious objections in the chaotic years after the 1840 schism, giving his own address endorsing slaves' determined resistance within weeks of Henry Highland Garnet's.[64]

More importantly, given the way his most puritanical disciples suppressed all news of that speech, Garrison also opened the pages of *The Liberator* to pieces that valorized violent martyrdom. Just three months after Garnet's August 1843 plea to the nation's slaves, *The Liberator* featured a story that distilled to its essence Garnet's understanding of slave suicide as an awful yet triumphant declaration of independence. "Liberty or Death" ran the headline, accompanied by a story of a black mechanic from Georgia who had been promised manumission on the death of his owner, only to be sold south by a cheating executor. Snatched from the cusp of freedom, George had been hastily herded onto a steamship by his new owner. But as dawn broke the next day, George was nowhere to be found, and the ship's grindstone was missing. The crew found both at the bottom of the river. "Death before slavery! George had tasted liberty!!!" the last line of the report read.[65]

The Liberator and its sister paper, *The Emancipator*, kept up a steady stream of similarly styled yet meticulously sourced news items throughout the 1840s. These reports struck indignant notes more often than not, demanding that readers interpret each Samson-like suicide as a deliberate rebuttal to what a column in *The Emancipator* called "the assertion, so often made by apologists for slavery, that the slaves are very happy in bondage and like it better than freedom." An item in the same sheet's August 12, 1846, issue was typical; it began by describing how a fugitive from a Baton Rouge plantation had recently been discovered "suspended with his feet dangling only a foot or two from the earth" by his owner's furious agents. Then, in a lengthy commentary that turned this slave's suicide into an accusation, the anonymous author fumed at the hypocrisy of southerners proud of Patrick Henry's eloquent call to resist tyranny at all costs yet unwilling to credit the heroism of "a rude and almost savage African [that] attempts to put in practice this principle of the great Virginian, and, rather than longer submit to the galling chains and blood-clotted cowskin of Slavery, deliberately and boldly meets death."[66]

By the time Garrison finally ended *The Liberator*'s flirtation with righteous violence in 1851, the cause had taken on a life of its own. The Compromise of 1850, which paved the way for the expansion of slavery into the Utah and New Mexico territories, and the brazen passage of the Fugitive Slave Act the same year, marked gigantic victories for proslavery interests in Congress. In the face of this onslaught, even the most committed pacifists began to waiver. In fact Henry C. Wright, the man who had written the "Non-Resistance" column in *The Liberator* for years, recanted his faith in the promise of peaceful persuasion in 1851, pledging that it was now his duty to go into the South and help African Americans resist their enslavement any way he could.[67]

The ratification of the Kansas-Nebraska Act in 1854, which repealed a thirty-five-year-old ban on slavery in territories north of the 36°30' parallel, set off a chain reaction of similar conversions. In a matter of months after the bill became law, several prominent white members of the recently disbanded Liberty Party endorsed militant action as a last resort.

Turning Patrick Henry's revolutionary rhetoric into a plan of action, men like James Redpath, Henry Ward Beecher, and Gerrit Smith began smuggling pistols, knives, and pocket compasses into Virginia, the Carolinas, and Georgia in hopes of encouraging their black brothers to rise up in armed revolt, escape to safety in the North, or summon the courage to die in the attempt. "Hitherto, I have opposed the bloody abolition of slavery," Smith declared in 1856, "But now, when it begins to march its conquering bands into the Free States, I and ten thousand other peace men are not only ready to have it repulsed with violence, but pursued even unto death, with violence."[68]

Planters and other proslavery interests watched the rise of a militant biracial coalition with horror and anger. During the 1830s, long before the abolition movement's disciplined commitments to pacifism and humanitarian realism had begun to waiver, supporters of the Slave Power had regularly (and mistakenly) accused Garrison and his allies of encouraging slaves to revolt. Now, as calls for violent resistance to slavery swept from the North toward the South and the West, planters had genuine reason to lose sleep. As Kansas bled in the mid-1850s, some there even imagined that itinerant abolitionists were sneaking onto their plantations to talk their slaves into acts of mass suicide:

> Circumstances have transpired within a few weeks past in this neighborhood which have placed beyond doubt the existence of an organized band of Abolitionists in our midst. We counsel our friends who have money in slave property to keep a sharp look out lest their valued slaves may be induced to commit acts which might jeopardize their lives. Mr. Graffam Thompson of this place lost a valuable Negro about a week ago, and we have not the least doubt that she was persuaded by one of this lawless band to destroy herself rather than remain in slavery. In fact, one of this gang was heard to remark, "that she did perfectly right in drowning herself," and just as he would have done, or "what any negro who is held in bondage should do."

While the scene strains credulity, this notice from an 1855 issue of the *Kansas Herald* demonstrates planters' acute awareness of the recent sea change in abolitionist engagement with slave suicide and the problem of resistance. Since the late seventeenth century, southern slaveholders had worked to shore up their power over their human property by brutally punishing every slave they discovered trying to kill themselves. In fact, deterring suicide on the plantation (and concealing the truth of its extent from northern visitors) was fundamental to preserving the grand illusion that bondsmen had not only consented to their enslavement but were also powerless to resist it. By 1855, many planters were coming to a dreadful realization: that militant abolitionists now considered acts of suicide in the single-minded pursuit of liberty worthy of some of the same assistance and encouragement they gave to slaves willing to risk their lives as rebels or runaways.[69]

By the eve of the Civil War, militant abolitionists had dug in everywhere. Although Garrison himself had returned to pacifism in the wake of the bloodshed in Kansas, more and more men and women from across the movement's splintered spectrum were moving in the opposite direction, leaving the aging leader increasingly isolated. John Brown's repeated attempts to spark slave revolts across the South after 1855 were simply the most extreme manifestations of the growing belief that blood sacrifice was a just and purifying rite for blacks as well as whites. In fact, the note that the leathery extremist passed to a jailer moments prior to his own martyrdom in Virginia in 1859 prophesized that more black blood—"the blood of millions"—would have to be spilled before the crimes of "this guilty land" could be purged away.[70]

It has become easy to dismiss John Brown's fanatical exploits as the product of his own sui generis conceptions of idealism and self-sacrifice. Yet as shifting depictions of slave suicides in antislavery writing make clear, Brown's ideas about the role of righteous resistance to race slavery had their roots in a decades-long debate about who had the power to challenge its corrupt and insidious authority and dispossess plantation owners who held human beings as private property. In this debate, perceptions of slave suicide played a central role.

In the immediate aftermath of the American Revolution, a handful of insurgent antislavery activists had used the pages of the new nation's literary magazines to forge a lyrical link between suicide and self-determination. They used this understanding of self-destruction as a noble and forceful response to slavery to try to undermine the pernicious mythology that the country's nonfree population had, through nonresistance, effectively consented to their enslavement. Stories of men imbued with what college-educated observers understood to be classical virtue, men who chose death over tyranny, thus dominated late eighteenth-century attempts to harness popular print culture for the limited, gradualist goals of early national antislavery.

These images of exceptional slaves committed to principled yet violent resistance did not disappear from antislavery writing in the nineteenth century. Activists resurrected stories of men like Quashi from time to time throughout the Jacksonian era. Yet by the 1830s, fear of slave revolts and the restrictions on representation that Garrisonians believed were necessary to effect a full-scale moral revolution ensured that these Caribbean Catos were banished to the margins of the movement. A growing cast of suffering servants instead took their place, many of them tearful women whose abject victimhood was rendered in pitiful descriptions of how they surrendered to death to staunch physical and emotional wounds. Constructed so as to make evangelical readers feel like Good Samaritans and compel them to intervene, these fatalistic and utterly unthreatening portrayals of slaves committing suicide were so widespread in abolitionist writing during the 1830s that they came to define nationwide efforts to undermine slavery's moral authority.[71]

Following the forced retrenchment of moral suasion activity after the Panic of 1837 and the fissuring of the abolitionist movement in 1840, the trope of the suicidal slave was remade once more. While writers such as Harriet Beecher Stowe would continue to trade on images of slave mothers trembling on the verge of oblivion until the eve of the Civil War, militant abolitionists active in the 1840s and 1850s rejuvenated the revolutionary-era connection between self-destruction, mastery, and manhood to serve a new and more radical liberationist creed that would settle the question of consent once and for all. First black and then white militants of the antebellum generation fused the example of Samson, the mighty Old Testament slave who brings down the temple roof upon the Philistines as he dies, to the rhetoric of Patrick Henry, the Virginia patriot who brooked no capitulation in the face of tyranny. In doing so they reached out to southern slaves and fearful fugitives alike with a simple and direct message: death is freedom, so declare your independence.[72]

Conclusion: Martyrs on the Altar of the Nation

In 1862, as the Civil War stretched into its second year, Union forces, under the command of Generals Grant and Buell, pushed their way into Tennessee. Their advance drove many slave owners in this frontline Confederate state to try to limit their potential losses by selling some of their human inventory to plantation owners in the Deep South. This, according to a report in the May 9 issue of the *Hartford Daily Courant*, was the cause that drove "a large and rather intelligent mulatto" to take his own life. Snatched away from his wife and children and sold at a Memphis auction to a Texas planter he knew to be a monster, the man in question shot himself with a pistol he had been concealing for the purpose. "The bondsman was free," the *Courant* declared, and the new owner of this "heroic martyr" had been thwarted. " 'D—n the cursed darkey,' " swore the Texas planter. " 'I am just so much out of pocket. If he'd come to life again, I'd give him forty lashes.' "[1]

By the early 1860s the *Courant* was one among a growing number of northern newspapers willing to publish occasional pieces that presented the suicides of fugitive blacks and rebel slaves as triumphant acts of dispossession. Earlier portrayals of suffering servants apologetically succumbing to oblivion to escape the psychic terrors of slavery now had to compete with increasingly bold and unrepentant depictions of sanctionable black suicide. These tidal changes in the representation of slaves who destroyed themselves reflect the shifting imperatives demanded by the increasingly radical agenda of militant abolitionists after the schism of 1840. Yet the same sea change also points to a larger transformation in the way many other early Americans had begun to respond to the divisive social and political implications most still perceived in acts of suicide.

Between the 1780s and the 1830s, throughout the Republic's faltering adolescence, parents, ministers, and magistrates had marshaled nearly every pulpit and printing press at their disposal to advance the self-serving claim that self-destruction was too damaging to the integrity of families, churches, and society itself ever to be countenanced. Alienated by the ascendency of Jeffersonian democracy, denominational pluralism, labor unrest, and smaller yet no less significant insurrections in domestic life and gender relations, many Calvinists and Federalists in particular were consumed with apocalyptic visions of total cultural collapse. "In what sense is it true that any people, however free, are self governed?" griped retired Massachusetts congressman Fisher Ames in an 1805 essay titled "The Dangers of American Liberty." "If they have in fact no government but such as comports with their ever-varying and often inordinate desires, then it is anarchy." In the age of the first-person singular, any self-destructive act—especially one committed by the young and willfully independent—seemed not only tragic but appallingly selfish. To Ames, suicide served as contemptible and contemptuous proof that all useful restraints on individual impulses had fallen away, that more and more of the American people lived beyond the reach of moral influence, and that the nation itself was set on a path to ruin.[2]

In this supercharged atmosphere, the language of suicide became a conspicuously common resource for the advancement of larger arguments about the proper relationship between liberty and order. Manifest in a startling variety of cultural expressions, suicide was the subject of incessant talk and debate in the newly United States, its salient power deriving in great part from its extremity, finality, and emotive force.

After the break with Britain, partisans succeeded in turning the subject of self-destruction into a vital vector for conflict and dispute. Perceived as an act of unadulterated individualism, suicide assumed unrivaled potency as a motif in public debates about the sorts of responsibilities that Americans should each have to themselves, to one another, and to the republican government they had together created. After all, as a polity built upon a voluntary contract among citizens, the nation derived its political health from the strength of the moral ties among its self-governing constituents. Thus as they tried to understand the meaning of freedom in this postrevolutionary order, more and more stakeholders found cause to link the precarious state of the Union to individual decisions to die, thereby turning public and private catastrophes into prisms of one another.

By such means, suicide became not simply a terminus for hysteria but also a locus for contesting some of the most consequential questions facing the new Republic during a cultural crisis as severe as any in American history. Placing suicide politics at the center of analysis thus provides keen insights into the struggles to produce new national conventions and aspirations. Indeed, the rich reservoir of rhetoric and imagery that invoking suicide made available was put to formative use in battles to determine the proper role of pervasive institutions like the media, private charity, the criminal justice system, organized religion, and slavery, precisely because it expressed the central dilemma facing the country and its citizens: how to walk the line between respecting individual liberty and preserving the integrity of the collective.

Animated by newspaper coverage suggesting that America was drowning in a sea of self-destructive behavior, many of the privileged men and women most unsettled by the atomizing dislocations peculiar to early national society used a string of very public debates about the meaning of self-destruction to bemoan the limits of their diminishing authority. Each time they decried the depiction of sentimental suicide in popular novels or denounced the frequency with which morally ambiguous reporting appeared in local newspapers, such once-powerful people found the means to express their deepest anxieties about the preservation of their own status, the decline of religious authority, and the crumbling of familial deference. Fanning the flames of the early national suicide panic, talking about its presumed causes, and racking their brains to find ways to prevent it gave husbands, fathers, doctors, and clergymen wedged between entitlement and insecurity a framework upon which to hang their hopes and fears at a time when their grasp on power seemed less and less certain.

For many Calvinist ministers and virtually every supporter of the Federalist Party, this was a rearguard action, a socially conservative means to lament a way of life already lost. Yet other aging revolutionaries took a more optimistic view, perceiving this unprecedented cultural crisis as a crucible of opportunity. Benjamin Rush is a case in point. A moderate, often maverick, Jeffersonian, Rush was as traumatized by the perceived breakdown of morality and virtue as Federalist totems like Fisher Ames. And, like Ames, Rush's own claim to moral influence in the new Republic derived definition and substance from his opposition to suicide and the socially subversive associations that he and many others perceived to accompany it. However, unlike Ames, Rush was not willing to surrender the new nation to anarchy without a fight. Instead, he put on a braver face and tried to muster faith that a sustainable political union could still be salvaged from this bubbling cultural ferment.

After the Revolutionary War, Rush devoted ever-greater energies to the search for new ways to foster cooperation in an open society. Strikingly, Rush's struggles to repair the ties of mutual obligation and cultivate new conditions of coexistence frequently found expression in the business of suicide prevention. As a foot solider of a republican revolution reliant upon a virtuous and well-informed citizenry, Rush argued for censoring newspaper coverage of suicide lest it dull the moral senses of malleable readers or stir them to bloody acts of imitation. As the father of nine voracious novel-readers and as a member of the Board of Visitors of a Young Ladies Academy, Rush strenuously attacked popular sentimental works that seemed to sabotage family bonds by portraying teenage suicide as exquisitely romantic. Likewise, as an early vice president of an antidrowning charity, Rush invested time and money in the cause of direct intervention to prevent the suicides of strangers, targeting considerable resources toward enacting his belief that well-meaning elites could and should interfere with the decisions of ordinary Americans determined to die.

Finally, as the author of the first American textbook to categorize self-destruction as a symptom of biological disease, and as the superintendent of the first purpose-built psychiatric ward, the doctor was instrumental in extending the authority of the medical establishment to encompass the custody of men and women, including his own suicidal son, John, who were deemed to be dangers to themselves.[3]

By founding or supporting a string of organizations and initiatives designed to drape coercive impulses in the garb of disinterested charity and cosmopolitan benevolence, Rush and other like-minded critics of unbridled democracy tried to nurture new bonds of empathy that could serve ordering functions without ever appearing to challenge the primacy of the rational individual in liberal society. The result was a battery of highly visible campaigns intended to transform individual character by promoting reflection, self-improvement, self-respect, and self-control. The cities of New England and the mid-Atlantic became the headquarters of most of these new experiments in moral stewardship because, as historian Sean Wilentz writes, "[it] was in these metropolises that the idealism and anxiety of what came to be called 'modern life' were most keenly felt and expressed."[4]

Rush's life's work derived much of its urgency from his enduring belief that self-destructive behavior was making "alarming progress" in the early United States. In this regard, the doctor was hardly sui generis. Evidence drawn from a cross section of heads of household and religious and political leaders attests that such convictions were widely held, deeply felt, and remarkably durable. Indeed, while the doctor would pass from the scene in 1813, anxiety that the new nation was in the grip of an unparalleled "epidemic" of suicide survived him by several decades. The panic seems to have peaked around 1805, at precisely the moment embattled elites seized upon newspaper coverage of suicide to act out their concerns about the rise of a secular press. Intermittent aftershocks, however, continued to shake public discourse throughout the 1810s, 1820s, 1830s, and beyond. "The land stinks with suicide," wrote Emerson as he surveyed the human carnage apparently produced by the financial collapse of 1837. "Ours is the age of suicide," a magazine columnist agreed soon afterward.[5]

It was not until the 1840s that expanding use of statistical methods by civil servants, social scientists, insurance agents, and medical investigators began to question this bone-deep, culture-shaping assumption. With the backing of ever-larger government bureaucracies, newly established scientific associations, and a cadre of medical institutions chasing prestige and respectability, America's first cohort of professional statisticians went to work trying to quantify all sorts of demographic patterns. No longer content to rely on unsystematic newspaper reports for assessments of the frequency of self-destruction, this pioneer generation succeeded in adding it to the list of means of violent death included in the 1850 census, and by 1860 the census went so far as to distinguish between five different methods of taking one's own life. As doctors, scientists, and statisticians slowly assumed responsibility for collecting suicide data, much of the debate about the meaning of self-destruction slowly migrated from the nation's pulpits and public prints to newly founded scientific and psychiatric serials, most notably the *Journal of Insanity*, founded in 1844.[6]

None of this is to say that public discourse on the subject evaporated after 1840. It did not. In novels and newspapers, and in poetry and in prose, a great many Americans continued to deploy the language of self-destruction as a resonant metaphor and to interrogate the meaning of individual decisions to die with forensic interest. There was, however, another way in which the antebellum era marked a turning point in the way ordinary citizens responded to the specter of suicide. Even as the reading public continued to reflexively condemn the great majority of suicides they encountered in print, some began to find room in their hearts to render a different verdict every once in a while. During the 1840s, as the business of interpreting why people kill themselves became ever more professionalized, and as ever more sophisticated data-gathering efforts undercut sensational claims about the frequency of self-destruction in America, it was becoming easier to publicly express compassion for men and women driven to suicide, albeit only in certain highly circumscribed situations. This small but significant shift in the way Americans responded to acts of individual suicide committed beyond their immediate circle of family and friends drew great strength from the rise of liberal and evangelical denominations in the decades after 1815, a development that had spurred more and more middling people to embrace humanitarian identities.[7]

Sensing opportunity, activists set about exploiting this burgeoning samaritanism to promote a range of liberal causes. Thus in the forty years after 1815, as reformers gained steadily greater access to the tools of print production, the northern reading public occasionally found themselves confronted with depictions of suicide that assumed that mature, sensible readers possessed the capacity to sympathize with stricken strangers who took their own lives to escape oppression or protest tyranny. Dismissing the colonial-era concerns that suicide was a crime against God and against nature while gingerly leveraging the early national obsession with suicide as a crime against society for their own purposes, reformers began presenting certain end-of-life decisions as imperfect challenges to entrenched interests that could be dislodged no other way. In this sense, the way successive generations of abolitionists promoted first pity and later esteem for black slaves and fugitives who committed suicide bore close relation to the efforts of Robert Rantoul, Charles Spear, and other antigallows campaigners to indict the death penalty. Stopping far short of any universal claim to a right to die, both movements succeeded in turning certain suicides into mobile signs filled with radical possibilities.

It was an uphill battle all the way. As they struggled to carve out a space in which the self-inflicted deaths of peculiarly degraded populations could be understood and identified with, campaigners against chattel slavery and the death penalty were careful not to overreach. Indeed, a mountain of evidence survives to demonstrate that antebellum Americans continued to heap contempt upon strangers who committed the act in most other circumstances. So fierce was that disdain that savvy partisans were able to exploit it to serve a range of social agendas throughout the 1840s and 1850s. The ongoing paper war between Universalists and their "partialist" opponents—a vitriolic campaign that rested on the shared belief that painting a rival faith group as a suicide cult was a toxic smear—provides one obvious example. For the same reasons, antebellum crusades to separate drunks from their drink, to alert well-to-do ladies of the perils of tightly bound corsets, and to denigrate lottery gambling each turned on a studied comparison between the vice in question and the "crime" of suicide. In one campaign after another, reformers played upon the urban reading public's enduring conviction that self-destruction remained, with some exceptions, a particularly heinous offense. Indeed, as American politics became engulfed in sectional acrimony and as the threat of secession and Civil War grew ever more tangible, a new generation of antebellum commentators spilled barrels of ink to decry disunion itself as a species of suicide.

"O America, thou has destroyed thyself!" wailed Rev. Daniel Steele during a fast-day sermon delivered five months after provisional Confederate forces attacked the US Army garrison at Fort Sumter. Standing before a large interdenominational audience gathered in the Baptist Church in Springfield, Massachusetts, in September 1861, the Methodist minister told those assembled that the brutal war now raging between the states was nothing less than an act of "national suicide." How had it come to this? "What evil times have we fallen upon," Steele asked, "when the greatest, happiest, freest and most envied government on earth puts the suicidal knife to her own throat, and lies, in sight of all the nations, weltering in her own blood?" He paused for barely a beat: "There is but one answer; there can be but one answer." Slavery, Steele said, was the cause of this "undisputed case of self-destruction."[8]

Of course states are not people. Contrary to constitutional arguments later popularized by Senator Charles Sumner, they cannot commit suicide. Yet the longer Steele spoke, the more he hammered home this strange and sobering comparison. For more than an hour—and for over thirty pages in the account of the sermon published later—Steele went to extraordinary rhetorical lengths to define the "stupendous rebellion" now rending the country in two as a species of self-destruction and to identify the spread of slavery as the toxic taproot of the nation's ruined health. "Our country has committed suicide by a slow poison," Steele asserted, before extending the analogy further still:

> In August, 1620, four months before the Mayflower dropped her anchor in Plymouth bay, [the] Virginia [colony], from the hands of a Dutch trader, received to her vitals a small dose of poison. Like most slow poisons, it produced a pleasing intoxication, alleviated the fatigue or hard toil, and threw a roseate hue over the asperities of colonial life. Again, and again, she quaffed the bewitching opiate, all unconscious of the pangs, the shame, the woe, the death lurking within that cup. Her sisters, the twin Carolines, Mary and Georgiana, see-

> ing her gay and easy life, followed her fatal example, and soon the insidious charmer had conquered the entire American family with the wine of this new inebriation. The symptoms were everywhere visible; the deadening of the natural sensibilities, the indurating of the conscience, and the beclouding of the reason. Some, seeing the hidden danger, drew back and saved themselves, by a desperate struggle, as from the outer circle of a whirlpool. But the others drank more deeply of the damning potion, till they fell into a deadly stupor, from which they have never awaked, not even now, when the final convulsions of death have seized upon them.

Drawing on imagery adapted from antebellum temperance literature, Steele compared slavery to an intoxicant, a poisoned "wine cup" that had numbed the nation's conscience and sent the country on a slow but steady path to self-destruction.[9]

As Steele himself explained, his purpose in dressing a decidedly familiar set of arguments about the causes of the Civil War in the language of embodied, self-directed violence served three aims. First, he intended this refrain to function as shorthand for the claims advanced by many northern abolitionists and evangelicals that the shocking cycle of violence now engulfing the continent was self-inflicted and unprovoked and thus singularly deplorable. "The trail of this serpent is upon us all," Steele declared, chiding his Massachusetts constituents for their own complicity in failing to stop the expansion of race slavery across the Deep South and the West in the decades since the Revolution:

> All the conceivable elements of guilt, which constitute a crime of the highest turpitude, combine in the suicide of our nation:—the absence of provocation, the unveiled wickedness of the purpose, the villainous means employed, the irreparable disasters consequent, and the satanic animus of the whole movement, mark this most outstanding act in the drama of history, as a stupendous national felony.

Embodying young America as a self-destructive soul that had drunk deep from slavery's poison chalice allowed Steele to emphasize collective guilt for the country's undoing.[10]

Second, Steele made the analogy between secession and self-destruction to communicate his repugnance for the bloody and brutal struggle that had followed that constitutional breach. "Suicide has always been considered, by Christian moralists, the most culpable form of murder," he explained. Thus to compare the martial violence of the past six months to the act of self-murder was to condemn it in the most damning terms imaginable. Indeed, while Steele and many other northerners had learned to respond to certain individual decisions to die with growing "pity" and compassion over the past few decades—he singled out those taken by "the scarred and bleeding Christian slave maiden"—in almost every other context the act remained a crime beyond the pale, a "crime against God," and a "crime against man" deserving "our intense abhorrence."[11]

Importantly, the same language also provided a set of images and precedents from which ordinary Americans might draw the inspiration and resolve necessary to quit the addiction to slavery that had driven this young nation to the very verge of extinction. By Steele's reckoning, the Union was in the "final convulsions of death" but had not yet completely succumbed. As long as the free states could muster the force of will to avert permanent disunion and vanquish the Slave Power, the nation's pulse remained. Its instinct for self-preservation endured, however faintly. "Our nationality is not destroyed beyond hope," Steele said, before beseeching his congregation to find "sufficient moral vigor to resist the insidious poison." Throw the poisoned bowl of slavery aside and wrestle anew for the soul of the nation, he urged them, in language borrowed, once again, from Washingtonian temperance. While other jeremiads on the subject of the war embraced images that gestured toward natural disaster and inevitable, irrepressible apocalypse—shipwrecks, cancers, and earthquakes—Steele's analogy encompassed the possibility of self-preservation and survival. Its aesthetic power not only underscored the destructive consequences of uncontested secession but also functioned as a call to action. "The God who has implanted in our nature, the instinct of self-defence," he explained, "is today summoning American Christians to march to the battle-field. . . . We must destroy [slavery] or be destroyed." In Steele's hands, suicide rhetoric functioned not simply as a prophetic warning of impending atrocity but also—and simultaneously—as an ardently hopeful reminder that ordinary Americans held the fate of the nation in their hands.[12]

In the dark and rancorous years prior to Daniel Steele's startling 1861 address, a growing number of concerned commentators, including Abraham Lincoln, had mustered similar language to characterize the gathering storm. Whether in literary or polemical contexts, whether from pulpits, in the pages of the press, or in private correspondence, a steadily increasing number of northern pundits had taken to likening the burgeoning prospect of violent disunion to the individual act of committing suicide. The newspapers published by Frederick Douglass illustrate the general pattern. Between August 1848 and September 1855, first the *North Star* and later *Frederick Douglass's Paper* took up the comparison with grim determination. The *North Star* equated proposals to extend slavery into California and New Mexico to "moral suicide." It informed free black readers that to withhold support from the Free Soil Party was "morally to commit suicide" and argued that the senators who had blocked the passage of the Wilmot Proviso "may have committed suicide." For its part, *Frederick Douglass's Paper*—the product of an 1851 merger between the *North Star* and Gerrit Smith's *Liberty Party Paper*—described the dissolution of the Whig Party over the slavery question as a felo-de-se and the use of popular sovereignty to determine the fate of the Kansas Territory as "the suicide of Slavery." That last phrase was then taken up as the title of an address delivered by Massachusetts congressman Eli Thayer in the House of Representatives on March 25, 1858, in which Thayer, a Republican, told his Democratic Party opponents that their efforts on behalf of the Slave Power to repeal the Missouri Compromise amounted to "a suicidal act," an overreach into once-neutral territory that compelled the Free States to respond and retaliate.[13]

The object of such purposefully provocative language was to persuade stakeholders that disunion was to be avoided at all costs. Similar motifs even inflected the language of the minority of slave owners who issued public warnings about the extremity of secession. For example, in September 1856 the *New Orleans Daily Creole* transcribed a speech made by Maryland congressman Henry Winter Davis that argued that constitutional separation "would be an act of suicide, and sane men do not commit suicide. The act itself is insanity. . . . Dissolution means death, the suicide of liberty, without a hope of resurrection." Embracing the opportunity to embody American liberty as a young woman who had recently succumbed to fatal derangement, Davis then went on imagine her body abandoned "with no sister to mourn her," only to be discovered and then unceremoniously buried "with a stake through the body, which men shun, cast out naked on the highway of nations."[14]

Despite its striking and insistent ubiquity in public discourse throughout the 1850s, 1860, and, most especially, in 1861, such restraining rhetoric, however visceral and emotive, proved wholly insufficient to diffuse the sectional crisis. It never became a transforming force. On the contrary, when the war came, Steele, Douglass, and men like them felt overwhelming pressure to embrace the Union's martial aims and soon turned their oratorical talents to the business of recruiting volunteer soldiers and buttressing northern morale. Here, too, suicide motifs provided useful ammunition, as boosters for the war effort promoted images of noble, romantic self-sacrifice in which battlefield slaughters of volunteer soldiers were reconfigured as acts of selfless martyrdom for a righteous cause. While the use of this sort of language had long been standard practice in western warfare, the scale of the Civil War, and the attendant push to mobilize hundreds of thousands of young men, was unprecedented. Even as northerners continued to understand all but a handful of noncombat suicides as selfish, antisocial deaths that denied their subjects the prospects of salvation, the romantic rhetoric of heroic self-sacrifice that began to spread as America went to war recast the meaning of one species of self-destruction, promising every volunteer soldier who succumbed to a martial death a glorious remembrance and the eternal comforts of heaven.[15]

As the Confederacy's early offensives made the prospects of Union victory appear ever more remote, clergymen across the Free States took to arguing that the blood of the fallen was necessary atonement for the sin of slavery. The blood sacrifice of "cheerful," God-fearing soldiers was required if the Union was to prevail and if America was to be cleansed, sanctified, and renewed. Through repetition, such claims soon became instinctual and reflexive. "A republic for which such sacrifices have been made," Albany, New York, pastor Rufus Clark declared at a memorial sermon delivered in July 1864, as the war finally began to turn in the Union's favor, "and upon whose altar such noble and precious lives have been laid, must live, must triumph over all its foes, and shine with new splendour in the ages yet to come." In this absolutist moral crusade, even Lincoln's assassination was an essential—and somehow voluntary—sacrifice for the larger cause.[16]

There was no place in this emerging civic religion for soldiers who drew knives across their throats or hanged themselves from tent poles. Unlike the tens of thousands of troops who surrendered their lives in the line of duty, soldiers who did so by other means seemed like cowards, deserters, or even traitors to the Union cause. In the midst of total war, their deaths seemed to telegraph a disconcerting dearth of self-discipline and mental vigor, a lack of faith in the power of prayer or the belief that God was on their side, and a deficit of honor and manly fortitude in the face of discomfort, privation, and atrocity. Their fatal disillusionment seemed also to signal their apparent surrender to childish, selfish fears, as well as their willingness to desert their comrades and disregard their place in a military hierarchy that, like a strict patriarchal family, rested upon unquestioned obedience.[17]

For these reasons, most northern newspaper editors paid little heed to mounting evidence that Union soldiers unable to cope with the debasements of the war were committing suicide in ever-greater numbers. Indeed, when stories of self-destruction in the Union army first began to surface in the northern press in 1861 and 1862, their authors typically declined to speculate as to the deceased's motive, or pointed instead to purportedly preexisting conditions such as intemperance, trouble at home, or ill health as the prime causal factor. Only as the war ground on and as pockets of opposition to forced conscription developed did some of the more critical Union newspapers begin to assert that the prospect of the draft, the trauma of combat, the toll of camp life, and disillusionment with the cause at hand had, in fact, driven many young men to suicide. After the war, the War Department would calculate that only three hundred enlisted men and twenty-four officers had taken their own lives during the fighting. This too seems like the result of undercounting. If the grim reportage collated from dissenting journalists and from piecemeal manuscript sources is anything to go by, it seems likely that almost every company in the Union army was touched by self-destruction or the threat of it.[18]

It was not until after the war that the majority of the reading public came to properly understand the true extent of soldiers' daily struggle to fight off the inclination to surrender to starvation, fear, and despair. As postwar memoirs and testimony demonstrate, that struggle was greatest among the 410,000 prisoners of war confined within crumbling cell blocks or overcrowded stockades. Asked to provide an account of his incarceration at Camp Butler, in Illinois, a Confederate prisoner named Francis Walker remembered "watching the bars of my window and wondering whether I should hang myself from them." At Andersonville, in Georgia, prisoners seized upon dull knives and worn-out suspenders to relieve what survivors referred to as hopeless suffering. "One morning after I had got up, I saw a man who had hung himself about fifteen or twenty feet from my tent to a stake that was in the ground, used partly to hang our blankets on," recalled J. Nelson Clark, a witness who testified at the trial of the prison's commandant in 1865. Although official records do not record a single self-inflicted death among 12,912 burials at Andersonville, firsthand accounts reveal that many inmates at the camp enacted a decision to die by walking deliberately across the stockade's "dead line" boundary and out into the no-man's-land patrolled by armed sentries, challenging them to open fire. If the guard missed or refused to be baited, "the suicide [would call] for him to do his duty and be done with it."[19]

In retrospect, there is little doubt that both sides sustained heavy numbers of self-inflicted casualties in the course of waging the Civil War. Yet while the mainstream northern press seemed reluctant to offer a full account of the many Union suicides committed during the five years of fighting, the same editors had no such qualms about reporting on the situation behind Confederate lines. Throughout the war, the pages of the most northern papers were often stocked with news and hearsay claiming that self-destruction directly attributable to the ongoing war was ravaging every rank of the Confederate army. In fact, as the Union army finally began to make inroads into enemy territory in 1864, more and more northerners began to write and speak of their expectation that the Confederacy's eventual collapse would coincide with a bloody tidal wave of suicide among its leaders, officers, and most committed supporters. This was certainly the assumption that guided a Union investigator dispatched to Cincinnati in June 1864 to infiltrate a group of southern sympathizers known as the Knights of the Golden Circle. To get their attention and secure their confidence, Edward Hoffman concocted a plan to pose as a Virginian refugee so distraught at the prospect of the Confederacy's imminent surrender that he had made an unsuccessful attempt on his own life by downing half a vial of laudanum. "The state of the times favored" such an extreme plan, Edward Hoffman wrote in a letter to his superiors, and so "for several days I . . . represented myself to the rebels as utterly discouraged."[20]

As the Union army advanced over the following twelve months, many northern papers, including Horace Greeley's *New-York Tribune*, came alive with rumors that various Confederate leaders and generals, including Robert Toombs, had assayed suicide to "prevent arrest by Federal forces." While most of these stories were fabricated or fanciful, the fact that a handful of prominent Confederates did take their own lives in the war's dying days only added fuel to the fire. In April 1865 dozens of northern papers relayed news that Florida governor John Milton had shot himself. A few weeks later, in June, the *Philadelphia Inquirer* reported that Edmund Ruffin, the uncompromising secessionist who had fired one of the first shots on Fort Sumter, had used a forked stick and musket to effect his suicide. "He had become very low spirited since the capture of Richmond," the *Inquirer* concluded, "and did not wish to live under Yankee rule."[21]

Whatever Ruffin's actual state of mind, the northern press worked tirelessly to forge a connection between such suicides and the defeat of the Confederate cause. Union editors informed their readers that the deaths of men like Ruffin and Milton were not fitting and masterful ends for proud warriors and patriots. Rather, they were effeminate, emotional, and cowardly admissions that the rebellion itself had been immoral, illegitimate, and treasonous from the very beginning. In a flood of reports detailing how Union officials placed their highest-profile rebel prisoners under suicide watches, northern editors taught their readers to assume that these captives were guilty of the war crimes attributed to them. As such, any attempt they made to take their own lives rather than face judicial retribution was equivalent to a signed confession and thus signal proof of the righteousness of the Union cause. In May 1865 several papers, including James Gordon Bennett's *New York Herald*, reported that Lewis Powell, the Alabama man accused of trying to assassinate Secretary of State William Seward, had tried "butting out his brains" "to save himself from being hung." After Powell had been restrained by Union guards, he and all the other suspected Lincoln conspirators were "ironed heavily hand to foot" and had to submit to "the padding of their heads with cotton" in case "fear or conscience" got the better of them.[22]

The same precautions featured prominently in northern press coverage of the imprisonment and trial of Henry Wirz, commandant of the infamous Confederate stockade at Andersonville. According to several Union papers, the prisoner had been handcuffed upon arrest and "is always attended by guards" because he had "threatened" to kill himself rather than face court-martial and almost certain execution. Bennett's *Herald* even published a wild and unsubstantiated story alleging that Wirz's wife had delivered to him in a kiss a dose of strychnine wrapped in licorice. The prisoner, the *Herald* alleged, was only prevented from swallowing the poison when a guard "caught him by the throat" and forced him to cough it up.[23]

The United States government had no more valuable prisoner than Jefferson Davis. After his capture in Georgia on May 10, 1865, Davis too found himself under round-the-clock surveillance while he awaited trial for war crimes. Ten days later, on May 20, Secretary of War Edwin Stanton personally dispatched a subordinate to Fortress Monroe, the Union garrison in Hampton, Virginia, where the disgraced former president was now being held, to "caution General Miles against leaving Davis any possible method of suicide; tell him to put him in fetters, if necessary—Davis must be brought to trial; he must not be allowed to kill himself." On those orders, Davis was shackled hand to foot and allowed only a wooden spoon to feed himself. News of Stanton's directives soon reached the northern press, whereupon editors concocted all sorts of stories testifying to the secretary's prescient wisdom. One San Francisco paper reported that Davis had put up stout resistance to being manacled and had "begg[ed] to be shot." Others, including the *Philadelphia Inquirer*, claimed that once Davis was in irons, he had refused all food, "essay[ing] suicide by starvation."[24]

A study of southern newspapers reveals that they rarely repeated these types of charges. On the contrary, several tried to refute them. After Wirz's execution on November 10, 1865, the *New Orleans Times* printed a diary entry purportedly written by Wirz, in which the disgraced commandant portrayed himself as an innocent and stoic scapegoat who would not countenance the thought of killing himself. "They are afraid I might

The noose in President Davis's cell in this undated Union envelope design may be read as both a taunting forecast of his likely fate at the hands of a military tribunal and as a miserable reminder that a self-inflicted alternative also existed. One account of the former president's captivity claims that guards once drew a figure hanging from a rope on the wall of the cell while Davis slept. *Jeff Davis's Private Tears* (n.d.). Courtesy of the American Antiquarian Society.

cheat them, and the public at large, from having their revenge and giving at the same time the masses the benefit of seeing a man hung," Wirz wrote, refusing to give them the satisfaction. Jefferson Davis and his supporters took a similar position. In a letter addressed to a northern journalist and dated June 6, 1865, Varina Davis indignantly denied that her prisoner-husband had ever been tempted to lay hands upon himself. "They need have taken no precaution against his suicide. He never has taken aught which was not his own. His life is his wife's, his children's, his country's, his God's. They may kill but can never degrade him." Confined to his cell at Fortress Monroe, Davis too fumed at the insinuation that he was looking for a way to evade justice. "If [my] wish were to commit suicide," Davis told a sympathetic visitor, even the most diligent surveillance "would prove wholly unavailing." By way of proof, Davis told the story of a French general imprisoned in England who was able to puncture his chest with nothing more than a small pin. "This was an instance of how absurd it was to attempt preventing suicide by watchfulness." At any moment, Davis declared, "[I could] have thrown down [my] burden of life, if wicked enough to have wished so rushing into presence of [my] Creator."[25]

Steadfast in his determination to have his day in court, Jefferson Davis understood how rumors that he was suicidal seemed to incriminate him. From his cell that summer, Davis accused Stanton of purposefully publicizing the suicide watch at Fortress Monroe in order to manipulate public opinion. "Taking it by your own hand is a confession of judgement to all that your worst enemies can allege," the former president—echoing Daniel Webster's famous closing statement at the trial of Frank Knapp in 1830—informed one visitor. "Denying [me] a knife and fork lest [I] should commit suicide was designed to represent [me] to the world as an atrocious criminal, so harrowed by remorse that the oblivion of death would be welcome." As Jefferson Davis was acutely aware, he had become a symbol for the entire Confederacy; the burden of responsibility and guilt not only for secession but also for the bloody war that had followed now rested on his shoulders. If he survived to see the day, his trial and likely execution would stand as a synecdoche for the Union's authority to dictate the terms of reunification and postwar Reconstruction. It was a humiliating prospect to be sure, but, Davis concluded, he owed it to himself, to his family, and to the cause he had led for so long to stand strong and face his accusers.[26]

In these ways, the passage of the first modern war recast the relationship between suicide and citizenship. In the decades after the American Revolution, it had been common, even fashionable, to represent individual acts of self-destruction as divisive attacks on the ties that bound citizens to one another and to the new Republic. The same understanding persisted throughout the Civil War, despite the success of antebellum activists in habilitating certain suicides as legitimate markers of institutional oppression. Yet the sheer magnitude of the blood sacrifice made by volunteer soldiers prior to the imposition of the draft required a partial reassessment of the long-standing assumption that self-destruction stands in fundamental opposition to the collective interest. Whether by invoking the attempted suicides of Confederate leaders as proof positive that the Union had been fighting a just and holy war, or by building a civic religion that drew strength, pride, and the possibility of collective, national redemption from the deaths of tens of thousands of heroic soldier-martyrs, the war enlarged the political meanings of self-destruction in important and lasting ways. In a realignment that could only be the result of a total war in defense of the homeland, civic leaders seeking to sustain the United States through the twin trials of Civil War and Reconstruction reconfigured voluntary death in the line of duty as a blood sacrifice upon the altar of the nation.[27]

Between the Revolution and Reconstruction, Americans engaged in an all-consuming ideological struggle to reconcile the expansion of individual liberty with the imperatives of coexistence and mutual obligation. To document the distinctive role that suicide politics played in this dynamic story is to understand how that politics came to shape and be shaped by all manner of related transformations in American society. Over the course of this crucial, formative period in the nation's early history, wide-ranging, intangible processes such as secularization, democratization, and medicalization altered how the reading public understood the meaning of suicide, even as these processes were simultaneously influenced by assumptions about self-destruction. By the same token, the rise of the novel, the twinned ascension of liberal and evangelical Christianity, the multifaceted development of the antislavery movement, and the growth of sectional interests drew strength and momentum from an evolving cultural politics of self-destruction, and, in turn, remade that politics.

The same dynamic exchanges inform our present moment. The vestigial traces of early American efforts to leverage decisions to die for political purposes linger on in many of today's headlines. The early national crusade to police sentimental novels deemed to be a deadly influence on weak and waxen young minds corresponds closely with modern assumptions about the copycat consequences of listening to expletive-laden rap music or playing violent video games. The same concerns that fired suicide prevention campaigns at the dawn of the nineteenth century are now manifest in attempts to overturn assisted suicide laws recently passed in Oregon and Washington. Likewise, the demagoguery and political gamesmanship first heard in debates over abolition, capital punishment, and revivalism now accompany news reports of the suicides of bullied students and ruined executives, as well as war veterans, cult members, terrorists, and hunger strikers. From this perspective, then, it seems that moral crises over self-destruction never entirely dissipate. Instead, they evolve and metastasize to serve the needs of those who stand to profit by them. Americans live in the midst of a seemingly unending series of suicide panics, each one more urgent and alarming than the last, and each one a damning "proof" that the country is benighted by ever more crippling social dislocations and by unprecedented extremes of atomization and alienation. If we are to better understand why opportunists in politics and the media continue to exploit certain species of suicide and the rhetoric of self-destruction more generally, we must attend to the origins of this morbid inclination in the decades after the Revolution, an era when the expansion of print culture made the fraught relationship between the self and society the subject of general conversation for the very first time.[28]

Notes

Acknowledgments

Index

Notes

Introduction

1. Samuel Miller Jr., *The Life of Samuel Miller, D. D., LL.D., Second Professor in the Theological Seminary of the Presbyterian Church, at Princeton, New Jersey* (Philadelphia: Claxton, Remsen, and Haffelfinger, 1869), 188–189. Reprints of the letter or excerpts from the pamphlet sermon it alluded to can be found in at least a dozen northeastern papers. The letter might have been a fake, a forgery of the preacher's own devising, or a fabrication by a friend to flatter his ego. If Miller knew, he never let on.

2. Samuel Miller, *The Guilt, Folly, and Sources of Suicide: Two Discourses, Preached in the City of New-York, February, 1805* (New York: T. and J. Swords, 1805), 5, 13.

3. "From the Chronicle," *New Hampshire Gazette*, June 23, 1807; "Mr. Willis," *Independent Chronicle and the Universal Advertiser*, January 30, 1783; "Postscript—Wednesday Evening," *Pennsylvania Evening Herald and the American Monitor*, June 15, 1785; "Miscellany," *Massachusetts Gazette*, August 1, 1788; "Observations on the Causes of Suicide," *Vermont Gazette or Freemen's Depository*, April 27, 1789; William Smith, ed., *History of New-York: From the First Discovery to the Year M. DCC.XXXII* (Albany: Ryer Schermerhorn, 1814), 325.

4. "Murders; Suicides; Humanity," *American and Daily Advertiser*, September 12, 1801; "The Subject of the Following Communication Is in Our Opinion of Considerable Importance," *Connecticut Gazette and the Commercial Intelligencer*, August 20, 1806; "Suicide," *People's Friend & Daily Advertiser*, May 18, 1807.

5. Susan E. Klepp, *"The Swift Progress of Population": A Documentary and Bibliographic Study of Philadelphia's Growth, 1642–1859* (Philadelphia: American Philosophical Society, 1991); Susan E. Klepp, "Zachariah Poulson's Bills of Mortality, 1788–1801," in *Life in Early Philadelphia: Documents from the Revolutionary and Early National Periods*, ed. Billy G. Smith (University Park: Pennsylvania State University Press, 1995); American Antiquarian Society, "Index of Marriages and Deaths

in the New York *Weekly Museum* 1788–1817" (Worcester, MA: American Antiquarian Society, 1952). Newspaper data are drawn from the cover-to-cover reading of hundreds of issues of thirty-six Maryland and Pennsylvania papers published between 1775 and 1784 and between 1795 and 1804.

6. [No headline], *Pennsylvania Journal*, April 2, 1772; Georges C. Minois, *The History of Suicide: Voluntary Death in Western Culture*, trans. Lydia G. Cochrane (Baltimore, MD: Johns Hopkins University Press, 1999), 179–209; "Sketch of a Moral and Political Map of Europe," *Massachusetts Spy*, December 20, 1770; Robert J. Taylor, Mary-Jo Kline, and Gregg L. Lint, eds., *Papers of John Adams* (Cambridge, MA: Harvard University Press, 1977–), vol. 9, 556; George Cheyne, *The English Malady: Or, a Treatise of Nervous Diseases of All Kinds, as Spleen, Vapours, Lowness of Spirits, Hypochondriacal, and Hysterical Distempers, &C* (London: G. Strahan and J. Leake, 1733); American Antiquarian Society, "Index of Marriages and Deaths." In the 1730s, 38 percent (31/81 in a representative sample) of newspaper items reporting a completed suicide were sourced domestically; by the 1810s, that proportion had risen to 88 percent (37/42 in a comparable sample).

7. "Windsor, (V.) Sept. 15," *The Mail; or, Claypoole's Daily Advertiser*, September 30, 1791; "Last Saturday Night," *Baltimore Evening Post*, October 19, 1792; "New London, December 15," *Philadelphia Minerva*, December 24, 1796; "Extraordinary Suicide," *Baltimore Evening Post*, November 15, 1792; "Thursday Last," *Pennsylvania Evening Post*, July 1, 1783.

8. Chas Critcher, *Moral Panics and the Media* (Buckingham, UK: Open University Press, 2003); Arnold Hunt, "'Moral Panic' and Moral Language in the Media," *British Journal of Sociology* 48, no. 4 (1997): 629–648; Charles Krinsky, ed., *Moral Panics over Contemporary Children and Youth* (Burlington, VT: Ashgate, 2008).

9. "Reflections on the Slavery of Negroes," *The Rural Magazine, or Vermont Repository* (June 1796); Paul H. Smith, ed., *Letters of Delegates to Congress, 1774–1789*, 25 vols. (Washington, DC: Library of Congress, 1976–2000), vol. 9, 57, vol. 14, 424; Jonathan Elliot, ed., *The Debates in the Several State Conventions on the Adoption of the Federal Constitution, as Recommended by the General Convention at Philadelphia, in 1787 . . .*, 5 vols. (Washington, DC: Taylor & Maury, 1836–1859), vol. 3, 9. See also Thomas Paine, *Common Sense* (Mineola, NY: Dover Thrift Editions, 1997), 7; "For the New Hampshire Gazette," *New-Hampshire Gazette*, March 4, 1785; Elliot, *The Debates*, vol. 2, 352, vol. 3, 203, vol. 5, 315, 487; Max Farrand, ed., *The Records of the Federal Convention of 1787* (New Haven, CT: Yale University Press, 1911), vol. 3, 319; "Toasts Drank on the 4th July by the Vice President," *Federal Republican*, August 15, 1808; "Extracts from Gen. Eaton's Speech," *Portsmouth Oracle*, September 24, 1808; "Williston Resolutions," *Vermont Centinel*, February 17, 1809; "Suicide," *Baltimore Patriot*, June 3, 1814.

10. "Messieurs Hall and Sellers," *Pennsylvania Gazette*, December 26, 1771; O. S. Fowler, *Fowler on Tight Lacing. Founded on Physiology and Phrenology; or the Evils Inflicted on Mind and Body by Compressing the Organs of Animal Life . . .* (New York, 1842). More than 170,000 copies of Rush's temperance pamphlets had been printed and distributed by 1850.

11. Samuel Spring, *Sixth Commandment Friendly to Virtue, Honor, and Politeness: A Discourse, in Consequence of the Late Duel . . .* (Newburyport, MA: E. W. Allen, 1804), 15; Samuel Low, *A Discourse on Duelling: Preached on Sunday, March 4, 1810, at the Capitol in the City of Washington . . .* (Richmond, VA: John O'Lynch, 1811), 18; Richard Bell, "The Double Guilt of Dueling: The Stain of Suicide in Anti-Dueling Rhetoric in the Early Republic," *Journal of the Early Republic* 29, no. 3 (2009): 383–410.

12. Lyman H. Butterfield, ed., *Letters of Benjamin Rush*, 2 vols. (Princeton, NJ: American Philosophical Society, 1951), vol. 1, 580–581; Lorna Ruth Wiedman, "Suicide in American Fiction" (PhD diss., University of Wisconsin-Madison, 1995), 24; "For the Weekly Chronicle," *Mott and Hurtin's New-York Weekly Chronicle*, February 12, 1795; Thomas Day, *The Suicide. A Dialogue Exhibited on the Stage at the Public Commencement of Yale-College* (Litchfield, CT: T. Collier, 1797); James Hillhouse, "Suicide," 1806, box 1, p. 6, James Abraham Hillhouse Papers, Beinecke Rare Book Library, Yale University; William Bentley, *The Diary of William Bentley, Pastor of the East Church, Salem, Massachusetts*, 4 vols. (Salem, MA: Essex Institute, 1905–1914), vol. 3, 468. Rush instructed Alexander McGillivray (1790), Timothy Pickering (1791), and Meriwether Lewis (1803) to gather information about the frequency of suicide in native populations. See George W. Corner, ed., *The Autobiography of Benjamin Rush, His "Travels Through Life" together with his Commonplace Book for 1789–1813* (Princeton, NJ: Princeton University Press, 1948), 188–189, 265–266; Drake E. Will, "The Medical and Surgical Practice of the Lewis and Clark Expedition," *Journal of the History of Medicine and Allied Sciences* 14, no. 3 (July 1959): 275; Benjamin Rush, "Medicine among the Indians of North America," in *The Selected Writings of Benjamin Rush*, ed. Dagobert D. Runes (Philadelphia: Philosophical Library, 1947), 264.

13. Corner, *Autobiography of Benjamin Rush*, 258; Eliza Cope Harrison, ed., *Philadelphia Merchant: The Diary of Thomas P. Cope, 1800–1851* (South Bend, IN: Gateway Editions, 1978), 196; Elaine Forman Crane, ed., *The Diary of Elizabeth Drinker*, 3 vols. (Boston: Northeastern University Press, 1991), 1922. Perhaps spurred by a similar interest, Philadelphia publisher Mathew Carey clipped more than fifty suicide stories for his scrapbooks before his death in 1839.

14. Corner, *Autobiography of Benjamin Rush*, 252; Christopher P. Bickford and Howard R. Lamar, eds., *Voices of the New Republic: Connecticut Towns 1800–1832* (New Haven, CT: Connecticut Academy of Arts and Sciences, 2003), vol. 1, 302; Samuel Latham Mitchill, "Summary View of the Modes by Which HUMAN LIFE Terminates in the City of New-York . . . ," *The Medical Repository, Comprehending Original Essays, and Intelligence Relative to Medicine, Chemistry, Natural History, Agriculture, Geography, and the Arts* (New York, 1808), 33–34.

15. Bentley, *Diary;* Robert R. McCausland and Cynthia MacAlman McCausland, eds., *The Diary of Martha Ballard, 1785–1812*, Maine Genealogical Society Special Publications No. 10 (Camden, ME: Picton Press, 1992); "Extracts from the Diary of Josiah Williston of Boston, 1808–1814," *New England Historical and Genealogical Register* 65 (1911): 366–371; John Pierce, "John Pierce diaries 1783–1847," Massachusetts Historical Society.

16. "Postscript-Wednesday Evening." See also, and for instance, Solomon Williams, *The Greatness and Sovereignty of God, Sufficient Reason to Silence Man's Complaints of His Providence, and Put a Stop to Our Striving against Him* . . . (Norwich, CT: John Trumbull, 1777); Nathan Perkins, *A Sermon, Occasioned by the Unhappy Death of Mr. Lloyd; a Refugee from Long-Island, and Published at the Request of His Friends* (Hartford, CT: Hudson and Goodwin, 1780); James Cogswell, *The Necessity of Repentance in Order to Avoid Destruction, Considered and Urged* . . . (Norwich, CT: John Trumbull, 1783); James Dana, *Men's Sins Not Chargeable on God, but on Themselves* . . . (New-Haven, CT: Printed by T. & S. Green, 1783); John Marsh, *The Great Sin and Danger of Striving with God: A Sermon Preached at Wethersfield, December 13th, 1782* . . . (Hartford, CT: Hudson and Goodwin, 1783); Abiel Abbot, *Self Preservation. A Sermon Preached before the Ancient and Honorable Artillery Company, in Boston, June 7, 1802* . . . (Boston: Russell, 1802); Joseph Lathrop, *Two Sermons on the Atrocity of Suicide and on the Causes Which Lead to It* . . . , 2d ed. (Springfield, MA: Henry Brewer, 1805).

17. Elizabeth R. Varon, *Disunion! The Coming of the American Civil War, 1789–1859* (Chapel Hill: University of North Carolina Press, 2008), 1–2; Daniel T. Rodgers, *Contested Truths: Keywords in American Politics since Independence* (New York: Basic Books, 1987), 4; Peter A. Dorsey, *Common Bondage: Slavery as Metaphor in Revolutionary America* (Knoxville: University of Tennessee Press, 2009), xi–17.

18. For an introduction to the vast amount of European and American scholarship arguing the meaning of self-destruction, see Émile Durkheim, *Suicide: A Study in Sociology*, ed. George Simpson, trans. John A. Spaulding and George Simpson (Glencoe, IL: The Free Press, 1951); Lester G. Crocker, "The Discussion of Suicide in the Eighteenth Century," *Journal of the History of Ideas* 13, no. 1 (1952): 47–72; A. Alvarez, *The Savage God: A Study of Suicide* (New York: Random House, 1972); Georgia Noon, "On Suicide," *Journal of the History of Ideas* 39, no. 3 (1978): 371–386; George Howe Colt, *The Enigma of Suicide* (New York: Summit Books, 1991); Robert Kastenbaum, "The Impact of Suicide on Society," in *The Impact of Suicide*, ed. Brian L. Mishara (New York: Springer, 1995).

19. Benjamin Rush, "An Address to the People of the United States on the Defects of the Confederation," *American Museum* 1 (1787): 12–13, "Suicide." In the 1890s, Émile Durkheim would label this interpretation of the meaning of suicide as egoistic. See Durkheim, *Suicide*, 14–15. Working from the same understanding, several twentieth-century communist dictatorships refused to report suicide rates.

20. William H. Gilman and Alfred R. Ferguson, eds., *The Journals and Miscellaneous Notebooks of Ralph Waldo Emerson*, 16 vols. (Cambridge, MA: Harvard University Press, 1963), vol. 3, 70.

21. Kastenbaum, "Impact of Suicide," 178; Varon, *Disunion*, 338.

22. "Notice," *Pennsylvania Gazette*, February 28, 1771. A subsequent notice suggests that the Arndorffs later reconciled, only to separate again in 1777.

23. Eric T. Carlsen and Jeffrey L. Wollock, "Benjamin Rush and His Insane Son," *Bulletin of the New York Academy of Medicine* 51, no. 11 (1975): 1316, 1325.

When John was a boy, his father had confined him to his room for days at a time to "maintain government" over him.

24. Ibid., 1317–1318. In 1828 the actor Edwin Forrest, who was studying for the part of King Lear, visited the hospital to observe the fifty-one-year-old patient. Forrest found him shuffling back and forth in the corridor, muttering to himself.

25. Overseers of the Poor, "Daily Occurrence Dockets," Philadelphia City Archives, May 23, 1795. See also "Daily Occurrence Dockets," July 13, 1800, and September 1800.

26. Rodgers, *Contested Truths*, 15.

1. Suicide and the State of the Union

1. "A Very Tragical Accident," *Publick Occurences*, September 25, 1690.

2. Increase Mather, *A Call to the Tempted: A Sermon on the Horrid Crime of Self-Murder* . . . (Boston: B. Green, 1723), 5, 7.

3. Ibid., 8; Samuel Phillips, *The Sin of Suicide Contrary to Nature. A Plain Discourse, Occasioned by the Late Perpetration of That Heinous Crime* . . . (Boston: Kneeland and Adams, 1767), 20; John Sym, *Life's Preservative against Self-Killing* (London: Routledge, 1988), 166.

4. Jonathan Edwards, *The Great Awakening*, vol. 4 of *The Works of Jonathan Edwards* (New Haven, CT: Yale University Press, 1972), 206–207. "[T]here are hundreds, and probably thousands of instances, of persons that have murdered themselves under religious melancholy," Jonathan Edwards explained to readers of *Some Thoughts on Religious Affections* in 1742. See Edwards, *Works*, vol. 4, 393–394.

5. Michael J. Crawford, "The Spiritual Travels of Nathan Cole," *William and Mary Quarterly* 33, no. 1 (1976): 101–102; Barbara E. Lacey, ed., *The World of Hannah Heaton: The Diary of an Eighteenth-Century New England Farm Woman* (De Kalb: Northern Illinois University, 2003), 48; John Owen King III, *The Iron of Melancholy: Structures of Spiritual Conversion in America from the Puritan Conscience to Victorian Neurosis* (Middletown, CT: Wesleyan University Press, 1983), 70–73; Owen C. Williams, *The Puritan Experience: Studies in Spiritual Autobiography* (New York: Schocken Books, 1972), 42.

6. William Whitmore, ed., *The Colonial Laws of Massachusetts. Reprinted from the Edition of 1660, with the Supplements to 1672. Containing Also, the Body of Liberties of 1641* (Boston, 1889), 137; Glanville Williams, *The Sanctity of Life and the Criminal Law* (New York: Knopf, 1966), 257–261; Vincent Brown, *The Reaper's Garden: Death and Power in the World of Atlantic Slavery* (Cambridge, MA: Harvard University Press, 2008), 131; Leon Radzinowicz, *A History of English Criminal Law and Its Administration from 1750. Volume 1: The Movement for Reform* (London: Stevens and Sons, 1948), 196–197. On punishments for suicide in Dutch New York, see Donna Merwick, *Death of a Notary: Conquest and Change in Colonial New York* (Ithaca, NY: Cornell University Press, 1999), 124–125.

7. Keith Burgess-Jackson, "The Legal Status of Suicide in Early America: A Comparison with the English Experience," *Wayne Law Review* 29, no. 1 (1982):

61–63; Williams, *Sanctity of Life*, 261–264. It was rare to punish those who survived an attempt to kill themselves.

8. John D. Cushing, ed., *The Earliest Acts and Laws of the Colony of Rhode Island and Providence Plantations, 1647–1719* (Wilmington, DE: M. Glazier, 1977), 19; Kenneth Scott, *Coroners' Reports, New York City, 1823–1842*, vol. 119, *Collections of the New York Genealogical and Biographical Society* (New York: New York Genealogical and Biographical Society, 1989), 1. For a useful analysis of a coroner's inquest as "a public drama," "a ritual of interpretation," and a "ceremony of objectification," see Daryl Edward Lee, "Suicide and the Subject of Modern Life" (PhD diss., University of Minnesota, 2001), 101–103.

9. David C. Brown, "The Decriminalization of Suicide in Massachusetts, 1660–1824: Overthrow of the Original Sin," unpublished paper in author's possession (2002), appendix. A more extensive study of similar records in early modern England revealed a comparable pattern of de facto decriminalization that Terence R. Murphy and Michael MacDonald attributed to growing resistance to property confiscations. See Michael MacDonald and Terence R. Murphy, *Sleepless Souls: Suicide in Early Modern England* (New York: Oxford University Press, 1990).

10. Thomas Jefferson Randolph, ed., *Memoirs, Correspondence, and Private Papers of Thomas Jefferson, Late President of the United States* (London: Henry Colburn and Richard Bentley, 1829), vol. 1, 127; Howard I. Kushner, *Self-Destruction in the Promised Land* (New Brunswick, NJ: Rutgers University Press, 1989), 29–30; Burgess-Jackson, "Legal Status of Suicide," 66. Across the Atlantic, several European jurisdictions, notably Geneva (1700), Tuscany (1786), France (1791), and Prussia (1796), went further, abolishing laws that prescribed bodily punishments. In England, such laws remained operative until 1823.

11. John Quincy Adams, *Life in a New England Town: 1787, 1788. Diary of John Quincy Adams . . .* (Boston: Little, Brown, 1903), 89–90.

12. Ibid., 90; John Pierce, "John Pierce diaries, 1783–1847," Massachusetts Historical Society, December 4, 1806; "Coroner's Inquest," *L'Oracle and Daily Advertiser*, September 6, 1808; Paul Revere, "Commonplace Book," Revere Family Papers, Massachusetts Historical Society; also see "Memorandum Book," Revere Family Papers; Susanna Hill, "Letter to Mrs. Betsey Russell Jenks, Both of Cambridge, Ma, December 5th, 1806," *Proceedings of the Cambridge Historical Society* 9 (1914): 15–16. When the new wife of Harvard president Henry Ware hanged herself in February 1807, the fact that she had destroyed herself was conveniently expunged from official records. See Stephen Paschall Sharples, ed., *Records of the Church of Christ at Cambridge in New England, 1632–1830* (Boston: Eben Putnam, 1906), 510; William Bentley, *The Diary of William Bentley, Pastor of the East Church, Salem, Massachusetts*, 4 vols. (Salem, MA: Essex Institute, 1905–1914), vol. 3, 277.

13. Samuel Spring, *Sixth Commandment Friendly to Virtue, Honor, and Politeness: A Discourse, in Consequence of the Late Duel . . .* (Newburyport, MA: E. W. Allen, 1804), 14–15; Samuel Miller, *The Guilt, Folly, and Sources of Suicide: Two Discourses, Preached in the City of New-York, February, 1805* (New-York: T. and J. Swords, 1805),

40–41. In England, one satirist observed that the frequency of suicide verdicts there might lead foreign observers to conclude that a country was a nation of lunatics. See Charles Moore, *A Full Inquiry into the Subject of Suicide. To Which Are Added . . . Two Treatises on Duelling and Gambling*, 2 vols. (London: J. F. and C. Rivington, 1790), vol. 1, 323–324.

14. "Coroner's Inquest"; Miller, *Guilt, Folly, and Sources of Suicide*, 17, 22, 13, 22, 26; William E. Nelson, *Americanization of the Common Law: The Impact of Legal Change on Massachusetts Society, 1760–1830* (Cambridge, MA: Harvard University Press, 1975), 37–39, 118. Like many of his contemporaries, Miller conflated the separate contracts of society and government.

15. "Coroner's Inquest." Acknowledging that activist juries had effectively decriminalized suicide, the Commonwealth of Massachusetts finally removed language about roadside burial from its statutes in 1824.

16. Louis P. Masur, "Age of the First Person Singular: The Vocabulary of Self in New England, 1780–1850," *Journal of American Studies* 25, no. 2 (1991): 193; Kenneth Silverman, *A Cultural History of the American Revolution* (New York: Crowell, 1976), 219–221. The same faith in the future extended to religion, commerce, and the arts.

17. W. S. Rossiter, *A Century of Population Growth: From the First Census of the United States to the Twelfth, 1790–1900* (Washington, DC: Government Printing Office, 1909), 9–10, 85; Joseph F. Kett, *Rites of Passage: Adolescence in America 1790 to the Present* (New York: Basic Books, 1977), 38; David T. Gilchrist, ed., *The Growth of the Seaport Cities, 1790–1825* (Charlottesville: University Press of Virginia, 1967), 26. Although the proportion of Americans living in urban areas rose steadily throughout the early national period, the country remained overwhelmingly agricultural and urban growth did not begin to overshadow the rural population until the 1830s.

18. Charles Lawrence, *History of Philadelphia Almshouses and Hospitals* (Philadelphia: Gaylord, 1905), 31; Douglass C. North, *The Economic Growth of the United States, 1790–1860* (Englewood Cliffs, NJ: Prentice Hall, 1961), 25–50.

19. Paul A. Gilje, *The Road to Mobocracy: Popular Disorder in New York City, 1763–1834* (Chapel Hill: University of North Carolina Press, 1987), 147, 69–70.

20. Sean Wilentz, *Chants Democratic: New York City and the Rise of the American Working Class, 1788–1850* (New York: Oxford University Press, 2004), 33, 63; Bruce Dorsey, *Reforming Men and Women: Gender in the Antebellum City* (Ithaca, NY: Cornell University Press, 2002), 7. Joseph Fichtelberg has identified fourteen significant economic panics and depressions between 1790 and 1865. See Joseph Fichtelberg, *Critical Fictions: Sentiment and the American Market, 1780–1870* (Athens: University of Georgia Press, 2003), 11.

21. Gilje, *Road to Mobocracy*, 92–94, 190–191; Wilentz, *Chants Democratic*, 25–27.

22. Joyce Appleby, *Inheriting the Revolution: The First Generation of Americans* (Cambridge, MA: Harvard University Press, 2000), 6, 15, 55–58.

23. John Adams, "Letter to John Taylor, April 15, 1814," in *The Works of John Adams*, ed. Charles Francis Adams (Boston, 1851), 484; Appleby, *Inheriting the*

Revolution, 6, 15, 55–58; Gordon S. Wood, ed., *The Rising Glory of America, 1760–1820* (Boston: Northeastern University Press, 1990), 10; Susan Branson, *These Fiery Frenchified Dames: Women and Political Culture in Early National Philadelphia* (Philadelphia: University of Pennsylvania Press, 2001), 55–60; Carroll Smith-Rosenberg, *This Violent Empire: The Birth of an American National Identity* (Chapel Hill: University of North Carolina Press, 2010), 88–135.

24. Gary B. Nash, "The American Clergy and the French Revolution," *William and Mary Quarterly* 22, no. 3 (1965): 392–412; Nathan O. Hatch, *The Democratization of American Christianity* (New Haven, CT: Yale University Press, 1989), 3–4, 9–11, 22; Ann Douglas, *The Feminization of American Culture* (New York: Papermac, 1988), 23–24.

25. Bentley, *Diary*, vol. 3, 544; Douglas, *Feminization*, 26, 36; Donald M. Scott, *From Office to Profession: The New England Ministry, 1750–1850* (Philadelphia: University of Pennsylvania Press, 1978), 7, 12, 18–31; Hatch, *Democratization of American Christianity*, 34, 56, 64; Emory Elliott, *Revolutionary Writers: Literature and Authority in the New Republic, 1725–1810* (New York: Oxford University Press, 1982), 36–40.

26. Clare A. Lyons, *Sex among the Rabble: An Intimate History of Gender and Power in the Age of Revolution, Philadelphia, 1730–1830* (Chapel Hill: University of North Carolina Press, 2006), 112, 89, 282–283. Ellen Rothman and Cathy Davidson each report a similar spike in premarital pregnancies in New England in the same period. See Ellen K. Rothman, *Hands and Hearts: A History of Courtship in America* (New York: Basic Books, 1984), 45–50; Cathy N. Davidson, *Revolution and the Word: The Rise of the Novel in America* (New York: Oxford University Press, 1986), 112–121.

27. Silverman, *Cultural History*, 504–510.

28. Mercy Otis Warren, *Sans Souci, Alias, Free and Easy, or, an Evening's Peep into a Polite Circle: An Intire New Entertainment in Three Acts* (Boston: Warden and Russell, 1785), 2; "Tea-Assembly," *Independent Chronicle*, January 27, 1785.

29. "Messr. Printers," *Herald of Freedom*, October 13, 1788; Tremaine McDowell, "Last Words of a Sentimental Heroine," *American Literature* 4 (1932): 174–177; Davidson, *Revolution and the Word*, chap. 5; Richard Walser, "Boston's Reception of the First American Novel," *Early American Literature* 17, no. 1 (1982): 65–74; Richard Walser, "More about the First American Novel," *American Literature* 24, no. 3 (1952): 352–357.

30. Jacob Rush, *Charges and Extracts of Charges on Moral and Religious Subjects, Delivered at Sundry Times by the Honorable Jacob Rush . . .* (Philadelphia: D. Hogan, 1803), 66; William Cushing, "Undelivered Speeches by William Cushing (February 4, 1788)," in *Documentary History of the Ratification of the Constitution*, ed. John P. Kaminski and Gaspare J. Saladino (Madison: State Historical Society of Wisconsin, 2000), 1439; Timothy Dwight, *Discourse on Some Events of the Last Century: Delivered in the Brick Church in New Haven on Wednesday, January 7, 1801* (New Haven, CT: Ezra Read, 1801), 19; Eliza Cope Harrison, ed., *Philadelphia Merchant: The Diary of Thomas P. Cope, 1800–1851* (South Bend, IN: Gateway Editions, 1978), 89.

31. Gordon S. Wood, "The Significance of the Early Republic," *Journal of the Early Republic* 8, no. 1 (1988): 18; Wood, *Rising Glory*, 9; Karen A. Weyler, *Intricate Relations: Sexual and Economic Desire in American Fiction, 1789–1814* (Iowa City: University of Iowa Press, 2004), 3–4.

32. Elizabeth R. Varon, *Disunion! The Coming of the American Civil War, 1789–1859* (Chapel Hill: University of North Carolina Press, 2008), 6–7, 38, 90, 132.

33. "On Newspapers. An Extract," *Federal Gazette and Baltimore Daily Advertiser*, November 20, 1797; Harrison, *Diary of Thomas P. Cope*, 301; "To the patrons of the Boston Daily Advertiser and Repertory," *Boston Daily Advertiser*, April 7, 1814; Carol Sue Humphrey, *The Press of the Young Republic, 1783–1833* (Westport, CT: Greenwood Press, 1996), 85, 132–135, 155; Frank Luther Mott, *American Journalism: A History of Newspapers in the United States through 260 Years: 1690 to 1950* (New York: Macmillan, 1950), 59, 167; Edward Connery Lathem, *Chronological Tables of American Newspapers, 1690–1820; Being a Tabular Guide to Holdings of Newspapers Published in America through the Year 1820* (Worcester, MA: American Antiquarian Society and Barre Publishers, 1972); John Bixler Hench, "The Newspaper in a Republic: Boston's *Centinel* and *Chronicle*, 1784–1801" (PhD diss., Clark University, 1979), appendix. Hale was nephew to the Revolutionary War hero of the same name.

34. Benjamin Rush, "To Andrew Brown: Directions for Conducting a Newspaper in Such a Manner as to Make It Innocent, Useful and Entertaining," in *Letters of Benjamin Rush*, ed. Lyman H. Butterfield, 2 vols. (Princeton, NJ: American Philosophical Society, 1951), vol. 1, 487; William B. Warner, "Communicating Liberty: The Newspapers of the British Empire as a Matrix for the American Revolution," *ELH* 72, no. 2 (2005): 345; Charles E. Clark and C. Wetherell, "The Measure of Maturity: The *Pennsylvania Gazette*, 1728–1765," *William and Mary Quarterly* 46, no. 2 (1989): 282, 301; Mott, *American Journalism*, 50–51; Allan R. Pred, *Urban Growth and the Circulation of Information: The United States System of Cities, 1790–1840* (Cambridge, MA: Harvard University Press, 1973), 20–22; Ian Kenneth Steele, *The English Atlantic, 1675–1740: An Exploration of Communication and Community* (New York: Oxford University Press, 1986), 167.

35. Richard B. Kielbowicz, *News in the Mail: The Press, Post Office, and Public Information, 1700–1860s* (New York: Greenwood Press, 1989), 6, 36–38, 141–146; Hench, "Boston's *Centinel* and *Chronicle*," 121–131; Richard R. John, *Spreading the News: The American Postal System from Franklin to Morse* (Cambridge, MA: Harvard University Press, 1995), 32–38; Pred, *Urban Growth and the Circulation of Information*, 39, 57–58, 80.

36. This study does not attempt to engage in the treacherous business of trying to ascertain why individuals kill themselves or whether or not suicide rates rise or fall over time. For a sampling of how historians interested in such questions have probed individual motives for suicide, see Daniel A. Cohen, "Homicidal Compulsion and the Conditions of Freedom: The Social and Psychological Origins of Familicide in America's Early Republic," *Journal of Social History* 28, no. 4 (1995): 747–750; Terri L. Snyder, "What Historians Talk about When They Talk about Suicide: The View from Early Modern British North America," *History Compass*

5, no. 2 (2007): 658–674, http://www.blackwell-synergy.com/doi/abs/10.1111/j.1478–0542.2007.00405.x. For a caution to social historians in this regard, see George Howe Colt, *The Enigma of Suicide* (New York: Summit Books, 1991), 39. For an expert analysis of the pitfalls of overdetermining from suicide statistics, see Jack D. Douglas, *The Social Meanings of Suicide* (Princeton, NJ: Princeton University Press, 1967), esp. 1–2, 183, 97, 207–213.

37. Harrison, *Diary of Thomas P. Cope*, 23; Marcus Daniel, *Scandal and Civility: Journalism and the Birth of American Democracy* (New York: Oxford University Press, 2009), 7–8. Many of the papers with the largest circulations were partisan organs. *The Aurora* claimed seventeen hundred subscribers in its prime, while in 1800 *Porcupine's Gazette* claimed two thousand.

38. Seth Ames, ed., *Works of Fisher Ames with a Selection of His Speeches and Correspondence*, 2 vols. (New York: Burt Franklin, 1971), vol. 2, 408; "The Subject of the Following Communication Is in Our Opinion of Considerable Importance," *Connecticut Gazette and the Commercial Intelligencer*, August 20, 1806; Elisha Douglass, "Fisher Ames, Spokesman for New England Federalism," *Proceedings of the American Philosophical Society* 103, no. 5 (1959): 713. Many trade books assume the existence of a powerful copycat effect. See, for instance, Loren Coleman, *The Copycat Effect: How the Media and Popular Culture Trigger the Mayhem in Tomorrow's Headlines* (New York: Simon and Schuster, 2003). However, an influential study of articles about suicide published in a national newspaper between 1910 and 1920 found no correlation between reporting and the rate of suicide. See Ira M. Wasserman, Steven Stack, and Jimmie L. Reeves, "Suicide and the Media: *The New York Times*'s Presentation of Front-Page Suicide Stories between 1910 and 1920," *Journal of Communication* 44, no. 2 (1994): 64–83. For an introduction to this large but factious field of research, see Émile Durkheim, *Suicide: A Study in Sociology*, ed. George Simpson, trans. John A. Spaulding and George Simpson (Glencoe, IL: The Free Press, 1951), 141; James B. Hittner, "How Robust Is the Werther Effect? A Re-examination of the Suggestion-Imitation Model of Suicide," *Morality* 10, no. 3 (2005): 193–200.

39. "Worcester, June 10," *Massachusetts Spy*, June 10, 1784; "Concord, July 13," *The Mail; or, Claypoole's Daily Advertiser*, August 11, 1791; "Effects of Bad Principles," *Carlisle Gazette*, August 12, 1814. The wide array of causes newspaper editors commonly ascribed to suicidal behavior and the tendency of editors to highlight nonculpable non compos mentis verdicts also struck many ministers and heads of household as deeply problematic.

40. "From the Patron of Industry," *Newburyport Herald*, September 12, 1821; "From the Patron of Industry," *Independent Chronicle and Boston Patriot*, September 12, 1821; "Editor," *Middlesex Gazette*, July 16, 1826. It was not until 1833 that anyone thought to question whether the decades-old habit of writing pro-life sermons and newspaper editorials might be contributing to "the stir about suicides." See "Frequency of Crime," *New Bedford Mercury*, August 16, 1833.

41. Karen Halttunen, "Early American Murder Narratives: The Birth of Horror," in *The Power of Culture: Critical Essays in American History*, ed. Richard Wrightman Fox and T. J. Jackson Lears (Chicago: University of Chicago Press,

1993), 67, 78; Michael MacDonald, "Suicide and the Rise of the Popular Press in England," *Representations* 22 (1988): 41–43, 51.

42. Daniel T. Rodgers, *Contested Truths: Keywords in American Politics since Independence* (New York: Basic Books, 1987), 8–15.

43. *An Essay on Marriage; or, the Lawfulness of Divorce, in Certain Cases, Considered* (Philadelphia: Zachariah Poulson, Junior, 1788), 2, 24. This anonymous author's agenda was to expand the basis for legal divorce in Pennsylvania beyond narrow, fault-based grounds.

44. Ibid., 24; Anthony Benezet, *A Caution and Warning to Great Britain and Her Colonies, in a Short Representation of the Calamitous State of the Enslaved Negroes in the British Dominions* . . . (Philadelphia: Henry Miller, 1766), 20; "Charleston, (S. C.) Jan. 18," *Independent Ledger*, February 27, 1786; "Philadelphia, May 21," *Pennsylvania Gazette*, May 21, 1788; Olaudah Equiano, *The Interesting Narrative of the Life of Olaudah Equiano, or Gustavus Vassa, the African. Written by Himself*, 2 vols. (New York: W. Durell, 1791), vol. 1, 56–57. The *Ledger*'s account was also taken up and reprinted by editors in Charlestown, Massachusetts, Baltimore, Maryland, Portsmouth, New Hampshire, and Burlington, New Jersey, over the following weeks.

45. "London, March 12. Slave Trade," *Dunlap's American Daily Advertiser*, May 25, 1792.

2. The Sorrows of Young Readers

1. "New-York, July 31, 1807," *New-York Gazette & General Advertiser*, July 31, 1807; Johann Wolfgang von Goethe, *The Sorrows and Sympathetic Attachments of Werter; a German Story* . . . (Philadelphia: Robert Bell, 1785), 70.

2. Amy Elizabeth Winans, "Slaves and Citizens: Early African America and the Discourse of Nations, 1770–1820" (PhD diss., Pennsylvania State University, 1998), 79; Rodney Hessinger, *Seduced, Abandoned, and Reborn: Visions of Youth in Middle-Class America, 1780–1850* (Philadelphia: University of Pennsylvania Press, 2005), 27.

3. Cathy N. Davidson, *Revolution and the Word: The Rise of the Novel in America* (New York: Oxford University Press, 1986), 73, 10, 42; Sarah Knott, "A Cultural History of Sensibility in the Era of the American Revolution" (DPhil, University of Oxford, 1999), 24–25; Herbert Ross Brown, *The Sentimental Novel in America, 1789–1860* (New York: Pageant, 1959), 15.

4. Davidson, *Revolution and the Word*, 27; David Kaser, *A Book for Sixpence: The Circulating Library in America* (Pittsburgh: Beta Phi Mu, 1980), 39, 48; Knott, "Cultural History of Sensibility," 28.

5. Kaser, *A Book for Sixpence*, 50; Brown, *Sentimental Novel in America*, 23.

6. John Davis, *Travels of Four Years and a Half Years in the United States* (London, 1803), 204; "Letter of Advice to a Young Lady. To Miss—," *New-York Magazine or Literary Repository* (August 1797), 398; Knott, "Cultural History of Sensibility," 28; Sarah Knott, *Sensibility and the American Revolution* (Chapel Hill: University of North Carolina Press, 2008), 52; R. B. Winans, "The Growth of a

Novel-Reading Public in Late 18th Century America," *Early American Literature* 9, no. 3 (1975): 271–272.

7. Emory Elliott, *Revolutionary Writers: Literature and Authority in the New Republic, 1725–1810* (New York: Oxford University Press, 1982), 36; Karen Halttunen, "Humanitarianism and the Pornography of Pain in Anglo-American Culture," *American Historical Review* 100, no. 2 (1995): 312; Davidson, *Revolution and the Word*, 42–43.

8. Benjamin Rush, *An Oration, Delivered before the American Philosophical Society . . . On the 27th of February, 1786* (Philadelphia: Cist, 1786), 33, 26; Davidson, *Revolution and the Word*, 113–116; G. J. Barker-Benfield, *The Culture of Sensibility: Sex and Society in Eighteenth-Century Britain* (Chicago: University of Chicago Press, 1992), 1–36, 104–153, 248, 276; Andrew Burstein, *Sentimental Democracy: The Evolution of America's Romantic Self-Image* (New York: Hill and Wang, 1999), xi–xviii, 14; Knott, *Sensibility and the American Revolution*, 1–18, 153–263.

9. Carla Mulford, ed., *"The Power of Sympathy" and "The Coquette"* (New York: Penguin, 1996), 62; Knott, *Sensibility and the American Revolution*, 17–18, 220–238; Mildred Davis Doyle, "Sentimentalism in American Periodicals" (PhD diss., New York University, 1941), 34–85; Tremaine McDowell, "Sensibility in the Eighteenth-Century American Novel," *Studies in Philology* 24, no. 3 (1927): 389–399; Martha Tomhave Blauvelt, *The Work of the Heart: Young Women and Emotion, 1780–1830* (Charlottesville: University of Virginia Press, 2007), 25.

10. Julian P. Boyd et al., eds., *Papers of Thomas Jefferson*, 23 vols. (Princeton, NJ: Princeton University Press, 1950), vol. 1, 74–75; Knott, *Sensibility and the American Revolution*, 109–151; Blauvelt, *Work of the Heart*, 32; John Tinnon-Taylor, *Early Opposition to the English Novel: The Popular Reaction from 1760 to 1830* (New York: King's Crown Press, 1943), 87–100.

11. Goethe, *Sorrows of Werter*, 70; Bruce Duncan, *Goethe's Werther and the Critics* (Rochester, NY: Camden House, 2005), 107–133.

12. Georges C. Minois, *The History of Suicide: Voluntary Death in Western Culture*, trans. Lydia G. Cochrane (Baltimore, MD: Johns Hopkins University Press, 1999), 267; Robyn L. Schiffman, "A Concert of Werthers," *Eighteenth-Century Studies* 43, no. 2 (2010): 208–209; Orie William Long, "English Translations of Goethe's Werther," *Journal of English and Germanic Philology* 14, no. 2 (1915): 169–203; Stuart Pratt Atkins, *The Testament of Werther in Poetry and Drama* (Cambridge, MA: Harvard University Press, 1949); Fritz Gutbrodt, "The Worth of Werther: Goethe's Literary Marketing," *MLN* 110, no. 3 (April 1995): 579–630.

13. "Classified Adv.," *Independent Journal*, July 7, 1784; Frederick H. Wilkens, "Early Influence of German Literature in America," *Americana Germanica* 3, no. 2 (1899): 136; O. W. Long, "Werther in America," in *Studies in Honor of John Albrecht Walz* (Lancaster, PA: Lancaster Press, 1941), 88; Brown, *Sentimental Novel in America*, 155; Schiffman, "A Concert of Werthers," 212.

14. *Literary Magazine and American Register* 6, no. 39 (1806): 451; Davis, *Travels of Four Years and a Half Years*, 149; "Classified Adv.," *Independent Journal*, January 21, 1784; "Classified Adv.," *Independent Journal*, January 31, 1784; "Diary of Anne Hume Shippen Livingston, March, 1784," in *Nancy Shippen Her Journal Book: The*

International Romance of a Young Lady of Fashion of Colonial Philadelphia with Letters: To Her and about Her, ed. Ethel Armes (Philadelphia: Lippincott, 1935), 312.

15. Long, "Werther in America," 106–107; O. W. Long, "English and American Imitations of Goethe's Werter," *Modern Philology* 14, no. 4 (1916): 193–216; Atkins, *Testament of Werther*, 251.

16. Benjamin Rush, *Essays, Literary, Moral and Philosophical*, 2d ed. (Philadelphia: Thomas and William Bradford, 1806), 82.

17. Susan Montgomery to Benjamin Rush, "The Speculator. No. XIII," *Massachusetts Magazine* (November 1795): 487; "The Ubiquitarian," *Weekly Magazine* (April 14, 1798): 331–332. See also "The Monitress," *Dartmouth Gazette*, September 12, 1810. This column was quickly reprinted in newspapers across New England and the mid-Atlantic.

18. "For the Merrimack Magazine," *Merrimack Magazine and Ladies' Literary Cabinet* (April 12, 1806): 137. Ironically, this editorial was actually an uncredited excerpt from another suicide novel, *The Hapless Orphan* (1793), at the climax of which one character commits suicide having read *The Sorrows of Young Werther*.

19. *Gentleman's Magazine* (1784): 876; Minois, *The History of Suicide*, 40.

20. Daryl Edward Lee, "Suicide and the Subject of Modern Life" (PhD diss., University of Minnesota, 2001), 16, 28; James B. Hittner, "How Robust Is the Werther Effect? A Re-examination of the Suggestion-Imitation Model of Suicide," *Mortality* 10, no. 3 (2005): 193; Lord George Byron, *The Poems and Dramas of Lord Byron* (New York: T. Y. Crowell, 1884), 527; A. Alvarez, *The Savage God; a Study of Suicide* (New York: Random House, 1972), 207–208.

21. "Charleston, Tuesday, November 16, 1784. Extract of a Letter from Kingston, Jamaica, Oct. 9," *South-Carolina Gazette and General Advertiser*, November 16, 1784.

22. Richard Cumberland, *The Mysterious Husband. A Tragedy in Five Acts. As It Is Acted at the Theatre-Royal, Covent-Garden* (London: C. Dilly, 1783), 64; "Extract of a Letter from Kingston."

23. "Mr. Printer," *New-Hampshire Mercury*, January 25, 1785; Margaret Hutchinson, "Letter to Mrs. Margaret (Holyoke) Mascarene," 1789, Mascarene Family Papers, Massachusetts Historical Society; "The Ubiquitarian." See also "From the New-Hampshire Mercury. Mr. Printer," *The Independent Ledger and the American Advertiser*, March 14, 1785.

24. "The Ubiquitarian."

25. "The Monitress."

26. Mulford, *Power of Sympathy*, 100. The *Massachusetts Magazine* reprinted Harrington's enthusiastic defense of self-murder under a laudatory headline later that year. See "Beauties of the Power of Sympathy," *Massachusetts Magazine* 1 (1789): 50–53.

27. Julia A. Stern, *The Plight of Feeling: Sympathy and Dissent in the Early American Novel* (Chicago: University of Chicago Press, 1997), 13; Elizabeth Barnes, "Affecting Relations: Pedagogy, Patriarchy, and the Politics of Sympathy," *American Literary History* 8, no. 4 (1996): 609.

28. *The Hapless Orphan; or, Innocent Victim of Revenge: a Novel, Founded on Incidents in Real Life* . . . , 2 vols. (Boston: Belknap and Hall, 1793), vol. 2, 194, 213. For similar tableaux, see Catherine Waltraud Proescholdt-Obermann, "The Reception of Goethe's Works in British Periodicals 1779 to 1805" (PhD diss., Anglia Polytechnic, 1990), 86; John Brewer, *A Sentimental Murder: Love and Madness in the Eighteenth Century* (London: Harper Perennial, 2005), 168; Lillie Deming Loshe, *The Early American Novel* (New York: Columbia University Press, 1907), 14.

29. Bibliographical data drawn from Henri Petter, *The Early American Novel* (Columbus, OH: Ohio State University Press, 1971); Brown, *Sentimental Novel in America;* "Early American Fiction 1789–1875," Chadwyck, http://collections.chadwyck.com.proxy-um.researchport.umd.edu/home/home_eaf2.jsp.

30. "An Instance of Female Heroism, Which Happened in New-York in May, 1773," *New-York Magazine; or, Literary Repository* (November 1791): 647; "THE SEDUCED FEMALE—A Sentimental Sketch," *New-York Magazine; or, Literary Repository* (January 1796): 14; Mulford, *Power of Sympathy*, 40; Hugh Henry Brackenridge, *Modern Chivalry: Containing the Adventures of Captain John Farrago and Teague O'Reagan, His Servant* (New York: Rowman and Littlefield, 2003), 127; James Butler, *Fortune's Foot-ball; or, the Adventures of Mercutio* . . ., 2 vols. (Harrisburg, PA: Wyeth, 1797), vol. 1, 58–59.

31. [Sukey Vickery], *Emily Hamilton: A Novel Founded on Incidents in Real Life* (Worcester, MA: Isaiah Thomas, 1803), 46; Caroline Matilda Thayer, *The Gamesters; or, Ruins of Innocence. An Original Novel, Founded in Truth* (Boston: Thomas and Andrews, 1805), 82–84.

32. Mulford, *Power of Sympathy*, 51; Susanna Rowson, *Charlotte: A Tale of Truth* (Philadelphia: Mathew Carey, 1794), 95; John Davis, *The Original Letters of Ferdinand and Elizabeth* . . . (New York: Caritat, 1798), 135; Thayer, *Gamesters*, 296–297.

33. *Hapless Orphan*, vol. 2, 199; Davis, *Original Letters of Ferdinand and Elizabeth*, 128; Susanna Rowson, *Reuben and Rachel: A Tale of Old Times* . . ., 2 vols. (Boston, 1798), vol. 2, 349.

34. Brown, *Sentimental Novel in America*, 58; "The Felo De Se. By Werther," *Massachusetts Magazine* (March 1790): 181.

35. Susanna Rowson, *The Inquisitor; or, the Invisible Rambler*, 2d ed., 3 vols. (Philadelphia: Mathew Carey, 1794), vol. 3, 188.

36. Samuel Miller, *A Brief Retrospect of the Eighteenth Century*, 2 vols. (New York: Swords, 1803), vol. 2, 175; also see *The Guilt, Folly, and Sources of Suicide: Two Discourses, Preached in the City of New-York, February, 1805* (New York: T. and J. Swords, 1805), 44–45; "Suicide," *People's Friend & Daily Advertiser*, May 18, 1807; "From the People's Friend," *Newburyport Gazette*, June 1, 1807; "Suicide," *Charleston Courier*, June 3, 1807. Miller considered trying to ban the sale of books like *Werther* but soon dismissed the idea as impractical. See Miller, *Brief Retrospect*, vol. 2, 179.

37. Thaddeus Mason Harris, *A Sermon Preached in the First Parish in Dedham, September 13, 1801: Being the Lord's Day after the Execution of Jason Fairbanks* (Dedham, MA: Herman Mann, 1801), 29; "Died," *National Recorder*, November 27, 1819; "Died," *Ladies' Literary Cabinet*, December 4, 1819. Later testimony revealed

that the young lady in question, Eliza Fales, had been reading *Julia Mandeville* (1764), a melodramatic British fiction in which two young lovers die at the climax, prior to her fateful meeting with Jason Fairbanks.

38. Elizabeth Barnes, *States of Sympathy: Seduction and Democracy in the American Novel* (New York: Columbia University Press, 1997), 87, 8–9, 14, 20, 35–36.

39. Ibid., 31, 40–41; Mulford, *Power of Sympathy*, 7; Davidson, *Revolution and the Word*, 44, 99.

40. John Mifflin, "Journal of 'Leander,'" January 18, 1787, James Gibson Collection, Historical Society of Pennsylvania; "Affected Sensibility," *Columbian Magazine* (1790): 252; "The Essayist No. 4," *Ladies Magazine* (September 1792): 159–161; Knott, *Sensibility and the American Revolution*, 145.

41. John Bennett, "Letter to a Young Lady. Letter XXII—a Lovely Fair One," *American Museum* (June 1792): 265; "Letter III. On the Practice of Reading Novels and Romances," *United States Magazine* (1794): 141.

42. *Watchman*, March 25, 1796; "Vancenza; or the Dangers of Credulity," *Lady's Magazine and Repository of Entertaining Knowledge* (November 1792): 296.

43. Davidson, *Revolution and the Word*, 42.

44. [Thomas Bellamy], "The Fatal Effects of Seduction: Exemplified in a letter from the Reformed Edmund, to His Friend. By Thomas Bellamy," *Gentlemen and Ladies Town and Country Magazine* (June 1789): 251; Charles Brockden Brown, *Edgar Huntley; or Memoirs of a Sleep-Walker* (Philadelphia, 1799); Sally Wood, *Dorval; or, The Speculator. A Novel, Founded on Recent Facts* (Portsmouth, NH, 1801); George Watterston, *Glencarn: or, the Disappointments of Youth* (Alexandria, VA, 1810).

45. "Despair; or the History of Delia and Lorenzo with an Engraving," *New-York Magazine* 2, no. 11 (1791): 691–692.

46. Susanna Rowson, *Trials of the Human Heart, a Novel*, 3 vols. (Philadelphia: Wrigley and Berriman, 1795), 99; Thayer, *Gamesters*, 280; *The History of Constantius and Pulchera; or Constancy Rewarded* (Salem, MA: Cushing, 1795), 15, 21, 60; Rebecca Rush, *Kelroy: A Novel* (Philadelphia: Bradford and Inskeep, 1812), 191; *Amelia: Or the Faithless Briton. An Original American Novel, Founded Upon Recent Facts* (Boston, 1798).

47. Butler, *Fortune's Foot-Ball*, vol. 1, 28; Mulford, *Power of Sympathy*, 223, 38.

48. Enos Hitchcock, *Memoirs of the Bloomsgrove Family: In a series of letters to a respectable citizen* . . . (Boston: Thomas and Andrews, 1790), 296; *The Slave of Passion, or, The Fruits of Werter: A Novel* (Philadelphia: J. Hoff, 1802), 4; Davidson, *Revolution and the Word*, 127–129; Karen A. Weyler, *Intricate Relations: Sexual and Economic Desire in American Fiction, 1789–1814* (Iowa City: University of Iowa Press, 2004), 33.

49. Charles Brockden Brown, *Arthur Mervyn; or Memoirs of the Year 1793* . . . , 2 vols. (Philadelphia: Maxwell, 1799), vol. 1, 187, 88; also see Brown, *Jane Talbot: A Novel* (Philadelphia: John Conrad & Co, 1801), 288.

50. Charles Brockden Brown, "Man at Home," in *The Rhapsodist: And Other Uncollected Writings*, ed. Harry R. Warfel (New York: Scholars' Facsimiles and Reprints, 1943), 90; William M. Manly, "The Importance of Point of View in Brockden Brown's Wieland," *American Literature* 35, no. 3 (1963): 320. In addition,

in *Jane Talbot*, Henry Colden is deemed unacceptable as a son-in-law because he is a proponent of rational suicide. See Brown, *Jane Talbot*, 99.

51. Davis, *Original Letters of Ferdinand and Elizabeth*, 62–63; *Hapless Orphan*, vol. 2, 205–206.

52. Charles Brockden Brown, "Criticism," *Literary Magazine, and American Register* (April 1805): 315–316; Miller, *Brief Retrospect*, vol. 2, 171; Bryan Waterman, *Republic of Intellect: The Friendly Club of New York City and the Making of American Literature* (Baltimore, MD: Johns Hopkins University Press, 2007), 231–241; Jane P. Tompkins, ed., *Reader-Response: From Formalism to Post-Structuralism* (Baltimore, MD: Johns Hopkins University Press, 1980); Leah Price, "Reading: The State of the Discipline," *Book History* 7 (2004): 303–320; Philip Goldstein and James L. Machor, eds., *New Directions in American Reception Study* (New York: Oxford University Press, 2008).

53. Charles Brockden Brown, "A Student's Diary. . . . No (VI)," *Literary Magazine and American Register* (March 1806): 404; Miller, *Brief Retrospect*, vol. 1, xi.

54. Shirley Samuels, ed., *The Culture of Sentiment: Race, Gender, and Sentimentality in 19th Century America* (New York: Oxford University Press, 1992), 6; Burstein, *Sentimental Democracy*, 308–323.

55. John Neal, *Keep Cool, a Novel: Written in Hot Weather. By Somebody*, 2 vols. (Baltimore, MD: Cushing, 1817), vol. 1, 73.

56. Andrews Norton, "Recent Publications concerning Goethe," *Select Journal of Foreign Literature* 1 (1833): 250; Henry Wadsworth Longfellow, "Journal," December 29, 1835, Longfellow National Historic Site; Lambert A. Wilmer, "Sorrows of Skwerter," *Atkinson's Casket* (October 1838): 449–455; Schiffman, "A Concert of Werthers," 219; Long, "Werther in America," 101; Matthew Lewis, *Journal of a West India Proprietor, Kept during a Residence in the Island of Jamaica* (New York: Oxford University Press, 1999), 20.

57. Clara Crowninshield, "Diary of Clara Crowninshield, August, 1836," in *Diary: A European Tour with Longfellow, 1835–1836*, ed. Andrew Hilen (Seattle: University of Washington Press, 1956), 304; Nina Baym, *Woman's Fiction: A Guide to Novels by and about Women in America, 1820–1870* (Ithaca, NY: Cornell University Press, 1979), 25.

58. Jane P. Tompkins, *Sensational Designs: The Cultural Work of American Fiction, 1790–1860* (New York: Oxford University Press, 1985), 124–125, 59, 76; Barnes, *States of Sympathy*, 94–95.

3. Saving Sinking Strangers

1. Thomas Barnard, *Discourse, Delivered before the Humane Society of the Commonwealth of Massachusetts, at the Semi Annual Meeting, June 10, 1794* (Boston: Jeremy Belknap, 1794), 23–24; Timothy Thompson Sawyer, *Old Charlestown: Historical, Biographical, Reminiscent* (Boston: J. H. West Co., 1902), 90.

2. Barnard, *Discourse*, 23–24.

3. Norman Fiering, "Irresistible Compassion: An Aspect of Eighteenth-Century Sympathy and Humanitarianism," *Journal of the History of Ideas* 37, no. 2

(1976): 195–218; Evan Radcliffe, "Revolutionary Writing, Moral Philosophy, and Universal Benevolence in the Eighteenth Century," *Journal of the History of Ideas* 54, no. 2 (1993): 221–240; Karen Halttunen, "Humanitarianism and the Pornography of Pain in Anglo-American Culture," *American Historical Review* 100, no. 2 (1995): 303–334; Amanda Bowie Moniz, "Saving the Lives of Strangers: Humane Societies and the Cosmopolitan Provision of Charitable Aid," *Journal of the Early Republic* 29, no. 4 (2009): 610–611.

4. Daniel Dana, *An Address to the Members of the Merrimack Humane Society, at Their Anniversary Meeting in Newburyport, September 7, 1813* (Exeter, NH: Charles Norris & Co., 1813), 4; Conrad Edick Wright, *The Transformation of Charity in Postrevolutionary New England* (Boston: Northeastern University Press, 1992), 5, 55, 64; Albrecht Koschnik, *"Let a Common Interest Bind Us Together": Associations, Partisanship, and Culture in Philadelphia, 1775–1840* (Charlottesville: University of Virginia Press, 2007), 1; Moniz, "Saving the Lives of Strangers," 615.

5. John Lathrop, *A Discourse before the Humane Society in Boston, Delivered on the Second Tuesday of June, 1787* (Boston: E. Russell, 1787), 18–19. Suicide had been decriminalized in Amsterdam in 1658. See Pieter Spierenburg, *The Spectacle of Suffering* (New York: Cambridge University Press, 1984), 56.

6. William Tudor, *A Discourse Delivered before the Humane Society, at Their Anniversary, May 1817* (Boston: John Eliot, 1817), 29; Amanda Bowie Moniz, "'Labours in the Cause of Humanity in Every Part of the Globe': Transatlantic Philanthropic Collaboration and the Cosmopolitan Ideal, 1760–1815" (PhD diss., University of Michigan, 2008), 80; M. A. DeWolfe Howe, *The Humane Society of the Commonwealth of Massachusetts: An Historical Review, 1785–1916* (Boston: Riverside, 1918), 6.

7. Moniz, "'Labours in the Cause of Humanity,'" 79–82, 363–364; "New Haven, March 16," *New-Haven Gazette, and the Connecticut Magazine*, March 16, 1786; *A Brief Account of the Humane Society, Instituted in the Year 1774. Laid before the Annual Meeting of the President, Vice-Presidents, and Directors, at Their Anniversary Festival, on the 24th Day of March, 1789* (London: Royal Humane Society, 1789), ix–x. The Humane Society of Philadelphia, to give it its legal title, was actually founded in 1780 by a group of physicians returning from medical training in Europe. Yet, for reasons that included the death of its president in 1783, the society lay almost dormant for seven years and only revived in 1787 following the much-trumpeted establishment of a similar society in Boston.

8. Humane Society of Massachusetts, *The Institution of the Humane Society of Massachusetts* (Boston, 1786?); E. H. Thomson, "The Role of Physicians in the Humane Societies of the Eighteenth Century," *Bulletin of the History of Medicine* 37 (1963): 47–48; Howe, *Humane Society*, 38; Merrimack Humane Society, *The Institution of the Merrimack Humane Society, with the Rules for Regulating Said Society, and the Methods of Treatment to Be Used with Persons Apparently Dead* (Newburyport: E. M. Blunt, 1803).

9. Humane Society of Philadelphia, "Annual Subscription Book for 1813," in Records of the Humane Society of Philadelphia, American Philosophical Society; Merrimack Humane Society, *Institution;* Howe, *Humane Society*, 43–44;

Humane Society of the Commonwealth of Massachusetts, *Humane Society of the Commonwealth of Massachusetts: Appendix* (Boston: n.p., 1810), 12–14. Among the twenty-three speakers at the Massachusetts Humane Society's annual meetings, fourteen were Harvard graduates, while another six were recipients of its honorary degrees.

10. David Hosack, *An Enquiry into the Causes of Suspended Animation from Drowning; with the Means of Restoring Life* (New York: Thomas and James Swords, 1791), iii–iv; Stefan Maria Timmermans, "Saving Lives: A Historical and Ethnographic Study of Resuscitation Techniques" (PhD diss., University of Illinois at Urbana-Champaign, 1995), 22–23; John Anthony Tercier, *The Contemporary Deathbed: The Ultimate Rush* (London: Palgrave Macmillan, 2005), chap. 3; Humane Society of the State of New York, *The Constitution of the Humane Society of the State of New-York* (New York: J. Buel, 1795), 19.

11. Benjamin Davis, *Some Account of the City of Philadelphia, the Capital of Pennsylvania, and Seat of the Federal Congress* . . . (Philadelphia: Richard Folwell, 1794), 51; Benjamin Say, *An Annual Oration Pronounced before the Humane Society of Philadelphia on the Objects and Benefits of Said Institution; the 28th Day of February, 1799* (Philadelphia: William Young, 1799), 21; Humane Society of Philadelphia, *Do Not Despair* (Philadelphia, 1806); John Clarke, *A Discourse Delivered before the Humane Society of the Commonwealth of Massachusetts, at the Semi-Annual Meeting* (Boston: Belknap and Hall, 1793), 33.

12. Benjamin Waterhouse, *On the Principle of Vitality. A Discourse Delivered in the First Church in Boston, Tuesday, June 8th, 1790, before the Humane Society of the Commonwealth of Massachusetts* (Boston: Thomas and John Fleet, 1790), 2.

13. Thomas Thacher, *A Discourse Delivered at Boston, before the Humane Society of the Commonwealth of Massachusetts, June 10th, 1800* (Boston: John & Thomas Fleet, 1800), 13.

14. William Hawes, *Annual Report Published for the Anniversary Festival* (London, 1795), 23; Martin Pernick, "Back from the Grave: Recurring Controversies over Defining and Diagnosing Death in History," in *Death: Beyond Whole-Brain Criteria*, ed. Richard M. Zaner (Dordrecht: Springer, 1988), 20–27; Erwin H. Ackerknecht, "Death in the History of Medicine," *Bulletin of the History of Medicine* 43, no. 1 (1968): 21.

15. *Brief Account*, xi–xii.

16. Lathrop, *Discourse*, 16; Lemuel Shaw, *A Discourse Delivered before the Officers and Members of the Humane Society of Massachusetts, 11 June 1811* (Boston: John Eliot, 1811), 6–8.

17. Humane Society of the State of New York, *Constitution*, 9–10; Isaac Hurd, *A Discourse Delivered in the Church in Brattle Street, in Boston, Tuesday, June 11th, 1799 before the Humane Society of the Commonwealth of Massachusetts* (Boston: John & Thomas Fleet, 1799), 15; Dana, *Address*, 19; Howe, *Humane Society*, 25.

18. Hurd, *Discourse*, 20; Moniz, "Saving the Lives of Strangers," 612; Barnard, *Discourse*, 9. On the demographics of rescuers and those rescued, see Moniz, "Saving the Lives of Strangers," 618–634.

19. Humane Society of the State of New York, *Constitution*, 20; Thomas Danforth, *A Discourse before the Humane Society, of the Commonwealth of Massachusetts, Boston, June 14, 1808* (Boston: Russel & Cutler, 1808), 14; *Order of Performances on the 22d Anniversary of the Massachusetts Humane Society* (1807); "Merrimack Humane Society," *Newburyport Herald*, September 4, 1807. On the activities of the Royal Humane Society to prevent suicide, see Luke Anthony Francis Davidson, "Raising Up Humanity: A Cultural History of Resuscitation and the Royal Humane Society of London, 1774–1808" (PhD diss., University of York, 2001), 227–228.

20. Lathrop, *Discourse*, 18; Eliphalet Porter, *A Discourse Delivered before the Humane Society of the Commonwealth of Massachusetts, at Their Semi-Annual Meeting, June 8, 1802* (Boston: Hosea Sprague, 1802), 11–12; John C. Howard, *A Discourse Delivered before the Humane Society of the Commonwealth of Massachusetts, at Their Semiannual Meeting, June 12, 1804* (Boston: Hosea Sprague, 1804), 14; Thaddeus Mason Harris, *A Discourse Delivered before the Humane Society of the Commonwealth of Massachusetts, June 10, 1806 . . .* (Boston: E. Lincoln, 1806), 9; also see Harris, *An Earnest Caution against Suicide* (Boston: Joshua Belcher, 1812).

21. Thomas Gray, *The Value of Life and Charitable Institutions, a Discourse Delivered before the Humane Society of the Commonwealth of Massachusetts, at Their Semi-Annual Meeting, June 11th, 1805* (Boston: Hosea Sprague, 1805), 7–8. See also Henry Colman, *A Discourse Delivered in the Chapel Church, Boston, before the Humane Society of Massachusetts, 9 June 1812* (Boston: John Eliot, 1812), 16.

22. Howard, *Discourse*, 61; William Bentley, *The Diary of William Bentley, Pastor of the East Church, Salem, Massachusetts*, 4 vols. (Salem, MA: Essex Institute, 1905–1914). Rev. Bentley recorded no less than 80 drownings and 209 other accidents in his diaries from 1784 to 1819; none involved hanging. Likewise, the Boston managers had read countless reports from the Royal Humane Society in London in which their surrogates had thwarted suicides by hanging.

23. "For the Centinel," *Columbian Centinel*, March 22, 1800. The column had first been published in papers in London. See, for instance, "A Caution for the Preservation of Life," *Times* (London), January 23, 1790. No record has been found to indicate whether or not Boston pharmacists paid this notice any heed.

24. "Philadelphia, August 27," *Pennsylvania Gazette*, August 27, 1730; "Philadelphia, Sept. 23," *American Weekly Mercury*, September 23, 1731.

25. "Effects of Bad Principles," *Spooners Vermont Journal*, June 27, 1814.

26. "Philadelphia, August 27," "New-York, June 26," *American Weekly Mercury*, June 29, 1732.

27. Francis G. Walett, ed., *The Diary of Ebenezer Parkman, 1703–1782* (Worcester: American Antiquarian Society, 1974), 202; Eliza Cope Harrison, ed., *Philadelphia Merchant: The Diary of Thomas P. Cope, 1800–1851* (South Bend, IN: Gateway Editions, 1978), 245.

28. "Philadelphia, Sept. 3," *American Weekly Mercury*, September 3, 1730; "Philadelphia," *American Weekly Mercury*, September 18, 1735.

29. Rescue data compiled from all surviving annual addresses and other published documents; data do not include any rescues that came to the attention of the society between June 1812 and June 1813, when no records are extant. Records for

the Philadelphia Humane Society are less comprehensive, though Amanda Moniz has pieced together what remains to show that between 1782 and 1815, that society rescued at least eighty-three persons. See Moniz, "'Labours in the Cause of Humanity,'" 218.

30. Clarke, *Discourse,* 35; John Bartlett, *A Discourse on the Subject of Animation. Delivered before the Humane Society of the Commonwealth of Massachusetts, June 11, 1792* (Boston: Isaiah Thomas, 1792), 23; John Brooks, *A Discourse Delivered before the Humane Society of the Commonwealth of Massachusetts, 9th June 1795* (Boston: T. Fleet, 1795), 25. The same ambiguities of intent surround many apparently accidental deaths or near misses. See, for instance, Paul E. Johnson, *Sam Patch, the Famous Jumper* (New York: Hill and Wang, 2003), 2, 115, 123–125.

31. William Walter, *A Discourse Delivered before the Humane Society of the Commonwealth of Massachusetts, at Their Semiannual Meeting, June 12th 1798* (Boston: John & Thomas Fleet, 1798), 41; Danforth, *Discourse,* 28. For a rare acknowledgment of a suicide by drowning that the Boston society's surrogates failed to restore to life, see Brooks, *Discourse,* 17–18.

32. Barnard, *Discourse,* 23; Chandler Robbins, *A Discourse Delivered before the Humane Society of the Commonwealth of Massachusetts, at Their Semiannual Meeting, June 14th 1796* (Boston: Thomas Fleet, 1796), 32; Colman, *Discourse,* 29; Tudor, *Discourse,* 53.

33. Humane Society of the State of New York, *Constitution,* 20; Howard, *Discourse,* 19.

34. "New-York, June 26."

35. Brooks, *Discourse,* 22; William Buchan, *Domestic Medicine: Or, a Treatise on the Prevention and Cure of Diseases, by Regimen and Simple Medicines with Appendix* (Philadelphia: A. Bartram, 1805), 483; Louise Foxcroft, *The Making of Addiction: The "Use and Abuse" of Opium in Nineteenth-Century Britain* (London: Ashgate Press, 2007), 171.

36. Brooks, *Discourse,* 22.

37. Ibid.

38. Ibid. Welsh was the first corresponding secretary of the Humane Society of the Commonwealth of Massachusetts and served as trustee from 1786 to 1798. See "Thomas Welsh," in *Sibley's Harvard Graduates,* ed. Conrad Edick Wright and Edward W. Hanson (Boston: Northeastern University Press, 1999), vol. 18, 183–88.

39. Brooks, *Discourse,* 22.

40. Ibid.

41. "Thomas Welsh," 188.

42. David J. Rothman, *The Discovery of the Asylum: Social Order and Disorder in the New Republic* (Boston: Little, Brown, and Company, 1971), chap. 6; Gerald N. Grob, *Mental Institutions in America: Social Policy to 1875* (New York: Free Press, 1973), chap. 1.

43. Steven Mintz, *Moralists and Modernizers: America's Pre–Civil War Reformers* (Baltimore, MD: Johns Hopkins University Press, 1995), 158; Rothman, *Discovery of the Asylum,* introduction.

44. Benjamin Rush, *Medical Inquiries and Observations, Upon the Diseases of the Mind* (Philadelphia: Kimber & Richardson, 1812); Rothman, *Discovery of the Asylum*, chaps. 2, 5; Grob, *Mental Institutions*, chaps. 1, 2; Mary Ann Jimenez, *Changing Faces of Madness: Early American Attitudes and Treatment of the Insane* (Hanover, NH: University Press of New England, 1987).

45. Grob, *Mental Institutions*, 39–42.

46. Jedidiah Morse, *A Sermon Preached before the Humane Society of the Commonwealth of Massachusetts, at Their Semi-Annual Meeting, June 9th 1801* (Boston: John & Thomas Fleet, 1801), 18–20; Grob, *Mental Institutions*, 52.

47. Porter, *Discourse*, 9–10; Danforth, *Discourse*, 14; Burton Spivak, *Jefferson's English Crisis: Commerce, Embargo, and the Republican Revolution* (Charlottesville: University of Virginia Press, 1979).

48. "Humane Society," *Boston Gazette*, June 16, 1808; Nathaniel I. Bowditch, *History of the Massachusetts General Hospital* (Boston: John Wilson and Son, 1851), 423–432; Grob, *Mental Institutions*, 52; Thomson, "Role of Physicians," 47–48.

49. Caleb Cushing, *The History of the Present State of the Town of Newburyport* (Newburyport: E. W. Allen, 1826), 41; "Humane Society," *Columbian Centinel*, May 10, 1817. These figures refer to donations of more than $100 made to the joint General and Mental Hospital fund prior to 1828. See Bowditch, *History of the Massachusetts General Hospital*, 423–432.

50. Bowditch, *History of the Massachusetts General Hospital*, 423–432. Ten women also made donations of $100 or more. While neither of the Bay State humane societies allowed female members, women were a frequent presence at annual meetings.

51. Tudor, *Discourse*, 55; "Subscriptions in Aid of the General and Humane Hospitals," *Newburyport Herald*, December 24, 1816; Bowditch, *History of the Massachusetts General Hospital*, 423–432.

52. Nathaniel Hawthorne, *The House of the Seven Gables* (New York: Penguin, 1986), 38.

53. Wright, *The Transformation of Charity*, 139; Humane Society of Massachusetts, *Sir, the Undersigned . . .* (Boston, 1830), 1; Thomson, "Role of Physicians," 48; Cushing, *History*, 41; "The Trustees of the Humane Society," *Independent Chronicle and Boston Patriot*, August 11, 1824; Sarah Smith Emery, *Reminiscences of a Nonagenarian*, ed. Sarah Anna Emery (Newburyport, MA: W. H. Huse, 1879). The Philadelphia Humane Society struggled on to the end of the 1820s, when it fell dormant; it formally dissolved in 1856.

54. Thomas Gale, *Electricity, or the Ethereal Fire, Considered* (Troy, NY: Moffit & Lyon, 1802), 127–128.

55. Rush, *Medical Inquiries*, 129–130. Rush provided multiple case studies in suicide prevention, including one he had gleaned from reading Philippe Pinel (see 130–131).

56. New York Lunatic Asylum, "Annual Report," in *New York Senate Documents* (Albany, 1842), 220–221; Rothman, *Discovery of the Asylum*, 146–149.

57. Edward Jarvis, *Insanity and Insane Asylums* (Louisville, KY: Prentice and Weissinger, 1841), 18; Elizabeth T. Stone, *A Sketch of the Life of Elizabeth T. Stone, and of Her Persecutions: With an Appendix of Her Treatment and Sufferings While in the Charlestown Mclean Assylum* [*sic*], *Where She Was Confined under the Pretence of Insanity* ([Boston?]: Printed for the author, 1842), 27–28.

58. Jarvis, *Insanity*, 9, 14, 10; Gerald N. Grob, *The State and the Mentally Ill: A History of Worcester State Hospital in Massachusetts, 1830–1920* (Chapel Hill: University of North Carolina Press, 1966), 20.

59. Barbara G. Rosenkrantz and Maris A. Vinovskis, "'Sustaining the Flickering Flame of Life': Accountability and Culpability for Death in Ante-Bellum Massachusetts Asylums," in *Health Care in America: Essays in Social History*, ed. Susan Reverby and David Rosner (Philadelphia: Temple University Press, 1979) 156; Grob, *Mental Institutions*, 98–131; Jimenez, *Changing Faces of Madness*, 114, 121; William B. Scott, *In Pursuit of Happiness: Americans' Conceptions of Property from the Seventeenth to the Twentieth Century* (Bloomington: Indiana University Press, 1977), 126–127.

4. Wounds in the Belly of the State

1. "Cephas Clap, Tailor," *Republican Spy*, November 12, 1805; "Jonathan Jewett; Belchertown," *Hampshire Gazette*, January 4, 1815; "Trial of Jewett," *Hampshire Gazette*, September 27, 1815; "Northampton, Nov. 1," *The Repertory*, November 7, 1815.

2. "Northampton, Nov. 15," *The Repertory*, November 25, 1815; "Hon. Ebenezer Mattoon; Sheriff," *Columbian Centinel*, June 11, 1796; "Ebenezer Mattoon," in Andrew R. Dodge, *Biographical Directory of the United States Congress, 1774–2005* (Washington, DC: Government Printing Office, 2005).

3. Frederick A. Packard, *Report of the Trial of George Bowen; for the Murder of Jonathan Jewett, Who Committed Suicide on the 9th of November, 1815, While Confined in the Common Gaol of the County of Hampshire, under Sentence of Death for the Murder of His Father* (Northampton, 1816), 12; "Jewett's Last Dreadful Act," *The Repertory*, November 25, 1815.

4. Packard, *Trial of George Bowen*, 4, 30.

5. "Execution," *Hampshire Federalist*, June 10, 1806; Nathan Strong, *The Reasons and Design of Public Punishments: A Sermon Delivered before the People Who Were Collected to the Execution of Moses Dunbar, Who Was Condemned for High Treason against the State of Connecticut, and Executed March 19, 1777* (Hartford, CT: Ebenezer Watson, 1777), 17; Packard, *Trial of George Bowen*, 4.

6. *Narrative of the Pious Death of the Penitent Henry Mills, Who Was Executed at Galesboro's, Penn, on the 15th of July Last, for the Murder of His Wife and Five Children . . .* (Boston: H. Trumbull, 1817), 5; Louis P. Masur, *Rites of Execution: Capital Punishment and the Transformation of American Culture, 1776–1865* (New York: Oxford University Press, 1989), 43.

7. Daniel Allen Hearn, *Legal Executions in New York State: A Comprehensive Reference, 1639–1963* (Jefferson, NC: McFarland, 1997); Hearn, *Legal Executions*

in New England: A Comprehensive Reference, 1623–1960 (Jefferson, NC: McFarland, 1999); Hearn, *Legal Executions in New Jersey: A Comprehensive Registry, 1691–1963* (Jefferson, NC: McFarland, 2005); also see Negley K. Teeters, *Scaffold and Chair: A Compilation of Their Use in Pennsylvania, 1682–1962* (Philadelphia: Philadelphia Prison Society, 1963), 63–64.

8. Benjamin Rush, *Considerations on the Injustice and Impolicy of Punishing Murder by Death Extracted from the American Museum with Additions* (Philadelphia: Mathew Carey, 1792), 3; Masur, *Rites of Execution*, 51–54; Stuart Banner, *The Death Penalty: An American History* (New York: Cambridge University Press, 2002), 91.

9. Robert James Turnbull, *A Visit to the Philadelphia Prison . . . With Observations on the Impolicy and Injustice of Capital Punishments* (Philadelphia: Budd and Bartram, 1796), 86; also see *Observations on the Penal Code* (Charleston, SC: Office of the Southern Patriot, 1816), 23.

10. Richard D. Brown and Irene Quenzler Brown, *The Hanging of Ephraim Wheeler: A Story of Rape, Incest and Justice in Early America* (Cambridge, MA: Harvard University Press, 2003), 193–195; David Brion Davis, *From Homicide to Slavery: Studies in American Culture* (New York: Oxford University Press, 1986), 23; Masur, *Rites of Execution*, 29, 58, 71–92.

11. *Narrative of the Pious Death of the Penitent Henry Mills*, 1; Masur, *Rites of Execution*, 105; Daniel A. Cohen, "Homicidal Compulsion and the Conditions of Freedom: The Social and Psychological Origins of Familicide in America's Early Republic," *Journal of Social History* 28, no. 4 (1995): 754; Michel Foucault, *Discipline and Punish: The Birth of the Prison*, trans. Alan Sheridan (New York: Vintage, 1995), 65–66.

12. James Dana, *Men's Sins Not Chargeable on God, but on Themselves . . .* (New-Haven: T. & S. Green, 1783), 20; Christopher Grasso, "Deist Monster: On Religious Common Sense in the Wake of the American Revolution," *Journal of American History* 95, no. 1 (2008): 43–68.

13. *Providence, January 1, 1783. The Following Is the Most Particular Account of the Late Cruel Murders* (Providence, RI: B. Wheeler, 1783); Stephen Mix Mitchell, *A Narrative of the Life of William Beadle, of Wethersfield, in the State of Connecticut . . .* (Hartford, CT: Bavil Webster, 1783), 11. This was not Beadle's final resting place. The body-snatchers moved the corpse twice more, first to bury it further away from a popular ferry and then once more after some children accidentally discovered it (12).

14. "Portland. Murder and Suicide," *Cumberland Gazette*, November 1, 1790; "Thomas H. Daniels," *Newport Mercury*, December 18, 1819; "The End of James Anthony," *Rhode-Island American and General Advertiser*, March 5, 1814.

15. "Boston, August 28," *Independent Ledger and the American Advertiser*, August 28, 1786; "Horrible Scene," *Eastern Argus*, December 30, 1828; William Dunlap, *Ribbemont; or, the Feudal Baron, a Tragedy in Five Acts, as Performed at the New York Theatre* (New York: D. Longworth, 1803), 50–51.

16. "Baltimore, August 21," *The Boston Gazette, and Weekly Republican Journal*, September 4, 1797; "Suicide," *National Messenger*, March 4, 1818; "Portland. Murder and Suicide." For other press accounts of extensive preparations, see "Suicide," *Baltimore Patriot*, September 15, 1817; Thomas H. Daniels, *Some Particulars of the*

Life of Thomas H. Daniels, Alias Daniel H. Thomas: Who Was Apprehended at Newport . . . on Suspicion of Being Concerned in the Robbery and Murder of Mr. Jacob Gould . . . and Who Put an End to His Existence by Hanging Himself . . . (Boston: William Chamberlain, 1819), 11; "Suicide," *Village Register and Norfolk County Advertiser*, October 2, 1828. In *Ribbemont*, Theodore enlisted his father to bring poison to his cell. See Dunlap, *Ribbemont*, 53.

17. Packard, *Trial of George Bowen*, 11.

18. "Communication," *Rhode-Island American and General Advertiser*, March 5, 1814; Abby Maria Hemenway, *The History of Rutland County Vermont: Civil, Ecclesiastical, Biographical and Military* (White River Junction, VT: White River Paper Co., 1882), 1070.

19. Hemenway, *History of Rutland County*, 851–852.

20. Patrice Higonnet, *Sister Republics: The Origins of French and American Republicanism* (Cambridge, MA: Harvard University Press, 1998), 256, 66.

21. Packard, *Trial of George Bowen*, 1; "Northampton, Sept. 25," *Dedham Gazette*, October 4, 1816; "Singular Trial. Trial of George Bowen, for the Murder of Jonathan Jewett," *Boston Intelligencer, and Morning & Evening Advertiser*, January 11, 1817; "Singular Trial," *Massachusetts Spy, or Worcester Gazette*, January 22, 1817; [no headline], *Washington City Weekly Gazette*, November 23, 1816.

22. Cathy N. Davidson, *Revolution and the World: The Rise of the Novel in America* (New York: Oxford University Press, 1986), 89–105. For a rare modern-day parallel to the charges leveled against Bowen, see Monica Davey, "Online Talk, Suicides and a Thorny Court Case," *New York Times*, May 14, 2010.

23. Packard, *Trial of George Bowen*, 7. Morton knew the Fairbanks case intimately. His wife, the poet Sarah Apthorp Morton, was the likely author of a sympathetic biography of the defendant. See Daniel A. Cohen, *Pillars of Salt, Monuments of Grace: New England Crime Literature and the Origins of American Popular Culture* (Amherst: University of Massachusetts Press, 2006), 189.

24. Packard, *Trial of George Bowen*, 7.

25. Ibid., 9.

26. Ibid., 17, 16, 13, 14, 30, 14.

27. Ibid., 18.

28. Ibid., 18, 20.

29. "Massachusetts; George Bowen; Jonathan Jewett," *The Evening Post*, January 25, 1817; Packard, *Trial of George Bowen*, 38; Jonathan H. Lyman, *An Oration, Delivered at Northampton, July 6, 1807, on the Anniversary Celebration of American Independence* (Northampton, MA: Thomas M. Pomroy, 1807).

30. Packard, *Trial of George Bowen*, 24, 25.

31. Ibid., 7, 31. Bates also suggested in passing that the sentimental novels might have put the idea of suicide in Jewett's head (40).

32. Ibid., 40–41.

33. Ibid., 47.

34. Ibid., 8, 55–56; also see "Jonathan Jewett; Northampton; Friday; Chief-Justice; Parker," *Concord Gazette*, October 10, 1815; Russell K. Osgood, "Isaac Parker: Republican Judge, Federalist Values," in *The History of the Law in Massa-*

chusetts: The Supreme Judicial Court, 1692–1992, ed. Russell K. Osgood, (Boston: Supreme Judicial Court Historical Society, 1992), 153–170; Banner, *Death Penalty*, 54–62.

35. Packard, *Trial of George Bowen*, 55–56; Michael Meranze, *Laboratories of Virtue: Punishment, Revolution and Authority in Philadelphia, 1760–1835* (Chapel Hill: University of North Carolina Press, 1996), 41–42.

36. Packard, *Trial of George Bowen*, 31, 7; "Jewett's Last Dreadful Act"; "Jewett's Tragical End, Northampton, Nov. 15," *Salem Gazette*, November 28, 1815.

37. Packard, *Trial of George Bowen*, 56. What happened to Bowen after the trial is difficult to ascertain, though he may have been the person of that name who popped up in New Haven in the 1820s as one of the managers of a series of shady lottery schemes. See advertisement, *Connecticut Herald*, April 9, 1822.

38. Daniels, *Life of Thomas H. Daniels*, 11.

39. "Adonijah Bailey," *Commercial Gazette*, June 2, 1825; "From the Boston Traveller Feb. 2: Marchant and Colson," *Republican Farmer*, February 7, 1827; *The Trial of Robert Bush for the Murder of Sally Bush, His Wife: Who Was Found Guilty and Sentenced to Be Hung at Springfield, Nov. 14th, 1828.—but Committed Suicide on the 12th* . . . (Springfield, MA, 1828). See also "Poughkeepsie, August 1," *The Evening Post*, August 2, 1821; "Meadville, Penn, July 29," *The Farmers' Cabinet*, August 16, 1823; "Imprisonment for Debt," *Village Register and Norfolk County Advertiser*, September 19, 1823; "Suicide," *Providence Patriot*, September 13, 1823; "I. B. Desha; Jail," *Middlesex Gazette*, September 13, 1826; "Suicide," *Baltimore Patriot*, March 7, 1829; "Suicide," *Baltimore Patriot*, August 13, 1830; "Salem, N.Y. Sept. 10," *Baltimore Patriot*, September 17, 1830.

40. David L. Ferguson, *Cleopatra's Barge: The Crowninshield Story* (Boston: Little, Brown, 1976); James Albert Winans and Howard A. Bradley, *Daniel Webster and the Salem Murder* (Columbia, MO: Artcraft Press, 1956).

41. John Torrey Morse, ed., *Life and Letters of Oliver Wendell Holmes: In Two Volumes* (Boston: Houghton Mifflin, 1896), vol. 1, 69; Wallace B. Eberhard, "Mr. Bennett Covers a Murder Trial," *Journalism Quarterly* 47, no. 3 (1970): 458; John W. Whitman, *Trial of George Crowninshield, J. J. Knapp, Jun. and John Francis Knapp, for the Murder of Capt. Joseph White, of Salem, on the Night of the Sixth of April, 1830* (Boston: Beals and Homer, and F. Ingraham, 1830), 3, 5; Charles P. Curtis, "The Young Devils and Dan'l Webster," *American Heritage* 11, no. 4 (1960): 53.

42. Eberhard, "Mr. Bennett Covers a Murder Trial," 457; *Atrocious Murder. $1000 Reward* (Salem, 1830); Curtis, "Young Devils and Dan'l Webster," 53.

43. Curtis, "Young Devils and Dan'l Webster," 53; Gordon Dean Ross, "The Crowninshield Family in Business and Politics, 1790–1830" (PhD diss., Claremont Graduate School and University Center, 1965); Ferguson, *Cleopatra's Barge*, 84, 129–137.

44. "Supplement," *Salem Observer*, May 29, 1830; Winans and Bradley, *Daniel Webster and the Salem Murder*, 17.

45. Ferguson, *Cleopatra's Barge*, 137, 141.

46. Ibid., 143.

47. Ibid., 142–143; also see *The Most Important Testimony Adduced on the Trial of John Francis Knapp, for the Murder of Capt. Joseph White, of Salem, on the Night of the 6th of April, 1830* (Providence: H. H. Brown, 1830), 36; Curtis, "Young Devils and Dan'l Webster," 101.

48. Curtis, "Young Devils and Dan'l Webster," 101.

49. *A Biographical Sketch of the Celebrated Salem Murderer, Who for Ten Years Past Has Been the Terror of Essex County . . .* (Boston, 1830), 24; *Death of Crowninshield, the Salem Murderer, Who Hung Himself in Prison, June 15, 1830, That He Might Avoid the Ignominy of a Public Execution* (Salem, 1830); Rita Pollard, "Against the Law and beyond the Evidence," *American Bar Association Journal* 63 (1977): 207; Ferguson, *Cleopatra's Barge*, 143.

50. Ferguson, *Cleopatra's Barge*, 144.

51. "Perez Morton," in *Sibley's Harvard Graduates*, ed. Clifford K. Shipton (Boston: Northeastern University Press, 1975), 561; "Supreme Court at Salem," *Newport Mercury*, July 31, 1830; "The Late Trial," *Ladies Miscellany*, August 25, 1830; "Richard Crowninshield," *Newburyport Herald*, August 13, 1830; Curtis, "Young Devils and Dan'l Webster," 55, 101; Winans and Bradley, *Daniel Webster and the Salem Murder*, 10.

52. Winans and Bradley, *Daniel Webster and the Salem Murder*, 28, 30.

53. Whitman, *Trial*, 16; Pollard, "Against the Law and beyond the Evidence," 209.

54. Daniel Webster, *Speeches and Forensic Arguments* (Boston: Perkins & Marvin, 1835), 452; Whitman, *Trial*, 103–104.

55. Ferguson, *Cleopatra's Barge*, 126; Eberhard, "Mr. Bennett Covers a Murder Trial," 457–463; Winans and Bradley, *Daniel Webster and the Salem Murder*, 9–11. Even a journal as high-minded as the *Ladies' Miscellany* ran eight stories that summer. Memoirs included John C. Palmer Jr., *Explanation; or Eighteen Hundred and Thirty. Being a Series of Facts Connected with the Life of the Author from Eighteen Hundred and Twenty-Five to the Present Day* (Boston: S. N. Dickinson, 1831).

56. Curtis, "Young Devils and Dan'l Webster," 102; [no headline], *New York Courier and Enquirer*, August 19, 1830; *Second Trial of John Francis Knapp, at Salem, for the Alleged Murder of Capt. Joseph White . . .* (Salem, MA, 1830); Charles W. March, *Reminiscences of Congress* (New York: Baker and Scribner, 1850), 178–179.

57. *A Report of the Evidence and Points of Law, Arising in the Trial of John Francis Knapp, for the Murder of Joseph White, Esquire* (Salem: W. & S. B. Ives, 1830), 35; March, *Reminiscences of Congress*, 174–175. Nathaniel Hawthorne wrote to a friend on September 1, 1830, that Frank Knapp's wife had twice tried to hang herself since the trials began, and his father had made his own attempt, only to be cut down by Phippen Knapp, the third of his sons. Edward B. Hungerford, "Hawthorne Gossips about Salem," *New England Quarterly* 6, no. 3 (1933): 455–456.

58. Eberhard, "Mr. Bennett Covers a Murder Trial," 463; Pollard, "Against the Law and beyond the Evidence," 210; "The Late Trial," *Essex Register*, August 23, 1830; *An Authentic Account of the Last Hours of John Francis Knapp. Containing Letters Written by Him Subsequent to Conviction . . .* (Milford, MA: Ballou & Stacy, 1831), 11; Ferguson, *Cleopatra's Barge*, 151.

59. Hungerford, "Hawthorne Gossips about Salem," 455–456.

60. Pollard, "Against the Law and beyond the Evidence," 210; Ferguson, *Cleopatra's Barge*, 151–153.

61. *Laws of the Commonwealth of Massachusetts Passed at the Several Sessions of the General Court, Commencing May, 1828, and Ending March, 1831* (Boston: Dutton and Wenworth, 1831), 562–563.

62. Robert DeGroff Bulkley, "Robert Rantoul, Jr., 1805–1852: Politics and Reform in Antebellum Massachusetts" (PhD diss., Princeton University, 1971), 75; Steven Mintz, *Moralists and Modernizers: America's Pre–Civil War Reformers* (Baltimore, MD: Johns Hopkins University Press, 1995), 94; Masur, *Rites of Execution*, 119–122.

63. A. C. Thomas, *A Lecture on Capital Punishment. Delivered in the First Universalist Church, Philadelphia, on the Evening of June 20, 1830* (Philadelphia: William Sharpless, 1830), 11; S. M. Stilwell, *The Report of the Honorable S. M. Stilwell . . . to Inquire into the Expediency of a Total Abolition of Capital Punishment* (Albany, NY: Packard, Hoffman and White, 1832), 7; Massachusetts General Court Committee on Capital Punishment, *Report and Bills Relating to the Abolition of Capital Punishment* (Boston, 1837), 16; Banner, *Death Penalty*, 104. Rantoul arranged for an extra thousand copies of his report to be printed and distributed to the press and others in Boston.

64. Attempts to refute Rantoul's natural rights argument included Benjamin Dole, *An Examination of Mr. Rantoul's Report for Abolishing Capital Punishment in Massachusetts* (Boston, 1835).

65. Committee on Capital Punishment, *Report Relating to Capital Punishment* (Boston, 1836), 72; John L. O'Sullivan, *Report in Favor of the Abolition of the Punishment of Death* (New York, 1841), 96–97.

66. "Capital Punishment," *New Yorker*, June 18, 1836; Masur, *Rites of Execution*, 109; "Public Executions," *The Hangman*, April 2, 1845; David Brion Davis, "The Movement to Abolish Capital Punishment in America, 1787–1861," *American Historical Review* 63, no. 1 (1957): 33; Edward Schriver, "Reluctant Hangman: The State of Maine and Capital Punishment, 1820–1887," *New England Quarterly* 63, no. 2 (1990): 271–287.

67. Andie Tucher, *Froth and Scum: Truth, Beauty, Goodness and the Ax Murder in America's First Mass Medium* (Chapel Hill: University of North Carolina Press, 1994), 149–155.

68. Ibid., 153–156; "Suicide of John C. Colt," *New York Herald*, November 19, 1842.

69. "John C. Colt," *New York Daily Tribune*, November 19, 1842; Lydia Maria Child, *Letters from New York*, 3d ed. (New York: C. S. Francis, 1845), 220–221.

70. John L. O'Sullivan, "Colt's Case," *Democratic Review* (1842): 652, 655; Paul Christian Jones, "The Politics of Poetry: The *Democratic Review* and the Gallows Verse of William Wordsworth and John Greenleaf Whittier," *American Periodicals* 17, no. 1 (2007): 1–25.

71. "Cheated the Gallows," *The Hangman*, May 7, 1845; "The Gallows Superseded," *The Hangman*, May 21, 1845; "Russia," *The Hangman*, September 17, 1845;

Masur, *Rites of Execution*, 136. *The Hangman* had more than two thousand subscribers in 1845.

72. "Russia"; "To the Wardens of State Prisons throughout the Union," *The Prisoner's Friend*, January 7, 1846.

73. "A Meeting in Prison," *The Hangman*, October 8, 1845. The healthy sales of Victor Hugo's *Last Days of a Condemned Man* (tr. 1840) testified to the ways in which middle-class sensibility now encompassed suffering inmates. See Davis, "The Movement to Abolish Capital Punishment," 30.

74. Charles Spear, *Essays on the Punishment of Death* (Littleton, CO: Fred. B. Rothman [1844], 1994), 200–201; James Richmond, *Petition to Abolish Capital Punishment* (Hudson, NY: P. Dean Carrique, 1844), 2; E. H. Lake, *Objections to Capital Punishment*, 2d ed. (Haverhill, MA: Essex Banner Press, 1844), 5–7, 12–13; Charles C. Burleigh, *Thoughts on the Death Penalty* (Philadelphia, 1847), 77; G. W. Quinby, *The Gallows, the Prison, and the Poor-House: A Plea for Humanity; Showing the Demands of Christianity in Behalf of the Criminal and Perishing Classes* (Cincinnati: G. W. Quinby, 1856), 62, 178–179.

75. George B. Cheever, *Capital Punishment. The Argument of Rev. George B. Cheever, in Reply to J. L. O'Sullivan, Esq., in the Broadway Tabernacle, on the Evenings of January 27th, and February 3d and 17th* (New York, 1843), 46–47; Philip English Mackey, "Reverend George Barrell Cheever: Yankee Reformer as Champion of the Gallows," *Proceedings of the American Antiquarian Society* 82, no. 2 (1972): 323–342; Robert M. York, *George B. Cheever, Religious and Social Reformer, 1807–1890* (Orono: University of Maine Press, 1955).

76. Tobias Purrington, *Report on Capital Punishment, Made to the Maine Legislature in 1836 . . .*, 3d ed. (Washington, DC: Gideon & Co., 1852), 47.

77. Davis, "Movement to Abolish Capital Punishment," 44–46; Mackey, "Reverend George Barrell Cheever," 341; Masur, *Rites of Execution*, 154–155, 60.

5. The Threshold of Heaven

1. William Bentley, *The Diary of William Bentley, Pastor of the East Church, Salem, Massachusetts*, 4 vols. (Salem, MA: Essex Institute, 1905–1914), vol. 4, 243–245; Hosea Ballou, *A Sermon Designed to Notice, in a Religious Manner, the Death of the Rev. George Richards, of Philadelphia . . .* (Portsmouth, NH: S. Whidden, 1814), 105; Russell E. Miller, *The Larger Hope: The First Century of the Universalist Church in America, 1770–1870* (Boston: Unitarian Universalist Association, 1979), 715.

2. Ernest Cassara, *Hosea Ballou: The Challenge to Orthodoxy* (Boston: Universalist Historical Society, 1962), 76; Miller, *Larger Hope*, 47, 68. The text for Richards's eulogy was Isaiah 53:3, "A Man of Sorrow and Acquainted with Grief." For friendly criticism of Richards's hymnody, see Bentley, *Diary*, vol. 3, 348.

3. Thomas Whittemore, *A Sermon, Delivered at the Funeral of the Reverend Alfred V. Bassett, Pastor of the Universalist Society in Dedham* (Boston: Printed and published at the Trumpet Office, 40 Cornhill, 1832); Nathan D. George, *Universalism Not of the Bible: Being an Examination of More Than One Hundred and Twenty*

Texts of Scriptures, in Controversy between Evangelical Christians and Universalists... (New York: Carlton and Phillips, 1856), 391–392.

4. Nathan O. Hatch, *The Democratization of American Christianity* (New Haven, CT: Yale University Press, 1989), 3–46; James D. Bratt, "Religious Anti-Revivalism in Antebellum America," *Journal of the Early Republic* 24, no. 1 (2004): 68.

5. The best survey of the founding moment of the Universalist movement in America is Ann Lee Bressler, *The Universalist Movement in America, 1770–1880* (New York: Oxford University Press, 2001). See also Janet Moore Lindman, "'Bad Men and Angels from Hell': The Discourse of Universalism in Early National Philadelphia," *Journal of the Early Republic* 31, no. 2 (2011): 259–282.

6. Lyman H. Butterfield, ed., *Letters of Benjamin Rush*, 2 vols. (Princeton, NJ: American Philosophical Society, 1951), vol. 1, 583–584; Miller, *Larger Hope*, 39. Universalist writers in the early nineteenth century liked to claim other revolutionary-era figures as supporters of or closeted believers in universal salvation, among them Benjamin Franklin and George Washington. See C. C. Burr, *A Review of Rev. Mr. Lane's Lectures against Universalism in Six Numbers* (Troy, NY: Cannon Place, 1844), 85.

7. Alfred V. Bassett, "Sermon on Universal Salvation," 1828, Papers of Thomas Whittemore, Harvard Divinity School; Bressler, *Universalist Movement*, 6–19; E. Brooks Holifield, *Theology in America: Christian Thought from the Age of the Puritans to the Civil War* (New Haven, CT: Yale University Press, 2003), 133–134, 220–231.

8. Hosea Ballou, *A Treatise on Atonement, in Which the Finite Nature of Sin Is Argued, Its Cause and Consequences as Such*... (Randolph, VT: Sereno Wright, 1805); Bressler, *Universalist Movement*, 16, 24–27; Stephen A. Marini, *Radical Sects of Revolutionary New England* (Cambridge, MA: Harvard University Press, 1982), 145; Charles A. Collier, "Aspects in the Growth of American Universalism" (AB thesis, Harvard College, 1952), 12.

9. Bressler, *Universalist Movement*, 30–33.

10. Andrew Royce, *Universalism: A Modern Invention, and Not According to Godliness*, 2d ed. (Windsor, VT: Chronicle Press, 1839), 105; Joseph Young, *Calvinism and Universalism Contrasted in a Series of Letters to a Friend* (New York: Samuel Campbell, 1793), 33, emphasis in original.

11. John H. Wigger, *Taking Heaven by Storm: Methodism and the Rise of Popular Christianity in America* (New York: Oxford University Press, 1998), 97; Hatch, *Democratization of American Christianity*, 3.

12. Jacob Frieze, "On the Arrogant Pretensions of the Orthodox Clergy," *Christian Telescope and Universalist Miscellany*, August 19, 1826, 9–10; Nathan D. George, *Examination of Universalism, Embracing Its Rise and Progress, and the Means of Its Propagation. By Rev. Nathan D. George, of the Maine Conference of the Methodist Episcopal Church* (Boston: Waite, Peirce and Company, 1846), 93–94; Bressler, *Universalist Movement*, 56, 60–63; Bratt, "Religious Anti-Revivalism," 86.

13. Miller, *Larger Hope*, 79–97, 273.

14. [No headline], *Trumpet and Universalist Magazine*, October 6, 1832; "Our Enemies Being Judges," *Trumpet and Universalist Magazine*, May 17, 1834; Miller, *Larger Hope*, 161–163; Bressler, *Universalist Movement*, 22–32; Holifield, *Theology in America*, 219.

15. Joel Hawes, *Reasons for Not Embracing the Doctrine of Universal Salvation. In a Series of Letters to a Friend* (New York: American Tract Society, 1826), 25. Hawes's work provoked a direct and lengthy riposte. See Russell Canfield, *A Candid Review of Ten Letters, Containing Reasons for Not Embracing the Doctrine of Universal Salvation* . . . (Hartford, 1827).

16. Collier, "Aspects in the Growth of American Universalism," 38; William Buell Sprague, *Wicked Men Ensnared by Themselves a Sermon Preached, December 16, 1825, in the Second Parish of West Springfield*, 3d ed. (Springfield, MA: Tannatt & Co, 1826), 22; John Murray, *Bath-Kol. A Voice from the Wilderness* (Boston: N. Coverly, 1783), 349; Timothy Merritt and Wilbur Fisk, *A Discussion on Universal Salvation: In Three Lectures and Five Answers against That Doctrine* (New York: B. Waugh and T. Mason, 1832), 226; Christopher Grasso, "Deist Monster: On Religious Common Sense in the Wake of the American Revolution," *Journal of American History* 95, no. 1 (2008): 47.

17. James M. Davis, *Universalism Unmasked, or the Spurious Gospel Exposed: Containing Three Lectures, in Reply to Three* . . . (Philadelphia: I. Ashmead & Co, 1837), 98. See also Andrew Crosswell, *Mr. Murray Unmask'd, In which, among other things, is shewn, that his doctrine of universal salvation, is inimical to vertue, and productive of all manner of wickedness* . . . (Boston: J. Kneeland, 1775), 9–10; Seth Crowell, *Strictures on the Doctrine of Universal Salvation* (New York: Hoyt & Bolmore, 1821), 61–62; Matthew Hale Smith, *Universalism Examined, Renounced, Exposed* (Boston: Tappan & Dennet, 1842), 325; George, *Examination of Universalism*, 101; A Western Layman, *The Serpent Uncoiled: or a Full Length Picture of Universalism*, rev. ed. (Philadelphia: American Baptist Publication Society, 1846), 85; Collier, "Aspects in the Growth of American Universalism," 38.

18. Edwin F. Hatfield, *Universalism as It Is; or, Text Book of Modern Universalism in America* (New York: J. A. Hoisington, 1841), iv; T. J. Sawyer, *Review of E. F. Hatfield's "Universalism as It Is"* (New York: P. Price, 1841); Miller, *Larger Hope*, 285; Charles A. Howe, *The Larger Faith: A Short History of American Universalism* (Boston: Skinner House Books, 1993), 40.

19. Butterfield, *Letters of Benjamin Rush*, vol. 1, 419; Bressler, *Universalist Movement*, 14, 26, 36; Holifield, *Theology in America*, 223–230; Thomas Whittemore, *Plain Guide to Universalism* (Boston: Thomas Whittemore, 1840), 290.

20. Henry Bacon, *A Plea for Charity: A Discourse, before the Universalist Female Charitable Institute, of Boston* (Boston: Abel Tompkins, 1836), 3; Miller, *Larger Hope*, 487–638.

21. "R. Crowninshield Opinions," *Trumpet and Universalist Magazine*, August 21, 1830; "Cause of Self Murder," *Gospel Advocate*, October 1, 1824; J. Aiken, *Review of the Serpent Uncoiled: or of the Full Length Portrait of Universalism* (Indianapolis: Indiana State Journal Steam Press, 1848), 65; Burr, *Review of Rev. Mr. Lane's Lectures*, 141; O. A. Skinner, *Skinner's Review of Hatfield. Seven Sermons,*

Delivered in the Orchard-Street Universalist Church, in the Winter of 1847 (New York: C. L. Stickney, 1847), 17–18.

22. Kenneth M. Johnson, "The Doctrine of Universal Salvation and the Restorationist Controversy in Early Nineteenth Century New England" (PhD diss., University of Ottawa, 1978), 214; Peter Hughes, "The Origins and First Stage of the Restorationist Controversy," *Journal of Unitarian Universalist History* 27 (2000): 1–57; see also Hughes, "The Second Phase of the Restorationist Controversy: Disciplinary Crisis and Schism, 1824–1831," *Journal of Unitarian Universalist History* 28, no. 2 (2001): 28–91.

23. Jacob Wood, *Universal Restoration Defended: Being an Examination of a Sermon Entitled the Future Punishment of the Wicked Certain and Endless . . .* (Worcester, MA: William Manning, 1818), 19; see also Wood, "To the World," *Christian Repository* (December 1822): 168.

24. Hawes, *Doctrine of Universal Salvation*, 110–112. See also Davis, *Universalism Unmasked*, 101.

25. "Judas Iscariot," *Christian Messenger*, September 9, 1820; "Of Judas Iscariot," *Christian Messenger*, August 14–21, 1819; "Reply to Berean," *Christian Intelligencer*, February 28, 1821; "Review of the Christian's Vade-Mecum," *Gospel Herald*, November 17, 1821; "To the Editor of the Gazetteer," *Gazetteer*, June 9, 1824.

26. Sprague, *Wicked Men Ensnared*, 37–41.

27. Ibid.

28. Ibid., 21, 16, 18–19.

29. "Postscript—Wednesday Evening," *Pennsylvania Evening Herald and the American Monitor*, June 15, 1785. My survey of representative pamphlet or book-length attacks on Universalism printed in America between 1820 and 1850 revealed that arguments connecting universal salvation to suicide appeared in 14 out of 18 texts (78 percent) in the sample.

30. Thomas C. Upham, *The Manual of Peace. Embracing I. Evils and Remedies of War, II. Suggestions on the Law of Nations . . .* (New York: Leavitt, Lord & Co., 1836), 242.

31. William Latta McCalla, *Discussion of Universalism: Or, a Defence of Orthodoxy against the Heresy of Universalism* (Philadelphia: John Young, 1825), 91; Merritt and Fisk, *Discussion on Universal Salvation*, 49–50. See also Luther Lee, *Universalism Examined and Refuted: And the Doctrine of the Endless Punishment . . .* (Watertown, NY: Knowlton & Rice, 1836), 17.

32. Adam Empie, *Remarks on the Distinguishing Doctrine of Modern Universalism: Which Teaches That There Is No Hell and No Punishment for the Wicked after Death* (New York: T. and J. Swords, 1825), 19; Merritt and Fisk, *Discussion on Universal Salvation*, 49–50. Rivals frequently tarred Universalism as a form of deism. See, for instance: Davis, *Universalism Unmasked*, 170–171; "From the Religious Enquirer," *Gospel Advocate*, May 2, 1829; "Deism and Universalism the Occasion of Suicide," *Home Missionary and American Pastor's Journal* (October 1828): 103–104.

33. Miller, *Larger Hope*, 115–123.

34. Merritt and Fisk, *Discussion on Universal Salvation*, 138–139; A. Wilson McClure, *Lectures on Ultra-Universalism*, 3d ed. (Boston: William Peirce, 1835),

11–13, 27–28, emphasis in original. While rivals had raised the question of suicide regularly since the early 1820s, after 1831 the subject came up in 9 out of every 10 books and pamphlets published by opponents of the controversial denomination. In a sample, 14 out of 16 (87 percent) anti-Universalist writings published between 1831 and 1850 discussed the problem of suicide in relation to universal salvation, while only 2 out of 6 (33 percent) works published between 1775 and 1831 did so.

35. McClure, *Lectures on Ultra-Universalism*, 20, 23, 15, 17, 24, 123. For Whittemore's response to the "course vulgarity" of McClure's sarcasm, see "McClure's Lectures," *Trumpet and Universalist Magazine*, February 23, 1839.

36. McClure, *Lectures on Ultra-Universalism*, 116–117.

37. Edwin F. Hatfield, *Universalism as It Is; or, Text Book of Modern Universalism in America* (New York: J. A. Hoisington, 1841), 125–126. See also Bernard Whitman, *Friendly Letters to a Universalist on Divine Rewards and Punishments* (Cambridge, MA: Brown Shattuck and Co., 1833), 342–343; Josiah Priest, *The Anti-Universalist, or History of the Fallen Angels of the Scriptures; Proofs of the Being of Satan and of Evil Spirits* (Albany, NY: J. Munsell, 1837), 399; Davis, *Universalism Unmasked*, 154–155, 212; A Western Layman, *Serpent Uncoiled*, 54; Alexander Hall, *Universalism against Itself, or an Examination and Refutation of the Principal Arguments Claimed in Support of the Final Holiness and Happiness of All Mankind* (St. Clairsville, OH: Alexander Hall, 1846), 372; Matthew Hale Smith, *Universalism Not of God: An Examination of the System of Universalism; Its Doctrine, Arguments, and Fruits . . .* (New York: American Tract Society, 1847), 206–209.

38. Hall, *Universalism against Itself*, 370–371.

39. Ibid., 374; Smith, *Universalism Not of God*, 303; Miller, *Larger Hope*, 68. Over the years, the murder-suicide committed by James Purrinton in Maine in 1806, the death by duel of Congressman Jonathan Cilley in 1838, the jail suicide of counterfeiter Cyrus Crawford in 1840, and the murder and jail suicide committed by John Colt in New York in 1842 were all imputed to Universalism.

40. Whittemore, *A Sermon*, 2; Whittemore, "Sermon on the Ordination of Alfred V. Bassett," June 17, 1830, Papers of Thomas Whittemore, Harvard Divinity School.

41. Whittemore, *A Sermon*, 12–13.

42. Ibid. When, in 1847, Matthew Hale Smith repeated the allegation that Bassett's religious beliefs had driven him to suicide, Universalist respondents made the same rebuttal. See Smith, *Universalism Examined, Renounced, Exposed*, 325; L. C. Browne, *Review of the Life and Writings of M. Hale Smith* (Boston: A. Tompkins, 1847), 239.

43. E. K. Hunt, "Statistics of Suicides in the United States," *American Journal of Insanity* 1 (1845): 234; "From the Buffalo (NY) Patriot," *Universalist Magazine*, July 29, 1820; "Cause of Self Murder," *Gospel Herald*, September 25, 1824. Versions of the *Herald*'s item subsequently appeared in many other Universalist papers, including the *Herald of Salvation*, *Christian Intelligencer*, *Universalist Magazine*, *Messenger of Peace*, *Christian Inquirer*, and *Gospel Advocate*.

44. Jonathan Wallace, *Sermon Delivered at the Funeral of Silas Bradley, Who Died by Suicide, on the Evening of the 11th April, 1826* (Potsdam, NY: Powell, 1826), 9–

10; see also Wallace, "An Examination of a Pamphlet Entitled a Brief Review of a Sermon Delivered by Jonathan Wallace," 1827, p. 43, Jonathan Wallace Collection, St. Lawrence University Library Special Collections.

45. "Calumny Detected. Murder and Suicide," *Evangelical Restorationist*, April 15, 1826; "Orthodox Fruits," *Gospel Herald*, December 16, 1826.

46. "Suicide," *Trumpet and Universalist Magazine*, August 31, 1833. See also "Cassel, June 25," *Gospel Herald*, September 14, 1822; "Lamentable Suicide," *Christian Intelligencer*, June 18, 1825; "Suicide," *Trumpet and Universalist Magazine*, January 28, 1832; "A Warning to Avaricious Priests," *Spirit of the Pilgrims and Messenger of Resurrection*, March 28, 1828; L. F. W. Andrews, *A Looking Glass for Fanatics, or, A Collection of Cases of Insanity, Suicide, and Murder, the Result of "Four Days, "Protracted," and Other "Meetings"* (1832?), 2; Browne, *Writings of M. Hale Smith*, 239. For a sample of reports dedicated to narrating the suicides of evangelical ministers, see "Suicide," *Trumpet and Universalist Magazine*, April 5, 1834; "Singular Suicide," *Trumpet and Universalist Magazine*, January 19, 1839.

47. "Another Victim to Religious Delusion," *Gospel Herald*, July 13, 1822.

48. Ibid. Also see "Afflicting Case of Suicide," *Trumpet and Universalist Magazine*, July 19, 1834; "Horrid Effect of Endless Misery," *Trumpet and Universalist Magazine*, July 26, 1834.

49. "Horrible Effects of the Doctrine of Endless Misery," *Universalist Magazine*, November 25, 1820; "The House of Terror," *Gospel Herald*, July 28, 1821; "The Suicide at Cambridgeport," *Trumpet and Universalist Magazine*, October 11, 1828; "Woburn Suicide," *Trumpet and Universalist Magazine*, August 15, 1829.

50. Russell Streeter, *Familiar Conversations: In Which the Salvation of All Mankind Is Clearly Exhibited and Illustrated* (Woodstock, VT: N. Haskell, 1835), 239–240, 198–199; "Another Victim," *Herald of Salvation*, March 8, 1823. See also "Another Offering to Moloch," *Gospel Herald*, April 21, 1821; "A Victim," *Gospel Herald*, October 12, 1822; "Another Victim," *Gospel Advocate*, February 28, 1823; "Influence of Endless Misery," *Trumpet and Universalist Magazine*, July 16, 1831; "Victims to Endless Misery," *Trumpet and Universalist Magazine*, January 28, 1832; "From the Sentinel and Star in the West," *Glad Tidings and Ohio Christian Telescope*, February 28, 1837; Browne, *Writings of M. Hale Smith*, 225. In 1836 Thomas Whittemore even claimed that Dick Crowninshield, the Salem murderer, had been a believer in what he referred to as "the doctrine of endless misery." See "A Guilty Conscience," *Trumpet and Universalist Magazine*, July 2, 1836. Data were drawn from 2,039 separate issues of the following Universalist titles published between January 1, 1820, and December 31, 1839: *Herald of Salvation, Gospel Advocate, Olive Branch, Olive Branch and Christian Inquirer, Messenger of Peace, Dialogical Instructor, Gazetteer, Evangelical Restorationist, Spirit of the Pilgrims, Candid Examiner, Gospel Inquirer, Philadelphia Universalist, Gospel Herald, Universalist Magazine*, and *Trumpet and Universalist Magazine*.

51. Richard Carwardine, *Trans-Atlantic Revivalism: Popular Evangelicalism in Britain and America, 1790–1865* (Westport, CT: Greenwood Press, 1978), 10; Roger Finke and Rodney Stark, *The Churching of America, 1776–1990: Winners and Losers in Our Religious Economy* (New Brunswick, NJ: Rutgers University Press, 1992), 54–56.

52. "Another Victim," *Gospel Herald*, August 16, 1823; "Insanity," *Trumpet and Universalist Magazine*, September 28, 1833. See also "Victims of Fanatacism," *Trumpet and Universalist Magazine*, March 15, 1834; "Religious Insanity," *Trumpet and Universalist Magazine*, March 22, 1834; Andrews, *Looking Glass for Fanatics*, 1; Miller, *Larger Hope*, 269.

53. "Religious Delusion," *Philadelphia Universalist Magazine*, September 1822. For a similar request from 1834, see "Request," *Trumpet and Universalist Magazine*, April 5, 1834. See also "For the Universalist Magazine," *Universalist Magazine*, August 10, 1822; "Melancholy Events," *Gospel Herald*, August 24, 1822; "Another Victim," *Gospel Herald*, May 22, 1824; "Sprague's Sermon," *Universalist Magazine*, March 4, 1826; "From the Religious Inquirer," *Gospel Advocate*, June 23, 1827. In 1837 Whittemore's paper advertised the existence of a pamphlet listing the names of 156 lives lost to revival fervor. See "Mirror of Partialism," *Trumpet and Universalist Magazine*, July 15, 1837.

54. McClure, *Lectures on Ultra-Universalism*, 32–33; "A Mate to the Temperance Ox," *Trumpet and Universalist Magazine*, May 2, 1835. Between 1820 and 1828, twenty-eight stories describing religious suicides appeared in Boston's *Universalist Magazine* and thirty in New York's *Gospel Herald*, two of the widest-circulating denominational papers of the era. Data were drawn from 549 issues of the weekly *Trumpet* between 1828 and 1839, 442 issues of the weekly *Universalist Magazine* between 1820 and 1828, and 289 issues of the *Gospel Herald* in the same period.

55. "And Another," *Trumpet and Universalist Magazine*, October 29, 1831. See also "Striking Effects of the Doctrine of Endless Misery," *Gospel Herald*, December 16, 1826; "Suicide," *Trumpet and Universalist Magazine*, January 28, 1832.

56. "Suicide," *Trumpet and Universalist Magazine*, October 17, 1829; "Another Victim," *Gospel Advocate*, May 24, 1828; "Victim to Orthodoxy," *Trumpet and Universalist Magazine*, April 13, 1833.

57. Andrews, *Looking Glass for Fanatics*, 2, 1.

58. Jonathan Edwards, *The Great Awakening*, vol. 4 in The Works of Jonathan Edwards (New Haven, CT: Yale University Press, 1972), 206–207; Jon Butler, "Enthusiasm Described and Decried: The Great Awakening as Interpretative Fiction," *Journal of American History* 69, no. 2 (1982): 311; Michael J. Crawford, *Seasons of Grace: Colonial New England's Revival Tradition in Its British Context* (New York: Oxford University Press, 1991), 210–211. For post-Revolution versions of this conversion archetype, see Barry O'Connell, ed., *On Our Own Ground: The Complete Writings of William Apess, a Pequot* (Boston: University of Massachusetts Press, 1992), 146, 49; David W. Kling, *A Field of Divine Wonders: The New Divinity and Village Revivals in Northwestern Connecticut, 1792–1822* (University Park: Pennsylvania State University Press, 1993), 213–217.

59. "Revivals," *Trumpet and Universalist Magazine*, April 23, 1831.

60. William B. Sprague and Leonard Woods, *Lectures on Revivals of Religion* (New York: D. Appleton & Co., 1833), 33–34; McClure, *Lectures on Ultra-Universalism*, 32–33. For similar defenses of camp meetings, see Hall, *Universalism against Itself*, 371; George, *Universalism Not of the Bible*, 392.

61. Benjamin Whittemore, *Universalism against Suicide: A Sermon Delivered in the Fourth Universalist Church in Boston, May 15, 1836* (Boston: Abel Tompkins, 1836), 3. An excerpt of Whittemore's sermon also appeared in the *Trumpet*, where he served as assistant editor. See "Sermon," *Trumpet and Universalist Magazine*, July 23, 1836.

62. Whittemore, *Universalism against Suicide*, 12, 10.

63. "The Case of the Suicide Reconsidered," *Expositor and Universalist Review* (July 1838): 288; Merritt and Fisk, *Discussion on Universal Salvation*, 156–157; Lee, *Universalism Examined and Refuted*, 118–119. See also Canfield, *Candid Review of Ten Letters*, 89; "The Murderer and Suicide," *Trumpet and Universalist Magazine*, May 19, 1838; Burr, *Review of Rev. Mr. Lane's Lectures*, 129–130.

64. Streeter, *Familiar Conversations*, 240; Sawyer, *Review of E. F. Hatfield's "Universalism as It Is,"* 139; Browne, *Writings of M. Hale Smith*, 221. See also Lucius R. Paige, *Universalism Defended. A Reply to Several Discourses Delivered by Rev. Timothy Merritt, in 1827, against That Doctrine* (Hartford, 1830), 117.

65. Hatfield, *Universalism as It Is*, 126; E. E. Guild, *The Universalist's Book of Reference: Containing All the Principal Facts and Arguments, and Scripture Texts, Pro and Con, on the Great Controversy between Limitarians and Universalists*, 2d ed. (Boston: Usher, 1853), 103–106.

66. Bressler, *Universalist Movement*, 47; Miller, *Larger Hope*, 123; Hughes, "Restorationist Controversy," 52.

67. Guild, *Universalist's Book of Reference*, 104.

68. K. M. Johnson, "Restorationist Controversy," 284–285, 94; Bressler, *Universalist Movement*, 71; Miller, *Larger Hope*, 164, 783–841.

69. Holifield, *Theology in America*, 272; Lewis O. Saum, *The Popular Mood in Pre–Civil War America* (Westport, CT: Greenwood Press, 1980), 44.

70. Bressler, *Universalist Movement*, 7; Dickson D. Bruce Jr., *And They All Sang Hallelujah: Plain-Folk Camp-Meeting Religion, 1800–1845* (Knoxville: University of Tennessee Press, 1974), 56; Charles A. Johnson, *The Frontier Camp Meeting: Religion's Harvest Time* (Dallas, TX: Southern Methodist University Press, 1955), 242–243; Randolph A. Roth, *The Democratic Dilemma: Religion, Reform, and the Social Order in the Connecticut River Valley of Vermont, 1791–1850* (New York: Cambridge University Press, 1987), 187–219.

6. The Problem of Slave Resistance

1. "The Desperate Negroe," *Massachusetts Magazine* (October 1793): 583–584.

2. "The Story of Quashi, an African Slave," *New-York Journal*, June 21, 1788; "The Story of Quashi, an African Slave," *Massachusetts Spy*, July 17, 1788; "The Story of Quashi, an African Slave," *Independent Gazetteer*, June 9, 1788.

3. Timothy Patrick McCarthy and John Stauffer, eds., *Prophets of Protest: Reconsidering the History of American Abolitionism* (New York: New Press, 2006), xi; William Lloyd Garrison, "To the Public," *The Liberator*, January 1, 1831; John Woolman, *Considerations on Keeping Negroes; Recommended to the Professors of Christianity of Every Denomination* (Philadelphia: B. Franklin and D. Hall, 1762), 40.

4. Anthony Benezet to John Pemberton, August 10, 1783, in *Friend Anthony Benezet*, ed. George S. Brookes (Philadelphia: University of Pennsylvania Press, 1937), 397; Gary B. Nash and Jean R. Soderlund, *Freedom by Degrees: Emancipation in Pennsylvania and Its Aftermath* (New York: Oxford University Press, 1991), 115.

5. Richard S. Newman, *The Transformation of American Abolitionism: Fighting Slavery in the Early Republic* (Chapel Hill: University of North Carolina Press, 2002), 18, 27; David N. Gellman, *Emancipating New York: The Politics of Slavery and Freedom, 1777–1827* (Baton Rouge: Louisiana State University Press, 2006), 56–77.

6. "Forum: Black Founders," *William and Mary Quarterly* 64, no. 1 (2007): 83–166.

7. Thomas Day and John Bicknell, *The Dying Negro: A Poem*, 3d ed. (London: W. Flexney, 1775), 24; "The Dying Negro," *Royal American Magazine* (February 1774): 71–72; "The Dying Negro," *Pennsylvania Magazine* (January 1776): 36–38; "The Dying Negro," *Universal Asylum and Columbian Magazine* (May 1790): 316–318; "The Dying Negro," *Massachusetts Magazine* (January 1791): 1; Olaudah Equiano, *The Interesting Narrative of the Life of Olaudah Equiano, or Gustavus Vassa, the African. Written by Himself*, 2 vols. (New York: W. Durell, 1791), vol. 1, 133–134; *Stephens's Catalogue of Books, &C. For 1795* (Philadelphia: W. W. Woodward, 1795); "Advertisement," *Columbian Centinel*, March 5, 1796; "Biographical," *Mirror of the Times, & General Advertiser*, April 20, 1805.

8. Thomas Branagan, *The Charms of Benevolence* (Philadelphia: Johnston, 1813), 296; see also Branagan, *A Preliminary Essay, on the Oppression of the Exiled Sons of Africa* (Philadelphia: John W. Scott, 1804), 26; Debbie Lee, *Slavery and the Romantic Imagination* (Philadelphia: University of Pennsylvania Press, 2002), 35; Lorenzo Dow Turner, *Anti-Slavery Sentiment in American Literature Prior to 1865* (Washington, DC: Association for the Study of Negro Life and History, 1929), 25.

9. Zephaniah Swift, *An Oration on Domestic Slavery. Delivered at the North Meeting-House in Hartford, on the 12th Day of May*, A.D. 1791 (Hartford, CT: Hudson and Goodwin, 1791), 14; "Reflections on the Slavery of Negroes," *The Rural Magazine, or Vermont Repository* (June 1796): 363; "The African Slave," *Weekly Museum*, March 27, 1802; Jonathan Edwards, *The Injustice and Impolicy of the Slave Trade, and of the Slavery of the Africans: Illustrated in a Sermon Preached before the Connecticut Society for the Promotion of Freedom* (New Haven, CT: Thomas and Samuel Green, 1791), 6; William Patten, *On the Inhumanity of the Slave-Trade, and the Importance of Correcting It. A Sermon* (Providence: J. Carter, 1793), 9; "London, March 12. Slave Trade," *Dunlap's American Daily Advertiser*, May 25, 1792.

10. Terri L. Snyder, "Suicide, Slavery, and Memory in North America," *Journal of American History* 97, no. 1 (2010): 47–53.

11. "Revenge," *Norwich Packet*, February 20, 1789; Branagan, *Preliminary Essay*, 54. On the evidentiary problems that plague the study of slave suicide, see Snyder, "Suicide, Slavery, and Memory," 43–47.

12. "The Gally Slave," *New York Packet*, May 29, 1786; "A Singular Reality," *New-Hampshire Mercury*, July 5, 1785; "For the Massachusetts Gazette," *Massachusetts Gazette*, October 5, 1787; Eran Shalev, *Rome Reborn on Western Shores:*

Historical Imagination and the Creation of the American Republic (Charlottesville: University of Virginia Press, 2009).

13. Quashi's story was told and retold so often that by 1807 it had appeared in papers from urban Philadelphia to rural Vermont, as well as in a textbook published by Mathew Carey and in Thomas Branagan's *Preliminary Essay* (1804).

14. Francois Furstenberg, "Beyond Freedom and Slavery: Autonomy, Virtue, and Resistance in Early American Political Discourse," *Journal of American History* 89, no. 4 (2003): 1295–1330.

15. George Buchanan, *An Oration upon the Moral and Political Evil of Slavery. Delivered at a Public Meeting of the Maryland Society, for Promoting the Abolition of Slavery, and the Relief of Free Negroes, and Others Unlawfully Held in Bondage. Baltimore, July 4th, 1791* (Baltimore: Philip Edwards, 1793), 10.

16. Clement Clarke Moore, *Observations upon Certain Passages in Mr. Jefferson's Notes on Virginia Which Appear to Have a Tendency to Subvert Religion, and Establish a False Philosophy* (New York, 1804), 23–24; David N. Gellman, "Race, the Public Sphere, and Abolition in Late Eighteenth-Century New York," *Journal of the Early Republic* 20, no. 4 (2000): 628; Frederic M. Litto, "Addison's Cato in the Colonies," *William and Mary Quarterly* 23 (1966): 431–449. Not all antislavers of this generation opposed post-emanicipation migration. Despite his commitment to ending the slave trade, Branagan was an avowed segregationist who, in 1805, advanced a plan to relocate all African Americans to the Louisiana Territory.

17. "Original Poetry," *New-Haven Gazette and Connecticut Magazine*, February 21, 1788.

18. Humanitas, *Reflections on Slavery; with Recent Evidence of Its Inhumanity. Occasioned by the Melancholy Death of Romain, a French Negro* (Philadelphia: R. Cochran, 1803), vi. For a merchant's account of the events that day, see Eliza Cope Harrison, ed., *Philadelphia Merchant: The Diary of Thomas P. Cope, 1800–1851* (South Bend, IN: Gateway Editions, 1978), 134. Marginalia suggest, albeit highly inconclusively, that William Darlington, a future representative for the state of New York, may have been the author of *Reflections on Slavery*.

19. Humanitas, *Reflections on Slavery*, 14, 17.

20. Ibid., 14–15; Rachel Hope Cleves, *The Reign of Terror in America: Visions of Violence from Anti-Jacobinism to Anti-Slavery* (New York: Cambridge University Press, 2009), 108–109. An investigation following Romain's suicide showed that Salaignac had applied to the mayor of Trenton for authorization to carry the family from New Jersey southward, and a jury eventually declared that Salaignac had broken no law.

21. United States Congress, *The Debates and Proceedings in the Congress of the United States* (Washington, DC: Gales and Seaton, 1834), 201; Gellman, "Race, the Public Sphere, and Abolition in Late Eighteenth-Century New York," 625. Notably, many Garrisonians, including Lydia Maria Child, were involved in the campaign to protest Indian removal. For an introduction to the depiction of native suicide in nineteenth-century American culture, see Brian W. Dippie, *The Vanishing Indian: White Attitudes and Indian Policy* (Middletown, CT: Wesleyan University Press, 1982); Gordon M. Sayre, *The Indian Chief as Tragic Hero: Native*

Resistance and the Literatures of America, from Moctezuma to Tecumseh (Chapel Hill: University of North Carolina Press, 2005).

22. Humanitas, *Reflections on Slavery*, 39; John Saillant, "The Black Body Erotic and the Republican Body Politic, 1790–1820," *Journal of the History of Sexuality* 5, no. 3 (1995): 403. Only a few revolutionary-era radicals dared to conflate slave suicide with armed insurrection. See Anthony Benezet, *Serious Considerations on Several Important Subjects: Viz. on War and Its Inconstancy with the Gospel. Observations on Slavery, and Remarks on the Nature and Bad Effects of Spiritous Liquors* (Philadelphia: Joseph Crukshank, 1778), 35; Swift, *Oration on Domestic Slavery*, 13–14; "Quashy; or, the Coal-Black Maid. A Tale," *Time-Piece*, January 24, 1798.

23. Steven Deyle, *Carry Me Back: The Domestic Slave Trade in American Life* (New York: Oxford University Press, 2005), 21, 283–296.

24. Jesse Torrey, *A Portraiture of Domestic Slavery, in the United States: With Reflections on the Practicability of Restoring the Moral Rights of the Slave . . .* (Philadelphia: J. Bioren, 1817), 33, 41; Josephine F. Pacheco, *The Pearl: A Failed Slave Escape on the Potomac* (Chapel Hill: University of North Carolina Press, 2005), 15–47.

25. Torrey, *Portraiture of Domestic Slavery*, 30–32, emphasis in original. The American Colonization Society was founded in 1816, the same year as Torrey's unsettling visit to Washington.

26. Ibid., 31, 42–44, emphasis in original. For other descriptions of slave suicide, see 11, 44–45.

27. "Portraiture of Domestic Slavery," *New-England Galaxy and Masonic Magazine*, December 19, 1817; "Notice of New Publications," *The National Register*, March 22, 1817; "Advertisement," *Columbian Centinel*, July 9, 1817; "Advertisement," *Hampden Federalist*, November 20, 1817.

28. "Portraiture of Domestic Slavery"; "Portraiture of Slavery," *Independent American*, July 16, 1817; "Portraiture of Domestic Slavery," *Christian Disciple*, July 5, 1817; "Boston. Saturday, November 2, 1833," *The Liberator*, November 2, 1833; Lydia Maria Child, *An Appeal in Favor of That Class of Americans Called Africans* (Boston: Allen & Ticnor, 1833), 190.

29. "Torrey's Portraiture of Slavery," *Genius of Universal Emancipation*, March 1832; "Black List," *Genius of Universal Emancipation*, August 1821.

30. "Horrid Suicide," *Genius of Universal Emancipation*, March 5, 1830; "From the Morning Post," *Genius of Universal Emancipation*, June 1822.

31. Deyle, *Carry Me Back*, 178–179; Merle L. Dillon, *Benjamin Lundy and the Struggle for Negro Freedom* (Urbana-Champaign: University of Illinois Press, 1966), 44, 69; Henry Mayer, *All on Fire: William Lloyd Garrison and the Abolition of Slavery* (New York: St. Martin's Press, 1998), 51–91; Trish Loughran, *The Republic in Print: Print Culture in the Age of U.S. Nation Building, 1770–1870* (New York: Columbia University Press, 2007), 315–319.

32. Dillon, *Benjamin Lundy*, 54–56; Loughran, *Republic in Print*, 310–316.

33. Dwight Lowell Dumond, *Antislavery: The Crusade for Freedom in America* (Ann Arbor: University of Michigan Press, 1961), 264–267, quote on 264; Maria Weston Chapman, *Right and Wrong in Massachusetts* (Boston: Dow and Jackson's Anti-slavery Press, 1839), inside cover; Merle L. Dillon, *Slavery Attacked: Southern Slaves and Their*

Allies, 1619–1865 (Baton Rouge: Louisiana State University Press, 1990), 178; James Brewer Stewart, *Holy Warriors: The Abolitionists and American Slavery* (New York: Hill and Wang, 1976), 70–71; Timothy Patrick McCarthy, "A Culture of Dissent: American Abolitionism and the Ordeal of Equality" (PhD diss., Columbia University, 2006), 229–231; Richard R. John, *Spreading the News: The American Postal System from Franklin to Morse* (Cambridge, MA: Harvard University Press, 1995), 257–281; Philip Lapsansky, "Graphic Discord: Abolitionist and Antiabolitionist Images," in *The Abolitionist Sisterhood: Women's Political Culture in Antebellum America*, ed. Jean Fagan Yellin and John C. Van Horne (Ithaca, NY: Cornell University Press, 1994), 202.

34. Theodore Dwight Weld, *American Slavery as It Is: Testimony of a Thousand Witnesses* (New York: American Anti-Slavery Society, 1839); Joseph Sturge, *American Slavery: Report of a Public Meeting Held at Finsbury Chapel, Moorfields, to Receive Frederick Douglass, the American Slave, on Friday, May 22, 1846* (London: C. B. Christian and Co., 1846), 17; Loughran, *Republic in Print*, 354–360; John Sekora, "Black Message/White Envelope: Genre, Authenticity, and Authority in the Antebellum Slave Narrative," *Callaloo* 32 (1987): 482–515; James L. Huston, "The Experiential Basis of the Northern Antislavery Impulse," *Journal of Southern History* 56, no. 4 (1990): 624–625; Augusta Rohrbach, *Truth Stranger Than Fiction: Race, Realism and the U.S. Literary Marketplace* (New York: Palgrave, 2002), 24–25; Jeannine Marie DeLombard, *Slavery on Trial: Law, Abolitionism, and Print Culture* (Chapel Hill: University of North Carolina Press, 2007).

35. Rohrbach, *Truth Stranger Than Fiction*, 4; Elizabeth B. Clark, "'The Sacred Rights of the Weak': Pain, Sympathy, and the Culture of Individual Rights in Antebellum America," *Journal of American History* 82, no. 2 (1995): 463–493, quote on 465; Huston, "Northern Antislavery Impulse," 627–629; Marcus Wood, *Slavery, Empathy, and Pornography* (New York: Oxford University Press, 2002); Karen Halttunen, "Humanitarianism and the Pornography of Pain in Anglo-American Culture," *American Historical Review* 100, no. 2 (1995): 303–334.

36. Charles Olcott, *Two Lectures on the Subject of Slavery and Abolition. Compiled for the Special Use of Anti-Slavery Lecturers and Debaters, and Intended for Public Reading* (Massilon, OH, 1838), 27; Clark, "The Sacred Rights of the Weak," 463–473; Bruce Dorsey, *Reforming Men and Women: Gender in the Antebellum City* (Ithaca, NY: Cornell University Press, 2002), 186–187.

37. Dickson D. Bruce Jr., "Print Culture and the Antislavery Community: The Poetry of Abolitionism, 1831–1860," in *Prophets of Protest: Reconsidering the History of American Abolitionism*, ed. Timothy Patrick McCarthy and John Stauffer (New York: New Press, 2006), 29; Eran Shalev, "Ancient Masks, American Fathers: Classical Pseudonyms during the American Revolution and Early Republic," *Journal of the Early Republic* 23, no. 2 (2003): 170.

38. Cynthia A. Hamilton, "Models of Agency: Frederick Douglass and 'the Heroic Slave,'" *Proceedings of the American Antiquarian Society* 114, no. 1 (2004): 122.

39. "Letters on Slavery, Addressed to Mr. Thomas Rankin, Merchant at Middlebrook, Augusta Co. Va.," *The Liberator*, October 6, 1832. In addition to the five editions of John Rankin's letters, this story was subsequently retold in "Remarks of Rev. Mr. Blain," in *Proceedings of the New-England Anti-Slavery Convention: Held*

in Boston on the 27th, 28th and 29th of May, 1834 (Boston: Garrison & Knapp, 1834), 56–59; "New-England Anti-Slavery Convention. Remarks of Rev. Mr. Blain," *The Liberator*, August 30, 1834; Julius Rubens Ames, *"Liberty." The Image and Subscription of Every Coin Issued by the United States of America* (New York: American Anti-Slavery Society, 1837), 128.

40. James Williams, *Narrative of James Williams, an American Slave, Who Was for Several Years a Driver on a Cotton Plantation in Alabama* (New York: American Anti-Slavery Society, 1838), 32; Deyle, *Carry Me Back*, 245–275; John Hope Franklin and Loren Schweninger, *Runaway Slaves: Rebels on the Plantation* (New York: Oxford University Press, 1999), 54–55.

41. "Report on the Domestic Slave Trade," *American Anti-Slavery Reporter* (July 1834) 100, 99.

42. William Grimes, *Life of William Grimes, the Runaway Slave* (New York, 1825), 16; "Desperation of a Mother," *Anti-Slavery Record* (September 1835) 97; Lydia Maria Child, "Children's Department—A Talk with My Young Readers," in *American Anti-Slavery Almanac for 1837* (Boston: Webster and Southard, 1836), 43–44; Deborah C. De Rosa, *Domestic Abolitionism and Juvenile Literature, 1830–1856* (Albany: State University of New York Press, 2003).

43. Lydia Maria Child, *Authentic Anecdotes of American Slavery* (Newburyport, MA: Charles Whipple, 1838), 3–4; Weld, *American Slavery as It Is*, 92; Child, *Appeal in Favor*, 190; "Report on the Domestic Slave Trade," 98–99; "The Poor Wife," *The Slave's Friend* (1837): 6–7; Marcus Wood, *Blind Memory: Visual Representations of Slavery in England and America, 1780–1865* (London: Routledge, 2000), 181; Deyle, *Carry Me Back*, 33–35.

44. Nathaniel Southard, *Why Work for the Slave?* (New York: American Anti-Slavery Society, 1838), 4. Lucy's story had first been picked up by the *Genius of Universal Emancipation* in October 1837 and then by New York's *Colored American* in February 1838.

45. "Letters from the South West to Mr. Tappen, Letter I. Natchez, 1833," *American Anti-Slavery Reporter* (February 1834): 28; "Suicide," *Anti-Slavery Record* 1 (1835): 152; Ames, *"Liberty,"* 136; Weld, *American Slavery as It Is*, 108; LaRoy Sunderland, *Testimony of God against Slavery: A Collection of Passages from the Bible . . .* (Boston, 1836), 93; LaRoy Sunderland, *Anti-Slavery Manual, Containing a Collection of Facts and Arguments on American Slavery* (New York: S. W. Benedict, 1837), 74; Charles Elliott, *Sinfulness of American Slavery: Proved from Its Evil Sources . . .* (Cincinnati: L. Swormstedt and J. H. Power, 1850), 268; Williams, *Narrative of James Williams*, 85.

46. Charles Ball, *Slavery in the United States: A Narrative of the Life and Adventures of Charles Ball* (New York: John S. Taylor, 1837), 328–329; Charles W. Nichols, "Who Read the Slave Narratives," *Phylon* 20 (1959): 150; Yuval Taylor, ed., *I Was Born a Slave: An Anthology of Classic Slave Narratives*, 2 vols. (Chicago: Lawrence Hill, 1999), vol. 1, 261; vol. 2, xx.

47. Ball, *Slavery in the United States*, 329, 31, 36.

48. Émile Durkheim, *Suicide: A Study in Sociology* (New York: Simon and Schuster, 1997), 276; [no headline], *Slave's Friend* (1837): 16. My analysis here fo-

cuses upon polemical representations of slave suicide, many of whose authors likely inferred, distorted, or largely invented the motives for suicide they attributed to individuals. For an introduction to American slaves' own understanding of what suicide represented, and when and why it might be committed, see Snyder, "Suicide, Slavery, and Memory," 53–59.

49. Ball, *Slavery in the United States*, 70, 36, 69.

50. Louis S. Gerteis, *Morality and Utility in American Antislavery Reform* (Chapel Hill: University of North Carolina Press, 1987), 19; Leonard Richards, *"Gentlemen of Property and Standing": Anti-Abolitionist Mobs in Jacksonian America* (New York: Oxford University Press, 1970), 54; Stewart, *Holy Warriors*, 74; Steven Mintz, *Moralists and Modernizers: America's Pre–Civil War Reformers* (Baltimore, MD: Johns Hopkins University Press, 1995), 131; Beth A. Salerno, *Sister Societies: Women's Antislavery Organizations in Antebellum America* (De Kalb: Northern Illinois University Press, 2004), 24; Susan Zaeske, *Signatures of Citizenship: Petitioning, Anti-Slavery, and Women's Political Activism* (Chapel Hill: University of North Carolina Press, 2007), 2–3.

51. John C. Nerone, *Violence against the Press: Policing the Public Sphere in U.S. History* (New York: Oxford University Press, 1994), 85–110; Stewart, *Holy Warriors*, 71–74; Aileen S. Kraditor, *Means and Ends in American Abolitionism: Garrison and His Critics on Strategy and Tactics* (New York: Random House, 1967).

52. Mayer, *All on Fire*, 261–284.

53. McCarthy, "A Culture of Dissent," 248; Harriet Beecher Stowe, *Uncle Tom's Cabin; or, Negro Life in the United States of America* (London: Richard Bentley, 1852), 135; Bruce E. Kirkham, *The Building of Uncle Tom's Cabin* (Knoxville: University of Tennessee Press, 1977), 101–103, 35.

54. For a penetrating analysis of the discursive model Garrisonians tried to build, see Robert Fanuzzi, *Abolition's Public Sphere* (Minneapolis: University of Minnesota Press, 2003).

55. Henry Highland Garnet, "Address to the Slaves of the United States (1848)," in *Pamphlets of Protest: An Anthology of Early American Protest Literature, 1790–1860*, ed. Richard Newman, Patrick Rael, and Philip Lapsansky (New York: Routledge, 2001), 162; Joel Schor, *Henry Highland Garnet: A Voice of Black Radicalism in Nineteenth-Century America* (Westport, CT: Greenwood Press, 1977), 47–67; Stanley Harrold, ed., *The Rise of Aggressive Abolitionism* (Lexington: University Press of Kentucky, 1995), x, 3–17, 29–52, 71; Robert S. Levine, *Martin Delany, Frederick Douglass and the Politics of Representative Identity* (Chapel Hill: University of North Carolina Press, 1997), 28–29; Furstenberg, "Beyond Freedom and Slavery," 1308, 1311–1312; James Brewer Stewart, "From Moral Suasion to Political Confrontation: American Abolitionists and the Problem of Resistance, 1831–1861," in *Passages to Freedom: The Underground Railroad in History and Memory*, ed. David W. Blight (Washington, DC: Smithsonian Books, 2004), 82–89.

56. Garnet, "Address to the Slaves," 164, emphasis in original; Harrold, *Rise of Aggressive Abolitionism*, 63–70, 91–96.

57. Houston A. Baker, ed., *Narrative of the Life of Frederick Douglass, an American Slave* (New York: Penguin, 1982), 124, 67; William L. Andrews, *To Tell a Free Story:*

The First Century of Afro-American Autobiography, 1760–1865 (Urbana: University of Illinois Press, 1986), 100; Herbert Aptheker, "Militant Abolitionism," *Journal of Negro History* 26, no. 4 (1941): 466; Levine, *Martin Delany, Frederick Douglass*, 28, 127.

58. "Doings in Maryland," *The North Star*, July 14, 1848; Levine, *Martin Delany, Frederick Douglass*, 18–57; Max Cavitch, *American Elegy: The Poetry of Mourning from the Puritans to Whitman* (Minneapolis: University of Minnesota Press, 2007), 212.

59. "Declaration of Sentiments of the Colored Citizens of Boston on the Fugitive Slave Bill," *The Liberator*, October 11, 1850; [no headline], *Pennsylvania Freeman*, October 31, 1850; Elizabeth R. Varon, *Disunion! The Coming of the American Civil War, 1789–1859* (Chapel Hill: University of North Carolina Press, 2008), 231; Carol Wilson, "Active Vigilance Is the Price of Liberty: Black Self-Defense against Fugitive Slave Recapture and Kidnapping of Free Blacks," in *Antislavery Violence: Sectional, Racial, and Cultural Conflict in Antebellum America*, ed. John R. McKivigan and Stanley Harrold (Knoxville: University of Tennessee Press, 1999), 115–118.

60. Jonathan Katz, *Resistance at Christiana: The Fugitive Slave Rebellion, Christiana, Pennsylvania, September 11, 1851* (New York: Thomas Y. Crowell Company, 1974), 86; Lois E. Horton, "Kidnapping and Resistance: Antislavery Direct Action in the 1850s," in *Passages to Freedom: The Underground Railroad in History and Memory*, ed. David W. Blight (Washington, DC: Smithsonian Books, 2004), 161; Stanley J. Robboy and Anita W. Robboy, "Lewis Hayden: From Fugitive Slave to Statesman," *New England Quarterly* 46, no. 4 (1973): 601.

61. Laura E. Richards, ed., *The Letters and Journals of Samuel Gridley Howe*, 2 vols. (Boston: D. Estes, 1906), vol. 2, 270; Anthony J. von Frank, *The Trials of Anthony Burns: Freedom and Slavery in Emerson's Boston* (Cambridge, MA: Harvard University Press, 1988); Samuel May, *The Fugitive Slave Law and Its Victims*, revised and enlarged ed. (New York: American Anti-Slavery Society, 1861), 30; "Give Me Liberty, or Give Me Death," *Provincial Freeman*, April 11, 1857; Mark A. Schantz, *Awaiting the Heavenly Country: The Civil War and America's Culture of Death* (Ithaca, NY: Cornell University Press, 2008), 152.

62. James O. Horton and Lois E. Horton, *In Hope of Liberty: Culture, Community, and Protest among Northern Free Blacks, 1700–1860* (New York: Oxford University Press, 1997), 240; see also Horton and Horton, "The Affirmation of Manhood: Black Garrisonians in Antebellum Boston," in *Courage and Conscience: Black and White Abolitionists in Boston*, ed. Donald Jacobs (Bloomington: Indiana University Press, 1993), 127–153; Steven Weisenburg, *Modern Medea: A Family Story of Slavery and Child-Murder from the Old South* (New York: Hill and Wang, 1998), 53, 89, 225.

63. William Wells Brown, *Clotel; or, the President's Daughter: A Narrative of Slave Life in the United States* (London: Partridge & Oakey, 1853), 220; Robert S. Levine, ed., *Clotel, or, the President's Daughter: A Narrative of Slave Life in the United States*, (Boston: Bedford/St. Martin's, 2000), 3–27. Portions of this verse were borrowed from Grace Greenwood's "The Leap from the Long Bridge."

64. William Lloyd Garrison, "Address to the Slaves of the United States," in Harrold, *Rise of Aggressive Abolitionism*, 169–178.

65. "From the Pittsburg Mistery. Liberty or Death," *The Liberator*, October 20, 1843; Harrold, *Rise of Aggressive Abolitionism*, 88–91.

66. "Liberty of Death," *Emancipator*, May 25, 1843; "Another Suicide by a Slave," *Emancipator*, August 12, 1846.

67. Aptheker, "Militant Abolitionism," 476.

68. "Letter from Gerrit Smith," *Syracuse Journal*, May 31, 1856.

69. "Kansas Herald," *Frederick Douglass' Paper*, August 31, 1855; Cavitch, *American Elegy*, 327, fn 96.

70. John Brown, *Address of John Brown to the Virginia Court, When About to Receive the Sentence of Death, for His Heroic Attempt at Harper's Ferry to Give Deliverance to the Captives, and to Let the Oppressed Go Free* . . . (Boston: C. C. Mead, 1859), 1; Franklin Benjamin Sanborn, ed., *The Life and Letters of John Brown: Liberator of Kansas, and Martyr of Virginia* (Boston: Roberts Brothers, 1891), 517.

71. Robert H. Abzug, "The Influence of Garrisonian Abolitionists' Fears of Slave Violence on the Antislavery Argument, 1829–40," *Journal of Negro History* 55, no. 1 (1955): 15–26; Peter Hinks, *To Awaken My Afflicted Brethren: David Walker and the Problem of Antebellum Slave Resistance* (University Park: Pennsylvania State University Press, 1997), 237–257.

72. Levine, *Martin Delany, Frederick Douglass*, 99–143; Eric J. Sunquist, "Slavery, Revolution, and the American Renaissance," in *The American Renaissance Reconsidered: Selected Papers from the English Institute, 1982–83*, ed. Walter Benn Michaels and Donald E. Pease (Baltimore, MD: Johns Hopkins University Press, 1985), 1–33; Russ Castronovo, *Fathering the Nation: American Genealogies of Slavery and Freedom* (Berkeley: University of California Press, 1995), 194–199.

Conclusion

1. "Memphis Items," *Hartford Daily Courant*, May 9, 1862.

2. Seth Ames, ed., *Works of Fisher Ames with a Selection of His Speeches and Correspondence*, 2 vols. (New York: Burt Franklin, 1971), vol. 2, 359.

3. On Rush's understanding of the strategic role of sympathy in this postrevolutionary crisis, see Jason Frank, "Sympathy and Separation: Benjamin Rush and the Contagious Public," *Modern Intellectual History* 6, no. 1 (2009): 27–57.

4. Sean Wilentz, *Chants Democratic: New York City and the Rise of the American Working Class, 1788–1850* (New York: Oxford University Press, 2004), 6; Joyce Appleby, *Inheriting the Revolution: The First Generation of Americans* (Cambridge, MA: Harvard University Press, 2000), 3, 5, 11, 231; Michael Meranze, *Laboratories of Virtue: Punishment, Revolution and Authority in Philadelphia, 1760–1835* (Chapel Hill: University of North Carolina Press, 1996), 3–4, 13.

5. "Postscript-Wednesday Evening," *Pennsylvania Evening Herald and the American Monitor*, June 15, 1785; John L. O'Sullivan, *Report in Favor of the Abolition of the Punishment of Death* (New York: J. and H. G. Langley, 1841), 96; Joel Porte, ed., *Emerson in His Journals* (Cambridge, MA: Harvard University Press, 1982), 164; C[ornelius] M[athews], "The Unrest of the Age," *Arcturus* (1841): 133; Scott A. Sandage, *Born Losers: A History of Failure in America* (Cambridge, MA: Harvard Uni-

versity Press, 2005), 6; Mathew Carey, "Excerpta," in Carey Scrapbook Collection, vol. 4, 299–300, Library Company of Philadelphia. The disappointments and reverses that befell many of the hopeful and desperate men who trekked west to find their fortune during the California Gold Rush were apparently acute enough to produce a spike in the official statistics for western districts. See *Eighth Census of the United States, Mortality* (Washington, DC: Government Printing Office, 1866), 253.

6. Sharon Ann Murphy, *Investing in Life: Insurance in Antebellum America* (Baltimore, MD: Johns Hopkins University Press, 2010), 13–46; Patricia Cline Cohen, *A Calculating People: The Spread of Numeracy in Early America* (Chicago: University of Chicago Press, 1982), 205; Susan E. Klepp, "Zachariah Poulson's Bills of Mortality, 1788–1801," in *Life in Early Philadelphia: Documents from the Revolutionary and Early National Periods*, ed. Billy G. Smith (University Park: Pennsylvania State University Press, 1995), 219; Mary Poovey, *A History of the Modern Fact* (Chicago: University of Chicago Press, 1998), 308–309; Stephen M. Stigler, *The History of Statistics: The Measurement of Uncertainty before 1900* (Cambridge, MA: Harvard University Press, 1986); *Eighth Census*, 253; Howard I. Kushner, *Self-Destruction in the Promised Land* (New Brunswick, NJ: Rutgers University Press, 1989), 38. For a pioneering statistical investigation of suicide, see E. K. Hunt, "Statistics of Suicides in the United States," *American Journal of Insanity* 1 (1845): 225–234. During the Civil War, the urge to count and to quantify would help many Americans make some sense of and impose some form of order upon the extraordinary scale of carnage the war produced. See Drew Gilpin Faust, *This Republic of Suffering: Death and the American Civil War* (New York: Knopf, 2008), 251.

7. For a flavor of popular writing about self-destruction after 1840, see Max Cavitch, *American Elegy: The Poetry of Mourning from the Puritans to Whitman* (Minneapolis: University of Minnesota Press, 2007), 224–225; James Gates Percival, *The Poetical Works of James Gates Percival*, 2 vols. (Boston: Ticknor and Fields, 1863), vol. 2, 156–171; H. Marion Stephens, *Home Scenes and Home Sounds; or, the World from My Window* (Boston: Fetridge and Company, 1854), 185–187; "The Atlantic Monthly, for February 1859," *National Era*, February 10, 1859.

8. Daniel Steele, *De Profundis Clamavi; the Cause, the Crime, and the Cure of Our National Suicide* (Springfield, MA: Samuel Bowles & Co., 1861), 10–11.

9. Ibid., 11, 14, 19; David Herbert Donald, *Charles Sumner*, 2 vols. in 1 (New York: Da Capo, 1996), 54–57, 138–140, 99. The language of "state suicide" became a fixture in the northern press and among private correspondence throughout the war.

10. Steele, *De Profundis Clamavi*, 14, 18–20.

11. Ibid., 18–20.

12. Ibid., 14, 20, 25, 30; Elizabeth R. Varon, *Disunion! The Coming of the American Civil War, 1789–1859* (Chapel Hill: University of North Carolina Press, 2008), 6; Terrie Dopp Aamodt, *Righteous Armies, Holy Cause: Apocalyptic Imagery and the Civil War* (Macon, GA: Mercer University Press, 2002).

13. "Speech of Hon. J. R. Giddings," *North Star*, August 4, 1848; "Free Soil Movement—Buffalo Convention," *North Star*, August 21, 1848; "Thirty First Congress," *North Star*, February 22, 1850; "Ex-Gov. Hunt and the Whig Party,"

Frederick Douglass' Paper, August 31, 1855; "Kansas the Suicide of Slavery," *Frederick Douglass' Paper*, September 28, 1855; Eli Thayer, *The Suicide of Slavery. Speech of Hon. Eli Thayer of Mass. Delivered in the House of Representatives, March 25, 1858* (Washington, DC: Buell and Blanchard, 1858), 5. In 1838 Abraham Lincoln had informed his audience at the Springfield Lyceum that "if destruction be our lot, we must ourselves be its author and finisher. As a nation of freemen, we must live through all time, or die by suicide." See Don E. Fehrenbacher, ed., *Abraham Lincoln, Speeches and Writings, 1832–1858* (New York: Library of America, 1989), 29. Even the most cursory dip into print culture sources from the antebellum period will reveal the stunning ubiquity of suicide motifs to describe all manner of moral, political, and constitutional choices facing elected officials and their supporters.

14. "Is Disunion Probable?" *New Orleans Daily Creole*, September 17, 1856. See also Joseph Grégorie de Roulhac Hamilton, ed., *Correspondence of Jonathan Worth*, 2 vols. (Raleigh, NC: Edwards & Broughton, 1909), vol. 1, 144, 151, 167.

15. Harry S. Stout, *Upon the Altar of the Nation: A Moral History of the American Civil War* (New York: Viking, 2006), 82–83; Reid Mitchell, *The Vacant Chair: The Northern Soldier Leaves Home* (New York: Oxford University Press, 1993), 141; Steven E. Woodworth, *While God Is Marching On: The Religious World of Civil War Soldiers* (Lawrence: University Press of Kansas, 2001), 46; Mark A. Schantz, *Awaiting the Heavenly Country: The Civil War and America's Culture of Death* (Ithaca, NY: Cornell University Press, 2008), 38–69. For comparisons between soldiering and suicide, see Lewis Henry Steiner, *Report of Lewis H. Steiner: Inspector of the Sanitary Commission, Containing a Diary Kept during the Rebel Occupation of Frederick, Md.* (New York: A. D. F. Randolph, 1862), 18; Lydia Minturn Post, ed., *Soldiers' Letters, from Camp, Battle-Field and Prison* (New York: Bunce & Huntington, 1865), 467. Civil War martyrology derived in part from the precedents set by antislavery martyrs like Elijah Lovejoy and John Brown and by the templates of heroic dying soldiers popularized in commercial literary culture during the Mexican War. See Alice Fahs, *The Imagined Civil War: Popular Literature of the North and South, 1861–1865* (Chapel Hill: University of North Carolina Press, 2001), 6. Once the war began, comparisons equating the political and strategic decision making to individual self-annihilation were increasingly confined to private correspondence, particularly among Union officers critical of the way the war was being waged. See, for instance, Amos Lawrence Mason, ed., *Memoir and Correspondence of Charles Steedman, Rear Admiral, United States Navy, with His Autobiography and Private Journals, 1811–1890* (Cambridge, MA: Riverside Press, 1912), 273; Robert Means Thompson and Richard Wainwright, eds., *Confidential Correspondence of Gustavus Vasa Fox: Assistant Secretary of the Navy, 1861–1865*, 2 vols. (New York: De Vinne Press, 1918–1920), vol. 1, 227; George Meade, *Life and Letters of George Gordon Meade, Major-General United States Army*, 2 vols. (New York: Charles Scribner's Sons, 1913), vol. 1, 239; Stephen Minot Weld, ed., *War Diary and Letters of Stephen Minot Weld, 1861–1865* (Cambridge, MA: Riverside Press, 1912), 227. Several Confederate correspondents also used suicide rhetoric to impugn the decisions of their own commanders, a practice that became more widespread after 1863. See, for example, Daniel Robinson Hundley, *Prison Echoes*

of the Great Rebellion (New York: S. W. Green, 1874), 99; Hamilton, *Correspondence of Jonathan Worth*, 324.

16. Rufus W. Clark, *A Discourse Commemorative of the Heroes of Albany: Who Have Fallen during the Present War in Defense of Our Country* (Albany, NY: C. Van Benthuysen, 1864), 8; Stout, *Altar of the Nation*, 249–251, 341, 84, 454–455; Fahs, *Imagined Civil War*, 83–87, 95. On the rhetoric of self-sacrifice in the Confederacy, see Drew Gilpin Faust, ed., *Macaria, or, Altars of Sacrifice* (Baton Rouge: Louisiana State University Press, 1992); Iver Bernstein, "Political Evil and the Body Politic in Mid-Nineteenth-Century America," in *The Problem of Evil: Slavery, Freedom, and the Ambiguities of American Reform*, ed. Steven Mintz and John Stauffer (Amherst: University of Massachusetts Press, 2007), 251; Schantz, *Awaiting the Heavenly Country*, 65–67, 97–125.

17. Mitchell, *Vacant Chair*, 7–8, 11; Gerald F. Linderman, *Embattled Courage: The Experience of Combat in the American Civil War* (New York: Free Press, 1987), 12, 31. When reporting the suicides of Union soldiers, northern newspaper editors gave considerable—surely disproportional—attention to those men in uniform known to be southern sympathizers, spies, deserters, or convicted felons. See, for instance, "Suicide of a Disgraced Soldier," *Philadelphia Inquirer*, June 17, 1861; "Attempted Suicide of a Soldier," *San Francisco Bulletin*, September 25, 1862; "News Summary," *New Hampshire Sentinel*, April 9, 1863.

18. Robert N. Scott et al., *War of the Rebellion: A Compilation of the Official Records of the Union and Confederate Armies*, 70 vols. (Washington, DC: Government Printing Office, 1880–1901), vol. 5, 665; Fahs, *Imagined Civil War*, 6, 107, 226; Linderman, *Embattled Courage*, 130–134, 69, 247. No similar tally exists for the Confederate Army. Extensive documentary evidence of the range and frequency of suicidal behavior in the two opposing armies is available via the *American Civil War: Diaries and Letters* online database, http://solomon.cwld.alexanderstreet.com/. For a sampling of news reports describing suicides committed by Union soldiers but attributing the act to nonservice-related causes, see "A Notable Suicide," *San Francisco Bulletin*, September 12, 1861; "Singular Attempt to Commit Suicide," *Baltimore Sun*, September 14, 1861; "Suicide in Camp," *Philadelphia Inquirer*, January 17, 1862; "Suicide of Colonel Henslow," *Philadelphia Inquirer*, April 9, 1862; "Suicide of a Soldier," *Philadelphia Inquirer*, May 21, 1862. For suicides purportedly committed to avoid the draft, see "To Avoid the Draft," *Constitution*, August 27, 1862; "Committed Suicide to Escape the Draft," *Baltimore Sun*, June 27, 1863; "Suicide of Mr. A. M. Ramsey," *New York Herald*, August 7, 1863; "The Suicide of Mr. Ramsey," *Wisconsin Daily Patriot*, August 15, 1863; "Suicide by Hanging," *New York Herald*, October 29, 1863. The Confederate press played the same game, reporting southern suicides infrequently, and typically failing to acknowledge how the tolls of war might have placed distinctive burdens on its soldiers and civilians. Yet the same Confederate editors often trumpeted northern suicides as pointed commentary on the divisions between Republicans and the antiwar opposition, and between Lincoln and his detractors. See "Late and Important," *Times-Picayune*, November 1, 1862; "A Man Named David Lamb," *Macon Telegraph*, November 5, 1862.

19. Lonnie R. Speer, *Portals to Hell: Military Prisons of the Civil War* (Omaha, NE: Bison Books, 2005), 60; "Trial of Henry Wirz," in *Executive Documents Printed by Order of the House of Representatives during the Second Session of the Fortieth Congress, 1867–1868* (Washington, DC: U.S. Government Printing Office, 1868), 157; William Marvel, *Andersonville: The Last Depot* (Chapel Hill: University of North Carolina Press, 1994), 157, 190; Dorence Atwater, *A List of the Union Soldiers Buried at Andersonville. Copied from the Official Record in the Surgeon's Office at Andersonville* (New York: Tribune Association, 1866). For other prison suicides, see John L. Maile, *Prison Life in Andersonville* (Los Angeles: Grafton Publishing, 1912), 31; Ovid L. Futch, *History of Andersonville Prison* (Gainesville: University of Florida Press, 1968), 42; Amos E. Stearns, *Narrative of Amos E. Stearns . . . A Prisoner at Andersonville* (Worcester, MA: Franklin P. Rice, 1887), 41–42; Robert Scott Davis, *Ghosts and Shadows of Andersonville: Essays on the Secret Social Histories of America's Deadliest Prison* (Macon, GA: Mercer University Press, 2006), 24; "The Wirz Trial. The Chapter of Horrors Continued," *Hartford Daily Courant*, September 6, 1865. For medical responses to soldiers who attempted suicide, see Surgeon General, *Medical and Surgical History of the Rebellion*, 3 vols. (Washington, DC: Government Printing Office, 1870), vol. 1, 440. On wartime press coverage of conditions in the military prisons, see Benjamin G. Cloyd, *Haunted by Atrocity: Civil War Prisons in American Memory* (Baton Rouge: Louisiana State University Press, 2010), 19–31.

20. *War of the Rebellion*, vol. 2, 303–307. "Give me liberty or give me death!" Hoffman's fabricated suicide note declared. For triumphant Union talk about the figurative self-immolation of the Confederacy in the closing months of the war, see James Hoyt, *The Suicide of Slavery. A Thanksgiving Sermon . . . in the First Baptist Church* (Cleveland, OH: Fairbanks, Benedict & Co., 1864), 15, 17–18. For Union press coverage of Confederate suicide, see "Suicide of Brigadier General Philip St. George Cooke," *New York Herald*, December 31, 1861; "Joseph Osterman," *San Francisco Bulletin*, November 19, 1861; "News and Other Items," *Pittsfield Sun*, March 20, 1862; "The Rebels," *Hartford Daily Courant*, March 17, 1862; "Unfortunate Suicide," *Philadelphia Inquirer*, September 16, 1861.

21. Myrta Lockett Avery, ed., *Recollections of Alexander H. Stephens: His Diary Kept When a Prisoner at Fort Warren, Boston Harbour, 1865* (New York: Doubleday, Page & Company, 1910), 186; "Washington," *Philadelphia Inquirer*, June 22, 1865; Dan T. Carter, *When the War Was Over: The Failure of Self-Reconstruction in the South, 1865–1867* (Baton Rouge: Louisiana State University Press, 1985), 33–34. On how southerners interpreted Ruffin's suicide as a statement of moral fortitude and political courage, see Kenneth S. Greenberg, *Honor and Slavery: Lies, Duels, Noses, Masks, Dressing as a Woman, Gifts, Strangers, Humanitarianism, Death, Slave Rebellions, the Proslavery Argument, Baseball, Hunting, and Gambling in the Old South* (Princeton, NJ: Princeton University Press, 1996), 93–95.

22. "Telegraphic," *Dallas Weekly Herald*, May 18, 1865; "The Plot the Press [illegible] from the Trial of the [illegible]," *New York Herald*, May 12, 1865; "Washington Letter," *Ohio State Journal*, May 15, 1865; "Protracted Cabinet Meeting," *Black Republican*, May 13, 1865. See also "Washington. The Treason

Trials!" *Philadelphia Inquirer*, May 13, 1865; "Washington the Coming Trial of the Conspirators Preparations Nearly Complete. The Manner of Their Confinement," *Philadelphia Inquirer*, May 9, 1865. According to several reports, Booth's suspected mistress, Mollie Turner, made an attempt to chloroform herself to evade capture during the manhunt. See "Editorial Correspondence New York, April 17, 1865," *San Francisco Bulletin*, May 16, 1865. The glee with which northern papers repeated rumors that Jefferson Davis had been wearing a woman's shawl when he was captured in Macon, Georgia, was further evidence of their interest in emasculating the Confederacy and its leaders.

23. "The Wertz Trial," *Macon Telegraph*, September 3, 1865; "Trial of Wirz," *New York Herald*, August 31, 1865; "W I R Z Details of His Execution," *New York Herald*, November 11, 1865.

24. Charles A. Dana, *Recollections of the Civil War, with the Leaders at Washington and in the Field in the Sixties* (New York: D. Appleton and Co., 1902), 282; "Letters from New York," *San Francisco Bulletin*, June 27, 1865; "The Manacling of Jeff. Davis," *Philadelphia Inquirer*, May 31, 1865; Clint Johnson, *Pursuit: The Chase, Capture, Persecution, and Surprising Release of Confederate President Jefferson Davis* (New York: Citadel, 2008), 213; Edward K. Eckert, ed., *"Fiction Distorting Fact," The Prison Life, Annotated by Jefferson Davis* (Macon, GA: Mercer University Press, 1987), xxiii; William A. Schmitt, *The Last Days of the Lost Cause: The Capture, Imprisonment and Trial of President Jefferson Davis* (Clarksdale: Mississippi Delta Pub. Co., 1949), 29–31. Rumors had circulated in the Union press during the war that Jefferson Davis was prone to self-destructive impulses. See "Eastern News by Overland Mail," *San Francisco Bulletin*, February 22, 1864; Joan E. Cashin, *First Lady of the Confederacy: Varina Davis's Civil War* (Cambridge, MA: Harvard University Press, 2006), 144; Edward Alfred Pollard, *Life of Jefferson Davis with a Secret History of the Southern Confederacy* (Bedford, MA: Applewood Books, 2008 [1869]), 320.

25. "The Diary of Wirz. Prison Reflections of the Andersonville Jailor," *New Orleans Times*, November 22, 1865; Felicity Allen, *Jefferson Davis: Unconquerable Heart* (Columbia: University of Missouri Press, 1999), 416; Eckert, *"Fiction Distorting Fact,"* 87.

26. Eckert, *"Fiction Distorting Fact,"* 12, 87. Some Confederates wished Davis would reconsider, voicing their hope that "God will take Mr. Davis to himself before our enemies can bring him to an ignominious death." See Dwight Franklin Henderson, ed., *The Private Journal of Georgiana Gholson Walker, 1862–1865, with Selections from the Post-War Years* (Tuscaloosa: Confederate Publishing Co., 1963), 123; "The Released Rebel Prisoners the Migration from Fort Warrens," *New York Herald*, June 15, 1865.

27. Stout, *Altar of the Nation*, 249; Franny Nudelman, *John Brown's Body: Slavery, Violence, and the Culture of War* (Chapel Hill: University of North Carolina Press, 2004), 39.

28. Many of the constitutional arguments marshaled by modern right-to-die advocates derive from their reading of the Due Process clause of the XIV Amendment, ratified in 1868. See Thomas J. Marzen et al., "Suicide: A Constitutional

Right?" *Duquesne Law Review* 24, no. 1 (1985): 3–242; see also Marzen et al., "'Suicide: A Constitutional Right?'—Reflections Eleven Years Later," *Duquesne Law Review* 35, no. 1 (1996–1997): 261–284. For the mid-nineteenth-century origins of recent anti-assisted suicide laws, see Marzen et al., "'Suicide: A Constitutional Right?'" 73–77. For an early accusation that teachers and students tormented a pupil to the point of suicide, see Jonas Greene, *The Crown Won but Not Worn; or, M. Louise Greene, a Student of Five Years at Kent's Hill, Me.* (Boston, 1867); Maine Wesleyan Seminary, *Libel Refuted: A Reply to Greene's Pamphlet* (Lewiston, ME: Journal Office, 1868). According to several new studies, the posttraumatic stress experienced by Civil War veterans often culminated in attempts at suicide. Eric Dean Jr., *Shook over Hell: Post-Traumatic Stress, Vietnam and the Civil War* (Cambridge, MA: Harvard University Press, 1997), 53–62, 112, 50–58; David Silkenat, *Moments of Despair: Suicide, Divorce, and Debt in Civil War Era North Carolina* (Chapel Hill: University of North Carolina Press, 2011); Diane Miller Sommerville, "'Will They Ever Be Able to Forget?': Confederate Soldiers and Mental Illness in the Defeated South," in *Weirding the War: Stories from the Civil War's Ragged Edges*, ed. Stephen Berry (Athens: University of Georgia Press, 2011), 411–435; Lee Ann Whites, *The Civil War as a Crisis in Gender: Augusta, Georgia, 1860–1890* (Athens: University of Georgia Press, 1995), 134–135; Stephen W. Berry II, *All That Makes a Man: Love and Ambition in the Civil War South* (New York: Oxford University Press, 2003), 9–11, 173–174. In Indiana at least five veterans' widows successfully petitioned the Pension Bureau for support on the basis that their husbands' postwar suicides were the direct consequence of their wartime service. See "Brooklyn City News," *New York Herald*, July 25, 1865.

Acknowledgments

After a decade spent thinking about what suicide meant and why it mattered to people in the past, I am happy, not to say relieved, to finally be able to thank all those who have shaped and enriched my life over the years consumed by this sobering project.

In graduate school I was fortunate to work under the supervision of Laurel Thatcher Ulrich, Joyce Chaplin, and Jill Lepore; it would be hard to imagine three finer scholars and mentors, and my debt to them is beyond measure. Other faculty at Harvard University and many fellow students have also influenced my intellectual development. Special thanks go to Vince Brown, Brian Delay, Lin Fisher, Becky Goetz, Kate Grandjean, David Hall, David Hempton, the late Bill Hutchison, Nadine Knight, Whitney Martinko, Phil Mead, Margot Minardi, Kirsten Sword, Adrian Weimer, and Katja Zalljadt. At the University of Maryland, I am grateful to my chair, Richard Price, for granting three semesters of research leave and, for their support of my scholarship, to my colleagues Ira Berlin, Janna Bianchini, Holly Brewer, Elsa Barkley Brown, Vin Carretta, Art Eckstein, Gary Gerstle, Jim Gilbert, James Henretta, Paul Landau, Clare Lyons, Whit Ridgway, Mike Ross, and Leslie Rowland.

In the course of this journey I received critical long-term research support from the John W. Kluge Center at the Library of Congress, the Huntington Library, the American Antiquarian Society, the University of Cambridge Mellon Fund, the McNeil Center for Early American Studies at the University of Pennsylvania, and the Library Company of Philadelphia. I have also benefited from valuable short-term fellowships granted by the Gilder Lehrman Center for the Study of Slavery, Resistance, and Abolition at Yale University, the College of Physicians of Philadelphia, the Historical Society of Pennsylvania, the New-York Historical Society, the Presbyterian Historical Society, the Massachusetts Historical Society, the American Philosophical Society, and the Harvard Law School. Among the small army of directors and curators who lent their time and expertise at these and other archives and foundations, several deserve particular recognition, namely, Karen Barzilay, Joanne Chaison, Peter Drummey, Paul Erikson, Jim Green, John Hench, Nicole Joniec, Melinda Kent, Connie King, Mark McMurray, Ed Morman, Frances O'Donnell, Jackie Penny, Dan Richter, Caroline Sloat, and Conrad Edick Wright.

I have, over the years, inflicted portions of this macabre manuscript on a variety of conference audiences in the United States, Britain, France, and Canada. The comments and suggestions offered by those in attendance have greatly improved the end result. Likewise, for sharing ideas, information, or their own research—and thereby helping me avoid some more egregious errors of fact and interpretation—my thanks go to Chris Beneke, David C. Brown, Dick Brown, Jacqui Cahif, Tom Carmody, Max Cavitch, Catherine Clinton, Leon Jackson, Sarah Knott, Bobby Lee, Bob Lockhart, Molly McCarthy, Meredith McGill, Amanda Moniz, Sharon Murphy, Matthew Osborn, Mark Peterson, Heather Repicky, Bill Rorabaugh, Eran Shalev, David Silkenat, Diane Miller Somerville, Terri Snyder, Catherine Stebbins, and John Tercier.

Earlier versions of Chapters 2 and 6 appeared as articles in *Early American Literature* and in *Slavery & Abolition*. As the book itself edged closer to publication, Joyce Seltzer, my editor at Harvard University Press, and Michael Meranze and Andrew Burstein, two external readers, each offered close readings and extensive, constructive criticism. Their enthusiasm for this project gave me courage and comfort.

I owe the greatest gratitude, however, to my friends, my students, and my family. David Hopper, Betty Wood, and Cathy Corman, three early teachers I remember fondly, each changed my life in ways they will never fully understand; their passion and high standards continue to inspire me. Believe it or not, the Harvard undergraduates I lived among during my years as a tutor at Pforzheimer House provided wonderful, engaging contrast to the wary, panicked, and proud early Americans whose cares I have spent so long trying to understand and unravel. More recently, my students at the University of Maryland, College Park, have energized both my teaching and my writing. My family—Gill, Stephen, and Julia Bell, Laura Perrett, and Judy, Marvin, and Kevin Lewis—offered love and much-needed perspective throughout the long life of this book about dealing with death. But one debt surpasses all others. It is to Monica Lewis, the bright star I follow on every journey. This is for her.

Index

www.ingramcontent.com/pod-product-compliance
Lightning Source LLC
LaVergne TN
LVHW091517200926
848483LV00005B/445/J
9780674063723